Gendered Infrastructures

GENDER, FEMINISM, AND GEOGRAPHY

Jennifer L. Fluri, Series Editor
Amy Trauger, Series Editor

TITLES IN THE SERIES

Critical Geographies of Youth: Law, Policy, and Power
Edited by Gloria Howerton and Leanne Purdum

Feminist Geography Unbound: Discomfort, Bodies, and Prefigured Futures
Edited by Banu Gökarıksel, Michael Hawkins, Christopher Neubert,
and Sara Smith

GENDERED
INFRASTRUCTURES

SPACE, SCALE, AND IDENTITY

Edited by

Yaffa Truelove and Anu Sabhlok

WEST VIRGINIA UNIVERSITY PRESS / MORGANTOWN

ISBN 978-1-959000-08-2 (paperback) / 978-1-959000-09-9 (ebook)

Library of Congress Control Number: 2023043224

Cover: design by Than Saffel / WVU Press; image by Anu Sabhlok; art
direction by Noor Sharma

CONTENTS

ACKNOWLEDGEMENTS

Gendered Infrastructures is dedicated to all those who have pushed boundaries in their quest toward a more socially just world. It has been a long time in the making and draws upon ideas that germinated long before the book was anywhere in the picture. We are indebted to the struggles and insights of all the feminists whose courage, care, and creativity continue to illuminate our paths. We are thankful to our students, teachers, friends, families, and interlocutors who participated in nurturing the ideas that constitute the book. These are too many to name, and so these acknowledgments, while unspoken, are deeply felt. Also deeply felt is our gratitude to our respective partners in life, Brijesh and Jitesh, for their love, support, and insights that sustained us through this journey.

This book would not have been possible without the support of a number of colleagues and editors who gave their time, critical thoughts, and enthusiasm to the book. We first wish to thank each of the authors who contributed to this collaborative book project for their enthusiasm and participation as well as their richly insightful perspectives on gendered infrastructures that inform their work. We are grateful for those who participated in and contributed to the two paper sessions on gendered infrastructures for the 2018 American Association of Geographers annual meeting that led to many of the chapters in this volume. The discussion around this theme began during Anu Sabhlok's term at the University of Colorado, Boulder as a Fulbright scholar. We acknowledge the Fulbright Nehru Academic and Professional Excellence Fellowship for enabling this conversation.

Many thanks to Subhashri Sarkar and Caitlin Ryan for helping out with making the edits and formatting required to make the manuscript ready for submission. We are also deeply appreciative of the editorial support at West Virginia University Press. The Gender, Feminism, and Geography series editors, Jennifer Fluri and Amy Trauger, provided impeccable support and incisive feedback that strengthened the book. We are immensely grateful for Derek Krissoff's ongoing support, feedback, and enthusiasm for this project from its very early stages. Last, we are grateful for the helpful feedback from two anonymous reviewers.

INTRODUCTION

Yaffa Truelove and Anu Sabhlok

From the kitchen faucet at home to the public tram in the city, infrastructures are gendered. Bridges and highways are built so as to conquer nature, unlit corners of an urban landscape are often the sites of sexual violence, and it is usually the women of a household who spend hours lining up for water. Infrastructures are not inert backdrops around which social activity happens. They shape and in turn are shaped by social and ecological processes. Such a view becomes apparent when we pay attention to relations between scales (such as intimate, national, global), between nature and culture, and between the material objects and the nonmaterial ideas and discourses surrounding them. Feminist scholars have been central to understanding how seemingly disparate realms might actually be co-constitutive. It is not a surprise then that the recent focus on critical approaches to infrastructure drew from the work of a feminist scholar when she asked methodological questions about studying infrastructure (Star 1999). Star pushed for an understanding of intersectionality, where marginalities are systemic consequences of socio-technical arrangements (Timmermans 2016). Her view of objects as ambiguous, relational, imbued with multiple meanings, and not unitary artifacts has pushed feminist methodologies and, one could argue, birthed a new infrastructural turn in critical scholarship (Bowker et al. 2016). Asking questions about the relationship between identities, social relations, and infrastructures is a "conduit to understanding the concrete force of abstract fields of power by allowing us to identify actually existing systems rather than a priori structures" (Wilson 2016, 248). Taking this call further, feminist geographers and political ecologists have, over the years, developed very sophisticated scholarship on space, place, and scale that has contributed to furthering the study of infrastructural assemblages. In this co-edited book, we bring together emerging scholarship on the socio-material dimensions of infrastructure with feminist and geographic theory in order to advance gendered approaches to infrastructure. In other words, we aim to bring together the numerous ways in which material infrastructures (electricity, water, internet, roads, etc.) and social infrastructures of everyday life connect to identities (gender, class, caste, race, etc.) as they both situate and spread across space.

Here we have three intentions. First, we intend to lay out the different ways in which infrastructures reproduce and/or rework gendered identities. How do infrastructures become sites for gendered social relations? How do the meanings associated with particular infrastructures allow for particular gender relations, and what is the social life of such gendered meanings? In what ways do established gender norms structure and make possible particular infrastructural configurations? Second, we intend to elucidate the convergences and divergences between the new infrastructural turn and feminist scholarship. In what ways do advances within feminist scholarship offer new frameworks that enable the critical study of infrastructure? How does an infrastructure-as-method approach enable insights that might otherwise have been subsumed? And what questions do such insights ask about identity? Third, as geographers both of us find the new infrastructural turn to be a productive site for thinking about space. We see space as social relations stretched out (Massey 2013, 22) and infrastructures as assemblages that move through and converge in space, which make circulations in space possible and that coalesce uneven geographies. Even as we focus on gender, our broader agenda is to explore these uneven geographies and the intersectionality of relations that these infrastructures enable or disable.

FEMINIST GEOGRAPHY AND THE CRITICAL TURN IN INFRASTRUCTURE: SPACE, PLACE, AND GENDER

The recent Netflix film *Gunjan Saxena* (2020) met with criticism for portraying the Indian Air Force in a bad light. The film shows Gunjan, the first female to be recruited into the Indian Air Force, running around the military grounds in search of a women's toilet and changing room. When she asks a senior officer where to find one, he tells her there is none, "because this place is not meant for women." A similar episode is recorded in the Hollywood movie *Hidden Figures* (2016), as it tells the biographical tale of three black female mathematicians at NASA who have to walk half a mile to the "colored people's" toilet in the adjacent building. Infrastructures, or their lack thereof, are explicit signals that convey who belongs to which place and who is to be kept out.

This infrastructural violence, especially when it relates to something as essential and intimate as toilets, has been grounds for revolution and for government intervention in the most private of our spheres. In a provocative speech given in 2013, Julius Malema, the former president of the African National Congress Youth League, calls out to the residents of the townships, "We need toilets, you must never be ashamed. If there is a need for a toilet revolution, we must engage in a toilet revolution." His speech came amid an ongoing "poo war," where residents of the Khayelitsha informal settlements threw buckets of sewage at prominent locations in Cape Town. Debates on the racial politics of sanitation and hygiene and images of women having to defecate in the open, unsafe, and inadequate toilets became central to the country's elections.

The United Nations has called for an end to open defecation by 2020, and in 2011 the Bill and Melinda Gates Foundation hosted a problematic "reinvent the toilet challenge" to reimagine toilets for the "developing world." An intimate and necessary act becomes a matter of global significance that reflects historical and contemporary asymmetries of power (Redfield and Robins 2016). Shit is political (Robins 2014; von Schnitzler 2015; McFarlane and Silver 2017; O'Reilly 2016). Around the same time, India's prime minister Narendra Modi allocated US$40 billion toward building toilets as part of a social awareness campaign titled "Swachh Bharat Abhiyaan." In India, the debate on toilets is embroiled in caste politics, differential access and class, and a gendered morality (Doron and Raja 2015). Powerful casteist and gendered discourses have resisted the incorporation of "impure" toilet spaces within the space of the house. This conceptualization appears as a counter to Western notions of what constitutes public and private (Chakrabarty 2002). Further, urban planning initiatives have often deliberately excluded informal settlements from connections to adequate sanitation infrastructures (Desai, McFarlane, and Graham 2015), and even their installation has at times produced infrastructural violence rather than alleviate it (Truelove and O'Reilly 2020). In the absence of the necessary and functional infrastructure within the house, women are forced to go out and relieve themselves. Modesty concerns regulate this activity to early mornings or late nights. In the dark and often in secluded spots, women have thus become targets of sexual violence when out to defecate. Indian television has picked up on this lack as part of Modi's political campaign, and fathers are urged in advertisements to not "give away" their daughters in marriage to households that do not have a toilet at home. The infrastructure of defecation has inspired revolutions and has become a technology of social control and surveillance where the state peeps into our very closets to model a civil society on bourgeois ideas of "purity," "progress," and "pathology."

This is an incomplete story of but one infrastructural object. When we start looking at infrastructures with a gendered lens, we begin to see how electrical connections, mobile technologies, public transport, and water pipes all have gendered stories to tell. Many of these stories would lie hidden if infrastructures were viewed as stagnant backdrops, as finished projects, and as apolitical material objects. More often than not, we think of infrastructures as engineering feats full of mundane technical specifications and mechanistic working drawings that have little to do with subjectivity or identity. They are commonly understood as a system of substrates (Star 1999) that serves as the ambient environment to modern life (Larkin 2013). In order to see how they work and how they structure our everyday lives, we need to make sense of infrastructures as inherently relational. The dual ontology of infrastructures as things but also relations between the things (Larkin 2013, 329) does not allow for linear thinking and instead pushes us to see them as constituted by materials (pipes, cables, wires, etc.), ideas (representations, meanings, symbols), and various forms of social relations that both enable their existence and result from their emplacement. Feminist commitments to relationality, to dismantling binaries such as subject/object, nature/culture, and material/discursive and instead viewing these as mutually constituted, offer methodological frames and theorizations that align well with the new conceptualizations of infrastructure. The infrastructural turn is therefore also a methodological turn. It involves the very tools that are so often associated with feminist and queer scholarship that excavate hidden, taken-for-granted ideologies and power relationships (Wilson 2016). A lot of work goes into this taken-for-grantedness, which relies on the efforts to "normalize, maintain, repair and stabilize" (Graham and McFarlane 2014, 12; Graham and Thrift 2007), and much of that work is gendered, though the literature thus far has not broadly or explicitly called it so. We have found feminist geographer Doreen Massey's pathbreaking work on space, place, and gender particularly productive for thinking through a gendered approach to understanding space, place and infrastructures. We draw upon this fundamental work of Massey to elaborate on the resonance between feminist geographic scholarship and the new infrastructural turn.

Feminist scholarship has challenged deterministic views of technology and insisted on a complex and relational understanding of the material world, weaving together the material and the symbolic to reveal the implicit workings of power (Boyer 2006). Research by feminist scholars of technology has demonstrated how gendered relations and gendered divisions of labor have shaped technology (Cockburn and Ormrod 1993; Bray 1997). Massey (2005) offered a non-Euclidean imagination of space that allows us to view spaces as social relations "stretched out," as a multiplicity where "distinct trajectories coexist" (9). Space, according to Massey, is a product of interrelations and is never really completed; it is always being produced and under construction. Such a view liberates space from a bounded view that situates spaces merely as a container of social life waiting to be liberated by time. One does not simply move through space or in space. In other words, space is not merely a static backdrop to social activity. Space is constantly produced through social relations even as it shapes social relations in particular ways. Massey also rejects the long-held notion of places as local and self-contained and instead shows how seemingly "local" places are networks of social relations that extend far beyond the place itself, stating, "there are no internal histories and timeless identities." Such a conceptualization of space as relational, as a process, as open-ended, as political, and as constituted by a "throwtogetherness" is pivotal to the understanding of infrastructures as assemblages, as systems that reach far beyond the object, as political, and as never-finished processes that are tied to specific temporalities.

Infrastructures need to be studied as systems (Larkin 2013) such that the presence of an electrical connection can be traced to the electric substation, to the hydropower dam, into government files, to labor journeys, to trucks carrying wires and meters, to the official who comes to read the meters, and to the computer that generates the bill. They can be traced to national policy related to electrification and to the World Bank loans that may enable the connection. The local electrician who forges an illegal connection has as much a role to play as the white-collar banker who sanctions the loan.

Feminist geographers have questioned the logic of scales as nested within one another or as a hierarchical conceptualization and have stressed the understanding of scales as mutually constituted. A global bank derives its meaning and work from projects at local scales. Localities reach out to the national governments to demand utilities and infrastructures, using regional analysis to determine technical details. And distantly produced electricity is experienced and altered at the very intimate scale of the home. Scholars have argued against the disembodied and masculinist idea of scale that premises the local/global binary as the norm. They instead show that the intimate and global are not separate (Smith 2012), abstract and bounded spheres. Instead, the local or the global are constituted through "people, processes and politics" that work through relationalities at multiple scales (Mountz and Hyndman 2006).

Feminist geographic understandings of space, place, and scale allow for an intersectional mapping of the geometries of power that underlie all infrastructural assemblages. Feminist scholars persistently argue for an understanding that highlights lived experience as opposed to abstract generalizations. They recognize that interlocking categories of experience (Collins 2015) shape lived realities and that it is not possible to separate gender, class, age, sexuality, caste, race, and other forms of identity if we are to explain inequalities (Valentine 2007). A feminist and intersectional approach to studying infrastructure makes visible deep-rooted questions of access and representation. It reveals ways in which infrastructures reproduce and perpetuate systemic inequalities even as they seek to flatten the field.

Infrastructures shape our embodied practices, intimacies, and everyday routines, and all of these are deeply intertwined with gender and sexualities. For example, the pervasiveness of digital infrastructures such as mobile phones, the internet, and other digital social networks have reworked existing spatial practices and created new spatialities that oscillate between digital and material worlds. The new spatial imaginaries that emerge are concomitant with emerging temporalities of the digital/material/social interface (Massey 2005). Infrastructures then are networked processes in multiple space-times. Nikhil Anand's (2017) work brings to the fore these multiple trajectories of space-time through his study of water supply in Mumbai. As water flows through miles of pipes to reach localities, residents negotiate with varying hydraulic pressure, restricted supply times, local leaders, plumbers, and gendered household divisions of labor to ensure that they have water in their homes for cooking, cleaning, and drinking. Anand's ethnography is so powerful precisely because of the way it connects the embodied to the abstract and meshes together space-time as he follows the flow of water from dams to households.

Infrastructures are assemblages of material artifacts; technological derivations; governance techniques of the social, political, economic, material, and ecological; the spatial, and the temporal. In a similar way, the new turn in infrastructure studies is a productive moment for geographers, anthropologists, political ecologists, sociologists, historians, engineers, and STS scholars to think together about the ways in which we understand infrastructures and how they mediate our lives.

Building on feminist geography's contributions to understanding infrastructure in relation to space, place, and gender, in the following sections we outline four specific subthemes to which the book and its chapters contribute. The first theme is gendered symbolisms and representations of infrastructure. Here we consider how gendered meanings and symbolisms are intimately connected to material infrastructures and in turn produce and reify social hierarchies, national imaginaries, private and public space, and masculinist triumphs. The second theme is material ecologies and intersectional social relations. Through drawing on feminist political ecology and other related scholarship, we examine how feminist approaches that undo binaries such as nature/culture, social/material make a number of critical contributions to understanding the complex ways ecologies, infrastructures, and social relations are mutually constituted. The third theme focuses on bringing the site and scale of the body to understanding infrastructural change, violence, and uneven citizenship. This section reveals how giving analytical attention to embodiment is critical for revealing the gendered violences and patterns of uneven citizenship that both enable and arise from infrastructural transformation. Finally, our fourth theme explores gendered infrastructures in the everyday, showing how feminist and gendered approaches to examining mundane practices and intimate spheres of life are critical for understanding the complex social, ecological, and political outcomes that arise from the making and unmaking of infrastructures across the globe.

GENDERED SYMBOLISMS AND REPRESENTATIONS OF INFRASTRUCTURE

> How then is "white men" built or even a building? Think about it. One practitioner relayed to me how they named buildings in her institution. All dead white men she said. We don't need the names to know how spaces come to be organized so they can receive certain bodies. We don't need the naming to know how or who buildings can be for. (Ahmed 2016)

Infrastructures serve as devices that make claims through their symbolic associations and aesthetics. STS scholars have long recognized how artefacts embody shared cultural meanings that play an important role in the naturalization of social relations (Latour 1992; Winner 1993). Research in infrastructure studies draws upon this tradition to bring attention to the ways in which "public sentiments of progress, modernity and wellbeing become attached to iconic buildings, highways, or new housing and shopping complexes, regardless of their functionality and material impact" (Amin 2014, 138; Harvey and Knox 2012). In the quote above Sara Ahmed turns the spotlight on the taken-for-granted domain of building names that reflect exclusions in institutional spaces based on gender, class, and race. Infrastructures may have material façades, but they are deeply infused with social meanings (Howe et al. 2016) and political power. Grand infrastructural projects such as those built during the Olympic Games in China and the Commonwealth Games in India are meant as geopolitical statements proclaiming the emergence of newer economies into the world stage (Cornelissen 2010). New bridges, buildings, and sports arenas reflect planning visions of world-class cities and are mobilized to reimagine particular kinds of urban futures. The association of infrastructures with progress has led several governments to adopt infrastructural development as their motto for election campaigning.

Research on transport infrastructure illustrates how gendered meanings are inscribed onto supposedly inert artifacts such as roads. Roads do the material and symbolic work of claiming territory and are touted as projects of nation-building and national defense (Sabhlok 2017). They project the idea of connectivity even when at times they disconnect (Harvey and Knox 2015; Murton 2017). According to Dalakoglou and Harvey, "Ethnographies of roads allow the ethnographer to tease out the practices and imaginaries that work across scales" (2012, 460). Sabhlok's (2017) work has shown how the national imaginations related to development and defense surface on road construction sites as gendered tropes celebrating a particular hegemonic masculinity. These gendered associations of roads and the mobilities/immobilities that they enable rely on accepted understandings of male as mobile and female as sedentary (Cook and Butz 2020). The construction of a road may reinforce such normalized gender codes while at the same time rework or challenge them. Moreover, infrastructures (particularly roads, bridges, and dams) are often seen as technological victories over Mother Nature. They are engineered and put in place through human ingenuity and labor. As figure I.1 demonstrates, it is not uncommon for infrastructures and their materialities to be coded as masculine triumphs (Schwenkel this volume). Such symbolisms have deep-reaching effects in the everyday lives of women and men.

For example, much of the advertising for domestic infrastructures continues to rely on gendered tropes or normative gendered divisions of labor. While infrastructural development may promise to ease labor, it does not challenge the association of women with the domestic sphere or men with the public sphere. Furthermore, gendered roles and the coding of women's bodies are often inscribed into how the temporalities of infrastructures are discursively framed. In July 2019, a billboard advertising repairs for an air-conditioning company appeared on a city street in Nottingham, UK. It sent a not-so-subliminal message about gendered roles (it's a man's job to get the air-conditioning fixed) and about women's bodies (as available for sexual comments). Meanings and symbolisms cannot be distanced from material infrastructures—these are built into and rely on each other to function as artefacts and as symbolic objects.

Illustrating the sometimes contradictory symbolic meanings that become imbued through gendered infrastructural labor, Schwenkel's chapter in this volume on the production of cement in Vietnam shows how women laborers in the concrete industry become "contradictory symbols of both the possibility

Fig. I.1. Associations of strength with masculinity reflect in advertisements for cement companies. (Photos by Anu Sabhlok)

of technological futurity and the potential for its failure." Traversing scales in her analysis, Schwenkel shows how decaying concrete structures "have come to symbolize the ruins of socialism's drab modernist utopias. In Vietnam, such ruins serve as a reminder of ways that women's labor shaped and was shaped by that very utopian promise of modernity as created materially through concrete infrastructures. They also bespeak of a state pedagogical apparatus aimed at the subjectivization of a female proletariat." Her chapter details how construction technologies in the city of Vinh that once symbolized the promise of progress now work to preclude it.

Further linking infrastructure's multifaceted gendered symbolism to the gendering of women's labor in Dakar, Senegal, Fredericks's chapter in this volume shows the powerful associations between waste and value in women's work to gather and dispose of waste in homes, lanes, and dump sites. Fredericks meticulously details how gendered meanings of waste work open up contradictory spaces for women, both offering opportunities to claim authority and expertise in their labor to dispose waste, and simultaneously "justifying [women's] positionality within low-paid, stigmatized work and, sometimes, their violent dispossession from the value they have so painstakingly constructed."

Infrastructures as part of material landscapes create powerful symbols and places of memory and, through processes such as street naming, demarcating tourist destinations, and other symbolic gestures, become instrumental in projects of cultural marginalization, erasure, or celebration of particular identities (Rose-Redwood 2009). For example, Kirk's chapter in this volume traces how the material infrastructures of tourist spaces such as zoos work to perpetuate a discursive violence against Palestinian bodies and lands. Her chapter exposes how the symbolic naturalization of settler indigeneity becomes articulated through "both material and discursive infrastructures at the zoo, all hidden in plain sight by the zoo's claims to being an apolitical tourist destination and environmental steward." Infrastructural spaces usually carry subtle signs that code who is an insider and who is an outsider, as well as what constitutes heterosexual or masculine/feminine spaces. Such coding often happens through the symbolic associations related to infrastructures present or absent.

MATERIAL ECOLOGIES AND INTERSECTIONAL SOCIAL RELATIONS

Infrastructures also challenge, and often have the potential to reveal and undo, socially constructed binaries such as nature/culture and social/material. When women queue at a tube well spigot in Delhi, waiting to fill and transport groundwater water from the spigot to their homes, their bodies become substitutes for absent pipes that might normally do this work. Where, then, does the body end and infrastructure begin if the body is in fact doing the work of augmenting absent infrastructure? And because patriarchal discourses shape whose bodies are responsible for procuring and moving water in India, water's circulation in the city operates through powerful gendered and cultural politics. Here, ecologies, infrastructures, and gendered social relations are mutually constituted, rather than distinct spheres that can be separated from each other. Bringing a social-material-ecological approach to infrastructure, scholarship aligned with feminist political ecology (FPE) contributes to gendering and embodying critical infrastructure studies through undoing binaries such as nature/culture and social/material, and further contributes to our volume.

FPE builds on political ecology's lineage to understand environmental change and access and control over resources as shaped by both human and more-than-human processes. For example, FPE brings a critical (and often

missing) gendered and intersectional approach to understanding the socio-
natural transformations of environments across geographic locations. This includes unpacking the socially constructed dichotomies of nature and culture, as
well as meticulously analyzing how resources such as food, water, energy, forests, and their related infrastructures are governed through, and productive of,
overlapping gender/class/race relations. Thus, FPE makes a number of important contributions to the complex ways ecologies, infrastructures, and social
relations are mutually reinforcing and coproduce each other. Consequently,
infrastructures as diverse as urban food systems (Havorka 2006; Jarosz 2011),
wells that distribute urban and rural water (Sultana 2009; Thompson, Gaskin,
and Agbor 2017), and the fragmented collection and circulation of waste
(O'Reilly 2016; Fredericks 2018; Desai, McFarlane, and Graham 2015) arise,
in part, through gendered, classed, and racialized power relations, and shape
the unequal ecological, material, and embodied consequences experienced by
differing social groups. Feminist political ecology thus offers an important
framework for analyzing gendered infrastructures. FPE provides a lens to understand how co-constituted social-material-ecological relations are embedded
in gendered forms of social power and affect, the production of masculinities/
femininities, and multiscalar political configurations.

While critical infrastructure studies have emphasized infrastructure's materiality as tied to both human and nonhuman agencies that shape social relations, FPE offers an important gendered and social-ecological perspective to
such analyses. In gendering and looking at the socio-natural dimensions of
materials like pipes, pumps, and toilets (which often unanticipatedly break,
rupture, and leak contaminants), FPE-aligned studies reveal how co-constituted social-material-ecological relations have important gendered dimensions
that often go overlooked. For example, Sultana's (2009, 2011) work on the
intersectional gender and class dimensions of well water access in Bangladesh
reveals how gendered and classed power relations, affects, and emotions are
reinscribed through men and women's everyday relations with differing types
of water wells, some of which hold water with high levels of arsenic. Sultana
demonstrates how arsenic contamination in wells produces differing types of
infrastructural and water-related agencies that combine with intersectional
social relations. Here, water ecologies, social power relations, and material
infrastructures are co-constituted in ways that create particular types of inequities for women and men in daily life. For example, the stress of trying to circumvent contaminated wells falls predominately on women but intersects with
class, marital status, and age, disproportionately affecting younger women and
daughters-in-law of poor households, whereas wealthier women are able to

mostly opt out of problems with well water by either negotiating access to deeper arsenic-free private wells or hiring another to do the work of fetching water (see also Thompson, Gaskin, and Agbor 2017, 1294).

Doshi's (2017) elaboration of an embodied urban political ecology of sanitation infrastructures in Mumbai reveals how the materiality of infrastructural breakdown and fragmentation shapes women's unequal embodied experiences of the city's sanitation. She gives the example of insufficient and unsafe public toilets in Mumbai's poorer neighborhoods, showing how such hazardous infrastructures reinscribe unequal gendered power relations and violences onto women's bodies. These women are often left with few alternatives to using toilets that sometimes unpredictably collapse on them and that have resulted in several deaths in the city. Desai, McFarlane, and Graham (2015), also studying sanitation infrastructures in Mumbai, illuminate how practices of gendered open defecation emerge from women's efforts to cope with absent, dangerous, expensive, and limited sanitation infrastructures. The authors also show that open defecation levels new types of risks onto the female body that differ significantly from risks faced by boys and men. Poor women's everyday routines and social relations are thus shaped by the unpredictable rhythms and agencies of sanitation infrastructures: the choked toilets, the unpredictable need for maintenance and repair, and even the collapse altogether of the infrastructure, all leading women to improvise and incur alternate hazards with regard to open defecation.

Schwenkel's (2015) work on the physical and affective labor to access water in the wake of the state's infrastructural breakdown and neglect in Vinh, Vietnam, is also aligned with FPE in demonstrating how urban water ecologies and infrastructures are co-constituted with gendered social and moral orders in the city. Specifically, Schwenkel reveals the reworking of gendered labor and moral orders in tandem with differing phases of water infrastructure's transformation over time. Schwenkel's study finds that breakdown, and the congruent need for maintenance and repair, shifts social and affective relations in highly gendered ways: "The everyday struggle for water required the collaborative efforts of both men and women, temporarily suspending the gendered division of labor around infrastructure and the expectation that women should secure critical resources, while men—like the plumber—repair and restore technical systems" (531). The reworking of gender relations in tandem with water infrastructure enables "new forms of solidarity and gendered social practice" (531), revealing the complex and sometimes positive affective and gendered outcomes of infrastructural failures.

Finally, in placing the body as a critical scale of analysis in infrastructure studies, studies aligned with feminist political ecology have begun to illuminate the gendered practices and labor that maintain and enable critical resources to be circulated and infrastructural networks to function. Stated most simply, this emerging new work shows how the (gendered) body itself constitutes infrastructure that helps circulate resources like water and accomplish waste disposal (Truelove and Ruszczyk this volume; Fredericks 2018; Alda-Vidal this volume). Beyond revealing how gendered practices, labor, and maintenance become embedded within and become key to the functionality of socio-material assemblages of water and waste, conceptualizing the body as infrastructure provides an important lens for unpacking patterns of inequality and sociopolitical transformation that often remain invisible within other scales of analysis (Truelove and Ruszcyzyk this volume). For example, Fredericks's chapter in this volume on waste infrastructures in Dakar shows how particular gendered bodies carry out the labor of waste within households, lanes, communities, and the city at large. In the absence of particular waste technologies, such as sorting machines, facilities, and sufficient trucks, women's bodies work to sort and manage waste at multiple sites within the city (including households, streets, and landfills), becoming a type of "prosthetic" (Truelove 2019c) that both extends and compensates for particular absences in the infrastructural network. The labor, repair, and affective and sensorial responses that surround the body acting as infrastructure helps reveal the multiple inequities and power relations of "infra-making" (Lancione and McFarlane 2016; Andueza et al. 2020) in the everyday (see figure I.2). Such interventions that draw attention to the relations between bodies and infrastructure help to productively address Desai, McFarlane, and Graham's observation that there remains limited scholarship "that explores people's everyday experiences and practices in relation to infrastructure and that deepens our understanding of the relationships between the body, infrastructure and the city" (2015, 7).

In addition, research on "beyond-the-network" fragmented systems has been particularly effective in demonstrating how care, maintenance, and labor shape social orderings of gendered/racialized/classed work that is critical to piecing together infrastructural fragments into functioning micro-networks (Fredericks 2018; Truelove 2021). While infrastructures often evoke the image of large-scale networks of roads, electricity, sewerage, and water, across the globe urban dwellers often rely on fragmented, fractured, and partial infrastructures to access key urban amenities. These infrastructural fragments not only show the disjunction between infrastructural imaginaries of world-class

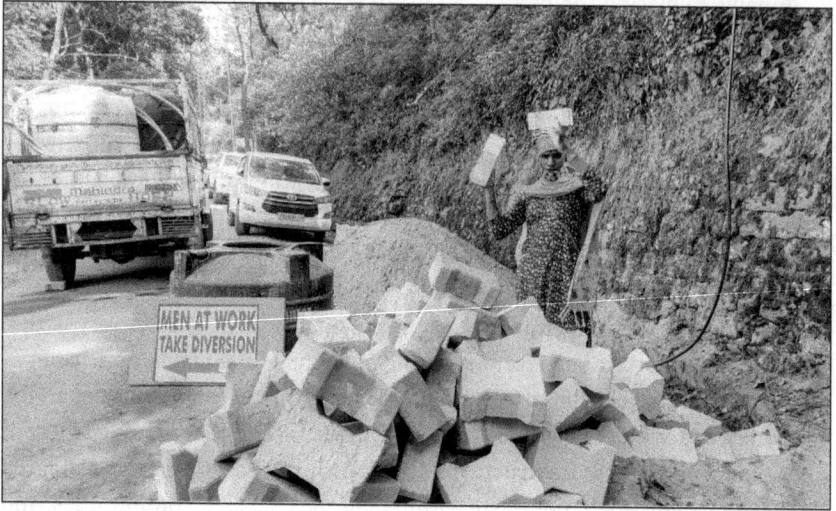

Fig. I.2. Gendered infrastructural work codes spaces in lingering ways. Here the sign "Men at Work" persists even as women laborers are seen working. (Photo by Anu Sabhlok)

and/or smart cities and the realities on the ground of heterogeneous infrastructural configurations (Lawhon et al. 2018) that function to varying degrees and effects; they also reveal the everyday politics and practices by which cities, materials, ecologies and gendered/classed/racialized bodies are co-produced. For example, Truelove's (2021) research on fragmented tube well and water tanker deliveries in Delhi's unauthorized colonies shows how "these fractured modalities ultimately constitute gendered socio-technical assemblages." Women's care and labor to pump water when wells are running and their work to segregate and distribute differing types of contaminated and potable water in the houses are critical to everyday water security in the neighborhood. Furthermore, women's use of social networks to determine when tankers will arrive provides a bridge to fractured infrastructures that enables their functionality but consequently deepens forms of gendered marginality and differentiation. This research illustrates how gendered infrastructural practices and labor "shape subjectivities and possibilities for social relations and urban claims-making" (Truelove 2021).

Within this book, scholars offer new research that expands a feminist and intersectional engagement with fragmented and temporally changing infrastructural materialities in significant new directions. Building on feminist political ecology scholarship that reveals the emotional geographies and gendered divisions of labor that undergird water access, Alda-Vidal, Browne, and Rusca's chapter in this volume unpacks women's gendered infrastructural labor at water kiosks in Lilongwe. These authors demonstrate how women's labor and the congruent gendered space produced at water kiosks are "fundamentally interwoven into the formal planning and running of water infrastructure" and reveal problematic patterns of gendered visibility and invisibility that keep infrastructures running. Thompson's chapter employs participatory and visual methods to tracking the feminist political ecology of small and fractured well water access in Cameroon. She shows how women's emotional care and labor is embedded in the functionality of wells within communities and "plays a fundamental role in ensuring the flow of water into households." Thompson's research provides a detailed account of how "gendered expectations shape the uneven distributions of embodied strain and responsibilities to negotiate the ambiguous quality of well water, often leaving women with difficult decisions and compromise in securing safe water for their households."

EMBODYING INFRASTRUCTURAL CHANGE, VIOLENCE, AND UNEVEN INFRASTRUCTURAL CITIZENSHIP

Attention to the scale and site of the body also yields important insights for a particular vein of scholarship within critical infrastructure studies that focus on infrastructural transformation, violence, and citizenship (see Rodgers and O'Neill 2012; Anand 2017; Lemanski 2019, 2020; Ruwanpura, Brown, and Chan 2020). A long lineage of feminist geographic and social science studies views the body as central to understandings of the intimate ways state power, subjectivities, and intersectional power relations become experienced and embodied in everyday practice (Mountz 2018; Silvey 2004; Smith 2009; Pain and Staeheli 2014; Sabhlok, Cheung, and Mishra 2015). Specifically, a set of relatively new studies takes an embodied approach to productively reveal not only how infrastructural transformations imprint bodies with gendered, raced, and classed subjectivities, but also level situated infrastructural violence on poor, lower-caste women's bodies (Truelove and O'Reilly 2020), and produce new forms of gendered infrastructural citizenship (Sultana 2020).

For example, recent efforts to situate "infrastructural violence" have helped reveal the unequal experiences and effects of differing kinds of violence on women's and men's bodies. Rodgers and O'Neill's (2012) important intervention (accompanied by a special issue on the same topic in *Ethnography*) first focused attention on conceptualizing and advancing an infrastructural violence framework. These scholars show both the structural and material forms of violence that become enacted by "broader processes of marginalization, abjection and disconnection" in relation to infrastructure. In defining infrastructural violence, Rodgers and O'Neill state: "Infrastructure is not just a material embodiment of violence (structural or otherwise), but often its instrumental medium, insofar as the material organization and form of a landscape not only reflect but also reinforce social orders, thereby becoming a contributing factor to reoccurring forms of harm" (404). Bringing an embodied and feminist political ecology lens to such a framework, Truelove and O'Reilly (2020) analyze what they call "situated infrastructural violence" in relation to India's Swachh Bharat Mission (SBM) in cities. This national initiative to improve sanitation, and in urban areas produce "India's Cleanest City," illustrates precisely the ways that the violence of infrastructural transformation impacts particular gendered, classed, and casted bodies unequally. Truelove and O'Reilly show that instead of ensuring more equitable and accessible sanitation infrastructures in Indore, which was awarded the SBM title of "India's Cleanest City" in 2017, poor, non-dominant-caste women experienced a worsening of both their sanitation and their housing infrastructures, as well as compounded forms of bodily harm, including urban displacement and the regular harassment and shaming associated with open defecation.

Expanding work on how differing infrastructures can either produce or alleviate specific kinds of gendered and embodied infrastructural violence, Datta and Ahmed (2020) demonstrate that a lack of access to infrastructure is a form of intimate violence. Through a study of Thiruvanathapuram, Kerala, these scholars show how infrastructural violence impacts gendered bodies through the "multiple scales, forms, sites and temporalities of infrastructural absence" (67). Building on a feminist critical geography of infrastructure, these authors call for approaches to infrastructural violence that "collapse hierarchies of intimate and structural violence" (67).

Elaborating further on embodied and affective approaches to gendered violence and infrastructure, Anshika Suri's chapter in this volume gives an ethnographic and gendered account of urban sanitation infrastructure. She shows that in the cities of Dar es Salaam and Nairobi, sanitation meanings, perceptions, and experiences are deeply intertwined such that the fear of violence defines women's relationship to material infrastructures as much as the violence associated with the lack of or inadequacy of infrastructure. Her ethnography also reveals how such a fear and feelings of insecurity produce particular gendered relations that manifest in furthering patriarchal control over women's bodies and movement. In a similar vein, Carroli and Grant-Smith's chapter in this volume expresses their frustration at the gap between the notion of infrastructure systems of support for a city and the apparent lack of care that technological systems exhibit. They aver that this gap produces material inequality and vulnerability. In particular they discuss gendered relations and women's safety surrounding public transportation. Carroli and Grant-Smith argue for a "feminist infrastructuring" that uses digital interventions to produce spaces of care within cities. One example of empowerment through reworking infrastructural assemblages is shown by Queirós, Leal, Fuzzi, and Vale (this volume). They discuss how the formation of women's collectives for waste recycling enabled women to escape the infrastructural violence otherwise embedded in the functioning of waste infrastructures.

In Ahmed and Datta's chapter on digital infrastructures in Thiruvananthapuram, Kerala, we see the complex (and underanalyzed) impacts of municipal digitalization on women's bodies, urban practices, and experience of violence. While their study finds, on the one hand, that mobile phones and data connectivity can provide information that has the potential to increase their safety in the city, on the other hand smart digital infrastructures also have deleterious consequences. Ahmed and Datta reveal that the same phones can also be weaponized "as tools of VAW [violence against women] across digital and material spaces in the home, neighborhood and city."

Finally, recent interventions within the infrastructure studies literature connects infrastructure to the production of broader patterns of unequal citizenship (Anand 2017; Lemanski 2019, 2020; Sultana 2020; McFarlane and Silver 2017). This vein of the literature has productively revealed the multiplicity of ways that infrastructures are embedded within, and produce, differentiated citizenship rights and complex relations between citizens and the state. Lemanski (2019), for example, shows how citizens, the state, and infrastructures become mutually constitutive: "For citizens, the state is materially and visibly represented though everyday (in)access to public infrastructure, while the state imagines and plans for citizens through infrastructure and maintenance" (115). In analyzing housing and public service delivery in Cape Town, she finds a "mismatch" of perceptions and political identities in both residents' and officials' practices related to infrastructure, connecting the production of competing infrastructural imaginaries and discourses to the material realities of both state actors' and residents' engagement with infrastructure governance. However, these complex configurations by which infrastructures manifest differing understandings, patterns, and experiences of uneven citizenship have only recently (and rarely) been explicitly gendered. Exceptions include a chapter in Anand's book *Hydraulic Citizenship*, in which he demonstrates how gendered time and labor are tied to hydraulic citizenship through the uneven pressures of Mumbai's sporadic water supply. More recently, Sultana (2020, 1407) demonstrates how embodied intersectionalities of socio-spatial differences, including gender, class, and migrant status, combine with the materialities of water and its infrastructure to shape urban citizenship in Dhaka, Bangladesh. This includes the lived citizenship practices of differing groups of residents, as well as community mobilizations and claims to recognition with regard to water. Such recent work shows the analytical imperative to apply an intersectional and gendered lens to how discourses, practices, and materialities of infrastructural citizenship become unevenly embodied across (and through) race, class, gender, ethno-religious, and other identities.

GENDERED INFRASTRUCTURES IN THE EVERYDAY

Feminist geographers have long given attention to the "everyday" as a primary methodological and conceptual focus, an area of inquiry that reveals often overlooked dimensions of infrastructure. Focusing on the everyday reveals not only how processes operating across scales (global, regional, urban) become situated and unevenly experienced, but also how mundane practices and intimate spaces of everyday life reveal important dimensions of power relations, intersectionality, and subjectivity. For example, research on the gendered production of private and public space (Datta 2016), the uneven gendered consequences of geopolitics in domestic life (Smith 2012; Silvey 2004; Fluri 2009), and situated knowledges and experiences of urban environments (Sultana 2020; Parikh 2020; Loftus 2007; Truelove 2019a, 2019b) brings attention to how wider political, economic, and environmental processes become unevenly lived and understood in everyday practice, often (re)producing gendered and racialized subject positions.

Feminist insights into the everyday also give attention to the ways that more conventionally understood structures of power become disrupted, or sometimes hold less overall explanatory value in understanding unequal lived experiences on the ground. For example, feminist political ecologists show how neoliberal socio-natural transformations of water at the global, regional, or city-scale often fail to fully explain water inequality in everyday practice (Kundu and Chatterjee 2020; Harris 2009; Truelove 2011). Sundberg (2016) asserts how the everyday reveals important but often neglected dimensions of environmental practices and engagements, showing how unequal gendered power relations operate in conjunction with other structures of power.

Feminist interventions into the everyday are thus well positioned to deepen infrastructure studies in several additional veins, to which all the chapters of this book contribute. While what we elaborate here is certainly not exhaustive, we particularly focus on how attention to the everyday reveals important dimensions of infrastructural space, the temporalities of infrastructure (decay, repair, maintenance, and the gendered labor and care work that often come into play in relation to these temporalities), and the affective relations and emotional geographies of infrastructure that often go overlooked in studies that focus more exclusively on wider (global, regional, state, city) structures of power.

First, feminist scholarship on the social construction of public and private space details how what is constructed as private and intimate space often normalizes patriarchal gendered relations and, in the case of infrastructures, relegates particular infrastructural practices, labor, and spaces as gendered. From waste that is informally managed in homes and neighborhood lanes as part of gendered household labor (see Fredericks 2018 and this volume), to social networks of care and health management within homes and communities (Truelove and Ruszczyk this volume), infrastructural space in the everyday is often highly gendered. These "intimate infrastructures" (Datta and Ahmed 2020) or "living infrastructures" (Berlant 2011) often are invisible in wider narratives regarding the ways key utilities circulate, particularly as they remain relegated to "private spaces" or reproductive work. However, the lived and intimate experiences of infrastructure profoundly shape how space, materials, and bodies are entangled and co-produce each other, structuring social power relations and situating the uneven lived experiences of large- and small-scale networks. For example, Dávalos and Gamble's work (this volume) shows how women's use of informal transport infrastructures for their everyday commute constitutes a gendered infrastructural assemblage that troubles taken-for-granted public/private binaries. Infrastructures that are not "spectacular" and do not work toward furthering hegemonic politics are rendered invisible. By bringing forth a discussion on informal transport networks, Davalos and Gamble draw attention to that which extends, augments, and subverts planned infrastructural networks.

Second, and relatedly, the infrastructural temporalities of the everyday, including breakdown, decay, maintenance, and repair, offer an opportunity for scholars to study the instability and change that undergirds (and enables) seemingly streamlined functional networks. Repair and maintenance, for example, are often "concealed tools" (Graham and Thrift 2007) that help give an infrastructure the appearance of smooth functionality (Jackson 2015). Similarly, Mattern (2018) goes a step further to show that even maintenance itself is propped up by often invisible spheres of gendered "care work" that enable both social and material infrastructures of life to continue. Connecting to our previous point above, the intimacy of the home, then, is often intricately tied to the operation of public infrastructures (Mattern 2018), for without the gendered care of women who carefully manage and circulate resources like water and waste, the necessary flows of materials and the care structures that enable public infrastructures to function would be absent.

Finally, understanding people's intimate experiences, labor, and knowledge of infrastructures also requires a closer investigation of the visceral, affective, sensorial, and emotional geographies of infrastructure as they are unevenly experienced in the everyday across differing social (race/class/gender/sexuality/etc.) groups. Explaining infrastructural affect, Ramakrishnan, O'Reilly, and Budds (2021) state: "Affect is related to 'how visceral experiences connect with structural and discursive spheres' (Doshi 2017, 126–7), and can be multiple—such as hope, frustration and longing—and fleeting. Affect is also connected to labor, in that infrastructural labor—in terms of the physicality, the barriers and risks involved, the gendered toll, and the anticipation of what is to come when such labor is performed—can compound feelings of neglect and marginality, or move people in more positive ways." Emotional geographies (see Sultana 2011) of infrastructure remain an important yet thus far underexamined aspect of how infrastructures unequally shape people's everyday experiences in gendered and racialized ways. For example, Sultana's (2009, 2011) work on water access in Bangladesh helps explain the complex relations between people, water, and wells, showing how water infrastructures become a force in shaping how social hierarchies are negotiated and addressed. Her examination of the emotional geographies of wells and water reveals differing types of micropolitics that shape unequal gendered experiences in the everyday. We hope this volume may point toward a number of new pathways to examine the everyday experience of infrastructure's absence. This includes the intimately experienced stress, risks, and difficult negotiations entailed in accessing and maintaining infrastructural networks (Ruszczyk 2019); the care and labor to be performed; and the potential emancipatory power of transforming daily interactions with infrastructures in more progressive ways surrounding the roads, waste, water, digital, and electricity networks that shape our existence on the planet.

The chapters in this book draw from varied experiences related to how infrastructures are gendered around the world, connecting the global to the everyday. From water kiosks in Malawi to waste infrastructures in Senegal, the chapters show that infrastructures exclude, reify, and symbolize particular gendered identities—locally and globally. As such, all of the chapters explore infrastructures through an intersectional lens at multiple scales even as they focus on gender in one particular place through one particular infrastructural object or assemblage. In the process, we consider how advances in feminist scholarship offer new frameworks for the critical study of infrastructure, and how such interdisciplinary thinking can move us forward in understanding the production of infrastructural space and its often uneven geographies.

REFERENCES

Ahmed, S. 2016. *Living a Feminist Life*. Duke University Press.

Amin, A. 2014. "Lively Infrastructure." *Theory, Culture, and Society* 31 (7–8): 137–61.

Anand, N. 2017. *Hydraulic City: Water and the Infrastructures of Citizenship in Mumbai*. Duke University Press.

Andueza, L., A. Davies, A. Loftus, and H. Schling. 2020. "The Body as Infrastructure." *Environment and Planning E: Nature and Space* 4 (3): 799–817.

Berlant, L. 2016. "The Commons: Infrastructures for Troubling Times." *Environment and Planning D: Society and Space* 34 (3): 393–419.

Bowker, G. C., S. Timmermans, A. E. Clarke, and E. Balka, eds. 2016. *Boundary Objects and Beyond: Working with Leigh Star*. MIT Press.

Boyer, K. 2006. "Introduction: Gender, Space, and Technology." *ACME: An International Journal for Critical Geographies* 5 (1): 1–8.

Bray, F. 1997. *Technology and Gender: Fabrics of Power in Late Imperial China*. University of California Press.

Chakrabarty, D. 2002. *Habitations of Modernity: Essays in the Wake of Subaltern Studies*. University of Chicago Press.

Cockburn, C., and S. Ormrod. 1993. *Gender and Technology in the Making*. Sage Publications.

Collins, P. H. 2015. "Intersectionality's Definitional Dilemmas." *Annual Review of Sociology* 41: 1–20.

Cook, N., and D. Butz. 2020. "'The Road Changes Everything': Shifting Gendered Mobilities, Spaces, and Subjectivities in Shimshal, Pakistan." *Gender, Place, and Culture* 28 (10): 1408–30.

Cornelissen, S. 2010. "The Geopolitics of Global Aspiration: Sport Mega-Events and Emerging Powers." *International Journal of the History of Sport* 27 (16–18): 3008–25.

Dalakoglou, D., and P. Harvey. 2012. "Roads and Anthropology: Ethnographic Perspectives on Space, Time, and (Im)Mobility." *Mobilities* 7 (4): 459–65.

Datta, A. 2016. *The Illegal City: Space, Law, and Gender in a Delhi Squatter Settlement*. Routledge.

Datta, A., and N. Ahmed. 2020. "Intimate Infrastructures: The Rubrics of Gendered Safety and Urban Violence in Kerala, India." *Geoforum* 110: 67–76.

Desai, R., McFarlane, C., and S. Graham. 2015. "The Politics of Open Defecation: Informality, Body, and Infrastructure in Mumbai." *Antipode* 47 (1): 98–120.

Doron, A., and I. Raja. 2015. "The Cultural Politics of Shit: Class, Gender, and Public Space in India." *Postcolonial Studies* 18 (2): 189–207.

Doshi, S. 2017. "Embodied Urban Political Ecology: Five Propositions." *Area* 49 (1): 125–28.

Fluri, J. L. 2009. "Geopolitics of Gender and Violence 'from Below.'" *Political Geography* 28 (4): 259–65.

Fredericks, R. 2018. *Garbage Citizenship: Vital Infrastructures of Labor in Dakar, Senegal*. Duke University Press.

Graham, S., and C. McFarlane. 2014. *Infrastructural Lives: Urban Infrastructure in Context*. Routledge.

Graham, S., and N. Thrift. 2007. "Out of Order: Understanding Repair and Maintenance." *Theory, Culture, and Society* 24 (3): 1–25.

Harris, L. M. 2009. "Gender and Emergent Water Governance: Comparative Overview of Neoliberalized Natures and Gender Dimensions of Privatization, Devolution, and Marketization." *Gender, Place, and Culture* 16 (4): 387–408.

Harvey, P. and H. Knox. 2012. "The enchantments of infrastructure." *Mobilities* 7 (4): 521–36.

Harvey, P., and H. Knox. 2015. *Roads: An Anthropology of Infrastructure and Expertise.* Cornell University Press.

Hovorka, A. J. 2006. "The No. 1 Ladies' Poultry Farm: A Feminist Political Ecology of Urban Agriculture in Botswana." *Gender, Place, and Culture* 13 (3): 207–25.

Howe, C., J. Lockrem, H. Appel, E. Hackett, D. Boyer, R. Hall, M. Schneider-Mayerson, A. Pope, A. Gupta, E. Rodwell, A. Ballestero, T. Durbin, F. el-Dahdah, E. Long, and C. Mody. 2016. "Paradoxical Infrastructures: Ruins, Retrofit, and Risk." *Science, Technology, and Human Values* 41 (3): 547–65.

Jackson S. 2015. "Repair: Theorizing the Contemporary: The Infrastructure Toolbox." *Cultural Anthropology* website, September 24. https://culanth.org/fieldsights/repair.

Jarosz, L. 2011. "Nourishing Women: Toward a Feminist Political Ecology of Community Supported Agriculture in the United States." *Gender, Place, and Culture* 18 (3): 307–26.

Kundu, R., and S. Chatterjee. 2020. "Pipe Dreams? Practices of Everyday Governance of Heterogeneous Configurations of Water Supply in Baruipur, a Small Town in India." *Environment and Planning C: Politics and Space* 39 (2): 318–35.

Lancione, M., and C. McFarlane. 2016. "Life at the Urban Margins: Sanitation Infra-Making and the Potential of Experimental Comparison." *Environment and Planning A: Economy and Space* 48 (12): 2402–21.

Larkin, B. 2013. "The Politics and Poetics of Infrastructure." *Annual Review of Anthropology* 42: 327–43.

Latour, B. 1992. "Where Are the Missing Masses? The Sociology of a Few Mundane Artifacts." In *Shaping Technology/Building Society: Studies In Sociotechnical Change*, edited by W. E. Bijker, and J. Law, 225–58. MIT Press.

Lawhon M., D. Nilsson, J. Silver, H. Ernston, and S. Lwasa. 2018. "Thinking through Heterogeneous Infrastructure Configurations." *Urban Studies* 55 (4): 720–32.

Lemanski, C. 2019. "Infrastructural Citizenship: The Everyday Citizenships of Adapting and/or Destroying Public Infrastructure in Cape Town, South Africa." *Transactions of the Institute of British Geographers* 45 (3): 589–605.

Lemanski, C. 2020. "Infrastructural Citizenship: (De)Constructing State-Society Relations." *International Development Planning Review* 42 (2).

Loftus, A. 2007. "Working the Socio-Natural Relations of the Urban Waterscape in South Africa." *International Journal of Urban and Regional Research* 31 (1): 41–59.

Massey, D. 2005. *For Space.* Sage.

Massey, D. 2013. *Space, Place, and Gender.* John Wiley & Sons. First published in 1994 by Polity Press.

Mattern, S. 2018. "Maintenance and Care." *Places Journal* (November). https://placesjournal.org/article/maintenance-and-care.

McFarlane, C., and J. Silver. 2017. "The Political City: 'Seeing Sanitation' and Making the Urban Political in Cape Town." *Antipode* 49 (1): 125–48.

Mountz, A. 2018. "Political Geography III: Bodies." *Progress in Human Geography* 42 (5): 759–69.

Mountz, A., and J. Hyndman. 2006. "Feminist Approaches to the Global Intimate." *Women's Studies Quarterly* 34 (1–2): 446–63.

Murton, G. 2017. "Making Mountain Places into State Spaces: Infrastructure, Consumption, and Territorial Practice in a Himalayan Borderland." *Annals of the American Association of Geographers* 107 (2): 536–45.

O'Reilly, K. 2016. "From Toilet Insecurity to Toilet Security: Creating Safe Sanitation for Women and Girls." *Wiley Interdisciplinary Reviews: Water* 3 (1): 19–24.

Pain, R., and L. Staeheli. 2014. "Introduction: Intimacy-Geopolitics and Violence." *Area* 46 (4): 344–47.

Parikh, A. 2020. "Urban Commons to Private Property: Gendered Environments in Mumbai's Fisher Communities." *Environment and Planning D: Society and Space* 39 (2): 271–88.

Ramakrishnan, K., K. O'Reilly, and J. Budds. 2021. "The Temporal Fragility of Infrastructure: Theorizing Decay, Maintenance, and Repair." *Environment and Planning E: Nature and Space* 4 (3): 674–95.

Redfield, P., and S. Robins. 2016. "An Index of Waste: Humanitarian Design, 'Dignified Living,' and the Politics of Infrastructure in Cape Town." *Anthropology Southern Africa* 39 (2): 145–62.

Robins, S. 2014. "The 2011 Toilet Wars in South Africa: Justice and Transition between the Exceptional and the Everyday after Apartheid." *Development and Change* 45 (3): 479–501.

Rodgers, D., and B. O'Neill. 2012. "Infrastructural Violence: Introduction to the Special Issue." *Ethnography* 13 (4): 401–12.

Rose-Redwood, R. S., 2008. "From Number to Name: Symbolic Capital, Places of Memory, and the Politics of Street Renaming in New York City." *Social and Cultural Geography* 9 (4): 431–52.

Ruszczyk, Hanna A. 2019. "Gendered Invisible Urban Resilience." In *The Routledge Handbook of Urban Resilience*, edited by Michael A. Burayidi, Adriana Allen, John Twigg, and Christine Wamsler. Routledge.

Ruwanpura, K. N., B. Brown, and L. Chan. 2020. "(Dis)Connecting Colombo: Situating the Megapolis in Postwar Sri Lanka." *Professional Geographer* 72 (1): 165–79.

Sabhlok, A. 2017. "'Main Bhi to Hindostaan Hoon': Gender and Nation-State in India's Border Roads Organisation." *Gender, Place, and Culture* 24 (12): 1711–28.

Sabhlok, A., H. Cheung, and Y. Mishra. 2015. "Narratives of Health and Well-Being." *Economic and Political Weekly* 50 (51): 71–6.

Schwenkel, C. 2015. "Spectacular Infrastructure and Its Breakdown in Socialist Vietnam." *American Ethnologist* 42 (3): 520–34.

Silvey, R. 2004. "Transnational Domestication: State Power and Indonesian Migrant Women in Saudi Arabia." *Political Geography* 23 (3): 245–64.

Smith, S. H. 2009. "The Domestication of Geopolitics: Buddhist-Muslim Conflict and the Policing of Marriage and the Body in Ladakh, India." *Geopolitics* 14 (2): 197–218.

Smith, S. H. 2012. "Intimate Geopolitics: Religion, Marriage, and Reproductive Bodies in Leh, Ladakh." *Annals of the Association of American Geographers* 102 (6): 1511–28.

Star, S. L. 1999. "The Ethnography of Infrastructure." *American Behavioral Scientist* 43: 377–91.

Sultana, F. 2009. "Fluid Lives: Subjectivities, Gender, and Water in Rural Bangladesh." *Gender, Place, and Culture* 16 (4): 427–44.

Sultana, F. 2011. "Suffering for Water, Suffering from Water: Emotional Geographies of Resource Access, Control, and Conflict." *Geoforum* 42 (2): 163–72.

Sultana, F. 2020. "Embodied Intersectionalities of Urban Citizenship: Water, Infrastructure, and Gender in the Global South." *Annals of the American Association of Geographers* 111 (5): 1407–24.

Sundberg, J. 2016. "Feminist Political Ecology." In *International Encyclopedia of Geography: People, the Earth, Environment, and Technology: People, the Earth, Environment and Technology*, edited by W. Liu and R. Marston, p. 112. Wiley-Blackwell.

Thompson, J. A., S. J. Gaskin, and M. Agbor. 2017. "Embodied Intersections: Gender, Water, and Sanitation in Cameroon." *Agenda* 31 (1): 140–55.

Timmermans, Stefan. 2016. "Working with Leigh Star." In *Boundary Objects and Beyond:*

Working with Leigh Star, edited by Geoffrey Bowker, Stefan Timmermans, Adele Clarke, and Ellen Balka, 1–13. MIT Press.

Truelove, Y. 2011. "(Re-)Conceptualizing Water Inequality in Delhi, India through a Feminist Political Ecology Framework." *Geoforum* 42 (2): 143–52.

Truelove, Y. 2019a. "Gray Zones: The Everyday Practices and Governance of Water beyond the Network." *Annals of the American Association of Geographers* 109 (6): 1758–74.

Truelove, Y. 2019b. "Rethinking Water Insecurity, Inequality, and Infrastructure through an Embodied Urban Political Ecology." *Wiley Interdisciplinary Reviews: Water* 6 (3): e1342.

Truelove, Y. 2019c. "The Body as Infrastructure: Gender and the Everyday Practices and Labour of Water's Urban Circulation." In *Labouring Urban Infrastructures: A Workshop Magazine*, edited by A. De Coss-Corzo, H. Ruszczyk, and K. Stokes, 21.

Truelove, Y. 2021. "Gendered Infrastructure and Liminal Space in Delhi's Unauthorized Colonies." *Environment and Planning D* 39 (6): 1009–25. https://doi.org/10.1177/02637758211055483.

Truelove, Y., and K. O'Reilly. 2020. "Making India's Cleanest City: Sanitation, Intersectionality, and Infrastructural Violence." *Environment and Planning E: Nature and Space* 4 (3): 718–35.

Valentine, G. 2007. "Theorizing and Researching Intersectionality: A Challenge for Feminist Geography." *Professional Geographer* 59 (1): 10–21.

von Schnitzler, A. 2015. "Infrastructure, Apartheid Techno-Politics, and Temporalities of 'Transition.'" In *The Promise of Infrastructure*, edited by Nikhil Anand, Akhil Gupta, *and* Hannah Appel, 134–54. Duke University Press.

Wilson, A. 2016. "The Infrastructure of Intimacy." *Signs: Journal of Women in Culture and Society* 41 (2): 247–80.

Winner, L. 1993. "Social Constructivism: Opening the Black Box and Finding It Empty." *Science as Culture* 3 (3): 427–52.

CHAPTER I

CONCRETIZING MODERNITY: THE GENDERED LABOR OF CEMENT INFRASTRUCTURES IN VIETNAM

Christina Schwenkel

> Nothing is more beautiful than your hands
> The hands of a builder fragrant with fresh mortar
>
> —Quang Thành, *Ng hệ An News,* 1978

Tim Ingold begins his 2007 article "Materials against Materiality," with a conundrum: that the "ever-growing literature in anthropology and archaeology [and, by extension, geography] that deals explicitly with the subjects of *materiality* and *material culture* seems to have hardly anything to say about *materials*" (1, emphasis in the original). By materials, he means the "stuff that things are made of" (1)—the stuff, for the purpose of this chapter, of infrastructure. Heeding Ingold's call to look not at things or infrastructures already made (the finished bridge, dam, or building) but at the materials involved in making them and their properties, this chapter examines the tangible materiality that has made much of our infrastructural worlds imaginable and possible: cement. By cement, I mean that powdery material "substance-in-becoming" (Barad 2003, 822) of finely ground limestone, shale, clay, iron ore, and other organic matter that, when heated at extremely high temperatures, chemically combine to produce that binding agent that we so depend on in our everyday, infrastructure-dependent lives. I take Ingold's provocation one step further, however, to examine the embodied labor attached to processes of transforming the raw, extracted materials of rationalized nature into modern concrete cities (Gandy 2002, 52). In so doing, I show cement to be a gendered substance of technological nation-building and a technic for the material and ideological building of socialism. Following Gibson-Graham, my approach displaces the "hegemonic framing of capitalism" (2008, 615) to understand how other infrastructural dreams materialized through concrete beyond colonialism and capital accumulation, informed by internationalist discourses of equality and liberation, failed to eradicate racial and gender hierarchies, but rather augmented them.

The rapidly expanding scholarship on infrastructure as a socio-material assemblage (e.g., Bennett 2005) has paid little attention to the ways in which gendered subjectivities and notions of femininity and masculinity have been anchored to infrastructure and its associated spatio-material and technical practices. On the one hand, this is surprising given that infrastructure is central to state- and nation-making projects, which *has* been the topic of much feminist scholarship (see Yuval-Davis 1997). On the other hand, scholars have rightly pointed to a lack of attention to women's urban lives and struggles in critical urban theory (Peake 2016). As technical objects and systems that have been historically coded masculine and linked, in essentialist ways, to male domains of science and technology (Wajcman 2010), infrastructures have been typically unmarked in their renderings and unaffixed to gendered bodies. Feminist literature that seeks to redress this gap often focuses on the "resource users" or consumers of infrastructure's value-added products as a means of social reproduction. Analyses of conflicts over access to water, for example, have shown how hydraulic infrastructures—including their breakdown (Anand 2017; Schwenkel 2015)—are tied to gendered divisions of labor and shifting relations of power across time and space (Sultana 2009; Truelove 2011). Less attention, however, has been paid to the gendered politics of *making* infrastructure. As Ingold (2012, 435) argues, to focus on the social lives and properties of materials is to "prioritize the processes of production . . . over those of consumption." To that end, while important work has pointed to the role of male laborers, for example in roadwork (Sabhlok 2017), including stratification among them (Harvey and Knox 2015), the labor of women in building and maintaining infrastructure remains largely invisible. For this reason, I argue that banal building materials like cement and concrete *are* a topic of feminist concern, not unlike water, precisely because they offer new ways to think about socio-material relations of infrastructure as tethered to particular divisions of labor. State retrenchment and neoliberalism, however, do not merely exacerbate gender inequalities in accessing everyday infrastructure, as the literature suggests. Rather, through an historical and ethnographic focus on the building materials industry in Vietnam, I show how such inequalities are constitutive of infrastructures and their harms, which have been dependent on gender disparities to concretize colonial and postcolonial nation-building.

There is arguably no other construction material more ubiquitous in Southeast Asia than cement. Cement is the stuff of dreams; stuffed into bags that find their way to all corners of the region through "supply chain capitalism" (Tsing 2009) and through logistical regimes of distribution under state socialism. These dreams are typically forward-looking and progress-oriented: "Development Is a Bag of Cement" is the title of an article on "infrapolitics" by John Cameron (2009). Like in Bolivia, where Cameron works, in Vietnam cement has been embraced as modern, rational, and urban, in contrast to the backwardness of traditional building materials, like thatch and bamboo, that did not allow for the same versatility and innovation in design (Nguyễn Quân 1982, 103–4). The association of cement with technological development has its limitations, however: cement is generally the stuff of lesser dreams—that is, *small-scale* public works (Cameron 2009, 694)—while concrete remains the matter of grander infrastructural and engineering possibilities (see figure 1.1).

As a marker of modernity (Forty 2012), cement is the primary ingredient in concrete, the technology most often used in public infrastructure projects to construct major highways, dams, bridges, and housing. Abidin Kusno, an architectural historian of Jakarta, once argued that such public infrastructures serve as visual signs of progress marked by straight lines, right angles, verticality, and reinforced concrete (2000, 68). As I show below, images of laboring migrant women as the procurers of postcolonial progress communicated similar messages about triumph over backwardness, though they did so from the bottom of the chain of global technology transfers meant to bring postwar Vietnam into modern time. When viewed through the affective lens of desires for national advancement, it becomes possible to see modern infrastructure as "the dream of social mobility captured in concrete," as the architect Reinier de Graaf once proclaimed (2015). These observations remind us that cement is not only a technical or even alchemical substance that takes on new properties (the paste that bonds with aggregates to generate concrete), but also *gendered* political and polarizing matter: it has been used to build empires and utopias, as well as to dismantle and destroy them.

In this chapter, I show how women's labor was key to materializing utopian dreamworlds through modern infrastructure that promised postcolonial liberation in two senses: first, through the mechanization of production, and second, through release from the domestic drudgery of social reproduction. I argue that on both accounts, these technological aspirations increased rather than decreased the labor-intensive conditions under which women lived and

Fig. 1.1. "For the solidity of reinforced concrete constructions, use the Haiphong Cement Plant." Colonial-era advertisement on display in Hải Phòng Cement Museum, Vietnam, 2022.

worked, thus offering new insights into the relationship between gender and infrastructural violence. In the pages that follow, I draw on the ongoing field and archival research in northern Vietnam between 2010 and 2022 to support this argument by first examining the history of cement production in Hải Phòng as a racial project of colonial subjectivization that led to revolution. I then show how the proletarianization of women and the import of new building technologies, such as prefabrication, were underpinned by particular power asymmetries that framed technology transfers from the socialist Global North ("Second World," at that time) to the decolonizing Global South ("Third World") as anticolonial projects of social and technological improvement—language that mirrored colonial discourses of uplift. Through a case study of Vinh, an industrial port city destroyed by US military violence and rebuilt with socialist development assistance where I have conducted fieldwork over the past twelve years, I look more closely at gender hierarchies and the overrepresentation of women in the building materials industry, who were conflicting symbols of both the possibility of a concrete futurity and the potential for its failure.

CEMENTING INDOCHINA'S DREAMS

French imperial power radically reconfigured landscapes and social relationships in colonial Indochina under the banner of "modernization." So, too, did cement. Developed in France in the 1850s, the alchemical production of cement had a "revolutionary effect on building construction" by eliminating geographical constraints: durable concrete was scalable anywhere (Forty 2012, 102). Materially, cement was the substance through which colonial visions of conquest became manifest in the built environment (Harvey 2010). Ideologically, cement was the civilizing "stuff" of subjectivization—the production of loyal colonial subjects—at the core of France's imperial mission to uplift, control, and govern the population.

One of the largest and earliest industrial projects in Vietnam was construction of the first cement factory in 1899 (Brocheux and Hémery 2009, 162). Founded by the Société des Ciments Portland artificiels de l'Indochine on the outskirts of Hải Phòng (and referenced in figure 1.1), the plant symbolized colonial expansion and ideologies of white superiority through the spread of French technology. The circulation across Indochina of bags of Portland cement, imprinted with a dragon logo—a quintessential sign of imperial strength and power—served as technologically persuasive "advertisements of the colonial project" (Starostina 2009, 182) that also naturalized colonial rule. Bags of "dragon cement" (*xi măng côn rồng*) would also provide the material scaffolding of modernity through French technological feats of construction and engineering (see Quang 2010).

As Marx predicted, experiences with industrial capitalism at this time were tied to dispossession and the creation of a class of landless wage workers whose survival depended on the sale of their labor power. In Vietnam, industrial workers at the turn of the twentieth century were mostly peasants who had lost their land to the expansion of colonial industry and other public works. This new proletariat was largely male owing to colonial gender ideologies that

Fig. 1.2. Women labor outside the Hải Phòng cement factory building auxiliary structures, 1927. Photo on display in the Vietnam Cement Museum on the site of the original factory in Hải Phòng, which is now an upscale housing settlement, 2022.

saw women's place as mothers in the household (Werner 2009). For example, railway workers in Vinh—my site of ethnographic study—were all men (Del Testa 2002), an observation that Frederick Cooper also made of colonial Africa's emergence of "industrial man" (1996, 2).

The preference for male labor in colonial factories did not mean that women were absent from infrastructure projects. Although there has been a "near total exclusion" of accounts of women's colonial experiences in Vietnam (Ha 1999, 96), there is a brief mention of female proletariats employed in mine work (115). Moreover, the gender bias in industry did not preclude the ways in which women were subjected to forced labor practices outside the factory to facilitate its daily operations (see figure 1.2). Like in Africa (Akurang-Parry 2000, 8), the role of compulsory female labor in colonial infrastructure development, such as mining or road-building to enable the transport of industrial goods, has largely been neglected by historians who pay more attention to women's domesticated labor and sex work under colonization.

Factory work floors in French Indochina became pivotal sites of anticolonial organizing. This would indelibly change the gender disparities in labor connected with industry and infrastructure. The cement plant in Hải Phòng, for example, transformed into a political space of uprisings by thousands of workers, also by those in the quarries, at the dawn of the Vietnamese revolution (Nguyễn Văn Quang 2015). The mass mobilization of men and women against French rule and exploitation would disrupt industrial operations, as colonial infrastructure became a target of sabotage and tactical resistance during the First Indochina War (1946–1954) that followed the founding of the independent Democratic Republic of (North) Vietnam (DRV). Such unrest is a reminder of the ways in which political matter, like cement, contributed to expanding empires, and was just as easily used to subvert them. As Braun and Whatmore remind us, technological objects are not only central to and constitutive of political life, but are also the stuff of "lively materialities" that mobilize collectivities and form the basis of their sociocultural arrangements (2010, xi–xii).

The fraught history of colonial cement production in Vietnam demonstrates how technologies of subjection quickly became the material politics of liberation. Workers would "emancipate" and gain control of the Hải Phòng cement plant on May 12, 1955 (Nguyễn Văn Quang 2015), heralding a new era of proletarianization, as women entered factories in unprecedented numbers. Women's labor force participation in revolutionary Vietnam was connected to both the postcolonial expansion of industry and the rehabilitation of war-ruined infrastructure. To decentralize the building materials industry and propel local production, regional cement factories were built across the provinces in the North, including one in the distant region of Nghệ An on the urban outskirts of Vinh with the support of China (which also provided assistance with construction of cement factories in and around Hanoi). Socialist urban policy sought to close the infrastructure gap—under French colonialism, infrastructure had primarily served industry and non-indigenous populations—by extending basic public services to the masses. Stable, accessible infrastructure would advance the cause of national development and liberate women from tedious domestic tasks that made them less productive in the factory. These initiatives were disrupted a decade later with the onset of US aerial warfare.

The Second Indochina War (1955–1975) would further transform gender relations and divisions of labor as men and women were mobilized once again for national defense (see figure 1.3). While men typically served on the front lines in the South (following the division of the country in 1954), women participated in efforts at the rear and along the forested corridors that made up the Hồ Chí Minh Trail. The Three Responsibilities Movement (Ba Đảm Đang)—maintain family (social reproduction), the economy (agricultural and industrial production), and sovereignty (defense and combat)—placed tremendous triple

Fig. 1.3. "Cement: Everything for Victory, 1973," pamphlet cover on display in Hải Phòng Cement Museum, Vietnam, 2022.

burdens on women in wartime (Turner and Hao 1999). Female youth volunteers (*thanh niên xung phong*) engaged in high-risk manual tasks as embodied practice connected to the labor of infrastructure maintenance and repair. In my interviews in Vinh—the most decimated city in the North—women recalled the grueling physical labor of digging tunnels, rebuilding roads, repairing bridges, detonating bombs, filling craters, carrying ammunition, growing rice, and evacuating industrial machinery to safer ground, all of which they carried out under the threat of enemy forces above. Tragically but not surprisingly, these undertakings resulted in a high rate of death; socialist equality presumed that women's lives were just as expendable as those of men.

The war was not only fought on the backs of women who served as fixers, producers, and carriers of military goods for the front lines; it was rebuilt with their hard labor as well. After the war, women did not return to their rural homesteads; there was no post-conflict restoration of a gender order that effaced women from the public sphere (cf. Campbell 2005). Rather, given the disproportionate numbers of male war dead, their acquired skills were needed more than ever in industry and in the rebuilding of demolished infrastructure. Socialist reconstruction would continue the trend toward feminization of the industrial workforce, as the state called on women to serve the nation through their manual labor once again.

MATERIALIZING POSTCOLONIAL GENDER HIERARCHY

While cement may have been the foundational matter of colonial dreams, concrete materialized the even bolder dreams of socialism and its grandiose industrial projects, including mass housing. Cheap, durable, and efficient, concrete was central to grand state visions of postcolonial nation building through Global North–Global South circulations of construction technologies intended to help Vietnam modernize and recover from the violence of US imperialism. Like cement, concrete was similarly entwined with geopolitical hierarchies and forward-looking narratives of progress that espoused "a better future." It, too, served as the "stuff of politics" that enabled new possibilities for relationships to form between political and technological practices (Braun and Whatmore 2010). In this section, however, I am interested in the ways in which socialist concrete indexed strategic realignments of power among competing communist countries vying for sovereign control over the development, use, and extraction of rational nature as industrial resource and commodity. Concrete, I show, served as a binding agent to draw materials, people, and technologies together into new social, political, and infrastructural arrangements that were not always feasible or even desirable. These hierarchical arrangements were as gendered as they were racialized: the (Eastern) European training of Vietnamese male technicians and female unskilled laborers in modern building technologies under the rhetoric of solidarity was central to the *global* Cold War project of socialist modernization. Taming a dangerous, unruly landscape devastated by a protracted air war would transform migrant worker-warriors into a skilled urban labor force. In this sense, infrastructure was not only a progressive, forward-looking civilizing strategy, but also a state pedagogical project that endeavored to produce certain kinds of gendered laboring subjects for socialist nation building, a point I come back to later in the chapter.

To set up my argument, it is important to note that historically, the DRV (North Vietnam) remained unrecognized and isolated for several years after its founding in 1945, until it entered into diplomatic relations with the major communist powers in early 1950 (Olsen 2006). Such geopolitical ambivalence allowed for the less powerful and younger state of the German Democratic Republic (GDR) or East Germany to play a prominent role in concretizing Vietnam's aspirations to socialist modernity. New alliances with the socialist Global North transformed the material and techno-infrastructural landscape of the struggling postcolony, as the leadership in Hanoi looked beyond the dominant powers of China and the Soviet Union for other sources of development support.

Given its own "ruin to development" teleology that was itself dependent on female infrastructural labor (Treber 2014), East Germany offered a scalar model of industrial growth that promised to swiftly and efficiently rebuild the country through mechanization of the building materials industry. The most ideal way proposed to accomplish this was prefabrication, or the import of precast concrete technologies. Prefabrication was enmeshed in, and productive of, a host of symbolic gender ideologies and racialized power asymmetries that resonated with earlier colonial discourses of national development. It would showcase East Germany's moral and technological superiority (also over capitalist West Germany), while rescuing Vietnam from the primitivity to which it had been bombed. This "progress" and reversal of backwardness, I show below, was coded through the female body, which was considered by many to be innately uncivilized and outside modernity (Leshkowich 2014).

At the time, prefabrication marked the built environment of socialist urban infrastructure, as this modern building technology was disseminated, adopted, modified, and applied across the Soviet Union, Eastern Europe, and the Global South. Often referred to as "panel" (*Platte*) construction, prefabrication was considered the most rational and resourceful means to build industry and deliver durable modern housing. Ideally, concrete components—from slabs to decorative elements—would be manufactured in factories, then transported to construction sites for assembly into complete modular structures referred to as "prefab" or "panel" housing. These experimental building technologies were exemplary of the fraught Cold War technopolitics of the time, whereby benevolent socialist infrastructure like housing was built in competition with the capitalist West (Zarecor 2011). As an architectural solution to Europe's own post–World War II housing crisis, the "prefab" model was exported to decolonizing countries, including Vietnam, which became East Germany's laboratory for standardizing the construction industry. In a telling display of global power hierarchies, Vietnam's demolished landscape became an Orientalist canvas for utopian dreams of "tropical modernism."

Until this point, brick construction—molded clay-fired blocks adhered by cement mortar joints—had been the go-to technology of reconstruction. Cement factories had been bombed, and production had come to a near halt. Because brickwork was more flexible and required fewer tools, technologies, and natural resources, it had continued during aerial bombardment and in subsequent periods of privation. Historically, bricks had been associated with architectural forms that were not readily available to the Vietnamese population, who lived predominantly in houses made of thatch and bamboo. Like cement, bricks symbolized the modern aesthetics of colonial power and rule, as well as commercial wealth. This changed with the revolution, when sun-baked, earthen bricks came to symbolize the nation's rebirth and regeneration. As I have argued elsewhere (Schwenkel 2013), bricks were gendered objects closely associated with female unskilled labor. Brickwork, too, was feminized: in Vinh, close to 80 percent of bricklayers involved in urban reconstruction were women (Purtak 1982). Images of female bricklayers rebuilding roads and infrastructure circulated in national media (see figure 1.4), along with poems that made explicit the metaphorical connections between women, bricks, and mortar (the binding paste), including the stanza by Quang Thành at the start of this chapter. Another example from 1974 romanticized brick production by linking it to the delicate care and touch of a woman, who—like its clay materiality—was intimately connected to earth and to reproduction: "You knead and care for each handful of soil . . . In the past [it] nourished people, while today it shelters them" (Schwenkel 2013, 266). Before mechanization, brick production remained too low, however, to realize grand visions of Vietnam's rise from ashes. An alternative technology that could achieve the desired scale and pace of recovery was necessary: concrete.

To break with bricks, in 1972 East Germany proposed to construct a large-panel concrete factory in Đạo Tú, Vĩnh Phúc province, fifty kilometers north of Hanoi, to assist with the rebuilding of the capital city after the war. This "gifted" infrastructure was framed as benevolent and part of a larger package of technical and vocational assistance to Vietnam. Yet, the resumption of mass bombing later that year forced the project's postponement until 1974. Prefabrication at the envisioned scale of "large panels" was new to Vietnam, and its promise to quickly and cheaply produce standardized social housing for workers appealed to government officials, given the urgent postwar need.

Fig. 1.4. Female bricklayers rebuilding infrastructure. (*Nghệ Tĩnh* News, July 21, 1978)

Architects and inhabitants were more skeptical of this transformative technology, however—a point I return to below.

For the GDR, Vietnam's first concrete panel factory held high political value, even though it was culturally incongruous and overly ambitious, given infrastructural constraints faced at the time. East German engineers who worked on site between 1974 and 1977 were also cynical about the project, which required the import of all machinery and equipment from abroad. According to Nguyễn Tham Thiện Kế (2011), at the inaugural handover of the factory in 1977 to the provincial party secretary, leery German technicians warned their Vietnamese colleagues that they would face many hardships if they did not appoint a technically competent cadre to run daily operations. The party secretary's son, who studied engineering in East Germany, was subsequently appointed as manager of the plant. This story is important for two reasons. First, it reveals that foreign experts sent to "transfer" expertise were not themselves optimistic about Vietnam's capacity for mechanization, and not only because of infrastructural lack. Rather, shaped by notions of European superiority, some foreign experts considered Vietnamese workers and management to be

Fig. 1.5. In situ prefabrication: women laboring on a construction site in Hanoi, November 1974. (Hubert Link. BArch Bild 183-N1105-425)

lacking in the skills necessary to use "their" modern technology. Second, and most important to my argument, it offers insights into the gendered and racialized division of labor that underpinned the masculine culture of technical-infrastructural expertise, whereby white European men trained Vietnamese male elites in new building technologies, while young migrant women took positions as low-skilled manual laborers.

Panel construction in Vietnam would become an example of the disconnect between a hopeful utopian future and a disenchanted dystopian reality. The concrete panel factory was envisioned as a harbinger of modernization. It was projected to build one thousand self-contained apartments annually, each measuring fifty-eight square meters, and equipped with basic infrastructure, including water, sanitation, and electricity, for reproduction of the modern nuclear family. In an interview, a Vietnamese architect who had studied in the Soviet Union maintained that this was far too ambitious, if not impossible. Because of the magnitude of the bombing, there was little technical infrastructure in place to build a new construction industry. The plant suffered from material shortages, and few workers were trained in the technique of concrete prefabrication. Decimated roads linked the remote factory with the city, making the transport of panels virtually impossible. Moreover, cultural unfamiliarity, and a tendency toward extended families, made prefabricated technologies and their embedded Eurocentric ideologies challenging to introduce to Vietnam. In the end, bricks remained the standard scaffolding technology, and the imperative to mechanize the building materials industry to reduce labor intensity and improve productivity was put on hold. Instead, small-scale prefab forms were produced on site by groups of mostly female unskilled workers (see figure 1.5). For women, this meant that the socialist state continued to rely on their hard manual labor for infrastructure development, despite promises of emancipation through industrial modernity.

INFRASTRUCTURE AS PEDAGOGICAL PRACTICE

There were similar difficulties—and gendered asymmetries—with the concrete factory built in 1975 on the edge of Vinh, three hundred kilometers south of Hanoi. This plant, also designed and equipped by the GDR as a gesture of "friendship," was anticipated to produce prefabricated concrete parts for both industry and a sprawling residential estate with three dozen standardized housing blocks. This integrated residential area was the first of its scale in Vietnam, where I conducted my fieldwork in 2010–2012, with follow-up visits biennially. New urban infrastructure, including social housing, was intended to reduce socioeconomic differentiation and the gendered division of domestic labor through universal access to basic public services following the city's annihilation. Given constrained technological capacity at the time, this plant did not aim to generate large concrete panels like the plant farther north, however. Instead, it would produce the key components of modular design, including ceiling plates, balcony slabs, floor tiles, supporting beams, stairways, and ornamental pieces to adorn uniform brick buildings. Prefabrication was both a temporal and technological solution to "de-modernization" as a result of infrastructural warfare (Graham 2005), and was intended to optimize the scale of urban recovery by cementing a new futurity. Like in Hanoi, such technologies were at odds with postwar conditions, however. Impassible roads and downed bridges made transport unfeasible. Steel for molds was in short supply, and machinery was lacking. Initially, there was a critical shortage of labor as volunteers—mostly women—worked to clear rubble, fill craters, and rebuild roads to create a stable foundation for new infrastructural projects made of concrete (Schwenkel 2020, 65).

Attention to the gendered bodies associated with the labor of infrastructure adds an important dimension to materiality that Ingold overlooked in his call to study transformations to materials and their properties. That is, everyday repetitive acts of hard manual work, such as extraction of gravel without machinery to produce cement as the basis of reinforced concrete buildings (or modular parts), are themselves gendered and dependent on entrenched divisions between masculine/skilled and feminine/unskilled labor. Such divisions are commonly seen in and beyond Vietnam in the labor of waste infrastructure, for instance (Minh T. N. Nguyen 2016; Schwenkel 2019; see also Fredericks 2014). One surprising finding in my historical-ethnographic research in Vinh was the degree to which women—mainly rural migrants, including the youth volunteers who had toiled in wartime on the Hồ Chí Minh Trail—were overrepresented in the buildings materials industry. In stone quarries, female unskilled laborers made up 51.7 percent of the manual workforce, in limestone 63 percent, and in brickwork 77 percent (Purtak 1982, 24). Of the two hundred workers at the concrete factory, a whopping 70 percent were women. Men, on the other hand, were more likely to hold management or skilled labor positions that required technical expertise, thus exacerbating—rather than eliminating—gender inequities under socialism.

There were challenges to creating a qualified workforce in a short period of time. To mechanize industry and shift from building by hand to machine-based manufacturing, workers were in urgent need of training. Infrastructure as pedagogical project and practice served to normalize gender difference and social hierarchy, even though training was couched in moral discourses of inclusion and equality. Training involved Western tutelage. At the highest level, elite Vietnamese men (and, to a lesser extent, women) went overseas to study in Soviet bloc countries to receive postgraduate degrees in engineering. Technical training also took place in Vietnam, with senior foreign experts (almost always men) acting as coaches or esteemed teachers, who passed down their knowledge and the charge of national development to Vietnamese apprentices. Above all, mechanization required a skilled and disciplined workforce. To this end, GDR experts built Vinh's first postsecondary vocational school in 1977, modeled on a German "hands-on" curriculum that stressed theory and practice, or studying and working simultaneously. The school offered two-year co-ed programs in mechanics, bricklaying, concrete work, carpentry, welding, and electronics. In an interview, one East German curriculum designer maintained that the school had attracted and trained equal numbers of men and women, who went on to find employment in the construction industry. His claims were backed by celebratory images I viewed in the press and in his own personal collection that showed female students in workshops operating machinery (see figure 1.6), or sitting attentively in classrooms with equal gender distribution. In this rescue narrative, Vietnamese women's participation in vocational training, and their handling of infrastructural technologies, was rendered emancipatory from feudal and colonial exploitation, as well as from gender exclusion in the work place—a necessary step on the pathway to socialist modernity. Women's proximity to infrastructure and technology would thus become constitutive of, rather than contradictory to, their femininity.

Women's participation in conventionally male-dominated sectors of infrastructure was promoted in images of female workers as the builders of Vietnamese socialism. These optimistic representations of a joyful, resilient workforce provide insight into the idealized labor women were expected to perform in the service of socialist nation-building. Gendered images and discourses that fit with the state's civilizing agenda communicated forward-looking and socially transformative values through posters and photographs of women close to infrastructural objects, including cranes, machines, and concrete beams, while highlighting increases in productivity and the surpassing of quotas. The gendered bodies of female laborers were meant to convey affects of hope coalescing around a prosperous modernity that was finally within reach of the population. At the same time, paternalist images of skills transfer from male foreign experts and local male elites to female migrant workers showed this technological worlding and North-South tutelage in building technologies to be contingent on gender, racial, and cultural differences.

Beyond labor, there were far more logistical complications with prefabricated technologies in Vinh than there had been in Hanoi, given the scale of aerial assaults inflicted on its landscape and population over ten years. Infrastructural warfare did not just switch the city off (see Graham 2005), but effectively shut it down. Factories, like the Chinese-built cement plant, were targeted and destroyed, forcing serial evacuations of civilians. Wide-scale devastation presented acute operational difficulties for the new concrete factory built on the outskirts of the city. In the initial years of reconstruction, the main element of concrete—cement—was unavailable and had to be imported from East Germany. The cement plant would not resume operations until outfitted with imported technologies that replaced ruined Chinese machinery more than two years after the cessation of bombing. Other materials that were lacking and needed to be imported to allow for concrete manufacturing included rebar to reinforce the concrete, tools and machinery to increase productivity,

Fig. 1.6. Acquiring technical knowledge and hands-on experience, 1979. (Photo by Raimer Buntrock)

trucks to transport prefabricated parts, cranes to lift those parts, and so on. Counter to the promise that mechanization and the shift from manual work to machines would improve lives and livelihoods, in the absence of material resources needed to rebuild, women's physical labor remained the crux of infrastructure (re)development.

The female bricklayers, concrete workers, and builders I met during my fieldwork in Vinh who had worked on the construction site of the housing estate and trained at the vocational school recalled their living and working conditions as *khổ* (miserable). This was a time of food insecurity and lack of basic goods and services. People worked hard to realize the promise of infrastructure as an escape from chronic scarcity and inequality on the forward-looking path to modernity. But those promises in the workplace (mechanization) and at home (indoor plumbing) did not materialize as planned, placing additional burdens on women to maintain both labor productivity and social reproduction in the home.

Despite celebrations of postcolonial and post-feudal equality, women remained at the bottom of the workplace hierarchy. The division of labor was such that women were responsible for the "unskilled" heavy work of infrastructure, such as producing, transporting, and laying bricks or filling and weighing bags of cement by hand under the watchful eyes of male supervisors (see figure 1.7). The women I came to know did not complain about this hierarchy or the years of arduous labor and pressure to increase productivity—the slow infrastructural violence that wore down their already exhausted bodies from the war. Rather, they tended to accept their lot as "fate"; such was the life of women from the countryside who came to the city, they said and chuckled uneasily, revealing entrenched beliefs about rural-urban difference, despite the revolution, which spoke of flattening such hierarchies. Recall that women had already been involved with the hard labor of infrastructure repair in wartime. The labor of national defense and national reconstruction was, from their perspective, continuous. More significant to the women was that the end of the air war had brought evacuations to a halt and thereafter allowed them to (re)settle with their families in newly built housing, but not without further difficulties. "What is there to say?" one woman mused, while pointing to my privileged disconnect from the violence of war and poverty that had pervaded her everyday life. "We never stopped working," she shared. Another female worker recalled, "We walked miles to our jobs every day, and then came home to haul water," despite the new indoor plumbing infrastructure (also quoted in Schwenkel 2015).

Like in Hanoi, infrastructural limitations meant that standardized mass housing—its striking similarity to housing blocks in Eastern Europe notwithstanding—was not made with modern prefabricated slabs, but with traditional brick. The women in my study recollected the barebones operations they were forced to endure. Before the concrete factory became operational in 1976, precasting and assembly were done on site with makeshift wooden frames, an adaption that was also necessary in Hanoi (see figure 1.5). Materials had to be transported by cart, and components were carried and emplaced by hand until imported cranes became more readily available. As one male engineer noted of the project's early years, these were not modern concrete buildings of the future, but labor-intensive, conventional brick structures assembled by the hands of women. It would take a few more years of recovery for mechanization of industry to be achieved. This would reduce the need for industrial workers over time as the postwar economy continued to decline. The female builders of infrastructure were eventually allocated units in the housing estate they built—a product of their unalienated labor in recognition of their contribution to nation building, confirmed by the framed certificates that hung on their walls. By the mid 1990s, however, most had been forced into early retirement, owing to declining health and downsizing that followed economic reforms (Đổi mới) in 1986. In Vietnam's post-reform labor climate, the women workers who struggled to put their aspirations into practice by first maintaining and then

Fig. 1.7. Gendered division of manual labor in the cement factory in Vinh, late 1970s. (Photo by Raimer Buntrock)

rebuilding urban infrastructure proved in the end to be the most expendable. These *gendered* dynamics to infrastructural violence, where "relationships of power and hierarchy translate into palpable forms of physical and emotional harm" (Rodgers and O'Neill 2012, 402), thus demand more attention in the literature as such harms, I have shown, disproportionately affect women.

CONCLUSION: DECOMPOSITIONS

The final undoing of the twentieth century finds concrete proof in the methodic removal of its physical substance. (de Graaf 2015)

What are we to make of infrastructural dreams of concrete and cement, those symbolically rich composite materials and binding agents that adhered gendered bodies to infrastructural technologies, and to one another relationally through shared aspirations to finally become "modern"? First, these material worlds decayed quickly—another infrastructural injustice that women endured. Concrete is hardly an inert matter with fixed attributes, but is actively "caught up in the currents" of urban lifeworlds and the ecologies of material transformation (Ingold 2007, 12), a process I have also shown to be highly gendered and generative of particular experiences of suffering and resilience. Exposure to corrosive atmospheres, like moisture, mold, salt, and air, induced radical chemical changes to cement and steel rebar, creating dystopian conditions of *unplanned obsolescence* with real social, material, and ideological consequences for governments and urban populations, especially women. At the global scale, these decaying structures have come to symbolize the ruins of socialism's drab modernist utopias. In Vietnam, such ruins serve as a reminder of ways that women's labor shaped and was shaped by that very utopian promise of modernity as created materially through concrete infrastructures. They also bespeak of a state pedagogical apparatus aimed at the subjectivization of a female workforce.

In Vinh, construction technologies that once embodied the promise of progress now seem to preclude it. In an ironic twist, the deteriorating city provides fodder for neoliberal logics of redevelopment as infrastructure has been reimagined as a tool for capital accumulation rather than a means to social equality. But capitalism itself cannot be held responsible for stratification and the respatialization of urban inequality, though it has played no small role. Rather, as I have shown, urban infrastructures have been dependent on, and also productive of, gender disparities across colonial, socialist, and now market economies, although to differing degrees and effects. National reconstruction deepened gender inequalities at the same time as the revolution made some important gains for women (Werner 2009). In the postwar years, the state's priority to industrialize and expand its hegemony over the South following reunification of the country, sidelined concerns about equality between women and men. The establishment of a classless society, in short, trumped the eradication of nationwide gender disparities.

Similarly, scholarship on infrastructure and infrastructural violence that foregrounds class and social status at the expense of gender risks not only silencing women's experiences, but also neglecting other indicators of inequality. This includes how gendered divisions of labor inform all stages of design, construction, use, and maintenance of infrastructure across time and space, or how infrastructural harms disproportionately affect women. Infrastructure and its technologies are often presumed to be the domain of men, unless the focus turns to "people as infrastructure" (Truelove and Ruszczyk 2022). Women's inclusion in the low-skilled labor of infrastructure was not gender progressive, however, but exploitative—and it continues to be so today. Like the uneven burdens and risks of water work in South Asia (Truelove 2011; Sultana 2009), women in Vietnam continue to bear disproportionately the burdens and risks associated with the labor of producing and maintaining urban infrastructure under the gaze of male supervision, from resource extraction to brick manufacturing, road-building, and construction (see figure 1.8). The raw materials from the earth—sand, gravel, slate, and clay—that female labor

Fig. 1.8. Female laborers engaged in road construction under male supervision in Hanoi, 2022. (Photo by Christina Schwenkel)

extracts and transforms into the stuff of infrastructure remain a topic of critical feminist concern and inquiry. Such materiality lays at the center of women's struggle for liberation as the users, consumers, and active builders of concrete infrastructural worlds.

REFERENCES

Akurang-Parry, Kwabena Opare. 2000. "Colonial Forced Labor Policies for Road-Building in Southern Ghana and International Anti-Forced Labor Pressures, 1900–1940." *African Economic History* 28: 1–25.

Anand, Nikhil. 2017. *Hydraulic City: Water and the Infrastructures of Citizenship in Mumbai.* Duke University Press.

Barad, Karen. 2003. "Posthumanist Performativity: Toward an Understanding of How Matter Comes to Matter." *Signs* 28 (3): 801–31.

Bennett, Jane. 2005. "The Agency of Assemblages and the North American Blackout." *Public Culture* 17 (3): 445–65.

Braun, Bruce, and Sarah J. Whatmore, eds. 2010. "The Stuff of Politics: An Introduction." In *Political Matter: Technoscience, Democracy and Public Life*, edited by Bruce Braun and Sarah J. Whatmore, ix–xl. University of Minnesota Press.

Brocheux, Pierre, and Daniel Hémery. 2009. *Indochina: An Ambiguous Colonization, 1858–1954.* University of California Press.

Cameron, John D. 2009. "'Development Is a Bag of Cement': The Infrapolitics of Participatory Budgeting in the Andes." *Development in Practice* 19 (6): 692–701.

Campbell, Patricia J. 2005. "Gender and Post-Conflict Civil Society." *International Feminist Journal of Politics* 7 (3): 377–99.

Cooper, Frederick. 1996. *Decolonization and African Society: The Labor Question in French and British Africa.* Cambridge University Press.

de Graaf, Reinier. 2015. "Architecture Is Now a Tool of Capital, Complicit in a Purpose Antithetical to Its Social Mission." *Architectural Review* (March 23). https://www.architectural-review.com/8681564.article.

Del Testa, David W. 2002. "Workers, Culture, and the Railroads in French Colonial Indochina, 1905–1936." *French Colonial History* 2: 181–98.

Forty, Adrian. 2012. *Concrete and Culture: A Material History.* Reaktion Books.

Fredericks, Rosalind. 2014. "Vital Infrastructures of Trash in Dakar." *Comparative Studies of South Asia, Africa, and the Middle East* 34 (3): 532–48.

Gandy, Matthew. 2002. *Concrete and Clay: Reworking Nature in New York City.* MIT Press.

Gibson-Graham, J. K. 2008. "Diverse Economies: Performative Practices for 'Other Worlds.'" *Progress in Human Geography* 32 (5): 613–32.

Graham, Stephen. 2005. "Switching Cities Off: Urban Infrastructure and US Air Power." *City* 9 (2): 169–93.

Ha, Marie-Paule. 1999. "Engendering French Colonial History: The Case of Indochina." *Historical Reflections/Réflexions Historiques* 25 (1): 95–125.

Harvey, Penelope. 2010. "Cementing Relations: The Materiality of Roads and Public Spaces in Provincial Peru." *Social Analysis* 54 (2): 28–46.

Harvey, Penelope, and Hannah Knox. 2015. *Roads: An Anthropology of Infrastructure and Expertise.* Cornell University Press.

Ingold, Tim. 2007. "Discussion Article: Materials against Materiality." *Archaeological Dialogues* 14 (1): 1–16.

Ingold, Tim. 2012. "Toward an Ecology of Materials." *Annual Review of Anthropology* 41 (1): 427–42.

Kusno, Abidin. 2000. *Beyond the Postcolonial: Architecture Urban Space and Political Cultures in Indonesia*. Routledge.

Leshkowich, Ann Marie. 2014. *Essential Trade: Vietnamese Women in a Changing Marketplace*. University of Hawai'i Press.

Nguyen, Minh T. N. 2016. "Trading in Broken Things: Gendered Performances and Spatial Practices in a Northern Vietnamese Rural-Urban Waste Economy." *American Ethnologist* 43 (1): 116–29.

Nguyễn Quân. 1982. *Nghệ thuật tạo hình Việt Nam hiện đại* [Modern Vietnamese plastic arts]. Hà nội: Văn hóa.

Nguyễn Tham Thiện Kế. 2011. "Người con trai cả long đong của Bí thư Kim Ngọc." *Tiền Phong* (February 7). http://www.tienphong.vn/xa-hoi-phong-su/nguoi-con-trai-ca-long-dong-cua-bi-thu-kim-ngoc-526944.tpo.

Nguyễn Văn Quang. 2015. "Xi măng Hải Phòng, biểu tượng của Thành phố Hoa Phượng đỏ 'Trung dũng—Quyết thắng.'" *Xây dựng* (December 25). http://www.baoxaydung.com.vn/news/vn/vat-lieu/xi-mang-hai-phong-bieu-tuong-cua-thanh-pho-hoa-phuong-do-trung-dung-quyet-thang.html.

Olsen, Mari. 2006. *Soviet-Vietnam Relations and the Role of China 1949–64: Changing Alliances*. Routledge.

Peake, Linda. 2016. "The Twenty-First-Century Quest for Feminism and the Global Urban." *International Journal of Urban and Regional Research* 40 (1): 219–27.

Purtak, Udo. 1982. *Voraussetzungen und Entwicklung des Wohnungsbaus unter humiden tropischen Bedingungen dargestellt am Beispiel des Aufbaus der Stadt Vinh in der Sozialistischen Republik Vietnam*. PhD dissertation, Technical University of Dresden.

Quang Hưng. 2010. "Xi măng Hải Phòng với thương hiệu Con Rồng." *Nhân Dân*, September 17. http://www.nhandan.com.vn/kinhte/item/3846802-.html.

Rodgers, Dennis, and Bruce O'Neill. 2012. "Infrastructural Violence: Introduction to the Special Issue." *Ethnography* 13 (4): 401–12.

Sabhlok, Anu. 2017. "'Main Bhi to Hindostaan Hoon': Gender and Nation-State in India's Border Roads Organisation." *Gender, Place, and Culture* 24 (12): 1711–28.

Schwenkel, Christina. 2013. "Post/Socialist Affect: Ruination and Reconstruction of the Nation in Urban Vietnam." *Cultural Anthropology* 28 (2): 252–77.

Schwenkel, Christina. 2015. "Spectacular Infrastructure and its Breakdown in Socialist Vietnam." *American Ethnologist* 42 (3): 520–34.

Schwenkel, Christina. 2019. "Governing through Garbage: Waste Infrastructure Breakdown and Gendered Apathy in Vietnam." In *Routledge Handbook of Anthropology and the City: Engaging the Urban and the Future*, edited by Setha Low, 318–31. Routledge.

Schwenkel, Christina. 2020. *Building Socialism: The Afterlife of East German Architecture in Urban Vietnam*. Duke University Press.

Starostina, Natalia. 2009. "Engineering the Empire of Images: Constructing Railways in Asia before the Great War." *Southeast Review of Asian Studies* 31: 181–206.

Sultana, Farhana. 2009. "Fluid Lives: Subjectivities, Gender and Water in Rural Bangladesh." *Gender, Place, and Culture* 16 (4): 427–44.

Treber, Leonie. 2014. *Mythos Trümmerfrauen: Von der Trümmerbeseitigung in der Kriegs- und Nachkriegszeit und der Entstehung eines deutschen Erinnerungsortes*. Essen: Klartext.

Truelove, Yaffa. 2011. "(Re-)Conceptualizing Water Inequality in Delhi, India through a Feminist Political Ecology Framework." *Geoforum* 42 (2): 143–52.

Truelove, Yaffa, and Hanna A. Ruszczyk. 2022. "Bodies as Urban Infrastructure: Gender, Intimate Infrastructures and Slow Infrastructural Violence." *Political Geography* 92. doi.org/10.1016/j.polgeo.2021.102492.

Tsing, Anna L. 2009. "Supply Chains and the Human Condition." *Rethinking Marxism* 21 (2): 148–76.

Turner, Karen Gottschang, with Phan Thanh Hao. 1999. *Even the Women Must Fight: Memories of War from North Vietnam*. Wiley.

Wajcman, Judy. 2010. "Feminist Theories of Technology." *Cambridge Journal of Economics* 34 (1): 143–52.

Werner, Jayne. 2009. *Gender, Household, and State in Post-Revolutionary Vietnam*. Routledge.

Yuval-Davis, Nira. 1997. *Gender and Nation*. Sage Press.

Zarecor, Kimberly Elman. 2011. *Manufacturing a Socialist Modernity: Housing in Czechoslovakia, 1945–1960*. University of Pittsburgh Press.

CHAPTER 2

GENDER RELATIONS AND INFRASTRUCTURAL LABORS AT THE WATER KIOSKS IN LILONGWE, MALAWI

Cecilia Alda-Vidal, Alison L. Browne, and Maria Rusca

INTRODUCTION

Since AbdouMaliq Simone (2004) conceptualized people as "infrastructures," numerous scholars have paid attention to the "human lives, labor, and bodies that are not only enrolled in but *constitute* infrastructure" (Doherty 2017, 194; emphasis original) (e.g., Anand 2020; Doherty 2017; Fredricks 2018; Truelove and Ruszczyk 2022). Against the myth of physical, automated, and reliable urban systems, Global South scholarship has shown that urban infrastructure depends on human inputs, including the labor required to operate, maintain, and repair infrastructures on a daily basis (Anand 2017; Björkman 2018; De Coss-Corzo 2021; Fredricks 2018) and the human bodies that substitute or make up for infrastructures when these are absent or fail (Truelove and Ruszczyk 2022). Emergent feminist inquiry into infrastructural labor has revealed the inequalities embedded in infrastructural labors and the gendered power relations that render some types of infrastructural work (e.g., repair) or workers (i.e., raced, classed, gendered) undervalued and disposable (Anand 2020; Fredericks 2014; Gidwani 2015; Mattern 2018). In this chapter, we build on and extend these feminist contributions by exploring the gendered dynamics of infrastructural work producing unequal patterns and unjust conditions of engagement at the water kiosks of Lilongwe, Malawi.

Water kiosks are booths in which residents can purchase a five- to twenty-liter bucket of water for drinking and other domestic uses (figure 2.1). They are a common infrastructure across many low-income areas in Southern African cities. As each facility is usually meant to serve many households they have been instrumental in increasing access to water in the low-income areas of urban Sub-Saharan Africa (WaterAid n.d.). Kiosks have been presented by donors as a low-cost and easily scalable solution (Klawitter et al. 2009), a quick fix for unserved, low-income populations in cities in the Global South. In contrast with the imaginary of the "automated" city, this infrastructure is heavily labor dependent for both water sellers and buyers. As we show in this chapter, the continued reliance on water kiosks and its framing as a successful model of water supply conceals the gendered power relations, meanings, and labors built into this water infrastructure.

Fig. 2.1. Gender relations and infrastructural labors at Lilongwe's water kiosks. (Illustration by Catalina Medarde)

In interrogating the gendered labors that enable the functioning of water kiosk systems, the chapter also brings attention to important policy implications. Governments and development partners are increasingly calling to invest in the construction of on-premises water facilities in the framework of the Sustainable Development Goals (WHO/UNICEF JMP 2017). Yet, the task is challenging, and kiosks are likely to remain a prominent technology for urban water supply in low-income areas (Adams, Sambu, and Smiley 2019; Contzen and Marks 2018). A deeper interrogation of the gendered politics and labors involved in these infrastructures is essential given the prevalence of kiosks in cities in Sub-Saharan Africa, their importance for residents' household water security, the multiple labors required to make this infrastructure viable, and the significance of kiosks in the global achievement of water security and gender equality.

We proceed as follows. We first review the ways in which different strands of critical feminist and urban scholarship conceptualize infrastructural labor. After introducing the methodology for this study, we draw on empirical work in Lilongwe to explore the gender and intersectional meanings and relations shaping the gendered infrastructural labors required to sustain water provisioning. We conclude by discussing the policy implications of the (in)visibility of women's infrastructural labor.

INFRASTRUCTURAL LABORS

Simone's (2004) conceptualization of people as infrastructures opened up the intellectual space to think about infrastructures beyond their technical dimensions and to consider the centrality of people's social relations and practices to the flow of resources in cities. This includes the social relations and practices of workers opening and closing valves, repairing pipes, clearing sewer blockages, or sorting trash who sustain functional urban services as well as broader sociopolitical systems (Anand 2017; Björkman 2018; De Coss-Corzo 2021; Fredricks 2018). As this scholarship has noted, these essential workers are often low paid, exposed to risks and harmful environments or practices, and unrecognized and undervalued by decision makers and users of infrastructures (Anand 2020; De Coss-Corzo 2021; Doherty 2017; Fredricks 2014). To illustrate, in many cities municipal waste services are kept at low cost or sustained through the underpaid or wageless labor of informal and precarious workers (Doherty and Brown 2019; Fredricks 2014; Millington and Lawhon 2018).

Several scholars have noted the patterns of visibility and invisibility surrounding infrastructural work (Anand 2020; De Coss-Corzo, Ruszczyk, and

Stokes 2019). Infrastructural construction jobs have been often used by decision makers to attract support or voters. These jobs are made highly visible and celebrated as part of the promises of progress that investments in infrastructures would bring about (Anand, Gupta, and Appel 2018). Once infrastructures are constructed, the mundane but essential labor that keeps infrastructures working becomes invisible (Anand 2020; De Coss-Corzo 2021). As Anand (2020) argues, the work of those who operate, maintain, and repair infrastructures—such as ensuring interruptions or malfunctioning impacts users as little as possible—tends to be "out of sight," rendering invisible both the labors that sustain infrastructures and the infrastructures themselves.

Responding to wider feminist calls to pay attention to embodiment and the scale of the body in urban politics (e.g., Doshi 2016), some scholars have developed the notion of "people as infrastructure" further. They demonstrate that not only do infrastructures rely on human labor, but there are also specific (gendered, raced, classed) bodies that are literally enrolled to become part of the urban infrastructure (Doherty 2017; Truelove 2019; Truelove and Ruszczyk 2022). A productive example of bodies that act as infrastructure is found in feminist water scholarship. This scholarship has extensively documented the gender stereotypes and constructs that, in most societies, situate women as primarily responsible for ensuring and managing household water (Harris et al. 2017; Sultana 2009; Truelove 2011). In the absence of pipes, the heavily labored responsibility of securing water access that entails finding suitable sources; waiting in long queues; negotiating with tankers, neighbors, or sellers; and hauling heavy containers and is often conducted by low-income women. Even when houses are connected to the water network, (often low-income) women must commit time and effort to compensate for water interruptions by for example constantly checking taps at odd hours to find out if water is back or turning on and off domestic suction pumps when the service has been reestablished (Truelove 2011; Truelove and Ruszczyk 2022; Sultana 2009; Velzeboer, Hordijk, and Schwartz 2017). As Truelove (2019) argues in the context of fragmented and unreliable water supply, women's bodies act as infrastructure becoming the "the material by which water [. . .] is made to circulate and arrive within homes" (27).

An embodied approach has also been useful to reveal the different forms of corporeal suffering experienced by those who become part of the infrastructure. Doherty (2017) shows that motorcycle taxi drivers in Kampala are constantly exposed to injuries and dead by traffic, and feminist water scholars have extensively documented the physical harm endured by the low-income women who substitute the pipes with their bodies, such as the fatigue, deformities, and illnesses caused by carrying large amounts of water (Sultana 2009; Truelove 2011). This feminist water scholarship has also called attention to other forms of emotional suffering embodied by having to navigate water access in context of water insecurity (Cole 2017; Sultana 2011, 2015, 2020; Truelove 2011; Wutich 2009). Examples of these are the stress of having to negotiate the conditions for borrowing water from employers, fear of harassment when collecting water from illegal sources, and the frustration of waiting for water tankers that do not come (Truelove 2011).

By engaging with feminist theory, scholars have revealed that the framing or naturalizing of specific types of infrastructural work as part of women's domestic duties has helped to exploit the voluntary labor of (often low-income) women (Fredericks 2009; Truelove 2011, 2019) and to erase these activities from the dominant descriptions of how services are provided in cities (Truelove and Ruszczyk 2022). Truelove (2011, 2019) highlights how framing water collection as a domestic duty allows states to avoid the costs of extending pipes into low-income neighborhoods. This body of scholarship provides different insights on water kiosks as socio-technical infrastructures that involve both material objects and labor (Doherty 2017) and calls for examinations of whose bodies and work are mobilized, concealed, and sacrificed to ensure that the kiosk system becomes a successful mode of water provision for Lilongwe's low-income areas.

METHODOLOGY AND CASE STUDY BACKGROUND

Two different sets of data, collected through two different research projects, have informed this chapter. The first set of data was collected from September to December 2017 and May to July 2018. Alda-Vidal conducted ten semi-structured interviews and a group interview with kiosk attendants to understand the conditions and experiences of work at the kiosk, including the risks and challenges attendants face and their relations with customers. Ten interviews with representatives from the Lilongwe Water Board, water user associations, and local nongovernmental organizations helped elucidate how they frame the work of women at the kiosk within the context of the water kiosks and the water user associations' systems. Finally, twenty interviews with kiosks users allowed understanding of the broader context of Lilongwe's kiosk system, the challenges of accessing water in low-income areas, and provided evidence of how the kiosk attendants and their bodily labors are an integral component of the water kiosk system in Lilongwe. Interview-based data was supplemented with review and analysis of urban plans, project documents, and other literature about Lilongwe's water sector.

The second set of data was collected through a videography project (February–March 2016), later developed into the documentary *Lilongwe Water Works?* (Rusca 2017), and the public screenings and film debates organized during the launching of the documentary in June 2018. The documentary explores Lilongwe's water kiosk system, focusing on the experiences of the women and men who access water through the kiosks and those who are involved in running them. During the filming of the documentary Rusca and the filming team conducted five further interviews with kiosk attendants. Two film screening and debate sessions were organized with representatives of water user associations in low income areas (one session in Area 50 with sixteen women and nine men, and one session in Tsabango with sixteen women and ten men) and with representatives of the water and sanitation sector (twenty-five participants, all men). These sessions were instrumental in eliciting lively discussions around the experiences of kiosk attendants and customers and in deepening the understanding of how the organizations supporting the water kiosks system perceive and react to the everyday challenges that attendants face. Notes and summaries of these group discussions have been used to support our arguments throughout the chapter.

THE WATER KIOSK SYSTEM AND WATER USER ASSOCIATIONS STRUCTURE IN LILONGWE'S LOW-INCOME AREAS

Around 60 percent of households in Lilongwe's low-income areas use kiosks as a primary source of water (Adams 2017). Kiosks were first built in Lilongwe during the relocation of the capital in 1968. Until 2006, these infrastructures were directly operated by the municipal water utility (Lilongwe Water Board) or by private operators. The Lilongwe Water Board was concerned with the high staffing costs for the direct operation of kiosks (Chirwa and Junge 2007), while private operators were failing to pay their bills to the Lilongwe Water Board (Rusca and Schwartz 2012). In 2006 a decision was made to establish a number of community-based water user associations to solve these financial challenges (Rusca and Schwartz 2012). Under the current operational model, the Lilongwe Water Board is in charge of delivering the bulk water and oversees the functioning of the kiosk system and of the water user associations are responsible for the operation of nearly a thousand kiosks that exist in the city (Pihljak et al. 2019).

Water user associations present a clear division of activities, which reproduces intersectional hierarchies based on gender and community status. The decision-making bodies of water user associations are populated by a majority of influential male community members, such as religious, political, and traditional leaders, or local businessmen (Rusca et al. 2015). Members of water user association management receive a monthly honorarium for their advisory role and are entitled to other economic benefits such as funeral allowances (Rusca et al. 2015). They also hold decision-making power over how to invest profits from water sales, what to prioritize in the negotiations with the Lilongwe Water Board, and whom to hire (Pihljak et al. 2019).

At the bottom of the water user associations' hierarchy are the more than eight hundred women employed as kiosk attendants and inspectors who perform the everyday activities of water provisioning at the kiosks (see also Adams, Juran, and Ajibade 2018). Kiosk attendants are recruited locally and are low-income women (Velzeboer 2015). They are responsible for opening and closing the taps, overseeing the amount of water collected, and gathering the payments from customers (Velzeboer 2015). They are in charge of ensuring that kiosks' surroundings are kept clean, helping users to lift buckets, and dealing with potential quarrels in the queue (Adams, Juran, and Ajibade 2018; Velzeboer 2015). Kiosk attendants work eight to nine hours a day (often in two shifts from 6:00 to 10:00 or 11:00 a.m. and 2:00 or 3:00 to 6:00 p.m.) seven days a week (ECA, PEM Consult, and TM Associates 2014). Once a week, attendants bring the money collected from water sales to the water user association offices, where revenues are compared to the meter reading done by a kiosk inspector (Adams, Juran, and Ajibade 2018; Velzeboer 2015).

The hierarchical structure and unequal power relations within Water User Associations and the wider contextual gendered dynamics—such as the lower levels of education and employment rates, as well as the mobility constraints faced by women in low-income areas and Malawi more in general (Castel, Phiri, and Stampini 2010)—situate kiosk attendants in a position of vulnerability in relation to the members of management. For example, Adams, Juran, and Ajibade (2018) and Velzeboer (2015) show that kiosk attendants do not participate in decision making and are afraid to complain about their working conditions to the powerful male members for fear of losing their jobs. Building on this outline of the infrastructural landscape and the resulting governance arrangements in Lilongwe, we move to examine the gendering of water labors and the embodied practices of water services provision at the kiosks.

GENDER RELATIONS AND INFRASTRUCTURAL LABOR AT THE KIOSK

Gendering Infrastructural Work: Reproducing Subjectivities

In Malawi, as in many other countries, due to gendered social norms, water collection is perceived as women's responsibility (Graham, Hirai, and Kim

2016; Mawaya and Kalindekafe 2010). In Lilongwe, water kiosks are constructed as gendered sites and infrastructures of water labor. The mobilization
of gender discourses and subjectivities frame water collection as an activity
conducted by women, with kiosks positioned as a feminine space in which
domestic duties of women are performed with "kiosk attendant" also framed
as a job role more suitable for women: "It is the nature of their job, they sell
to fellow women, very few men go there. And also men are not trustworthy in
keeping the money, they can drink it[. . . .] In the past we used to have some
men selling water but men feel shy to serve women, and we had a lot of problems with missing money" (interview, water user association administrator,
2017). These framings are shaped by existing gender roles and expectations
for both men and women, which reinforce stereotyped femininities and masculinities and naturalize women's presence—and men's absence—from kiosks
spaces.

As the interview fragment suggests, an important part of the smooth operation of kiosks depends on cordial relations between attendants and customers. Some participants also revealed how men who were previously employed
in attendant roles used physical violence to end conflicts with women. One
kiosk attendant (interview, kiosk attendant, woman, 2017) explained how
sometimes male attendants "when a woman wastes water[1] they would beat
her for that." Members of water user association management also frame men
as inadequate for the job. One member suggested that "sometimes men are
too rude they do not understand women, so it is a problem to put men in that
kiosk" (interview, representative of water user association, man, 2017). This is
reinforced by incidents with male kiosk attendants stealing money from water
user associations, something water user associations doubt women would dare
to do. As a water user association member explained, "sometimes they [male
kiosk attendants] would be turning the meter and for two three hours they
would be selling the water and pocketing themselves, women do not do that,
they cannot do that, they are shy" (interview, representative of water user association, man, 2017). Rather than sanctioning these attitudes, the water user
associations use these cases to naturalize women's temperaments and behaviors as more suited to the role as kiosk attendants.

This framing is further reinforced by water user association policies that
contribute to the reproduction of particular female subjectivities and the existing division of roles that position women as house carers, mothers, and wives.
The working schedule of kiosk attendants is set in a way that allows them to
continue to perform domestic work traditionally attributed to women. To illustrate, kiosks are closed at lunchtime, so that attendants can go home to

prepare meals and have lunch with the family. To further facilitate the integration of domestic role responsibilities and water labor at the kiosk, attendants are often assigned working locations near their home and offered the possibility of bringing their children to work (interview, water user association network representative, 2016). While ensuring that kiosk attendants can juggle work and family responsibilities, this policy also reproduces the idea that the job is a "natural" fit for women. As a result, the prevalence of women in kiosk operation and maintenance is also naturalized.

However, as we further elaborate in the next sections, the naturalization of the kiosk attendant job as a gendered activity conceals the power dynamics that construct these roles and the material implications thereof.

Subsidizing Lower-Cost Water Infrastructures through Women's Infrastructural Labors

The naturalization of the kiosk attendant job as a women's activity alongside the wider context of limited employment opportunities for low-income women enables water user associations to recruit women to this kiosk work as cheap, flexible labor. This cheap, flexible labor is necessary both to make the water kiosks system a financially viable water provisioning infrastructure and to reduce the costs of selling water.

Historically, kiosks have been developed as a formal node of provision within the centralized water system. This system implicitly relies on women's bodies to ensure water access to low-income users with low public investment while limiting consumption to what women's bodies are able to carry. In the late 1980s the possibility of substituting low-income area's kiosks with in-house piped connections was explored; however, maintaining the system of kiosks was suggested as a strategy to "control water demand" and to "delay capital and operating expenditures" such as in water source development or network infrastructure extension (Stanley International 1986, 4). Women already performed the function of maintaining access to and making up for inefficiencies and uneven access in the existing water systems. As we continue to explore in this section, this strategy overlooks the implications for women's lives, with the celebration of the "success" of kiosks as a key water infrastructure in Lilongwe concealing the risks and challenges women face as they perform these activities.

The current kiosk operational model involving the water user associations is presented as a success within local policy circles, on the grounds that "All the money is being collected, taken to office, banks, water bills are being paid. In areas where water user associations are getting enough water, members of the community are able to receive their salaries, also other members receive salaries with no problem. Extensions are being done and kiosk built with water sales" (interview, representative of the Lilongwe Water Board, 2017). Indeed, in low-income areas formal job opportunities such as those provided within water user associations are very limited. This is particularly the case for women, who, in Malawi more in general, constitute a greater part of the population with no formal employment. This is due to both lower levels of education and women's care responsibilities (Castel, Phiri, and Stampini 2010; Mkandawire-Valhmu and Stevens 2007). It is, therefore, no surprise that women's participation and empowerment are key elements on which the narrative of success is constructed by water user associations, the Lilongwe Water Board, and other development partners.

Undoubtedly, these jobs do represent a unique and highly sought-after prospect. Beyond a source of income, the kiosk offers a space to create and cultivate social networks and connections. At the kiosk, attendants constantly interact with other neighbors, and in particular with other women, who come to buy water. In this way, beyond providing a wage, the relations cultivated at work allow them to expand their social capital within the community. Throughout a number of the interviews, participants talked about how their position at the kiosk enabled them to make money on the side by selling charcoal or soap or how they have been offered the opportunity to participate in NGO initiatives such as saving groups or training. Kiosk attendants also hold a relative position of power and authority in relation to other low-income women in the community who come to the kiosk to buy water. For example, they may allow friends and relatives to draw water on credit or give them priority during water shortages (Velzeboer, Hordijk, and Schwartz 2017). Interviews with kiosk users show that sometimes kiosk attendants may even deny access to customers they are on bad terms with.

The relative benefits of the kiosk roles should not conceal the power dynamics and extractive relations underlying their position within the wider water system. In 2019, the monthly salary of attendants was MKW 30,000 (US$41.26), and for years it consistently remained under the minimum wage established by the government. These financial conditions contrast significantly with the economic incentive members of water user association management receive. On average the monthly wage of kiosk attendants working on a full-time basis is only one-third higher than the monthly honorarium of these members, who have an advisory role that involves attending four meetings per year (Pihljak 2014). While not explicitly mentioned in the success narrative of the kiosk system, it is evident that the reliance on cheap labor is needed to ensure the systems' success: "When we opened this [the water user association managed kiosk system] we needed people who can work as employee who can accept low salaries, and those are women. We wanted to help those people that are in need and most people that are in need are women, so by employing women we are helping people. That is why women accepted, men would have not" (interview, representative of water user association, man, 2017). The devaluation of their labor also materializes in their monthly salary. Water user associations have consistently rejected the demands of kiosk attendants for pay raises, despite the sustained increment in profits (Pihljak et al. 2019; Velzeboer 2015). Keeping wages low allows water user associations to use water revenues for development activities and investments that will benefit the leadership of the water user associations such as construction of offices, purchasing of cars, and other activities to consolidate their status in the community.

A second way in which women's labor "subsidizes" the inefficiencies of the system is through the expectation for kiosk attendants to work flexible hours. The technical characteristics of the network, together with everyday decisions about its operation, have led to a highly uneven water distribution in the city, with low-income areas suffering from frequent service interruption (Alda-Vidal, Kooy, et al. 2018; Boakye-Ansah et al. 2016; Tiwale, Rusca, and Zwarteveen 2018). Kiosk attendants must adapt their schedules to the erratic tempos of water supply. When pressure is low, they must extend their working hours to allow for all customers to fill their buckets. During water shortages, attendants must quickly return to their post when water is available.

Given these service deficiencies, attendants' adaptability was seen as a major advantage of the water user association kiosk model (Chirwa and Junge 2007). Flexibility of service delivery not only is important to ensure access to water, but it is also crucial to the financial sustainability of water user associations. To sustain their fixed operational costs and ensure a profit, water user associations must sell a minimum amount of water each month. Water shortages, therefore, are a loss of profit to be compensated for, and the financial viability of the system heavily relies on the flexibility of kiosk attendants to open the kiosks whenever water is available, including night hours. In this way the responsibility and labors of ensuring financial sustainability is passed on to kiosk attendants. As further elaborated in the next section, alongside the burdens of needing to adjust working schedules in accordance with unpredictable water supplies, kiosk attendants also have to assume the personal and physical risks of working odd hours.

Although the labor of kiosk attendants has been crucial for maximizing profits, ensuring low-income residents can access water, and reducing the financial impact of water shortages, kiosk attendants are increasingly considered expendable. An electronic system of water prepayment is being piloted to reduce the cost-of-service provision and dependence on attendants: "Previously people were accessing water through our kiosk which were being run by attendants; one could only buy water from those traditional kiosk if the attendant was around to serve them, meaning people in low-income could only have water during some hours of the day" ("Lilongwe Water Board Partners TNM on E-Madzi Initiative, Customers Pleased," 2017). Prepaid kiosks, it is argued, will reduce the cost of water by cutting down the operational costs associated with kiosk attendants. Strikingly, there is no mention of the implications that other water user association expenses—development activities and investments managed by the leadership—have for the final price of water (see Pihljak et al. 2019).

As a representative of the Lilongwe Water Board explained in an interview, "The plan is to have this [system] with no kiosk attendants. The same way an ATM works, there is no cashier there. So, the salary for the cashier will bring the price down" (interview, representative of Lilongwe Water Board, man, 2017). This shift to digital water provisioning systems including prepaid kiosks (also often known as water ATMs) is an increasing feature in low-income communities across the Global South (see Amankwaa, Heeks, and Browne 2021). When confronted with the loss of employment and what this will mean for women, the interviewee argued that water user associations are aware, but "they have accepted the idea and all they have said is that they are interested in seeing the price going down. They know people will not be employed, but their interest is that the price should go down and the access should improve" (interview, representative of Lilongwe Water Board, man, 2017). This section reveals the narrative that frames women's enrollment in kiosk attendant jobs as beneficial and emancipatory for them is a charade that hides that women are used for their cheap and flexible labor, labor that becomes easily expendable in reducing the costs of water provisioning, rather than for real concerns with their empowerment. As discussed below, these narratives also conceal the risks and emotional distress borne by kiosk attendants because of the frequent interruptions and shortages of water in low-income areas and the requirement to work on flexible schedules.

Emotional Water Labors: Risks and Distress during Water Shortages

Water shortages are common in low-income areas. Often water is only available at night, and attendants are exposed to risks of robbery and violence to meet their job expectations. As an attendant explained, "We face the risk of meeting thieves. They think we have money and want to rob us. Also, customers buying water at night [usually women] face the same risk" (interview, kiosk attendant, woman, 2016). Different cases of violent assault or harassment by drunk men have been reported in previous research (Velzeboer 2015). Women describe these night encounters as traumatizing experiences: "At the kiosk I worked before there was water only at night and I had a lot of problems. Once I met a ghost on my way home. Sometime men throw stones at me, once I could not even see who was throwing the stones" (interview, kiosk attendant, woman, 2016). The darkness also complicates counting money: "I cannot check if they are giving me the right amount. Once they gave me a broken 1,000 bill. I didn't know because it was folded so I gave the change" (interview, kiosk attendant, woman, 2016). This adds to the anxiety of attendants who are expected to pay any imbalances in the collection of payments from their own pocket.

During water shortages attendants, like other women, must complete their housework, including the extra burden of walking to the kiosk during their evening resting hours: "Even if I had a tiresome day instead of resting and sleeping, I am required to go work" (interview, kiosk attendant, woman, 2017). Leaving the house in the middle of the night to attend work on short notice may lead to tensions and household conflicts because family members perceive the job is distracting them from their domestic duties. As a community leader engaged in counseling a number of attendants and their families explained, "At whatever time the water comes the kiosk attendant is supposed to go, to leave the family behind and go to attend the customers. So it means that it does not allow for the time needed to attend to the family. If there are schoolchildren, she does not have time to feed them or to bathe them before they go to school. She does not have time for the husband" (group meeting, water user association, Area 50, community leader, man, 2018). This intersects with other wider issues of labor conditions in local neighborhoods. For example, in low-income areas it is common for men to work night shifts as security guards in the higher-income residential areas. This means children remain alone at home when attendants must go to the kiosk, which intensifies their concerns and suffering: "Selling water at night is difficult. Sometimes women come to my house and ask me to sell them water. We go there together but then they draw water and leave me there alone, I wait until morning and think of my kids that I left home alone, anything can happen" (interview, kiosk attendant, woman, 2016).

Furthermore, leaving the house at night often means a breach of social expectations of modesty imposed on women. For some attendants this is a source of anxiety and can even translate into conflicts with husbands, who may have suspicions of infidelity. "When water stops coming and resumes at night, our families are at risk. When our wives leave at night to get water, some women might take advantage of this problem and use that time to meet other men. Also, such families can easily break up because there might be cases of men fighting over suspicions that the other man had slept with another man's wife" (group meeting, Area 56, community member, 2018).

In concluding this section, we note that in claiming the success of this model, water utility staff, donors, and high-ranking members of water user associations overlook the multiple challenges faced by women who are responsible for selling and buying water at the kiosks. The odd working hours, the physical burden, the everyday violence, as well as the emotional distress associated with this task are concealed in discourses of success, measured in terms of high revenue collection and employment rates.

CONCLUSIONS

The chapter extends feminist scholarship on urban water by exploring the gender and intersectional meanings and relations shaping the paid gendered labors required to sustain water provisioning infrastructures. This is an underexplored area in comparison to the attention paid by feminist scholars to the gendered responsibilities and hardships associated to the work of securing water for households (Alda-Vidal et al. 2017). Drawing on this literature we have emphasized how the bodies and (paid and unpaid) labors of women are fundamentally interwoven into the formal planning and running of the water infrastructure in low-income areas. Water kiosks have proven to be a financially sustainable solution to extend and ensure access to water in low-income areas, and to date the success of water kiosks has been predicated on their construction as gendered spaces and infrastructures of water labor. Not only are they framed as such because they are more frequented by women, who have traditionally been responsible for the domestic labor of water collection, but also the labor required for their operation is framed by multiple actors as being more suitable to women. The feminization of these water labors has material implications for women working as kiosk attendants, who, despite having an income opportunity and the possibility to build on social relations, have to deal with low-paid jobs, reduced decision-making power in water user associations, and the physical and emotional risks of working odd hours to ensure both neighbors' access to water and the financial viability of the system.

Drawing on notions of bodies as infrastructure (Truelove 2019; Truelove and Ruszczyk 2022), we have revealed a different way in which low-income women act as urban infrastructures. The framing of kiosks as female spaces and the vulnerability of women as population who are unemployed or under-employed has turned the low-income women who work as kiosk attendants into cheap appendages to the kiosk (cf. Truelove 2019). Their work as add-on devices is essential to ensure water flows out of tap and into the buckets of other women, to the extent that their mobilities and temporalities are con-strained to the proximity of the kiosks and the capricious rhythms of water in the city. The system, however, is currently in flux, with women's bodies and labors within the water kiosk systems at risk of replacement from automated technologies and systems (i.e., prepaid systems, water ATMs). This highlights the little value and concern given by the organizations supporting the kiosk system to women's work and to the struggles they face to access livelihood opportunities.

Recent studies on infrastructural labors have invited researchers to pay at-tention to the embodied dimension of infrastructural inequalities (Doshi 2016; Truelove 2019), including the corporeal suffering by those who become infra-structures (Doherty 2017; Truelove and Ruszczyk 2022). With the example of kiosk attendants, we have extended this work, emphasizing that acting as infrastructures also has an emotional toll, such as the fears of violence, anxiety, and stress (Cole 2017; Sultana 2011, 2015, 2020; Truelove 2011; Wutich 2009) caused by having to work during the night or breaching social expectations on their role as family carers and modest wives.

Recent contributions from feminist inquiry into infrastructural labor have allowed us to bring into discussion questions around the (in)visibility of wom-en's infrastructural labor and the role this invisibility plays in subsidizing the failures of the kiosk system. On the one hand, women's labor is made visible and celebrated in dominant narratives about the water kiosks system to discur-sively produce the success of the water user association model and the promise of kiosks as inclusive and even empowering water supply infrastructures (see also Anand, Gupta, and Appel 2018; O'Reilly 2006). The performance of this success, however, relies on erasing from this dominant narrative the physical and emotional risks and burdens borne by female bodies to make up for the inefficiencies of the system (Truelove and Ruszczyk 2022).

From a policy and planning perspective, a more critical consideration of the infrastructural work of women within the kiosk system is essential, given how significant kiosks are as water provision infrastructures in Global South cities. This requires making visible the reliance of infrastructural systems on women's labor and moving beyond the current tokenist approach that celebrates the recruitment of women as attendants to addressing their demands for just and safe working conditions. Furthermore, as we have shown, in Lilongwe there are indications that digitization of water services and a shift to prepaid kiosks may supplant women's low-cost labor. As the water supply system transitions to a new technology (Amankwaa, Heeks, and Browne 2021), kiosk attendants become disposable, while water user association management is likely to play an important role in the prepaid kiosk system. Being already excluded from negotiations and decision-making processes within the water system, women's rights and interests as water users, collectors, and workers are also unlikely to be heard and protected within this digital transition. Continued attention to the gendered and labor dynamics of these water kiosk digitization projects will be needed as they are trialed and tested.

ACKNOWLEDGMENTS AND FUNDING

We are grateful for the invaluable fieldwork support provided by Charles Mkula (development journalist and founder of Hyphen Media Institute). We would like to thank participants who shared their time and experiences with us. This article was written in the framework of the PhD project of the first author, which has been funded by the Sustainable Consumption Institute, University of Manchester. Furthermore, the research builds on two larger projects conducted in Lilongwe as part of the European Union's Horizon 2020 research and innovation program under the Marie Skłodowska-Curie grant agreement INHAbIT Cities, No 656738 and the DGIS-UNESCO IHE Programmatic Cooperation under the Uncovering Hidden Dynamics in Slum Environments (UNHIDE). The manuscript was much improved by the thoughtful, supportive comments of book editors and reviewers. Cecilia would also like to thank her PhD examiners, Saska Petrova and Antje Bruns, who provided insightful and encouraging feedback on this chapter.

NOTES

1. Wasted water here refers to water that runs out of the kiosk tap but cannot be accounted for in the price paid by the customer, such as, for example, the water that is used to wash the bucket or spillages during collection.

REFERENCES

Adams, E. A. 2017. "Thirsty Slums in African Cities: Household Water Insecurity in Urban Informal Settlements of Lilongwe, Malawi." *International Journal of Water Resources Development* 34 (6): 869–87. https://doi.org/10.1080/07900627.2017.1322941.

Adams, E. A., L. Juran, and I. Ajibade. 2018. "'Spaces of Exclusion' in Community Water Governance: A Feminist Political Ecology of Gender and Participation in Malawi's Urban Water User Associations." *Geoforum* 95: 133–42. https://doi.org/10.1016/j.geoforum .2018.06.016.

Adams, E. A., D. Sambu, and S. L. Smiley. 2019. "Urban Water Supply in Sub-Saharan Africa: Historical and Emerging Policies and Institutional Arrangements." *International Journal of Water Resources Development* 35 (2): 240–63. https://doi.org/10.1080/07900627.201 7.1423282.

Alda-Vidal, C., M. Kooy, and M. Rusca. 2018. "Mapping Operation and Maintenance: An Everyday Urbanism Analysis of Inequalities within Piped Water Supply in Lilongwe, Malawi." *Urban Geography* 39 (1): 104–21. https://doi.org/10.1080/02723638.2017.1292664.

Alda-Vidal, C., M. Rusca, M. Z. Zwarteveen, K. Schwartz, and N. R. M. Pouw. 2017. "Occupational Genders and Gendered Occupations: The Case of Water Provisioning in Maputo, Mozambique." *Gender, Place, and Culture: A Journal of Feminist Geography*, 24 (7): 974–90. https://doi.org/10.1080/0966369X.2017.1339019.

Amankwaa, G., R. Heeks, and A. L. Browne. 2021. "Digital Innovations and Water Services in Cities of the Global South: A Systematic Literature Review." *Water Alternatives* 14 (2): 619–44. https://www.water-alternatives.org/index.php/alldoc/articles/vol14/v14issue2/637-a14-2-15/file.

Anand, N. 2017. *Hydraulic City: Water and the Infrastructures of Citizenship in Mumbai*. Duke University Press.

Anand, N. 2020. "After Breakdown: Invisibility and the Labour of Infrastructure Maintenance." *Economic and Political Weekly* 55 (51). https://www.epw.in/journal/2020/51/review-urban-affairs/after-breakdown.html.

Anand, N., A. Gupta, and H. Appel, eds. 2018. *The Promise of Infrastructure*. Duke University Press.

Björkman, L. 2018. "The Engineer and the Plumber: Mediating Mumbai's Conflicting Infrastructural Imaginaries." *International Journal of Urban and Regional Research* 42 (2): 276–94. https://doi.org/10.1111/1468-2427.12526.

Boakye-Ansah, A. S., G. Ferrero, M. Rusca, and P. van der Zaag. 2016. "Inequalities in Microbial Contamination of Drinking Water Supplies in Urban Areas: The Case of Lilongwe, Malawi." *Journal of Water and Health* 14 (5): 851–63. https://doi.org/10.2166/wh.2016.258.

Castel, V., M. Phiri, and M. Stampini. 2010. *Education and Employment in Malawi*. Working Paper Series, African Development Bank. https://core.ac.uk/download/pdf/6220443.pdf.

Chirwa, E., and N. Junge. 2007. *Poverty and Social Impact Analysis: Private Sector Participation in the Distribution and Management of Water Services: A Study of Low Income Areas in Blantyre and Lilongwe*. Ministry of Economic Planning and Development and Ministry of Irrigation and Water Development, Republic of Malawi.

Cole, S. 2017. "Water Worries: An Intersectional Feminist Political Ecology of Tourism and Water in Labuan Bajo, Indonesia." *Annals of Tourism Research* 67: 14–24. https://doi.org/10.1016/j.annals.2017.07.018.

Contzen, N., and S. J. Marks. 2018. "Increasing the Regular Use of Safe Water Kiosk through Collective Psychological Ownership: A Mediation Analysis." *Journal of Environmental Psychology* 57: 45–52. https://doi.org/10.1016/j.jenvp.2018.06.008.

De Coss-Corzo, A. 2021. "Maintain and Repair: Rethinking Essential Labor through Infrastructural Work." *Exertions*. https://doi.org/10.21428/1d6be30e.1220879d.

De Coss-Corzo, A., H. Ruszczyk, and K. Stokes, eds. 2019. *Labouring Urban Infrastructures. A Workshop Magazine*. https://www.urbanstudiesonline.com/resources/resource/urban-studies-online-presents-the-labouring-urban-infrastructures-digital-magazine.

Doherty, J. 2017. Life (and Limb) in the Fast-Lane: Disposable People as Infrastructure in Kampala's Boda Boda Industry. *Critical African Studies* 9 (2): 192–209. https://doi.org/10.1080/21681392.2017.1317457.

Doherty, J., and K. Brown. 2019. "Labor Laid Waste: An Introduction to the Special Issue on Waste Work." *International Labor and Working-Class History* 95: 1–17. https://doi.org/10.1017/S0147547919000048.

Doshi, S. 2016. "Embodied Urban Political Ecology: Five Propositions." *Area* 49 (1): 125–28. https://doi.org/10.1111/area.12293.

ECA, PEM Consult, and TM Associates. 2014. Lilongwe Water Board Tariff Review and Willingness to Pay Study. Lilongwe, Malawi.

Fredericks, R. 2009. "Wearing the Pants: The Gendered Politics of Trashwork in Senegal's Capital City. *HAGAR Studies in Culture, Polity and Identities* 9 (1): 29.

Fredericks, R. 2014. "Vital Infrastructures of Trash in Dakar." *Comparative Studies of South Asia, Africa and the Middle East* 34 (3): 532–48. https://doi.org/10.1215/1089201X-2826085.

Fredericks, R. 2018. *Garbage Citizenship: Vital Infrastructures of Labor in Dakar, Senegal.* Duke University Press.

Gidwani, V. 2015. "The Work of Waste: Inside India's Infra-Economy." *Transactions of the Institute of British Geographers* 40 (4): 575–95. https://doi.org/10.1111/tran.12094.

Graham, J. P., M. Hirai, and S. S. Kim. 2016. "An Analysis of Water Collection Labor among Women and Children in 24 Sub-Saharan African Countries." *PLOS One* 11 (6): e0155981. https://doi.org/10.1371/journal.pone.0155981.

Harris, L., D. Kleiber, J. Goldin, A. Darkwah, and C. Morinville. 2017. "Intersections of Gender and Water: Comparative Approaches to Everyday Gendered Negotiations of Water Access in Underserved Areas of Accra, Ghana, and Cape Town, South Africa." *Journal of Gender Studies* 26 (5): 561–82. https://doi.org/10.1080/09589236.2016.1150819.

Klawitter, S., S. Lorek, D. Schaefer, and A. Lammerding. 2009. *Case Study: Water Kiosks: How the Combination of Low-Cost Technology, Pro-Poor Financing, and Regulation Leads to the Scaling Up of Water Supply Service Provision to the Poor.* Federal Ministry for Economic Cooperation and Development, Germany. https://www.giz.de/expertise/downloads/gtz2009-0193en-water-kiosks.pdf.

"Lilongwe Water Board Partners TNM on E-Madzi Initiative, Customers Pleased." 2017. *Nyasa Times.* July 24. https://www.nyasatimes.com/lilongwe-water-board-partners-tnm-e-madzi-initiative-customers-pleased.

Mattern, S. 2018. "Maintenance and Care." *Places Journal.* https://placesjournal.org/article/maintenance-and-care.

Mawaya, C., and M. P. Kalindekafe. 2010. "Access, Control, and Use of Natural Resources, in Southern Malawi: A Gender Analysis." In *Natural Resource Management: The Impact of Gender and Social Issues,* edited by F. Flintan and T. Šeberu Tadlá, 88–125. Fountain Publisher.

Millington, N., and M. Lawhon. 2018. "Geographies of Waste: Conceptual Vectors from the Global South." *Progress in Human Geography* 43 (6): 1044–63. https://doi.org/10.1177/0309132518799911.

Mkandawire-Valhmu, L., and P. E. Stevens. 2007. "Applying a Feminist Approach to Health and Human Rights Research in Malawi: A Study of Violence in the Lives of Female Domestic Workers." *Advances in Nursing Science* 30 (4): 278–89. https://doi.org/10.1097/01.ANS.0000300178.25983.e1.

O'Reilly, K. 2006. "'Traditional' Women, 'Modern' Water: Linking Gender and Commodification in Rajasthan, India." *Geoforum,* 37 (6): 958–72. https://doi.org/10.1016/j.geoforum.2006.05.008.

Pihljak, L. H. 2014. Water Pricing Regimes and Production of Urban Waterscape. MSc thesis, UNESCO-IHE Institute for Water Education. https://ihedelftrepository.contentdm.oclc.org/digital/collection/masters2/id/87570.

Pihljak, L. H., M. Rusca, C. Alda-Vidal, and K. Schwartz. 2019. "Everyday Practices in the Production of Uneven Water Pricing Regimes in Lilongwe, Malawi." *Environment and Planning C: Politics and Space* 39 (2): 300–317. https://doi.org/10.1177/2399654419856021.

Rusca, M. 2017. *Lillongwe Water Works?* Whales That Fly. https://vimeo.com/240647554.

Rusca, M., and K. Schwartz. 2012. "Divergent Sources of Legitimacy: A Case Study of International NGOs in the Water Services Sector in Lilongwe and Maputo." *Journal of Southern African Studies* 38 (3): 681–97. https://doi.org/10.1080/03057070.2012.711106.

Rusca, M., K. Schwartz, L. Hadzovic, and R. Ahlers. 2015. "Adapting Generic Models through Bricolage: Elite Capture of Water Users Associations in Peri-urban Lilongwe." *European Journal of Development Research* 27, 777–92.

Simone, A. 2004. "People as Infrastructure: Intersecting Fragments in Johannesburg." *Public Culture* 16 (3): 407–29. https://doi.org/10.1215/08992363-16-3-407.

Stanley International. 1986. Lilongwe Water Supply and Sanitation Master Plan—Supplementary Work Paper. Lilongwe, Malawi.

Sultana, F. 2009. "Fluid Lives: Subjectivities, Gender, and Water in Rural Bangladesh." *Gender, Place & Culture* 16 (4): 427–44. https://doi.org/10.1080/09663690903003942.

Sultana, F. 2011. "Suffering for Water, Suffering from Water: Emotional Geographies of Resource Access, Control, and Conflict." *Geoforum* 42 (2): 163–72. https://doi.org/10.1016/j.geoforum.2010.12.002.

Sultana, F. 2015. "Emotional Political Ecology." In *The International Handbook of Political Ecolo*, edited by R. Bryant, 633–45. Edward Elgar Publishing.

Sultana, F. 2020. "Embodied Intersectionalities of Urban Citizenship: Water, Infrastructure, and Gender in the Global South." *Annals of the American Association of Geographers* 110 (5): 1407–24. https://doi.org/10.1080/24694452.2020.1715193.

Tiwale, S., M. Rusca, and M. Zwarteveen, M. 2018. "The Power of Pipes: Mapping Urban Water Inequities through the Material Properties of Networked Water Infrastructures—The Case of Lilongwe, Malawi." *Water Alternatives* 11 (2): 314–35.

Truelove, Y. 2011. "(Re-)Conceptualizing Water Inequality in Delhi, India through a Feminist Political Ecology Framework." *Geoforum* 42 (2): 143–52.

Truelove, Y. 2019. "Rethinking Water Insecurity, Inequality, and Infrastructure through an Embodied Urban Political Ecology." *Wiley Interdisciplinary Reviews: Water* 6 (3): e1342. https://doi.org/10.1080/doi/epdf/10.1002/wat2.1342.

Truelove, Y., and H. A. Ruszczyk. 2022. "Bodies as Urban Infrastructure: Gender, Intimate Infrastructures, and Slow Infrastructural Violence." *Political Geography* 92: 102492. https://doi.org/10.1016/j.polgeo.2021.102492.

Velzeboer, L. 2015. *The Everyday Power of Water: A Case Study on Water Inequalities in Lilongwe, Malawi from the Perspective of Consumers.*

Velzeboer, L., M. Hordijk, and K. Schwartz. 2017. "Water Is Life in a Life without Water: Power and Everyday Practices in Lilongwe, Malawi." *Habitat International* 73: 119–28. https://doi.org/10.1016/j.habitatint.2017.11.006

WaterAid. N.d. *Managing Communal Water Kiosks in Malawi: Experiences in Water Supply Management in Poor Urban Settlements in Lilongwe.* https://www.ircwash.org/sites/default/files/Wateraid-2012-Managing.pdf.

WHO/UNICEF JMP. 2017. *WASH in the 2030 Agenda: New Global Indicators for Drinking Water, Sanitation, and Hygiene.* WHO/UNICEF JMP. https://washdata.org/sites/default/files/documents/reports/2017-07/JMP-2017-WASH-in-the-2030-agenda.pdf.

Wutich, A. 2009. "Intrahousehold Disparities in Women and Men's Experiences of Water Insecurity and Emotional Distress in Urban Bolivia." *Medical Anthropology Quarterly*, 23 (4): 436–54. https://doi.org/10.1111/j.1548-1387.2009.01072.x.

CHAPTER 3

GENDERED INFRASTRUCTURES OF DISCARD IN DAKAR, SENEGAL

Rosalind Fredericks

GENDERING INFRASTRUCTURE

From the household to the city dump, men and women play central but differentiated roles in infrastructures for managing domestic waste in Dakar. Infrastructures of disposal are deeply labor intensive, entailing sweat, ingenuity, opportunity, and, more often than not, uneven burdens of bodily strain, disease, and stigma. This chapter traces the infrastructural labors involved in the disposal process in Dakar through tracing people's waste labors—paying particular attention to the relational construction of masculinities and femininities in the space of trash work. In so doing, it illuminates how infrastructures are gendered, and, in turn, how gender is rendered infrastructural. At each link in the chain of disposal, it aims to flesh out the gendered material expertise, burdens, desires, and subjectivities imbued in Dakar's infrastructures of discard. Though the observations are specific to Dakar, insight is gleaned for thinking about the gendering of infrastructures anywhere. Waste is a particularly illuminating field to examine the gendered life of infrastructure because of the powerful associations between waste and value (Gidwani and Maringanti 2016) and the strong cultural notions of who is responsible for doing the dirty work.

This research builds on a vibrant set of recent debates broadening the purview of how infrastructure is understood. Instead of an inert, technical supporting structure, infrastructure should be seen as a lively, embodied sociotechnical system (see Fredericks 2018; see also Graham and McFarlane 2015; Larkin 2013; Murphy 2013; Simone 2004; Star 1999; Truelove and Ruszczyk 2022). This allows for a much broader understanding of infrastructures as vital socio-technical gatherings and foregrounds laboring bodies, systems of sociality, and hierarchical divisions on which these systems are built. Focusing on the social life of infrastructure—including how labor is rendered infrastructural—helps to flesh out the differentiated burdens and benefits of infrastructure for different people in the city. Infrastructure "attracts people, draws them in, coalesces and expends their capacities" (Simone 2012)—but people's capacities may be expended unevenly, especially along gender, class, or other social-power divisions. A focus on infrastructural labors, thus, helps to "flesh out" infrastructures' vitality (Fredericks 2018). The materiality of different infrastructures is consequential, moreover, because the matter being organized by infrastructures (be it waste, water, electricity, etc.) has direct implications for the organization, benefits, burdens, and politics of those socio-technical systems. Relatedly, their affective address—conjuring modernity and progress or, conversely, backwardness and state failure, for instance—is deeply intertwined with both their sociality and materiality. Infrastructural systems themselves may be discursively gendered with deep implications for infrastructural politics.

Attention to how human labor is rendered infrastructural is especially relevant in the non-networked, often informal, fragmented infrastructural systems that dominate in many parts of Africa and, for that matter, across the global South. Austerity, economic stagnation, and uneven development often result in urban residents picking up the slack of insufficient urban infrastructures through different forms of salvage bricolage.[1] The waste sector in Dakar, Senegal is a primary example. After structural adjustment decimated urban public services in the 1980s, the city's household waste management infrastructure was increasingly devolved onto the laboring bodies of specific Dakarois. Even in the context of the recent infrastructure boom in Dakar (see Melly 2016), certain neighborhoods remain deeply disadvantaged with regard to waste services and certain people play an outsized role in the labor of discard. Especially in poor areas, insufficient waste management services have necessitated bricolage infrastructures that stretch from the household all the way to the dump. A central organizing factor in these infrastructures is gendered divisions of labor in their intersection with gendered discourses of waste.

A closer look at the material, social, and affective elements forming infrastructure demands attention to the multiplicity of ways that infrastructure is gendered. From divisions between men's and women's labor, to the embodied experience of infrastructural violence (Chaplin and Kalita n.d.; Rodgers and O'Neill 2012; Truelove and O'Reilly 2021), to the gendered imaginaries conjured by projects of state improvement (Sabhlok 2017; Schwenkel 2015), gender is a key feature shaping infrastructures' form and politics. Waste infrastructures are particularly revealing, owing to the negative associations between waste and value (Gidwani and Maringanti 2016) and the intersections between waste's "gritty," course materiality (Kirsch 2013) and gendered bodies. Waste, like water, is "symbolic infrastructural matter" (Schwenkel 2015, 522) that gets caught up in biopolitical projects of state engineering as well as the everyday embodied politics of city-making by diverse urban residents. Discard labor is a process of organizing the environment and, thus, is implicated in the reproduction of the social order (Douglas 1966). Waste management requires disposable people and places, but these relations of disposability are complex and contradictory. "The work entailed in trash management repels, yet the risk and danger inscribed in the process render it a vital labor at the base of urban development. Though it is by definition dirty, polluted labor, trash work can be seen simultaneously as a process of cleaning and purification" (Fredericks 2018, 21).

This chapter specifically zooms in on gendered labor in Dakar's trash infrastructure in order to illuminate the ways that gendered bodies and desires are coalesced and expended as well as the specific burdens they carry. Discard infrastructure in Dakar is deeply gendered owing to the gendered discourses of waste and cleaning in Senegal. The specific burdens and benefits of forms of discard labor, then, are conditioned by differentiated experiences of embodied precarity in the context of infrastructural decay. Although there has recently been a surge of research recognizing the importance of the decay and maintenance of infrastructure (Anand 2012; Carse 2014; Chu 2014; Corwin and Gidwani forthcoming; Graham and Thrift 2007; Jackson 2014), much less attention has been paid to the "pronounced ways that the technical and affective labor of improvisation and repair is corporeally grounded and gendered in practice" (Schwenkel 2015, 522). This chapter examines decaying infrastructures of waste through an attention to gendered embodiment. Although much of the chapter focuses on women waste workers, because of women's associations with waste in Dakar and the particular burdens they bear, it does so from a perspective of gendered relationality and intersectionality. Gender operates in intersection with other forms of difference, including class, religion, ethnicity, and age, to structure the value and power struggles surrounding different kinds of waste work in Dakar.[2] In the rest of the chapter, I endeavor to unpack the relationship between identities, social-power relations, and waste infrastructures in Dakar through examining the specific burdens and opportunities for different waste workers in the space of the household, street, and the city dump. These spaces are not distinct from each other but, rather, forge a gendered infrastructural socio-technical system. In each, I consider laboring bodies as both site and scale crystalizing the wider material, social, and affective dimensions of infrastructure (see Truelove, under review).

HOUSEHOLD

> I have a lot to say about garbage—I think about it every day! Garbage is women's work because we are in charge of sweeping and cleaning the house. When things are running well, the main challenge is timing it right to get the garbage out of the house. In times when the [garbage] workers have a problem, we really have to get creative. There is nothing I haven't thought of. Really garbage makes us very tired.
>
> —Awa (resident, HLM Fass neighborhood)

The infrastructure of domestic waste management necessarily starts in the home. As those chiefly responsible for cleanliness in the home, women are exclusively in charge of managing household garbage in Dakar. Even in times and places with good collection, the management of household waste is a thorny task that requires a dedicated system. Much of the waste produced by Dakar homes consists of organic materials, including fish bones, animal entrails, and plant refuse, which can become rank and dangerous fast in the Senegalese heat. Adequate storage materials like trash bags and cans are too expensive for most Dakarois, so families rely on open plastic bins, rice sacks, or flimsy plastic bags to store and transport wastes. Even when disposal happens regularly, households must manage decomposing wastes to keep them from endangering household members in increasingly cramped spaces. These management systems require careful efforts to slow or contain the sticky processes of decomposition—or waste's "toxic vitality" (Harvey 2017). Owing to fastidious sweeping practices and the sandy, dusty ecology, a large component of Dakar trash also consists of sand, which can make the garbage heavy. Transferring garbage from the home to the garbage truck entails its own challenges. Dakar's collection method consists of trucks driving on predetermined neighborhood routes, rhythmically honking to signal their arrival so that household members can transport and dump their garbage directly into the truck. This collection process means that garbage is generally not left in anonymous piles to be later collected but, instead, requires a direct handoff between household members and municipal collectors.

Household maids or women lower on the family hierarchy—like younger sisters or wives—are often responsible for getting the garbage out of the house and, ideally, into the back of the trash truck as it passes. This can be a profoundly onerous labor, especially when the municipal trash system is in crisis, as it has been periodically over the last few decades.[3] The requirement of intersecting with the trash truck is premised on the idea of someone always being at home and can seriously constrain women's mobility. For those who live farther from the collection route—for instance, down inaccessible narrow sandy roads—this can be especially challenging. In this way, the temporal rhythms of waste management interface with the territoriality of these systems to forge the distinct materiality of these infrastructures for different users (Desai, McFarlane, and Graham 2015; Truelove 2016). As a result, in actual times of crisis, including strikes by the municipal garbage collectors or just periods of uneven service, women become increasingly preoccupied with how to manage their festering garbage. They have developed elaborate systems for keeping their families safe during periods of poor service through storing, burying, or dumping their garbage out of sight. Dumping into ditches or nearby vacant lots can be carried out by family members or for exorbitant fees by the increasingly numerous *charrettes* (horse carts) profiting from people's desperation. For families operating on highly circumscribed household budgets, these kinds of investments can be a significant and unfortunate expense. Women without the means to pay to have their accumulating garbage carted away in these difficult moments are forced to dump it themselves. This can be arduous and nervewracking and can even elicit formal sanction by local authorities.[4] Increasing costs of household trash management, moreover, have been seen to precipitate marital discord as male and female household members fight over tight budgets and divergent priorities.[5]

Austerity breeds new relations of social reproduction as the duties usually fulfilled by the state are devolved onto neighborhood women (Meehan and Strauss 2015; Mitchell, Marston, and Katz 2004). During the periodic trash crises precipitated by austerity that have paralyzed the collection of household waste in Dakar and caused the decay of physical infrastructures, more and more pressure is placed on household women to spend their time, money, and ingenuity in the realm of managing their families' waste. Their daily labors to reduce, bury, or transport garbage serve as an essential element of the wider infrastructure of discard. Gender operates in intersection with class to place particular pressure on poor women, who may live in more dense quarters and have fewer options in times of crisis. These women spend an inordinate amount of time, sweat, and money just trying to rid their homes of its most mundane yet potentially dangerous daily product, and they can often be stigmatized by the system's weaknesses. When homes, courtyards, and community spaces become inundated with the filth of rotting garbage, women are on the front lines of blame for the stench and rot of waste out of place. The uneven burdens of stigma and disease they may bear are the slow infrastructural violence and corporeal suffering precipitated by state neglect and politicking (see Desai, McFarlane, and Graham 2015; Truelove and O'Reilly 2021).

Unearthing the benefits and burdens of waste infrastructure in Dakar necessitates a close look at the household as both the site at which discard labors originate and a key locus of forms of gendered sociality that shape the wider system of garbage collection, as we shall see below. In the context of poverty, scarce resources, and inadequate municipal waste management, the disposal, storage, and transformation of materials through reuse and recycling begin in the home. Sometimes, in the context of collapsed or inadequate municipal service provision, household strategies fully replace municipal garbage collection. The home must thus be considered infrastructural, because the labors of managing waste in the home are deeply shaping of the wider infrastructural system and are infrastructural labors demanding time, management systems, and exposure, in their own right. Considering household labors, moreover, brings our attention to the scale of the body and the social power relations that construct embodied burdens and opportunities. Viewing the household and its gendered bodies as part of infrastructure reveals the gendering of infrastructure and the very real differentiated burdens of embodied precarity. A definition of precarity here should, moreover, be encompassing enough to include not just the body burdens entailed in frequent contact with wastes but also the investments in time, money, and mental energy demanded of female residents responsible for managing their household trash.

STREET

> I never thought I would actually become a municipal trash collector as a profession. We [women] all jumped at the opportunity because we didn't have any job prospects and it was work we cared about. Women sweep [clean] the homes so it was easy for us to move out and sweep the streets. What was exciting was getting paid for it! For the guys, it was much more complicated because they were not used to working with waste. Then, everyone wanted the job and we [women] had to defend our rights to these positions.
> —Marieme (municipal garbage worker, Niari Tali)

The municipal garbage sector in Dakar has seen tumultuous transformations over the last thirty years in the wake of structural adjustment. As detailed in Fredericks (2018), the brunt of this tumult has been borne by the street sweepers and trash collectors,[6] who have seen their job security and the value of their labor become subject to vicious political battles between the local and national state that have fomented over control of the sector. At least twelve distinct institutional reconfigurations during the period—ranging from privatization to full nationalization of the sector—have rendered their positions decidedly insecure and precarious in specific moments across this history. Austerity and party politics have, thus, resulted in a devolution of infrastructure onto labor, where workers' bodies have been made to bear the brunt of increasingly uneven investments in this ever-demanding foundational public service. In the face of decreasing investment into the physical elements of the infrastructure (trucks and collection equipment) and their consequent decay, increasing pressure has been placed on labor to pick up the slack, with profound consequences for workers' communities and bodies. A detailed history of labor in the sector illustrates the gendered experience of opportunity and burden enabled by this tumultuous history.

The unlikely founding of the contemporary garbage sector in a social movement known as *Set/Setal* ("Be Clean/Make Clean" in Wolof) brought women workers into the municipal trash collection force for the first time in the early 1990s, and they remain about a quarter of the sector's almost two thousand workers.[7] Women's connection to cleaning in the home justified their incorporation into the municipal collection force, because they were seen as natural waste managers, even if they were occupying new roles in the public space and getting paid for the first time for this work. In this sense, the formalization of their cleaning labors masculinized their cleaning labor and rendered it a legitimate labor deserving of compensation. The first women workers in certain parts of Dakar were known as *les Amazons* and had a celebrated reputation for their strength and fearless dedication to difficult, dirty labor. Many wore masculine clothing like trousers and baseball caps for the first time and played a key role in winning the respect and compliance of the residents they served. Their history in the sector is recalled with pride by today's garbage workers, men and women alike. For the young men who became trashworkers in the new system in the early 1990s, entering into formal trashwork was less smooth. The negative associations of waste work were, at first, a liability. Embarrassed to be seen by their families and friends, these men covered their faces and tried to hide their work. Eventually they got used to being seen as trashworkers, and their battle for respect over the coming years would diminish the stigma associated with the work. Their profoundly different experiences of entering into formal trashwork for the first time, however, are illustrative of the profoundly gendered differences structuring the subjectivities of infra-structural labor. Who does what work and for what benefit is deeply shaped by the gendered division of labor and the structure of work and responsibility in the household.

The devolution of infrastructure onto labor over the course of the last thirty years has conditioned systems of salvage bricolage in which workers make do and work around increasingly rickety, decaying physical infrastruc-ture. This has had profoundly consequential impacts on the lives and bodies of Dakar's municipal garbage workers. In the most precarious times, workers were provisioned with minimal equipment under conditions of increasing demands on garbage service, and many workers suffered ill health or were hurt on the job. The specific risks were often different for women and men. Women were eventually moved off the most labor-intensive jobs (like riding on the back of trucks) and concentrated instead in street-sweeping positions. As a result, men had to deal more with garbage trucks breaking down, most of which were im-ported used from Europe, and all of the dangers this entailed as they employed their own bodies to buttress the dilapidated steel infrastructure. The more de-graded the equipment they worked with, the more risk to their bodily integrity. Bodies, in this instance, served as a sort of material subsidy to disinvestment.

For their part, women had particular struggles related to the lack of bath-room access and the insecurities connected to working on the street. For cer-tain periods, certain zones required their street sweepers to work at night, which was particularly perilous for women workers. Rumors of nighttime assaults testified to the severity of the specific risks for women and quickly led to an exclusively daytime working policy in the sector. The strains on all workers extended to their families and communities as well, as the people who depended on them on were subject to the vicissitudes of an unstable, highly politicized sector. Men complained of their inability to graduate into adult-hood by becoming solid breadwinners capable of taking care of their families.[8] Whereas identifying as youth before had been a source of power, they became stuck within the social category of youth, their masculinity compromised by their inability to realize societal expectations of adult manhood. They spoke of deep strain in their families caused by late salary payments or injuries on the job. In addition to the financial and bodily strain of the work, women re-counted the difficulties of managing childcare duties while at work and the spe-cific household responsibilities they struggled to manage while holding down a full-time job. Regardless of the particular strain encountered, these conditions of precarity and insecurity quickly incited the workers to action.

Though by and large the sector's workers entered into formal trashwork as inexperienced young people, over time they developed a sophisticated and savvy union movement to defend their rights and lobby for respect and better pay and protections. From the founding of the union in 2000 through a decade of conducting regular strikes and public campaigns to sway the public to their cause, the union gained important recognition from the mayor of Dakar in 2009 and finally won the signing in 2014 of their collective bargaining agreement, which gave them formal contracts, improved salaries, and medical and other benefits. Although there is certainly much room for improvement and the union continues to lobby for higher pay and better protections, one can certainly trace a marked improvement in their work lives and reputations since the late 1990s. The professionalization of the sector has gone hand in hand with an overall masculinization of its image and reputation. The all-male leadership of the union has often framed its battle for labor rights in gendered terms—justifying a demand for better salaries and respect through underlining the upstanding nature of this brotherhood of "fathers of the nation" and heads of households. In an era of extreme job insecurity, when many young men board flimsy boats destined for Europe or languish in a state of "waithood" (Honwana 2012) with no ability to get married or found families, it's no surprise that the image of progress and formalization of the city's waste sector—a last remaining bastion of formal municipal labor—is yoked to an ideal of adult masculinity.

One of the more interesting elements of a close look at men and women trashworkers' political subjectivities in this battle to improve the sector and its reputation is the decidedly gendered invocation of Islamic piety by workers aiming to validate their cause. A common platform among male workers, including the all-male leadership of the union, was the idea that trashwork, as cleaning work, is a labor of piety and thus that workers deserved fair remuneration and respect for this work because of its religious value. Though they did personally value their labor because of its religious worth, women, on the other hand, didn't invoke their work's religious value in a public forum. In this case, "Public articulations by male workers of the value of their labor in religious terms served to at least partly offset some of the stigma of becoming garbage men" (Fredericks 2018, 146). This can be seen as a part of the "bricolage of the self" (146) required of bricolage labor systems, or the important modes of meaning making that workers draw upon as they cobble together infrastructural labor out of fragmentary systems. Spirituality served an important and valuable resource that men especially drew upon in the context of the demoralizing universe of austerity and its calamitous social consequences. Public pronouncements of Islamic fraternity both reflected the more public nature of Islamic practice for men in Senegal and the specific intersections of religious identity, gender, and generation sculpting experiences of stigma related to wastework.[9]

Though women workers also saw their religious practice as a personal resource in the face of stigmatized labor, their claims to the value of their work were more often rooted in assertions to gender equality and fair labor. When, as Marieme mentioned above, their jobs became more desirable in an increasingly inaccessible formal labor market, their main challenge was defending their right to work in the sector at all. In specific zones, women workers were let go and replaced by men, justified by men's supposedly more important roles as family breadwinners and the so-called inappropriateness of the work for women. In other words, although women were encouraged to become trash-workers at the beginning of the new sector and were even celebrated for their brazen strength and dedication in that era, later on gender difference became politicized to justify replacing women's jobs with men. Women's labor was less valued and their income wrongly understood as less essential to their families' economic security.

Together, this brief history reveals the important ways that gender shapes formal municipal trash work and its associated opportunities and burdens in Dakar. This speaks to the intersectionality of identities and political positionalities at play in this infrastructural sector. Men's and women's political positionalities were deeply shaped by the shifting constructions of masculinity and femininity at different moments, as they intersected with the waste infrastructure over time. Instead of remaining static, gendered labor took on different meanings and values in relation to infrastructure at different moments. Infrastructural lives are deeply shaped by the lives people live at home, with real implications for how their formal work in the street is valued and remunerated. Workers' political subjectivities, moreover, are rooted in gendered modes of apprehending the value of labor and articulating those claims in a public setting.

DUMP

This work is very hard. Often, I take medicines to combat the fatigue. . . . You know, it's not easy for a woman to carry a large tub [full of food waste] on her head, to walk a long way before dumping—it's not easy. But we don't have an alternative, a job that would be easier for us. But also, working at Mbeubeuss is a work without pressure. You are not a prisoner. You see—like me, this morning, I woke up, washed clothes, took my child to

the doctor, and now, here I am looking to gain a little something, to find what God has reserved for me today. And if I was someone's employee?
—Aida (food waste collector and pig farmer, Mbeubeuss)

About thirty kilometers from downtown Dakar in a dry lake bed sits the city's sprawling dump, Mbeubeuss, which has received Dakar's household and commercial waste since 1968. As the sole repository for Dakar's now 3.5 million inhabitants' garbage, Mbeubeuss has grown into one of the largest open-air dumps in Africa. The number of people depending on the dump includes an estimated 1,800 self-employed men, women, and children who survive on the dump's decentralized recycling network, an unknown number of whom (perhaps in the hundreds) live on the dump in dilapidated shacks made out of found materials (Cissé 2012; WIEGO 2019). For decades, the state conveniently ignored Mbeubeuss, including its vast informal recycling networks and the community of reclaimers working and even living on the dump, but more recent plans have been devised to upgrade the dump as part of a modernist development agenda for cleaning up undesirable elements of the city and fashioning Dakar into a world-class metropolis.

Over the last fifty years, reclaimers at Mbeubeuss have forged the dump landscape, molding intricate salvage economies that extend across the country and beyond. The vast 120-hectare area of the dump is a complex live-work space where Dakarois from different walks of life carve out niches built upon specific forms of material expertise. It is a vital living infrastructure primarily composed of people's labor. The constant threat of fire and the possible closure of the dump render any built-up structures temporary at best and disincentivize investments in equipment and tools. People's bodies are the primary equipment at work on the dump.[10]

Far from a uniform infrastructure, the dump is a complex composite of different recycling economies and their associated social systems, material practices, expertise, and authority. The majority of reclaimers work with plastics or metal, with some specializing in even more specific materials, like PET or PP plastics, and others working as more generalists. Beyond the main plastics and metal recycling networks, a host of specialist niches have developed around materials that often require particular expertise to recycle—like soap, textiles, or food waste. Historically, recycling on the dump has been highly decentralized, with reclaimers enjoying a high level of autonomy in their discrete reclaiming activities. Labor is most generally divided between those people who work the active dumping "platform" behind the trucks—the most dangerous and physically onerous work—and those who work elsewhere at a *baraque*, a cordoned off space, often with a semi-permanent shack for shelter, used for sorting, stockpiling, trading, and generally hanging out. Individuals may work independently, for a boss, or together with family members or friends. More often than not, even if they are mostly working for themselves, people group together by age, hometown, and, importantly, by gender. Gender is an important feature structuring the dump's division of labor as well as the embodied precarities of dump work and the political subjectivities of individual workers faced with new dump policy. About a quarter to a third of the workers on Mbeubeuss are women, and by and large, these women occupy some of the dirtiest and least lucrative niches on the dump. They are, moreover, the least well represented in the formal association that is engaged in defending pickers' rights and consulting with the governmental and international organizations shaping dump policy.

Perhaps the dirtiest niche on the dump is the reclamation of food waste, which is conducted exclusively by women to feed to pigs raised nearby the dump. Christian women, especially of the Mandjack ethnicity, which originates in southern Senegal, dominate this niche because of the stigma associated with raising pigs in Islam. Food waste collection is incredibly onerous labor that often involves working directly behind the trucks on the active dumping platform, the most dangerous part of the dump. Extracting food waste requires coming into contact with all kinds of sharp, putrid, and toxic materials, and women insist that this can only be done with bare hands. Once they fill a plastic bin with the food waste, this must be carried on the head to a nearby sorting area for further processing to ensure that no non-organic materials remain in the waste. The sorted food waste is then packed into rice sacks for transport off the dump, usually by horse cart. Many women gather food waste to feed directly to their own pigs, but others sell the feed. One rice sack of food waste currently sells for around 1,000 CFA (~US$2.00), and an individual woman might gather enough food waste to fill one to three sacks in a day.

Despite layering clothing to protect the skin and fastidious efforts to clean up at the end of the work day, the work is absolutely filthy, and these women are in constant contact with rotting matter. Their bodies suffer as a result. Notwithstanding a reluctance to speak of ill health for fear of it being used against them and their right to work at the dump, some workers have admitted that they suffer from a range of issues they believe are connected to the work, including skin problems, deep cuts that wouldn't heal, and even unexplained stillbirths. The returns on their labor are thin, at best. For Aida (quoted above), a divorced mother of six who raises her own pigs in an empty building a ten-minute walk from the back side of the dump, collecting food waste to raise pigs has allowed her to get her own room and had given her a measure of financial security. She still struggles, however, to pay her monthly rent of 17,500 CFA (US$30) and was unable to pay school fees for her youngest child. In addition to the burden of dirty labor is the stigma of raising pigs in a predominantly Muslim culture. Aida is a rare Muslim doing this work, and she knows it is looked down upon. She says she has no choice but to keep going in the only job that consistently earned her a living. Times have improved, she insisted, from the days when she had to bring her small children to the dump with her while she worked. Her story is a familiar one. Most of the women working on the dump are deeply disadvantaged—widows, divorcées, or young women with no employment prospects—who found their way to the dump out of a desperate lack of other options. Patriarchal social-power relations render these women more vulnerable financially, and their only recourse is to take on more precarious work. Echoing Aida's quote above, many are attracted by the flexibility allowed by working for oneself on one's own clock, which allows them to manage their household social reproductive duties (cooking, cleaning, childcare) as well. The temporality of waste reclamation, then, is directly related to the gendered rhythms of the household. For those conducting food waste reclamation, moreover, the all-female niche serves as a refuge for women unwilling to face stiff competition in other spheres, especially with men. The power of intersecting forms of discrimination, however, makes their labor especially precarious.

As the bottom of the dump's social hierarchy—and in a disgraced niche within an already stigmatized profession—the women food waste collectors are also perhaps the most vulnerable to impending changes on the dump. A major loan was signed in 2018 by the World Bank and other international funders to upgrade the dump in the coming years. Plans for the dump upgrade show that it will dramatically reconfigure recycling on the dump, especially the reclamation of food waste. After a delay due to COVID-19, construction will break ground early 2022 to wall off the main parts of the dump and build a sorting factory that will formalize the labor of recycling and a composting center that will transform the reclamation of food waste for pork production into a more palatable "green" composting center (Banna 2021). If the food waste sector is indeed fully converted to compost, it could imperil the livelihoods of the women food waste collectors and the whole nearby neighborhood, which depends on the pork economy. These women's lack of representation within the pickers' association, which is incorporated to a degree in the World Bank's stakeholder consultation process, means that they are not only mostly in the dark about impending upgrade plans but also lack a voice in how the upgrade process unfolds. With little recourse to other professions, they sit as those with the most to lose in the upgrade process.

Dakar's garbage dump is a vital, living infrastructure consisting primarily of the hard labor of some of the city's most disenfranchised citizens. But the value, meaning, and precarity of that infrastructural labor varies dramatically within the population of pickers that make their living there. Though they may have started out sweating it out behind the trucks on the dangerous dumping platform like everyone, a class of male recyclers have capitalized on the dump's lucrative recycling networks to moved up the ranks to become fairly well-off plastics and metal traders. They report that this success has enabled them to fulfill their obligations as men, sons, and fathers—to found families and become responsible heads of households. Very few women have advanced up the recycling commodity chain to the more lucrative positions. By and large, especially for the food waste workers, women reclaimers remain the dump's most disenfranchised workers; their infrastructural labors are profoundly less lucrative than those of their male compatriots and their positions are intensely precarious.

Although the government has conveniently ignored the vast networks of recycling at Mbeubeuss for most of the dump's history, the dump is coming into view not just as an obstacle that stands in the way of the city's modern image but also as a potential resource mine (Samson 2015). As scholars have noted in diverse locations, waste infrastructures—and dumps, in particular—can be host to some of the most violent processes of accumulation by dispossession (Arefin forthcoming; Demaria and Schindler 2016; Gidwani and Reddy 2011; Samson 2015). The upgrade of the dump and the formalization of picking labor will have profound implications for laborers on the dump. But the contours of that infrastructural violence will be deeply uneven.

Feminist scholars have long emphasized how urban change and particularly modernist projects to sterilize urban space and control abject elements of the social body are deeply gendered (see the introduction to this volume and also Bingaman, Sanders, and Zorach 2001; Kern 2010; Massey 1994). This volume draws special attention to the gendered nature of infrastructural politics, emphasizing the differential embodied burdens as well as the affective address of infrastructure. Plans to modernize Dakar's dump are aimed at regularizing what are viewed as backward informal economies through patriarchal notions of modern infrastructures and their associated labors. The gendered implications of this particular form of urban renewal are especially evident with regard to the food waste sector at Mbeubeuss. Women food waste collectors are the epitome of the messy, informal, feminized vision of the current dump that stands in contradistinction to the masculinist vision of a planned, formal, modern landfill that planners are hoping to usher forth in the coming years. Food waste reclamation for pork production is seen not only as particularly dirty and contaminated because of negative Islamic associations with pigs but also as especially dispensable because it is the domain of poor, illiterate women who are devalued in their roles as laborers and breadwinners. Much like the women municipal waste collectors who were fired when that system was formalized, these waste pickers may become casualties of efforts to upgrade Dakar's dump. Eradicating the pork micro-industry of Mbeubeuss may be a convenient way to cleanse a particularly polluted infrastructure, with devastating impacts on these women and their families.

CONCLUSIONS

A broader understanding of infrastructure that is attentive to its affective, material, and social elements lends insight into the variegated burdens and opportunities emplaced by infrastructure onto laboring bodies and the ways that gendered associations come to represent infrastructural systems as a whole. This chapter has endeavored to paint a vibrant picture of Dakar's waste infrastructure, paying particular attention to infrastructural labor and the deeply gendered experiences of working trash in Dakar. In this sense, this history has illuminated how infrastructures are gendered and, in turn, how gender comes to be rendered infrastructural. The particular materialities and symbols associated with waste are especially important to framing the value of waste work and conditioning its infrastructural politics. Gendered discourses of cleaning are deeply consequential in shaping not just the division of labor surrounding waste but also the particularities of men's and women's experiences of embodied precarity and their political subjectivities as they rally to improve their conditions. Gendered associations of waste work have provided contradictory spaces for women—both affording them strategic openings to take on new labor roles and to claim authority and expertise, and, at the same time, justifying their positionality within low-paid, stigmatized work and, sometimes, their violent dispossession from the value they have so painstakingly constructed. At the same time, different elements of the waste infrastructure as a whole have come to be gendered, conditioning political possibilities around infrastructural change.

This research has thus demonstrated how both the underinvestment and modernization of infrastructure are deeply gendered processes. Decaying infrastructure devolves infrastructure onto labor and community systems, placing people in more direct contact with their wastes and conjuring a sense of backwardness. Men and women have different experiences of the embodied precarities engendered as infrastructure breaks down and as they are called upon to deploy their bodies to buttress infrastructure in differentiated ways at the scale of the home, the street, and the dump. Given the toxic materiality of waste, the intimacy often bred between laborers and the waste itself as infrastructure degrades can be a deep source of bodily exposure and uneven burdens. The upgrade of infrastructure, furthermore, may be part and parcel of a gendered visioning process. In the case of Dakar's dump, for instance, infrastructural modernization can be partly understood as an endeavor to masculinize a polluted and feminized sphere. The formalization and professionalization of waste labor may be envisioned through gendered imaginaries of the household and family, which may, in effect, codify or entrench gendered inequities. Infrastructural violences—whether slow or abrupt—are thus conjured and experienced in and through the particular precarities of gendered bodies.

ACKNOWLEDGMENTS AND FUNDING

This chapter draws on ongoing ethnographic research conducted in Dakar since 2004 with support provided by the National Science Foundation, Social Science Research Council, Fulbright-Hays, and NYU. The author is grateful for research assistance and for insightful editorial comments from Ndeye Binta Laye Ndoye, Ousmane Diouf Sane, and Rachael Mattson. She would also like to thank the municipal waste collectors, Mbeubeuss reclaimers, and members of SNTN and Bokk Diom, in addition to others involved in the waste sector in Dakar who shared their time and insight. All mistakes in the text are the author's responsibility.

NOTES

1. This is developed more fully in Fredericks (2018). *Bricolage* is derived from the French verb *bricoler*, which means to tinker or piece together and is often associated with do-it-yourself (DIY) systems.
2. The value and relative burdens related to infrastructural labors of waste management have been shown to derive from power relations surrounding intersecting forms of difference in diverse locations (e.g., Beall 2006; Fahmi and Sutton 2010; Gidwani and Reddy 2011; Millar 2018; Nagle 2013; Samson 2010). See the introduction to this volume for a more fulsome discussion of intersectionality, power relations, and infrastructures.
3. See Fredericks (2018) for a history of the periodic trash crises that have gripped Dakar over the last few decades, brought on by institutional politicking, budget cuts, and striking municipal garbage workers.
4. For example, as I detail in chapter 3 of *Garbage Citizenship* (2018), women have been fined for dumping garbage on the beach in the Yoff district. To avoid sanction, some have resorted to hiding garbage in wastewater dumped at the water's edge or dumping at night.
5. When household garbage collection fees were increased in Yoff, for instance, this precipitated disagreements between men and women heads of household over household budget priorities. Women were often invested in paying more for garbage collection services but were less able to pay.

6. The formal title for these workers is *techniciens de surface* (surface technicians).
7. This is considered more fully in Fredericks (2018). See ENDA (1991) and Diouf (1996) for more on *Set/Setal*.
8. See Fredericks (2014, 2018) for more discussion of youth as a social category and young male trashworkers' struggles to become "full" adults through being able to get married and sufficiently take care of their families.
9. See Fredericks (2018) for more details.
10. See Fredericks (forthcoming) for more details on infrastructural labor at the dump.

REFERENCES

Anand, N. 2012. "Municipal Disconnect: On Abject Water and Its Urban Infrastructures." *Ethnography* 13 (4): 487–509.

Arefin, M. R. Forthcoming. "The Commodification of Waste: From Threat to Frontier," *Antipode* special issue, "Anthropocene: Apotheosis of Waste," edited by M. R. Arefin, R. Fredericks, and G. Hecht.

Banna, F. M. 2021. *Disclosable Version of the ISR—Senegal Municipal Solid Waste Management Project—P161477—Sequence No: 03 (English)*. World Bank Group.

Beall, J. 2006. "Dealing with Dirt and the Disorder of Development: Managing Rubbish in Urban Pakistan." *Oxford Development Studies* 34 (1): 81–97.

Bingaman, A., L. Sanders, and R. Zorach, eds. 2001. *Embodied Utopias: Gender, Social Change and the Modern Metropolis*. Routledge.

Carse, A. 2014. *Beyond the Big Ditch: Politics, Ecology, and Infrastructure at the Panama Canal*. MIT Press.

Chaplin, S., and R. Kalita. N.d. *Infrastructure, Gender, and Violence: Women and Slum Sanitation Inequalities in Delhi*. Centre for Policy Research.

Chu, J. Y. 2014. "When Infrastructures Attack: The Workings of Disrepair in China." *American Ethnologist* 41 (2): 351–67.

Cissé, O. 2012. *Les Décharges d'Ordures en Afrique: Mbeubeuss à Dakar au Sénégal*. Karthala.

Corwin, J. E., and V. Gidwani. Forthcoming. "Repair Work as Care: On Maintaining the Planet in the Capitalocene," *Antipode* special issue, "Anthropocene: Apotheosis of Waste," edited by M. R. Arefin, R. Fredericks, and G. Hecht.

Demaria, F., and S. Schindler. 2016. "Contesting Urban Metabolism: Struggles Over Waste-to-Energy in Delhi, India." *Antipode* 48 (2): 293–313.

Desai, R., C. McFarlane, and S. Graham. 2015. "The Politics of Open Defecation: Informality, Body, and Infrastructure in Mumbai." *Antipode* 47 (1): 98–120.

Diouf, M. 1996. "Urban Youth and Senegalese Politics: Dakar 1988–1994." *Public Culture* 8: 225–49.

Douglas, M. 1966. *Purity and Danger: An Analysis of the Concepts of Pollution and Taboo*. Routledge.

ENDA. 1991. *Set Setal, Des Murs Qui Parlent: Nouvelle Culture Urbaine à Dakar*. ENDA Tiers Monde.

Fahmi, W., and K. Sutton. 2010. "Cairo's Contested Garbage: Sustainable Solid Waste Management and the Zabaleen's Right to the City." *Sustainability* 2: 1765–83.

Fredericks, R. 2014. "Vital Infrastructures of Trash in Dakar." *Comparative Studies of South Asia, Africa, and the Middle East* 34 (3): 532–48.

Fredericks, R. 2018. *Garbage Citizenship: Vital Infrastructures of Discard in Dakar, Senegal*. Duke University Press.

Fredericks, R. Forthcoming. "Anthropocenic Discards: Embodied Infrastructures and Uncanny Exposures at Dakar's Dump," *Antipode* special issue, "Anthropocene: Apotheosis of Waste," edited by M. R. Arefin, R. Fredericks, and G. Hecht.

Gidwani, V., and A. Maringanti. 2016. "The Waste-Value Dialectic: Lumpen Urbanization in

Contemporary India." *Comparative Studies of South Asia, Africa and the Middle East* 36 (1): 112–33.

Gidwani, V., and R. N. Reddy. 2011. "The Afterlives of "Waste": Notes from India for a Minor History of Capitalist Surplus." *Antipode* 43 (5): 1625–58.

Graham, S., and C. McFarlane, eds. 2015. *Infrastructural Lives: Urban Infrastructure in Context.* Routledge.

Graham, S., and N. Thrift. 2007. "Out of Order: Understanding Repair and Maintenance." *Theory, Culture, and Society* 24 (3): 1–25.

Harvey, P. 2017. "Waste Futures: Infrastructures and Political Experimentation in Southern Peru." *Ethnos* 82 (4): 672–89.

Honwana, A. 2012. *The Time of Youth: Work, Social Change, and Politics in Africa.* Kumarian Press.

Jackson, S. J. 2014. "Rethinking Repair." In *Media Technologies: Essays on Communication, Materiality, and Society*, edited by T. Gillespie, P. Boczkowski and K. Foot, 221–39. MIT Press.

Kern, L. 2010. *Sex and the Revitalized City: Gender, Condominium Development, and Urban Citizenship.* University of British Columbia Press.

Kirsch, S. 2013. "Cultural Geography I: Materialist Turns." *Progress in Human Geography* 37 (3): 433–41.

Larkin, B. 2013. "The Politics and Poetics of Infrastructure." *Annual Review of Anthropology* 42: 327–43.

Massey, D. 1994. *Space, Place, and Gender.* University of Minnesota Press.

Meehan, K., and K. Strauss, eds. 2015. *Precarious Worlds: New Geographies of Social Reproduction.* University of Georgia Press.

Melly, C. 2016. *Bottleneck: Moving, Building, and Belonging in an African City.* University of Chicago Press.

Millar, K. M. 2018. *Reclaiming the Discarded: Life and Labor on Rio's Garbage Dump.* Duke University Press.

Mitchell, K., S. A. Marston, and C. Katz, eds. 2004. *Life's Work: Geographies of Social Reproduction.* Blackwell.

Murphy, M. 2013. Chemical Infrastructures of the St. Clair River. In *Toxicants, Health, and Regulation Since 1945*, edited by S. Boudia and N. Jas, 103–15. Pickering and Chatto.

Nagle, R. 2013. *Picking Up: On the Streets and behind the Trucks with the Sanitation Workers of New York City.* Farrar, Straus and Giroux.

Rodgers, D., and B. O'Neill. 2012. "Infrastructural Violence: Introduction to the Special Issue." *Ethnography* 13 (4): 401–12.

Sabhlok, A. 2017. "'Main Bhi to Hindostaan Hoon': Gender and Nation-State in India's Border Roads Organisation." *Gender, Place, and Culture* 24 (12): 1711–28.

Samson, M. 2010. "Producing Privatization: Re-articulating Race, Gender, Class, and Space." *Antipode* 42 (2): 404–32.

Samson, M. 2015. "Accumulation by Dispossession and the Informal Economy: Struggles over Knowledge, Being, and Waste at a Soweto Garbage Dump." *Environment and Planning D: Society and Space* 33 (5): 813–30.

Schwenkel, C. 2015. "Spectacular Infrastructure and Its Breakdown in Socialist Vietnam." *American Ethnologist* 42 (3): 520–34.

Simone, A. 2004. "People as Infrastructure: People as Intersecting Fragments in Johannesburg." *Public Culture* 16 (3): 407–29.

Simone, A. 2012. "Infrastructure: Commentary by AbdouMaliq Simone." *Cultural Anthropology Online*, November 26, 2012, https://journal.culanth.org/index.php/ca/infrastructure-abdoumaliq-simone.

Star, S. 1999. "The Ethnography of Infrastructure." *American Behavioral Scientist* 43 (3): 377–91.

Truelove, Y. 2016. "Incongruent Waterworlds: Situating the Everyday Practices and Power of Water in Delhi." *South Asian Multidisciplinary Academic Journal* 14.

Truelove, Y. Under review. "Embodied Infrastructure: Towards Bodies that 'Matter' and a Corporeal Geography of Infrastructure." *Transactions of the Institute of British Geographers*.

Truelove, Y., and K. O'Reilly. 2021. "Making India's Cleanest City: Sanitation, Intersectionality, and Infrastructural Violence." *Environment and Planning E* 4 (3): 718–35.

Truelove, Y., and H. A. Ruszczyk. 2022. "Bodies as Urban Infrastructure: Gender, Intimate Infrastructures, and Slow Infrastructural Violence." *Political Geography* 92: 1–10.

WIEGO. 2019. *Report on the 2018 Mbeubeuss Census*.

CHAPTER 4

PLACING OPPRESSION (WITH)IN PUBLIC INFRASTRUCTURES: TRACING AN INTERSECTIONAL RELATIONSHIP BETWEEN GENDER, VIOLENCE, AND TECHNOLOGY

Anshika Suri

INTRODUCTION

Eighteen-year-old Eunice lives in a shared household with six other people at 4A village in Mathare informal settlement in Nairobi. Her day starts with counting the number of jerry cans she has that still contain water. With no toilets or running water in her dwelling, and the nearest community shared toilet more than a ten-minute walk away, she heads to a nearby school to use their toilet facilities. Living in an informal settlement with inadequate water, sanitation, and hygiene (WASH) infrastructure, she carries her own jerry can of water to the toilet facilities. Although a neighboring shared dwelling has a toilet, her requests to use this facility have been repeatedly denied.[1]

Additionally, Eunice, like many other women in the Global South, is also responsible for fetching water for drinking and sanitary usage. As a means to purchase water, she is undergoing skills training to find employment as a hairdresser. Being one of the participants of the Teenage Mothers Empowerment program run by the local NGO MCFPanairobi, she is undergoing a six-month training that includes sessions in cosmetology and garment making. Since the program insists on mothers bringing their children along, she takes her two-year-old to the training center. Participants have access to the center's toilets,

Fig. 4.1. A water kiosk in Kibera, Nairobi. (Photo by Anshika Suri)

which she prefers to use, as it means a lower risk of catching infections like diarrhea (for which her child is particularly at risk) or urinary tract infection (a risk to her). While the MCFPanairobi training center has private toilets, most dwellings in the informal settlement rely on a shared ablution block, with around 140 households having access to one public toilet,[2] often leading to health and hygiene issues.

While returning home from training, Eunice frequently stops to purchase water. With one bucket of water (roughly one twenty-liter plastic jerry can) costing 2–5 KSH (roughly 2–5 US cents),[3] she can at most afford one jerry can per day. Moreover, with water provision limited to water kiosks in the settlement, the lines are long and can often lead to kiosks being locked by the (mostly male) youth groups[4] who manage them. Consequently, she often forgoes "drinking water after 6:00 p.m. at night" to avoid using the shared toilet. There is an added complexity of shared toilets inducing a fear of violence, especially when accessed at night, with Eunice recounting women being sexually assaulted by men and locked inside toilets. Women like Eunice thus often stand on an intersection of multiple categories: poverty, infrastructural inadequacy,

Fig. 4.2. Women washing clothes at shared water tank in Mathare. (Photo by Anshika Suri)

and gender violence, among others. The everyday embodied practices of women residents of urban informal settlements illustrate the daily contestations, negotiations, and coping mechanisms they employ to mediate gender inequality in urban infrastructure. These everyday encounters of women residents' also highlight the complex interweaving of WASH infrastructural inadequacy with narratives of violence, leading me to inquire whether inadequate public infrastructure is becoming oppressive due its gendered usage.

Considering this infrastructural inadequacy in informal settlements through a gendered lens offers an in-depth view on the global sanitation crisis, wherein 2.3 billion people still lack access to basic sanitation services (World Health Organization and UNICEF 2017). While access to sanitation was measured globally by the WHO/UNICEF Joint Monitoring Programme for Water Supply and Sanitation according to targets set by the Millennium Development Goals, this monitoring did not provide a disaggregated breakdown of access for men and women, despite well-documented gender-based inequalities in WASH. Subsequently, the 2030 Agenda for Sustainable Development was restructured to "to leave no one behind" (World Health Organization and UNICEF 2017, 34). Nevertheless, the slow pace of progress has highlighted the adverse impact of inadequate sanitation provision and access on women, with poor sanitation significantly influencing safety and well-being of women (Domestos, WaterAid, and Water Supply and Sanitation Collaborative Council 2013; Reddy and Snehalatha 2011) and leaving them vulnerable to sexual violence if they practice open defecation. These highlighted inequalities have prompted policymakers and development practitioners to provide "solutions," including shared sanitation facilities to curb open defecation and repurposed water projects to reduce women's time spent fetching water. My work adds to the emerging research on perceptions and meanings women associate with their everyday practices, particularly around precarious infrastructures.

Therefore, through the case studies of informal settlements in the capital cities of Dar es Salaam, Tanzania, and Nairobi, Kenya, this chapter describes the everyday urban routines of female and male residents that intersect with infrastructural inadequacy. Through residents' embodied and lived experiences, I aim to illustrate the oppressive nature of infrastructural inadequacy and gendered aspects of vulnerability to violence linked with WASH infrastructure. This chapter thus focuses on examining how adopting an intersectional approach can enrich gendered analyses of the technical infrastructures. Sanitation infrastructure further aids this investigation because sanitary facilities are inherently classified into binary notions of gendered usage—i.e., male and female (although recent scholarship has criticized this normative assumption, with analyses on transgender usage adding another layer of complexity within the normative binary analysis [Bender-Baird 2015]).

This chapter begins with a discussion of debates on everyday lived experiences of women with precarious infrastructures, through which I build the case for an intersectional approach toward analyses of urban infrastructure regimes. In the following sections, I examine intersections of narratives of fear and insecurity with infrastructural inadequacy. Through a discussion of embodied experiences of residents of informal settlements in cities of East Africa, I seek to examine whether the said inadequacy is turning public infrastructure oppressive, especially for women.

EVERYDAY LIVED EXPERIENCES WITH TECHNOLOGY

Earlier research on everyday life has highlighted how the urban poor are not solely excluded from the material necessities of life (Marcuse 2009, 190), but are often also deprived from articulating the access to critical services (Harvey 2012; Purcell 2002). This resonates in debates that examine the exclusion of women and poor people from infrastructure services. Much of the earlier scholarship on women and technology "fail(ed) to capture or explain women's ambivalence about technologies they encounter" (Faulkner 2001). However, recent research in feminist technology studies has been instrumental in analyzing gender and technology (Bray 2007), emphasizing the need to focus on women's lived experience as a way to give women a voice in the construction of new knowledge (Fonow and Cook 2014) though with limited attention to experiences from the Global South (Wamala-Larson and Stark 2019, 3).

Additionally, it has been argued that technologies gain gender identities when they enter into our everyday structure and culture by becoming actors in the material and symbolic practices of everyday lives (Lohan 2013, 158). Recent scholarship on infrastructural systems has demonstrated how everyday socio-material interactions with technologies have led to contested forms of citizenship (Anand 2011), wherein infrastructures influence the way of living (Von Schnitzler 2013). In this regard, women residents, through their everyday contestations and negotiations with urban infrastructural regimes, provide a diverse and gendered outlook on spatial practices (Beebeejaun 2017), which in turn can further provide insights into different forms of belonging to the city (Fenster 2005).

What makes these everyday interactions with urban infrastructures insightful is the often precarious provision in the cities of the Global South. This precarity in everyday life has further countered the notion of infrastructures as being implicitly "invisible" and becoming visible only upon breakdown (Star 1999; Kooy and Bakker 2008). Consequently, these interactions with varied infrastructures (such as water, sanitation, etc.) have become major sites of the production of the everyday, with infrastructural inadequacy mobilizing visibility (Von Schnitzler 2008). Sanitary infrastructure's socio-material configuration, especially when faced with precarious provision, highlights the complexity of (in)visibility, from both a technical and a social perspective. Sanitation is an act/action that is universally perceived to be conducted in private. When the lack of a private space forces the action/act (i.e., open defecation) to become a matter of public intervention (i.e., provision of shared/communal toilets), prefigurative roles for the urban poor are often revealed. Under the guise of aesthetic and unsanitary practices, studies show notions of shame being attached to open defecation due to sociocultural constructs of the female body (Desai, McFarlane, and Graham 2014, 14), highlighting the female body as a site of oppression, contestation, and negotiations and a sociopolitical tool within urban infrastructure regimes.

Nevertheless, research has also highlighted the various ways in which women creatively use these often cheaper technologies "to reshape local social structures, reorganize social geographies and recreate social institutions" (Scott, Semmens, and Willoughy 2013, 16), potentially affecting socio-technical and political geographies of access. In addition, their routines can also shed light on how publicness and privacy are negotiated through embodied spatial practices and the negotiation of access to public space (Truelove 2011). The everyday appropriations of urban public spaces such as communal/shared toilets by marginalized groups also represents their claim for a space of privacy and security. Therefore, the different ways in which spaces are invested by individuals and groups puts an emphasis on how they seek to shape the city to their needs.

Feminist critiques of development discourses that emerged in 1970s highlighted how earlier strategies were often focused on how to incorporate women within varied models instead of implicit inclusion (Reeves 2002; Valentine 2007; Beebeejaun 2017). Women were often represented as "incapable of thinking for themselves, requiring mediation and representation" (Spivak 1988 as cited by Caretta and Riano 2016, 259). Consequently, feminist geographers in the early 1990s argued for a shift away from the "women only" focus of feminist scholarship, stressing that such "simplistic formulations can be reductive and ineffectual in innovating strategies to combat oppressions" (Mohanty 1984). Many feminist scholars also contested the notion of a universal "woman," due to the experiences of women being varied and diverse, making it implausible to explain them through a single framework (Nash 2008). In addition, women's spatial and temporal experiences of the city not only highlight the micro-politics of urban life but also articulate how cities differ through the gendered mediation of space (Beebeejaun 2017).

Therefore, it became imperative to explain inequalities mediated by a complex framework of oppressive categories such as race, class, gender, and so on to uncover the pluralities in women's everyday encounters with urban precarious infrastructure regimes. The next section will discuss the potentials of an intersectional approach to critical infrastructures.

AN INTERSECTIONAL APPROACH TO CRITICAL INFRASTRUCTURES

Instead of merely summarizing the effects of a singular oppressive category, intersectionality has emerged as a concept to theorize on and empirically analyze the relationship between different social categories (Crenshaw 1991; Davis 2008; Winker and Degele 2011). An intersectional lens deconstructs "woman" as category by highlighting that while women mutually experienced oppression, it was not necessarily the same kind of oppression (Cho, Crenshaw, and McCall 2013, 800). In addition, intersectional analyses demand diversity in the voices of women as subjects and advocate for the further inclusion of women within other disciplines, as well through shedding a light on the material realities of women's lives. Intersectionality has traveled into spaces and discourses that are constituted by contested power relations (especially within debates on everyday life, among others). This inclusion has allowed an in-depth analysis into how acts of discrimination and hidden power relations further construct identities through interventions of multiple categories (McCall 2005; Valentine 2007; Winker and Degele 2011). However, earlier research on intersectional approaches in feminist geography and social sciences illustrated limited attention to the significance of space in the process of subject formation (Fernandes 2004; Valentine 2007). Conversations about intersectionality have also transcended the disciplines of women's/gender/feminist studies and critical race studies and are aiming at bridging this theory with other disciplines in determining how relevant intersectionality is in shaping individual experiences (Clarke and McCall 2013). The existing literature on intersectionality, therefore, highlights how this theory can be a useful analytical tool (1) to address the diversities of everyday urban lived experiences of women with service provision in informal settlements, and (2) to examine often precarious urban infrastructure provision through the everyday lived perceptions of the residents of cities of the Global South.

While recent scholarship in critical infrastructure debates has highlighted the need of incorporating everyday lived experiences (Graham and McFarlane 2014) to reveal existing urban inequalities, it lacks an in-depth analysis of how these everyday experiences inform and mediate manifested gendered inequalities in accessing basic services. This illuminates the need for intersectional approaches in critical infrastructure debates to further pinpoint how the intersection of multiple categories (such as race/class/gender, etc.) that emerge in everyday contestations and negotiations of residents as users of infrastructures can enrich understanding of the prefigurative and performative role of infrastructure access/provision. Larkin (2013, 330) has highlighted how the analysis of infrastructures has evolved from merely organizing everyday life to include accounts of translations, which have further implications on technological systems becoming entangled in contestations on citizenship and rights to access services. While there is extensive research illustrating these contestations, they fail to capture the magnitude and role of technological scripts in furthering these conflicts, more specifically, what Dutch and Norwegian feminists in science and technology studies have identified as "gender scripts" in technological artifacts (Oudshoorn, Saetnan, and Lie 2002). An intersectional approach in this aspect could also improve our understanding of critical infrastructures through the complexities of designer-user relations, where "end users" aid and influence technological development and make visible any specific practices in provision that may lead to the exclusion of specific users (Oudshoorn and Pinch 2003, 10). One such observed exclusion is through the risk poor women residents face when interacting with precarious infrastructure. Often, inadequate access to sanitation services and existing infrastructure designs can expose women to acts of violence, and reports indicate increased violence around sanitation infrastructures (Abrahams, Mathews, and Ramela 2006; O'Reilly 2016). Such gender-based violence instills a mobilizing fear and insecurity in the public space (O'Reilly 2016). Hence, the next section discusses the intersection of women's everyday routines with narratives of fear, insecurity, and gender violence.

ENCOUNTERS WITH VIOLENCE: WOMEN'S EVERYDAY URBAN ROUTINES

Everyday urban life encompasses an infinite range of routines. However, within the cities of the Global South, these routines are often characterized by disruptions of access to public space, as the everyday embodied and lived experiences of the urban poor (especially women) are tethered to spatialities and temporalities. Most literature pertaining to women's (lack of) access to public spaces concerns the fear of crime as the key constraining factor (Paul 2011; Pain 2001). Fear emanates from feelings of uncertainty, helplessness, and vulnerability and can vary depending upon the level of social well-being, as well as race and class affiliations (Koskela and Pain 2000). This is particularly true with regard to inadequate sanitation infrastructure; previous studies reveal that one of the challenges women face is their need to look for a secluded place to defecate in poor areas (Reddy and Snehalatha 2011), which is often marred with increased risk of them being subjected to gender-based violence (Joshi, Fawcett, and Mannan 2011). Earlier research in South Asia particularly illustrates the complexity in how gender is articulated, contested, and negotiated through lived experiences of water and sanitation provision (O'Reilly 2016; Truelove 2011). Studies have also often identified the two most critical aspects related to sanitation as space (where one lives) and gender, or the complexities of gendered identities and related sanitation needs and re-sponsibilities in these diverse settings (Joshi, Fawcett, and Mannan 2011, 1).

Fear is also experienced differently by men and women. Women often fear public places because of a "fear of shame and dishonor associated with being out-of-place" (Paul 2011, 419) and thereby can demonstrate practices of resis-tance in everyday spatial encounters (Pain 2001, 904). Moreover, Narayanan (2012, 19) points out how gendered violence occurs in the city's public spaces, where often the lack of gender-sensitive planning is observed. This is observed more than ever in public sanitation infrastructure: public facilities that women access are often inappropriately located, and inappropriate design often deters their use (Rakodi 1991; Corburn and Karanja 2014). In addition, the failure to involve women in the design of infrastructure facilities may result in inap-propriate standards and technological artefacts and can restrain their commit-ment to maintenance (O'Reilly 2016; Desai, McFarlane, and Graham 2014). Lastly, along with higher health risks of women, inadequate access to these services and existing infrastructure designs can also expose women to acts of violence around sanitation infrastructures (Abrahams, Mathews, and Ramela 2006). Thus, while sanitation needs are indeed universal, more research is needed on the gender-related constructs and implications in the design and promotion of basic sanitation infrastructure within diverse groups (Abrahams, Mathews, and Ramela 2006).

Therefore, each action of women as users highlights the various contesta-tions and negotiations they have to face within technological determinism: ambivalent relationships with technologies, imaginaries of them created by innovators of infrastructures and unintended consequences of their perfor-mative role as user, lack of privacy leading to public interventions, and lack of inherent inclusion within design and planning process. With numerous earlier studies highlighting the intersection of violence with infrastructural inadequacy, especially for women users, in the next sections through empirical evidence I will demonstrate how women navigate their everyday encounters with public sanitation infrastructure.

INFORMALITY AND PRECARIOUS INFRASTRUCTURES IN CITIES OF EAST AFRICA

I approached the question of gender inequality in sanitation to (1) substanti-ate the need to tackle the growing gender-based violence around communal/

shared sanitation facilities in informal settlements, and (2) furnish the study with some qualitative depth that brings forth the voices and experiences of male and female residents in the cities of Dar es Salaam and Nairobi. The selection of the research contexts was based on the fact that both cities had a similar colonial and postcolonial trajectory and have been previous sites of infrastructure upgrading programs led by the World Bank. However, despite the apparent similarities in the context—namely, the language, population size, and urban development trajectory—the cities also have a contrasting view of tackling the growing informal settlements and provision of formal services to its residents. Informality is a deregulated state where temporalities of ownership, use, and purpose of land are exacerbated by lack of mapping and regulations (Roy 2009, 80). In addition, informality is embedded far more deeply in East African society than formal systems (UN-Habitat 2014, 175). This intersection was observed within both of these cities through the lens of collaborative and co-productive arrangements of informal and/or self-organized provision of services that coexist (with some contestation) with municipal service provision. Therefore, for this study, Mlalakuwa informal settlement in Dar es Salaam and 4A ward of Mathare informal settlement in Nairobi were chosen as case studies. Before turning to an analysis of everyday interactions and mediations, it is important to situate residents' diverse experiences within broader processes of historical development trajectories of their settlements.

Although Mlalakuwa is a subward within the Makango Ward in Dar es Salaam, its development trajectory has led it to become an informal settlement. The 1968 Dar es Salaam Master Plan had designed Mlalakuwa as a light industrial area.[5] However, there was a gradual rise in the construction of residential units, which led to the creation of subdivisions in the settlement. In 1982, a residential layout scheme was prepared by the Ministry of Lands and Human Settlements Development in collaboration with the city council, but it proved difficult to implement because it disregarded existing land rights as well as access roads. Presently, the informal settlement of Mlalakuwa is based in the Kinondoni municipality in Dar es Salaam, consisting of ten villages.

Public spaces in Mlalakuwa include complex concepts of semipublic and semiprivate space, framed sometimes as private space (Rasmussen 2013, 9). The informal settlement is based along the Mlalakuwa River, which is a major water source in the city (International Water Stewardship Programme 2015). However, due to inadequate sanitation infrastructure, openly discharged sewage of liquid and solid waste is often dumped directly into the river by local residents. The informal settlement has seen interventions done for cleaning up the river and has been also a part of an innovative sanitation management solution, done in collaboration with the Dar es Salaam Water and Sewerage Company, the municipal body responsible for sanitation, and the Bremen Overseas Research and Development Agency, an international NGO working in collaboration with the local residents (see figure 4.3).[6] Hence, within the informal settlement, the provision of sanitation infrastructure is collaboratively arranged by the local municipality, NGOs, and residents.

In the case of Nairobi, I chose Mathare informal settlement, which comprises thirteen different villages. Mathare is often considered a hotbed of violence and has not seen as much investment from developmental agencies and NGOs as Kibera. As an informal settlement, it faces a scarcity of networked infrastructure provision, with residents relying on water kiosks and shared ablution blocks for access to water and sanitation. Moreover, since 2008, the Informal Settlements Department (ISD) under the Nairobi Water and Sewerage Company has been responsible for the Water and Sanitation Improvement Programme in various informal settlements across the city. Mathare Valley, where the chosen 4A village is based, has seen interventions aided by the ISD and a local NGO called Mathare Children's Fund has been running a Reusable Sanitary Pads program. The ISD also has a sociology subdepartment, which is responsible for engaging with the community on a daily basis to help facilitate

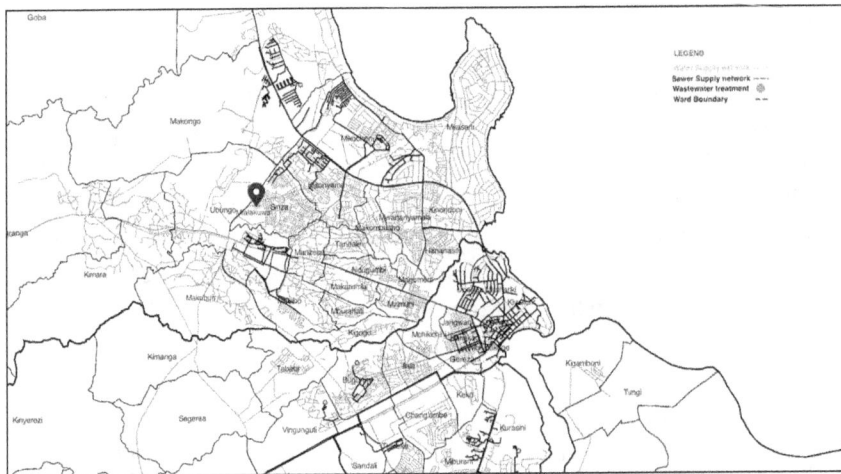

Fig. 4.3 Map showing innovation sanitation management tool developed in collaboration with DAWASA from City Sanitation Planning, citysanitationplanning.org. (Content created by Bremen Overseas Research and Development Association-Tanzania)

construction of sewers, water kiosks, and ablution blocks. The next section will now articulate the interactions, contestations, and negotiations in detail.

EVERYDAY EMBODIED URBAN SANITARY PRACTICES OF RESIDENTS IN MLALAKUWA, DAR ES SALAAM

Residents across Mlalakuwa resort to a wide variety of contestations and negotiations when accessing the precarious infrastructure provision. In addition, the responsibility for gaining and managing household water often falls to women. The values associated with accessing sanitation differ significantly between men and women. Because the residents engage in a diverse range of practices, the section below describes inquiries into varied avenues of everyday life.

In Mlalakuwa in Dar es Salaam, residents had access to shared facilities, which were mostly squatting latrines, often referred to as "multi-family private toilet" by the residents (see figure 4.4).[7] The everyday embodied experiences of women residents with the precarious provision revealed how they imbibed fear and insecurity due to inadequate lighting in the settlement and at the facility. With enhanced darkness at night, the interactions of the women residents were severely restricted and propelled the feeling of putting their lives at risk. The women felt that the darkness provided potential perpetrators a sense of anonymity and the ability to get away with a crime. Additionally, due to this fear of violence, women often asked their husbands or sons to accompany them at night or resorted to other ways of defecating such as "using a tin bucket," thus transforming the infrastructure provision into a space emanating fear.

Furthermore, the women felt that the existing conditions of the provided shared sanitation facilities also contributed to their insecurity. The women specifically pointed out the lack of proper doors, waste disposal methods, and cleanliness issues as the conditions that made them feel uncomfortable. Also, poor construction of the toilets, shortage of water, and inadequate lights in the toilets made the women hesitant to use the facilities at night. This highlighted how spatial interaction and the materiality of the provided infrastructure provision was experienced by women.

Women within these settlements and generally within the cities of Global South have an intricate relationship with water infrastructure (Van Houweling 2015). They are the ones mostly responsible for fetching water for households. My responses from the field revealed that the women residents were responsible for water collection for their households. In order to conserve water, most women restricted their own consumption by using buckets at night to defecate,

Fig. 4.4. Shared toilets in Mlalakuwa with waste collection bucket (*left*) and temporary doors (*right*). (Photos by Anshika Suri)

which they then emptied out in the Mlalakuwa river as a coping mechanism. Based on this, I inquired about their preferred sanitation facility. Almost all of them preferred a squatting flush toilet if they had to share with other tenants, to keep communicable diseases like urinary tract infections (UTIs) at bay. However, if it was within their own household, they all preferred a "sitting flush toilet." This particular observation highlighted how women users reinterpreted design scripts of sanitation infrastructure to have different uses and meanings, to potentially subvert oppressive health challenges.

However, what made these interactions more intriguing was the perspective of male residents,[8] who asserted shared toilets to be unsafe for women unless they were accompanied by a male. This observation reveals how everyday encounters of women with technological infrastructure can lead to imagined violence being used as a social construct to exert control over women's urban routines and access to public spaces. Additionally, male residents were more forthcoming on issues being faced by their wives and daughters like contracting UTIs, which also revealed that sociocultural norms may have been prohibitive toward women residents discussing their experiences. Thus, the disclosures from men about the fears of their wives and daughters helped shed a light on oppressive infrastructure inadequacy.

EVERYDAY EMBODIED URBAN SANITARY PRACTICES OF RESIDENTS IN MATHARE, NAIROBI

Along similar lines, in Mathare 4A Village in Nairobi, women residents' interactions (see note 1) with shared sanitation infrastructure were frequently marred by acts of gendered violence. The women residents mostly had access to shared ablution blocks, which were not readily accessible (more than a ten-minute walk). They were very vocal about the cases of violence and described in detail a case where an old woman was attacked and another case where the victim had been left on the street or dismembered inside a shared toilet, and how they had experienced intimidation tactics through the use of force or with guns and knives. They further described cases of rape and harassment around the toilets, openly discussed the difference between "rape" and "molestation," and debated which they felt was more severe. In contrast to the assumed silence and taboos around sexual violence, these women were not afraid to speak up about their everyday intersections and interaction with violence that was perpetuated through them trying to access sanitary infrastructure. While expressing their fears and insecurities about being faced with these risks every day, the women also demonstrated resilience in dealing with these fears through varied coping mechanisms like not eating or drinking after six in the evening to avoid having to defecate or urinate all together or using a "flying toilet" (see figure 4.5).[9]

However, as was in the case of Dar es Salaam, the lived experiences of the male residents[10] also shed insights into challenges such as overcrowding at ablution blocks due to inadequate provision, poor maintenance and repair, unaffordable user fees, and lack of running water. The male residents also displayed an indifference to the risks faced by women (health risks, bodily harm). They emphasized how gender-related differences played a role in how users interacted with an infrastructure—for example, women being responsible for cleanliness of toilets. Hence, infrastructural inadequacy might have been perceived as oppressive by the women, but for men, it just relayed an inconvenience and not a barrier to their freedom to access public space without fear and insecurity.

EVERYDAY EXPERIENCES WITH OPPRESSIVE INFRASTRUCTURAL INADEQUACY

The conjectures on everyday lived experiences of residents exhibit a perspective of a growing normalization of violence in public life in the city and little being done to break this paradigm. While urban settings in these cities offer women opportunities, their freedom is tempered with violence. Evidence from Nairobi and Dar es Salaam highlights that the fear of violence is far

Fig. 4.5. Makeshift toilets (*left*) and openly discarded sanitary napkins (*right*) in Mathare. (Photos by Anshika Suri)

greater than actual violence and ends up controlling the perception of the women's rights to the city. Thus, an intersectional perspective can help provide an analytical lens to the growing urban violence against women. With the incorporation of an intersectional perspective, the female body can be understood as a category of analysis, especially how the female body may interact with the materiality of infrastructure regimes. This can further allow women residents of informal settlements to be invested as full participants in projects to contribute their knowledge from their everyday encounters to determine what they want and need more explicitly.

Additionally, the chronic state of vulnerability of the women residents and the varied coping mechanisms employed by them highlight how the maintenance of body (and bodily waste) becomes a challenge for women residents, who lack a safe and hygienic place to defecate. This challenge is further exacerbated by state interventions that shape the infrastructure provision by choosing interventions like shared toilets over its citizens, which do not address issues emanating from inadequate infrastructure provision in the first place. Rather, as pointed by Brown (2014, 169) such provisions are often "embedded within hierarchies of knowledge and expertise," with designers, planners, and service providers "assuming poverty means grateful acceptance of infrastructure without debate" (169). This is echoed by Desai et al. (2014, 2) who highlight the contestations the urban poor (especially women) have to contend with when "using unbearably dirty public toilets," emphasizing the nexus of the materiality of the body versus infrastructure. Hence, based on the findings, it can be argued that the infrastructure becomes implicitly complicit in adding a spatial dimension to fear and insecurity, thereby adding another layer of oppression through their inadequacy.

However, while the narratives of women residents highlighted their daily interactions with multiple systems of oppression, they also brought forth evidence of everyday resilience and resistance. Both sets of women, despite admitting oppressive everyday interactions with shared sanitation facilities, showed their own interpretations of how small acts of being able to purchase water or being vocal about dealing with everyday violence empowered them. To exemplify, women residents in Dar es Salaam engaged in the informal economic activity of selling homemade sweets (fried sweets made of white flour and sugar called *mandazis*) and used the money they earned to purchase water for their households. Similarly, women residents in Nairobi undertook skills training to work as beauticians or tailors, which helped them in purchasing water from kiosks. This finding could also possibly provide an encouraging view toward possible shifts in analytical lens on how women users are written about and depicted within urban infrastructure debates. However, I must also state that this observation is in no way done to romanticize the notion of empowerment of women overshadowing their experiences of oppression. Rather, it is to shed a light on how within academic constructs, empirical evidence can potentially highlight subtle complexities in everyday experiences and lead to further inquisition. The next section will underline how the contestations with precarious sanitary facilities highlighted the presence of gender scripts within the infrastructure provision.

USER PREDETERMINATION BY SERVICE PROVIDERS

My observations from the field illuminate the presence of gender scripts in shared/multifamily sanitation facilities in the informal settlements, discerned through the intersection of violence with usage and access patterns of female users. The presence of gender scripts is part of the process of technological determinism for a city. While there is no concrete evidence pointing at the incorporation of a masculine gender script, there is predetermination of users and user attitudes that is inferred through the provision of fast solutions like shared toilets, wherein provision of said infrastructure is a governmental response to curb open defecation. However, these fast but ultimately temporary solutions could be described as reductive design strategies that may have contributed to the failure in curbing violence against women in places of inadequate service provision. In the case of Dar es Salaam and Nairobi, the provision of shared sanitation in informal settlements did not curb the narratives of violence usually associated with open defecation. Rather, women residents resorted to coping mechanisms that were developed through their interactions with the shared toilets, thereby potentially rewriting the user script of the infrastructure. The coping mechanisms and limited usage of shared toilets in both settlements provided insights into how the glaring lack of user involvement in design and site selection of shared toilets can lead to infrastructure becoming redundant or, worse, complicit in propelling fear or violence.

Hence, the role women residents play in shaping infrastructure through their everyday usage needs to be incorporated within user scripts of urban infrastructure service provision. The intention here is to not put forth a romanticized notion a feminine gender script to be incorporated. Rather, it is to shed a light on whether technological design can mediate inadequacy in service provision through a more inclusive process that does not restrict the envisioned users to predetermined access and usage patterns. Along these lines—i.e., imaginaries of women users—identification of gender scripts within the service provision and evidence of acts of violence bring forth the question on whether these precarious infrastructure provisions are becoming oppressive for women residents or whether this intersecting violence might be an unintended consequence of reductive planning strategies.

UNINTENDED CONSEQUENCES OF FAST SOLUTIONS

Women often found themselves marginalized within infrastructure provision (Haraway 1996, 37 as cited by Scott, Semmens, and Willoughby 2013, 7). This marginalization often results in imaginaries of women that don't match the realities of the everyday lived experiences of the women.[11] This mismatch can sometimes lead to unintended outcomes of choices in the design process (Oudshoorn, Saetnan, and Lie 2002, 481).

As discussed in earlier sections, the imaginaries of users led to the identification of gendered scripts within sanitation infrastructure that was provided to residents of the informal settlements. However, these scripts evoke inquiries into whether the predetermination of users and the subsequent limited interaction of women users with the provided facilities could lead to some unintended consequences, which often end up constraining instead of facilitating the technical infrastructure (i.e., the shared toilets).

Based on this, the intersection of violence with the shared toilets could be understood as an unintended consequence of technological determinism. Empirical evidence collected from cities in East Africa and Southeast Asia (Anand and Tiwari 2006; Arku, Angmor, and Seddoh 2013; Kareem and Lwasa 2014) highlight the presence of violence intersecting with inadequate urban infrastructure provision of water, sanitation, and transportation. All studies highlight the lack of access to infrastructure exacerbating inadequacy and forcing women to travel longer distances to seek the infrastructure provision. Within this research, the data gathered from both settlements highlighted how water collection for drinking and sanitary usage is a highly gendered landscape in both cities, with women often waiting in long lines at water kiosks.

This leads me to prompt for more detailed inquiry into urban infrastructure planning to determine in-depth whether inadequate infrastructures are themselves turning into systems of oppression or whether the reported violence is an unintended consequence of infrastructural inadequacy and reductive design strategies.

CONCLUSION

In this chapter, I have analyzed the everyday embodied experiences, practices, and perceptions of residents of informal settlements that emerge in relation to the materialities of sanitation infrastructures. By interrogating these embodied materialities, this chapter seeks to better articulate how an intersectional approach to critical infrastructures can reveal gender inequalities manifested in precarious infrastructure provisions.

The case studies illuminate how residents (both male and female) have diverse experiences in their everyday interaction with sanitation infrastructure. Both conflict and negotiation are elements in how residents engage with and through shared infrastructure services. The narratives of individual women in informal settlements and their lived experiences shed a light on how women inform, interact with, and transform infrastructure in informal settlements. Their negotiations explicate how sanitation for women users is determined by not only health and hygiene concerns but also a growing fear of facing violence while accessing shared toilets. However, the continued advocacy for shared toilets by governmental and developmental agencies to counter claims of fear, insecurity, and violence experienced in open defecation has not shown a decrease in the violence faced by women. Rather, these provisions raise questions of reductive design strategies, which can help in enabling appropriate policies and design strategies to be articulated and implemented.

Critical feminist technology assessment has led to calls for the voice of the users to be included in a more dominant manner. This study highlights the need to acknowledge the emerging power of women residents as knowledge producers in design and planning of infrastructure.

Additionally, both the cases help me advocate the use of intersectional analyses within the discipline of urban (infrastructure) design and development. With rapidly urbanizing cities especially in emerging economies in the Global South, I believe that the subject of the urban infrastructure regimes from a violence and feminist perspective must be researched from a new analytical lens. Working with feminist discourses within urban infrastructure policy planning and implementation, I consider the incorporation of an intersectional perspective within the multiscalar framework of the infrastructure service providers (formal and informal) to be an asset. This can (1) provide a deeper understanding to the growing complexities and (2) help innovate unique resolutions that are also interdisciplinary in nature.

NOTES

1. Name changed; information gathered through focus group discussion conducted with women residents of Mathare 4A village during fieldwork in March 2015.
2. Interview, community health assistant, Starehe subcounty health clinic, Mathare informal settlement, Nairobi, March 27, 2016.
3. Kenyan shilling. US$1 is approximately 114.15 KSH.
4. Focus group discussion, male residents, Mathare 4a village, Mathare informal settlement, Nairobi, March 22, 2016.
5. Interview conducted with the ward executive officer of Mlalakuwa on March 1, 2016.
6. Until their merger in 2018, the responsibility for the provision of networked sanitation services was divided between the Dar es Salaam Water and Sewerage Authority (DAWASA) and the Dar es Salaam Water and Sewerage Corporation. Today, DAWASA is the sole provider of piped water and sanitation services in Dar es Salaam.
7. Semi-structured interviews were conducted with female residents in Mlalakua during two field visits in March–April 2015 and February–April 2016.
8. Semi-structured interviews were conducted with male residents in Mlalakua during two field visits in March–April 2015 and February–April 2016.
9. A flying toilet is when a person defecates in a plastic bag, which is then tied up and discarded outside their living space, mostly on streets and open areas.
10. Focus group discussion, male residents, Mathare 4A village, Mathare informal settlement, Nairobi, March 22, 2016.
11. Male and female residents wanting to use these shared toilets is the prefigurative mode here, their performative mode is the coping mechanisms. As referenced earlier, the prefigurative role/user script is also heavily influenced by the idea that being poor means accepting means acceptance of provision without contestations (Brown 2014, 169).

REFERENCES

Abrahams, N., S. Mathews, and P. Ramela. 2006. "Intersections of 'Sanitation, Sexual Coercion, and Girls' Safety in Schools." *Tropical Medicine and International Health* 11 (5): 751–56. https://doi.org/10.1111/j.1365-3156.2006.01600.x.

Anand, Anvita, and Geetam Tiwari. 2006. "A Gendered Perspective of the Shelter–Transport–Livelihood Link: The Case of Poor Women in Delhi." *Transport Reviews* 26 (1): 63–80. https://doi.org/10.1080/01441640500175615.

Anand, N. 2011. "Pressure: The Politechnics of Water Supply in Mumbai." *Cultural Anthropology* 26 (4): 542–64. https://doi.org/10.1111/j.1548-1360.2011.01111.x.

Arku, F. S., E. N. Angmor, and J.-E. Seddoh. 2013. "Toilet Is Not a Dirty Word: Close to Meeting the MDGs for Sanitation?" *Development in Practice* 23 (2): 184–95. https://doi.org/10.1080/09614524.2013.772121.

Beebeejaun, Y. 2017. "Gender, Urban Space, and the Right to Everyday Life." *Journal of Urban Affairs* 39 (3): 323–34. https://doi.org/10.1080/07352166.2016.1255526.

Bender-Baird, K. 2015. "Peeing under Surveillance: Bathrooms, Gender Policing, and Hate Violence." *Gender, Place, and Culture* 23 (7): 983–88. https://doi.org/10.1080/0966369X.2015.1073699.

Bray, F. 2007. "Gender and Technology." *Annual Review of Anthropology* 36: 37–53. https://doi.org/10.1146/annurev.anthro.36.081406.094328.

Brown, S. T. 2014. "Kampala's Sanitary Regime: Whose Toilet Is It Anyway?" In *Infrastructural Lives*, edited by S. Graham and C. McFarlane, 153–73. Routledge.

Caretta, M. A., and Y. Riano. 2016. "Feminist Participatory Methodologies in Geography: Creating Spaces of Inclusion." *Qualitative Research* 16 (3): 258–66. https://doi.org/10.1177/1468794116629575.

Cho, S., K. W. Crenshaw, and L. McCall. 2013. "Toward a Field of Intersectionality Studies: Theory, Applications, and Praxis." *Signs: Journal of Women in Culture and Society* 38 (4): 785–810. https://doi.org/10.1017/CBO9781107415324.004.

Clarke, A. Y., and L. McCall. 2013. "Intersectionality and Social Explanation in Social Science Research." *Du Bois Review: Social Science Research on Race* 10 (2): 349–63. https://doi.org/10.1017/S1742058X13000325.

Corburn, J., and I. Karanja. 2014. "Informal Settlements and a Relational View of Health in Nairobi, Kenya: Sanitation, Gender, and Dignity." *Health Promotion International* 31 (2): 258–69. https://doi.org/10.1093/heapro/dau100.

Crenshaw, Kimberle. 1991. "Mapping the Margins: Intersectionality, Identity Politics, and Violence against Women of Colour." *Stanford Law Review* 43 (6): 1241–99. https://doi.org/10.2307/1229039.

Davis, K. 2008. "Intersectionality as Buzzword: A Sociology of Science Perspective on What Makes a *Feminist Theory* Successful." *Feminist Theory* 9 (1): 67–85. https://doi.org/10.1177/1464700108086364.

Desai, R., C. McFarlane, and S. Graham. 2014. "The Politics of Open Defecation: Informality, Body, and Infrastructure in Mumbai." *Antipode* 36: 98–120. https://doi.org/10.1111/anti.12117.

Domestos, WaterAid, and Water Supply and Sanitation Collaborative Council. 2013. *We Can't Wait: A Report on Sanitation and Hygiene for Women and Girls.* https://washmatters.wateraid.org/sites/g/files/jkxoof256/files/we%20cant%20wait.pdf.

Faulkner, W. 2001. "The Technology Question in Feminism: A View from Feminist Technology Studies." *Women's Studies International Forum* 24 (1): 79–95. https://doi.org/10.1016/S0277-5395(00)00166-7.

Fenster, T. 2005. "The Right to the Gendered City: Different Formations of Belonging in Everyday Life." *Journal of Gender Studies* 14 (3): 217–31. https://doi.org/10.1080/09589230500264109.

Fernandes, L. 2004. "The Politics of Forgetting: Class Politics, State Power, and the Restructuring of Urban Space in India." *Urban Studies* 41 (12): 2415–30. https://doi.org/10.1080/00420980412331297609.

Fonow, Mary Margaret, and Judith A. Cook. 2005. "Feminist Methodology: New

Applications in the Academy and Public Policy." *Signs: Journal of Women in Culture and Society* 30 (4): 2211–36. https://doi.org/10.1086/428417.

Graham, S., and C. McFarlane, eds. 2014. *Infrastructural Lives: Urban Infrastructures in Context*. Routledge.

Haraway, Donna J. 1996. *Modest_Witness@Second_Millennium.FemaleMan_Meets_OncoMouse™: Feminism and Technoscience*. London: Routledge.

Harvey, P. 2012. "The Topological Quality of Infrastructural Relation: An Ethnographic Approach." *Theory, Culture, and Society* 29 (5): 76–92. https://doi.org/10.1177/0263276412448827.

International Water Stewardship Programme. 2015. *Tanzania: Restoration of Mlalakua River*. http://www.iwasp.org/what-we-do/partnership/tanzania-mlalakua-river-restoration-project.

Joshi, D., B. Fawcett, and F. Mannan. 2011. "Health, Hygiene, and Appropriate Sanitation: Experiences and Perceptions of the Urban Poor." *Environment and Urbanization* 23 (1): 91–111. https://doi.org/10.1177/0956247811398602.

Kareem, B., and S. Lwasa. 2014. "Gender Responsiveness in Infrastructure Provision for African Cities: The Case of Kampala in Uganda." *Journal of Geography and Regional Planning* 7 (1): 1–9. https://doi.org/10.5897/JGRP2013.0424.

Kooy, M., and K. Bakker. 2008. "Splintered Networks: The Colonial and Contemporary Waters of Jakarta." *Geoforum* 39 (6): 1843–58. https://doi.org/10.1016/j.geoforum.2008.07.012.

Koskela, H., and R. Pain. 2000. "Revisiting Fear and Place: Women's Fear of Attack and the Built Environment." *Geoforum* 31 (2): 269–80.

Larkin, B. 2013. "The Politics and Poetics of Infrastructure." *Annual Review of Anthropology* 42 (1): 327–43. https://doi.org/10.1146/annurev-anthro-092412-155522.

Lohan, M. 2013. "Men, Masculinities, and 'Mundane' Technologies: The Domestic Telephone." In *Virtual Gender: Technology, Consumption, and Identity*, edited by E. Green and A. Adam, 149–61. Routledge.

Marcuse, Peter. 2009. "From Critical Urban Theory to the Right to the City." *City* 13 (2–3): 185–97. https://doi.org/10.1080/13604810902982177.

McCall, L. 2005. "The Complexity of Intersectionality." *Signs: Journal of Women, Culture, and Society* 30 (3): 1771–800.

Mohanty, C. T. 1984. "Under Western Eyes: Feminist Scholarship and Colonial Discourses." *Boundary 2* 12 (3): 333–58. Retrieved from https://www.jstor.org/stable/302821.

Narayanan, Yamini. 2012. "Violence against Women in Delhi: A Sustainability Problematic." *Journal of South Asian Development* 7 (1): 1–22. https://doi.org/10.1177/097317411200700101.

Nash, J. C. 2008. "Rethinking Intersectionality." *Feminist Review* 89: 1–15.

O'Reilly, K. 2016. "From Toilet Insecurity to Toilet Security: Creating Safe Sanitation for Women and Girls." *Wiley Interdisciplinary Reviews: Water* 3 (1): 19–24. https://doi.org/10.1002/wat2.1122.

Oudshoorn, N., and T. Pinch. 2003. "How users and non-users matter: Introduction." In *How Users Matter: The Co-construction of Users and Technologies*, N. Oudshoorn and T. Pinch, eds., 340. MIT Press. https://doi.org/10.1287/isre.1030.0016.

Oudshoorn, N., A. R. Saetnan, and M. Lie. 2002. "On Gender and Things: Reflections on an Exhibition on Gendered Artifacts." *Women's Studies International Forum* 25 (4): 471–83. https://doi.org/10.1016/S0277-5395(02)00284-4.

Pain, R. 2001. "Gender, Race, Age, and Fear in the City." *Urban Studies* 38 (5–6): 899–913. https://doi.org/10.1080/00420980120046590.

Paul, T. 2011. "Space, Gender, and Fear of Crime: Some Explorations from Kolkata." *Gender,*

Technology and Development 15 (3): 411–35. https://doi.org/10.1177/09718524
1101500305.

Purcell, M. 2002. "Excavating Lefebvre: The Right to the City and Its Urban Politics of the
Inhabitant." *GeoJournal* 58: 99–108.

Rakodi, C. 1991. "Cities and People: Towards a Gender-Aware Urban Planning Process?"
Public Administration and Development 11: 541–59.

Rasmussen, M. I. 2013. "The Power of Informal Settlements: The Case of Dar Es Salaam,
Tanzania." *Planum, the Journal of Urbanism* 1 (26): 1–11.

Reddy, B. S., and M. Snehalatha. 2011. "Sanitation and Personal Hygiene: What Does It Mean
to Poor and Vulnerable Women?" *Indian Journal of Gender Studies* 18 (3): 381–404.
https://doi.org/10.1177/097152151101800305.

Reeves, D. 2002. "Mainstreaming Gender Equality: An Examination of the Gender Sensitivity
of Strategic Planning in Great Britain." *Town Planning Review* 73 (2): 197–214.

Roy, A. 2009. "Why India Cannot Plan Its Cities: Informality, Insurgence and the Idiom of
Urbanization." *Planning Theory* 8 (1): 76–87. https://doi.org/10.1177/14730952
08099299.

Scott, A., L. Semmens, and L. Willoughby. 2013. "Women and the Internet: The Natural
History of a Research Project." In *Virtual Gender: Technology, Consumption and Identity*,
edited by E. Green and A. Adam, 3–22. Routledge.

Spivak, Gayatri Chakravorty. 1988. "Can the Subaltern Speak?" *Die Philosophin* 14 (27):
42–58.

Star, S. L. 1999. "The Ethnography of Infrastructure." *American Behavioral Scientist* 43 (3):
377–91.

Truelove, Y. 2011. "(Re-)Conceptualizing Water Inequality in Delhi, India through a Feminist
Political Ecology Framework." *Geoforum* 42 (2): 143–52. https://doi.org/10.1016
/j.geoforum.2011.01.004.

UN-Habitat. 2014. *The State of African Cities 2014 Re-imagining Sustainable Urban Transitions.*
United Nations Human Settlements Programme.

Valentine, G. 2007. "Theorizing and Researching Intersectionality: A Challenge for Feminist
Geography." *The Professional Geographer* 59 (1): 10–21.

Van Houweling, E. 2015. "Gendered Water Spaces: A Study of the Transition from Wells to
Handpumps in Mozambique." *Gender, Place, and Culture* 22 (10): 1391–407. https://doi
.org/10.1080/0966369X.2014.970140.

Von Schnitzler, A. 2008. "Citizenship Prepaid: Water, Calculability, and Techno-Politics in
South Africa." *Journal of Southern African Studies* 34 (4): 899–917. https://doi.org
/10.1080/03057070802456821.

Von Schnitzler, A. 2013. "Traveling Technologies: Infrastructure, Ethical Regimes, and the
Materiality of Politics in South Africa." *Cultural Anthropology* 28 (4): 670–93. https://
doi.org/10.1111/cuan.12032.

Wamala-Larson, C., and L. Stark. 2019. "Rethinking Gender and Technology within
Intersections in the Global South." In *Gendered Power and Mobile Technology: Intersections
in the Global South*, edited by Caroline Wamala-Larson and Laura Stark, 1–122.
Routledge. https://doi.org/10.4324/9781315175904-1.

Winker, G., and N. Degele. 2011. "Intersectionality as Multi-Level Analysis: Dealing with
Social Inequality." *European Journal of Women's Studies* 18 (1): 51–66. https://doi.org
/10.1177/1350506810386084.

World Health Organization and UNICEF. 2017. *Progress on Drinking Water, Sanitation and
Hygiene: 2017 Update and SDG Baselines.* http://www.who.int/iris/handle/10665
/258617.

CHAPTER 5

SEVERING THE SPATIAL LEASH: PROMOTING WOMEN'S RIGHT OF MOBILITY THROUGH DIGITAL DISRUPTION AND A FEMINIST ETHICS OF CARE

Linda Carroli and Deanna Grant-Smith

INTRODUCTION

The right to the city demands that citizens be able to participate in, "live in, play in, work in, represent, characterize and occupy urban space" (Fenster 2005, 219). Yet, when transport choices and access are concerned, women experience significant obstacles in enacting their right to the city. The right to mobility demands freedom of movement and the removal of barriers to such movement. Ensuring women's right to mobility is essential to meeting the New Urban Agenda (United Nations 2017) and United Nations Sustainable Development Goals (UN-Habitat, UNEP, and SLoCaT 2015), which prioritize safety for women in all life domains, including transport (UN Women n.d.), and enshrining these as principles for sustainable cities. To achieve these rights an infrastructural response is required that recognizes the socio-technical dynamics of infrastructure systems and how infrastructure and spatial systems reproduce uneven and gendered power relations that may limit women's mobility. Furthermore, while the right to mobility has significant gendered implications, these are generally overlooked in infrastructure and urban planning and policy.

Although significant differences in men's and women's transport demands and experiences are sufficiently evident to justify attention (Hamilton and Jenkins 2000), for decades women's needs have largely been overlooked in the planning and delivery of public transport services (Buiten 2007; Grant-Smith, Osborne, and Johnson 2017; Greed 2008; Hanlon 1996). In part this is because responsibility for transport and mobility falls to planning systems that neglect gender mainstreaming, despite the emergence and development of feminist planning scholarship (Beebeejaun 2017). Indeed, in urban and infrastructural administrative systems an ethics of care attentive to gender remains absent despite overtures to a communicative or participatory turn in planning theory and research. This gender blindness has shaped the material and technological dimensions of mobility infrastructure systems just as it has shaped other dimensions of the urban environment. Digital disruption, understood as the changing of fundamental expectations and behaviors through digital channels, has the potential to enable this ethics of care in respect of women's mobility.

In examining feminist interventions in mobility systems that draw on critical infrastructure studies, feminist geography, and technofeminism, we apply an ethics of care perspective to mediate the infrastructural, technological, and spatial dimensions of women's experiences of mobility. These case studies are drawn from existing literature and media accounts of women's mobility experiences. The analysis of these cases applies theory to address rights from a feminist ethics of care perspective. We propose that, due to the multiscalar complexity of infrastructure systems, the examination necessitates merging feminist understandings of space and of technology. The framing of women's agentic actions and interventions as an ethics of care emerges as feminist infrastructuring that highlights gendered experiences of mobility. Other gendered histories and experiences of organization and infrastructure provisioning, such as self-organization and movements for women's shelters and other women's services and resources, are inflected in the ways in which digital disruption responds to women's mobility. This view reflects Simone's (2004, 241) proposition that infrastructures extend to include their intersections with people's activities that flexibly determine how the city is lived and used. Women's action has disrupted and sought to radically alter the contours of inequality that shape women's lived spatial and socio-technological experience, particularly in relation to the public sphere, public space and freedom of movement. For women, disruption is an imperative and strategic in the development of infrastructures and platforms emerging from the social, everyday and lived dimensions of infrastructures and cities (Amin 2014; Graham and McFarlane 2014; Simone 2004).

In recent years, technology-enabled interventions in and reconfigurations of transport systems and spatial relationships have emerged to provide women with choices and information in relation to practices of mobility and their rights. In this chapter, we examine three sets of interventions, each with a digital infrastructure dimension that, when combined with a feminist ethics of care, have the potential to safeguard and promote the needs of individuals in consideration of their risk exposure and vulnerability. The first set of interventions are social media campaigns focused on sexual harassment and race-based harassment related to public transport use. The second set of interventions are digital innovations, including the emergence of women's safety reporting and mapping apps and women-only ridesharing services. The third considers attempts to reshape spatial relationships through the development of digital work centers and similar infrastructure that reduce the need for transport.

The emergence of these technology-enabled interventions is a move toward the development of a feminist infrastructure. Such a feminist infrastructure acknowledges and cares for women's experiences of transport, enacts a feminist right to the city, and disrupts the gender blindness that proliferates urban and infrastructure system development. These interventions illustrate the potential for digital disruption to address gaps in existing transport infrastructure solutions and merge feminist socio-technical practices and care as "infrastructuring." We interrogate each set of interventions through the following questions: Why were these initiatives established? How are they organized? How are they infrastructural? And how do they care? We conclude by discussing the need for more systematic and far-reaching policy engagement with the gender dimensions of mobility systems, particularly at a time when policymakers are focusing on the "disruption" of such socio-technical systems.

WHY INFRASTRUCTURE MATTERS FOR WOMEN'S MOBILITY

Mobility and access to transport are necessary conditions of the urban environment that afford citizens access to a diverse range of social, economic, and recreational needs. Mobility is significantly shaped by access to infrastructures and technologies, yet not all citizens have equitable access to mobility and transport. Mobility is ordinarily understood in terms of movement involving travel and distance, and shaped by a range of technological and spatial assumptions, such as car ownership and automobility in the urban context (Johnson, Andrews, and Warner 2017). However, gender, race, ability, and class can also structure mobility and access to transport through the uneven distribution of power, wealth and security (Clarsen 2014; Johnson, Andrews, and Warner 2017; Yon and Nadimpalli 2017).

Men's and women's mobility patterns differ, with women's travel behavior recognized as more diverse and complex (Grant-Smith, Osborne, and Johnson 2017), Gendered patterns of (im)mobility can restrict the distances women commute and their modal choices. Women are also disadvantaged by the socio-technical transport system, which inhibits their access to essential services, employment, and leisure opportunities. Travel patterns are highly gendered as women continue to bear the primary responsibility for caring for and transport-ing family members (McDonald 2006) and for household purchasing (Dobbs 2005). Thus, women's mobility is constrained by a "spatial leash" (Pocock, Skinner, and Williams 2012) attributable to a need to be available for others and to consider their own and others' safety. This greater transport burden and more complex transport requirements to meet the demands of women's multi-ple roles (Greed 2008) and mobilities of care (Sánchez de Madariaga 2013) also limit women's ability to adopt alternative forms of commuter transport such as cycling, which continues to be dominated by men (Osborne and Grant-Smith 2017; Scheiner 2014). Women tend to have less access to private transport than men (Hjorthol 2008; Næss 2008), and as a result, women rely strongly on public transport (Morris, Roddis, and Spiridonos 2010), even though public transport is not always safe for women (Gardner, Cui, and Coiacetto 2017). For example, the Australian Human Rights Commission (2017) found that public transport journeys to and from university campuses were the most common setting where female university students experienced incidents of sexual harassment and the second most common location where they experienced sexual assault.

Importantly, the incidence of gendered violence and fear of violence in public space and on public transport challenge and diminish women's mobil-ity: infrastructures are not gender aware or responsive. Gendered barriers to mobility are most evident in active transport and public transport, forms of transport that are also more sustainable and affordable than automobility (Whitzman 2013). For example, in Port Moresby, Papua New Guinea, it was found that more than 90 percent of women and girls experienced some form of violence when accessing public transport (UN Women 2014). A response was to introduce bus services restricted to women and children only (UN Women 2016). Similar women-only public transport services, including women-and-children-only carriages on trains, have been trialed in India, Japan, Egypt, Brazil, Mexico, the Philippines, and Pakistan (UN Women 2016).

Despite its immediate need and appeal, gender segregation of this kind cannot be a long-term solution as it does little to address the deeper causes of gender inequity and problematically places responsibility for women's safety on individual women rather than society. The threat or fear of sexual violence is an intrusive and unwelcome incursion on women's lived public and private experience, causing women to exist in a "geography of fear" and self-defense, mentally plotting safe and unsafe movements, times, and spaces (Valentine 1989). Fear and threat influence women's mobility and use of space, creating a hyperawareness of potential and actual threats (Whitson 2017). The sources of the fear—which is often associated with particular types of spaces and infrastructures and perceptions of safety associated with isolation, lighting, opportunity, and exposure—needs to be delineated (Whitson 2017). Fear and social vulnerability are not produced by built environments but rather by gendered power relations, which are embedded in built environments and infrastructure systems (Whitson 2017).

Transport planning and policy rarely reflect gendered differences in mobility, with transport planning tending to focus on peak hour movements, direct journeys between home and work, and movements into and out of the central business district—that is, the trips middle-class men of working age are likely to take (Grant-Smith, Osborne, and Johnson 2017). These transport infrastructure and service systems are designed around patterns of mobility that are inherently gendered and classed yet deemed to be universal and neutral. As a result, public transport systems may be not only inaccessible and impractical for women but also unsafe for women. Indeed, women are more likely to perceive public transport and the spaces around it (e.g., bus stops, walking between stops, and destinations) as dangerous (particularly at night), which may affect their usage (Rosenbloom 2005; Wekerle 2005). Ethnicity, age, and dis/ability also shape women's sense of safety and how accessible public transport may be (Sweet and Escalante 2010). However, even women who attempt to mirror male commuter travel patterns and take advantage of the services provided are not afforded equal access, and women often have negative transport experiences (Fritze 2007).

Women's Mobility and the Right to the City

Mobility is a key dimension of the right to the city encompassing issues of affordability and availability, safety and security, and physical access to infrastructure and services (Levy 2013). Infrastructure systems enact social relationships, display social selectiveness, and shape social identities (Tonkiss 2013; Amin 2014). Indeed, "the physical organization of the city, as well as access to and control over its spaces, are critical aspects of the construction of gendered and sexualized identities and inequitable power relations" (Whitson 2017, 78). For Levy (2013, 53–54), the act of traveling is a form of appropriation of public space in the city in its own right. The freedom to move in public space without physical or verbal threat has both literal and symbolic meaning to women.

Transport and mobility, as both spatially and technologically shaped, are integral dimensions of the physical organization of the city and the structuring of urban space. For example, the use of active transport, like cycling, has technological elements including lighting, crossings, and paths. Spaces for mobility are ordinarily infrastructural spaces that are intended for public access and use. Ubiquitous built forms and artifacts like roads and bridges not only play a role in socio-spatial inequality and gendering, but they also exert their power and influence as long-lived obdurate infrastructures that act in space and place (Wajcman 1991). Mobility is shaped by spatial, technological, and social relations that coalesce in infrastructure systems to produce and reproduce gendered power relations. Infrastructure aims for invisibility, to be taken-for-granted, or to recede from view, but this assumes neutrality that is not possible for women whose experiences expose its failures (Star 1999; Wilson 2016).

Where feminist geographers have interrogated the gendered spatial dimensions of transport and cities, technofeminism and feminist digital geography examine the technological dimensions of gender, space, infrastructure, and power. Space and technology are dynamic forces in cities that reinforce normative social hierarchies. This merging of feminist spatial and technological thinking has underpinned other studies of women's mobility and right to the city (Jha 2018) as a way of "grappling with the messiness of digital mediation of everyday lives" (Elwood and Leszczynski 2018, 631). Spatial and technological determinism and neutrality are rebuked by feminist methodologies and epistemological interventions that examine the social and historical context and construction of gender, space, and technology (Wajcman 1991; Elwood and Leszczymski 2018). As Elwood and Leszczynski (2018, 640) emphasize, immanent and latent liberatory potentials of technology can be exerted relationally and through appropriation. The liberatory digital politics to which they refer points to possibilities for "re-making our technologies and ourselves as digital subjects." In Simone's (2004) concept of "people as infrastructure," the relational dimensions of liberation can also involve a tentative and precarious process of remaking urban ensembles and relations. We propose this is foundational for feminist infrastructuring as an articulation of emancipatory politics and transformative modes of organization.

Feminist Infrastructuring

Infrastructure systems are large technical systems that support cities. They are formed of diverse social and technical elements, and they are constitutive of socio-spatial relations. Infrastructures are understood as imposing gendered, spatial, and technological implications. They include physical structures and services that support the functioning of a city or region and are necessary for human and social development. Critical infrastructure studies examine the social, everyday, and lived dimensions of infrastructures (Amin 2014), in which infrastructure is understood as "a complex social and technological process" rather than as "a thing," indicating their contingency and power dynamics (Graham and McFarlane 2014, 1). Following Haraway's (1985, 1997) overtly optimistic assertion that technologies are intrinsically part of us, transformative relations between women and technology manifest as both necessary and possible.

As infrastructures are intended as systems of support that make cities work, we question whether and how, as spatial-socio-technical configurations, they can be made to care. This recognition of the gendered dimensions of infrastructure systems, like mobility, through the use of digital technology or through digital geography, is understood as feminist infrastructuring. Infrastructuring refers to "the socio-technical mechanisms for constituting and supporting a public" (le Dantec and DiSalvo 2013, 242), and it suggests ongoing processes that resist power through an ethics of care and participation in a feminist "counter-public" (Salter 2013, 226). Feminist infrastructuring is underpinned by an ethics of responsibility and care for women and rights. The interaction between gender, technology, and space productively reinscribes relatively fixed and static infrastructures.

Questions of care, ethics, and responsibility have resounded in geographic thinking through the work of Massey (2005), Lawson (2007), Cloke (2002), and others, who examine the spatial formation of social, technological, and economic structures in which power is reproduced. Lawson (2007, 6) asks, "Can care ethics move beyond the interpersonal, the near and familiar, to care for distant others?" Ideas of care may also relate to Wilson's (2016) conception of infrastructural intimacy, which also suggests proximity and relation. The relationship between intimacy and infrastructure produces other contours of power and exchange where infrastructure brings people closer together across spatial divides (Wilson 2016) while also enabling people to organize and "situate themselves" (Simone 2004, 245). Where infrastructure potentially produces material inequality and vulnerability, such intimacy or proximity calls for an ethics of care in the exchange of individual rights and mutual responsibility (Caswell and Cifor 2016). Infrastructures do not act alone. An ethics of care situates relations between and responsibilities for each other in the ways in which infrastructures are planned, built, and experienced. Lawson entreats spatial thinking and engagement with Massey's challenges of geographies of responsibility to consider "how we in our ordinary lives are implicated in inequality" in order to excavate our own political responsibility (Massey 2005 cited in Lawson 2007, 6). Drawing on Tronto's (1993) recasting of care as political relations, Lawson and Massey both argue that ethics of care have inherently spatial and relational implications. The spatial is formed or mediated through technologies as a socio-spatial technological configuration, which includes institutions and infrastructures through which care can be inflected and embedded. Restructured relationships and spatial dynamics result from the introduction of a women-only ridesharing service to provide safe and convenient travel for urban women. Such alternate formations of socio-technological relations and services can constitute a repair to systems that do not work for women; they shape geographies of responsibility (Massey 2005). Fisher and Tronto (1990, 103) describe this restitution as constitutive of care, defined as "everything we do to maintain, continue, and repair our world so that we may live in it as well as possible." Care, in this sense, unfolds as multiple practices, processes, contexts, and relations.

RESPONDING TO WOMEN'S MOBILITY THROUGH DIGITAL DISRUPTION

The three sets of interventions that are examined in this chapter demonstrate varying degrees of responsiveness to barriers to women's mobility. Such barriers are the result of a range of socio-technical decisions and flows of power that shape the development of infrastructure systems in cities. All these interventions not only acknowledge sexual harassment and lack of gender awareness in transport, but also recognize that women's increased visibility in public life has not meant ready access to public space and mobility (Jha 2018). Of the socio-spatial and cultural factors that can inhibit women's mobility, safety is primary. Indeed, safety concerns are likely to be a major consideration in modal choices and transport routes for women. Despite this, Greed (1994, 43) argues that "[w]omen's lack of mobility is often seen as their own fault and not an urban structural issue."

Digital Campaigns against Sexual and Race-Based Harassment

The first set of interventions we examine here focus on grassroots and government campaigns against sexual harassment and race-based harassment in relation to public transport use. Women are more likely than men to be victims of violence and sexual harassment while taking public transport (Levy 2013). Government campaigns in Singapore, Melbourne, London, and New York have focused on drawing attention to sexual harassment and assault on public transport and encouraging women to report incidents to authorities. In Melbourne, a partnership of government and nongovernment agencies initiated an anti-harassment campaign on public transport titled "Hands Off" in 2017. The campaign was initiated in response to a significant increase in reports of sexual offences. During the two-week "Hands Off" campaign in Melbourne, Australia, images of suspected perpetrators of sexual harassment or assault on public transport in twenty unsolved cases were circulated. A police unit focusing on sexual offenses on public transport was also established. The intention was to signal that sexual offending is a crime and to encourage the public to share information that could lead to the arrest of perpetrators. The campaign resulted in the extensive circulation of the images, community provision of information, and identification of suspected perpetrators. However, it took a 40 percent increase in reports of sexual assault to trigger the "Hands Off" campaign in Melbourne, despite several years of increased reports, indicating a lag in policy attention and agency resistance in combating sexism in urban systems (Mills 2017).

Hashtag campaigns like #IllRideWithYou and "Hands Off" have attracted criticism for their limited efficacy and impact (Bahrawi 2014; Fileborn 2017). However, through informational and communicative strategies, they stake out a problem space that acknowledges women's experience, and these strategies can be bundled for ongoing systemic reform designed to transform everyday experiences of mobility (Fileborn and Vera-Gray 2017).

Internationally, the #BoardtheBus, #WhyLoiter, #EverydaySexism, and #StopStreetHarassment activist campaigns are designed for women to (re)claim public space, public transport, safety, and mobility through collaborative action and sharing stories (Bowles Eagle 2015; Jha 2018). In Delhi, India, both #WhyLoiter and #BoardtheBus campaigns were instigated in 2014. Both were responses to the gang rape and murder of women on public transport (Bowles Eagle 2015; Jha 2018). Through these campaigns, women were encouraged to occupy space and speak out about rape culture, and in #BoardtheBus women were asked to ride the bus together in groups. Similarly, #EverydaySexism and #StopStreetHarassment elicit worldwide women's reports of practices that ultimately restrict their access to space and their movement. In response to safety threats, ongoing activism, awareness-raising, and advocacy, systemic and structural reforms are in play in various Indian states and cities. Some responses include gender awareness training for bus drivers initiated by Breakthrough (Bowles Eagle 2015), an all-woman police unit in Jaipur (*Hindustan Times* correspondent 2017), and an all-woman staffed Metro station in Kolkata (Javed 2018). This networked organization confers a platform for women's experiences that evokes Simone's idea of people as infrastructure and through which the ensemble of the city is remade.

Although gender as a lens for analysis in planning has received some attention, intersectionality as a theory and practice remains marginal in planning (Bosman, Grant-Smith, and Osborne 2017) and feminist digital geography (Elwood and Leszczynski 2018). This is problematic as the risk of violence and sexual harassment on public transport is heightened for those belonging to visible minorities. Increased bigotry toward Muslims following the 2014 Martin Place hostage crisis and shooting in Sydney, Australia (Jacobs 2014), perpetrated by a self-identified Muslim man, led to a grassroots social media campaign. Using the Twitter hashtag #IllRideWithYou, the campaign recognized that Muslim people—particularly Muslim women who wear religious attire, which makes them more visible—could face increased danger and hostility on public transport. Individuals offered themselves as escorts on public transport routes to Muslim people who were concerned about using public transport alone. This campaign was a moving display of support for the Muslim Australian community; however, it also highlighted the increased danger they face while traveling on public transport and the fact that public spaces are more or less safe (or perceived to be so) depending on one's positionality and identity (Grant-Smith, Osborne, and Marinelli 2016).

Digital Disruption in Service Provision and (Personal) Mobility Planning

The second set of interventions are digital innovations, including the emergence of map-based safety reporting apps for women and women-only ridesharing services through which women's experiences of urban and infrastructural space are brought to the fore (Elwood and Leszczynski 2018). A survey of fifteen-to-nineteen-year-old women by Plan International Australia (2018b) found that one-quarter of respondents thought that young women should be accompanied on public transport and one-third were afraid to be in public spaces at night. Shared knowledge about safety threats plays a role in supporting women's mobility in cities. A research collaboration between Plan International Australia and the XYX Lab at Monash University resulted in an interactive map on which women could identify their experiences and perceptions of safety in select Australian capital cities. The project, Free to Be, notably identified public transport stops and stations as unsafe or undesirable locations (Plan International Australia 2018a). Project participants are invited to drop digital pins onto an online map and to include a description of their experience there. For example, comments about Flinders Street Rail

Station in central Melbourne, Australia, include descriptions of harassment by groups of drunk or aggressive men, poor-quality lighting, assault, intimidation, lack of security presence, and feeling unsafe. Along the main transit routes through the suburbs, participants comment about isolated train stations, being followed by men, and lack of safe road crossings when leaving a tram station.

These accounts reveal current ideas and practices of urbanism, mobility, and urban planning as lacking gender awareness. Kipfer (2009, 80) describes this as "gendered 'phallocentric' links between macro-levels of the social order and the contradictory realities of everyday life." Where policy and planning have failed to engage women and address gender inequality, initiatives such as Free to Be present experiences of the city that belie the "inclusive and safe city" rhetoric of neoliberal urban management and policy (Wekerle 2013; Beebeejaun 2017).

Mobility is experiencing significant technological change, and ridesharing is among the first wave of changes that enable users to develop more customized experiences and itineraries. Ridesharing disrupts traditional mobility services by providing a demand-responsive personal service that is accessed through a mobile phone app and where privately owned vehicles take passengers for a fare. However, it is not only public transport where women feel uncomfortable or are subjected to unsafe situations and unwanted sexual advances. It also occurs in taxis and Uber rides, where there have been instances of women passengers being raped, sexually assaulted, or physically intimidated (Marsh 2017; O'Brien et al. 2018). Indeed, the incidence of sexual harassment, misconduct, and assault on public transport is so pervasive that the National Sexual Violence Resource Center and the Urban Institute developed a system of categorization for such incidents by users of Uber and other app-driven ridesharing services (Sniffer, Durnan, and Zweig 2018).

Established as an alternative to Uber in 2016, Australian digital ridesharing service Shebah is an all-female network of drivers and passengers. Both services identify women and children's safety as a central priority. Shebah operates in most Australian capital cities through a mobile phone app. The introduction of the service was praised by political, community, and media figures, with several media reports in which women revealed their experiences of harassment and assault while using other mobility services (Fidge 2016; Gilmore 2017; Martin 2017). The company website stresses feminist principles in its service provision, including convenience and safety for women passengers, as well as economic opportunities for drivers, who retain more of their fares than Uber drivers. Shebah also uses an inclusive definition of "women" that includes transgender and queer women and nonbinary people who are significantly femme-identified.

Digitally enabled interventions like Shebah and the *Free to Be* project are founded on the belief that women and girls have a right to travel safely and free from unwelcome attention. They attend to and rectify a gendered gap in current urban and transport infrastructure system and service provision. This type of feminist infrastructuring, developed as a service and network by women and for women and as a response to abuses of power by and in other transport services, frees women and girls from the burden of precautionary and defensive behaviors while in transit as either passengers or drivers. All-women ridesharing eliminates the greatest source of threat to women's personal safety. It is grounded in an ethics of care in which an alternative to a broken and hostile system is introduced so that women can live, work, and move better. Women both use and work in the service to collaboratively create safer places, safer mobility systems, and gender-aware transport. In the absence of other societal and institutional responses to women's mobility needs and combined with safety mapping, all-female ridesharing can be bundled into mobility-as-a-service apps to further develop gender-aware and integrated mobility and infrastructure.

Reshaping Spatial Relationships through Digital Practices

The third set of interventions we look at are based on attempts to reshape the spatial relationships involved in work and mobility, including digital or "smart" work centers and coworking spaces that reduce the need for commuting. Digital work centers are a hybrid infrastructure arising from innovations in information communications technologies (ICT), public-private venturing, building typology and architecture, gender mainstreaming, and sustainable urban development. They enable telecommuting, an established feature of flexible and decentralized employment that is generalized as an ICT enabled residentially based work arrangement. Digital work centers shift teleworking from the home to a workplace or office space that can be hired by companies for their staff or by self-employed individuals. In Australia, the introduction of digital work centers is supported by all levels of government, particularly for outer suburban and regional areas with linkages to metropolitan centers (QUT Urban Informatics Lab/Smart Services CRC 2015; Buksh and Mouat 2015). These facilities mean some women, particularly professionals, can reconfigure the spatial flows of career, commuting, and care through the use of an ICT.

Women's workforce participation is partly influenced by place of residence. There is a correlation between access to work, type of work, and place of residence that results in the perpetuation of gendered stereotypes and disadvantage (Williams et al. 2009). Historically, urban planning has emphasized development patterns and transport networks that can entrench long commutes and expensive infrastructure investments. Women who live in outer suburban areas must make trade-offs between employment, transport, and care. This results in "a clear division of labour, with many highly educated and skilled women forced to abandon careers in the city and take lower-skilled jobs close to home in order to be available to their children" (Williams et al. 2009, 5). Consequently, spatiotemporal arrangements, described as a "spatial leash," result in the gendering of workforce participation by place of residence.

The geographic distribution of employment in most Australian metropolitan areas is concentrated in city centers. Women with families living in outer suburban areas where housing is affordable have reduced access to employment and transport. This results in women assuming home-based and low-skilled jobs "in lieu of good local jobs which employed their skills and experience and provided career scope as well as family-oriented flexibility" (Williams et al. 2009, 5). Digital work centers provide a facility that enables women to better negotiate the complexities of career, commuting, and care by relocating the place of work, reducing the need to travel and remaining closer to home. Two-parent/carer households are also better able to negotiate work locations to better support women's employment opportunities.

For such facilities to be considered as feminist infrastructuring, which enacts an ethics of care, women need to be prioritized with appropriate scaffolding for employment pathways and access to services such as childcare, ICT, and transport, rather than one of many co-beneficiaries or a by-product as occurs in some of the commentary about digital work centers (Buksh and Mouat 2015). Even though some of these facilities have been established to support women with care responsibilities and women use them at a higher rate than men (QUT Urban Informatics Lab/Smart Services CRC 2015), user analysis of gender-oriented services and outcomes seems to be lacking. Without considering gender and power in the evaluation, location, and design of such facilities, there is a risk of reproducing or "retraditionalising" established gender and power relations rather than achieving gender mainstreaming through flexible labor arrangements (Banks and Milestone 2011; Wajcman 2004). The COVID-19 pandemic triggered shifts in work practices in which teleworking became much more accepted for those able to work from home or remotely. While working from home exacerbated domestic inequalities, the learning from COVID-19 is that a range of teleworking opportunities with access to appropriate services can support women's employment (Soubelet-Fagoaga et al. 2021).

REALIZING FEMINIST INFRASTRUCTURING

Through the identification of digitally enabled interventions in mobility, this chapter has examined feminist infrastructuring as an interplay of care, gender, technology, and space. It recognizes that gendered experiences of cities and mobility are both technological and spatial. While a technological or technofeminist perspective is important for feminist geography, the lens of ethics of care enlivens the gendered dimensions of infrastructure systems. It is also essential for feminist approaches to be intersectional to recognize the terms on which diverse women assert citizenship (Yon and Nadimpalli 2017). These perspectives are fundamental to the production of gender-aware space and systems. We concur with other feminist scholars who have identified failures in urban and infrastructure management and planning systems to analyze and address the gendered dimensions of the right to the city and right to mobility. In particular, there is a failure in understanding the linkages between gender, urban design, transport, and safety.

The interventions discussed in this chapter occur both outside and within the institutions that compose the socio-technical system. They are hybridized through digital capabilities, including neo-geography, mobile devices, high-speed broadband, and social networks, and can involve organizations that are marginal in the mobility system such as NGOs, digital innovation sectors, and research institutions. Such marginal organizations have pooled diverse capabilities to assert gender awareness in the mobility system and inform women's transport choices. Alternative feminist infrastructures and organization are defending women's mobility and right to the city through the provision of services and information. However, digital technologies are not solely liberatory and cannot be relied upon for reconfiguring gender relations or systemic sexism. While new technologies have demonstrably been used to support women's mobility, they have also been deployed by stalkers, trolls, and other abusers to infringe upon women's space, privacy, and mobility.

In the campaigns described here, it is vital to acknowledge that care and change are dimensions of a feminist ethics of care. In voicing and recognizing inequality, a feminist ethics of care strategically stresses the urgency of change in uncaring or neutral systems and practices. While the campaigns are a necessary acknowledgment of a global problem, they raise questions about whose behaviors should change. Many of them direct women to act by reporting incidents of harassment and assault or advising women to alter their travel behavior. However, women's behavior is not necessarily the problem, as one of the most visible and tangible ways of exercising power is to occupy or to control space (Tonkiss 2005). Targeting men to change their behavior to respectfully share space with women, some activist campaigns have focused on the practice of "manspreading," or taking up additional space by sitting on public transport with their legs wide apart. These have included a controversial YouTube campaign that saw a social activist splashing a mixture of water and bleach on the groins of men who were sitting with their legs akimbo on the St Petersburg metro (BBC Trending 2018). On-vehicle campaigns attempting to change the practice of manspreading have also been approached by transit authorities around the world.

CONCLUSION

Women have the right to access public spaces and infrastructures and to not have their lives restricted by fear or actual violence (Peake and Rieker 2013, 4). The social media and other activist platforms reported in this chapter have supported women in raising these issues and increasing awareness of them. However, these rights must also have a formal place in planning systems and understanding of lived space and infrastructure.

Despite claims for communicative and participatory turns in planning and governance theory, authoritarian urban management prevails (Yon and Nadimpalli 2017). It has not enacted gender participation and mainstreaming in infrastructure systems. Women are rarely specifically canvassed through stakeholder consultation and passenger surveys by transport authorities or providers; *Free To Be*, through the XYX Lab, included design thinking workshops with women and girls to explore solutions (Kalms et al. n.d.). Consultation processes can offer opportunities for contribution within protected enclaves before bringing these back into mainstream consultation to inform and educate other stakeholders present another arena for disruption and participation by women (Cameron and Grant-Smith 2005).

Mobility systems are continuing to undergo significant technological and infrastructural change, but women continue to be denied their rights to mobility. Some of these changes, such as hybrid, electric, and autonomous vehicles, are likely to affirm safety in automobility rather than reconfiguring a socially and environmentally fairer transport system. It is important to understand the impact of interventions such as those examined in this chapter. They have played a necessary role in raising awareness of issues and strengthening feminist networks. However, it is difficult to ascertain whether structural change has resulted without more detailed impact assessment. Feminist infrastructuring highlights the systemic dimensions of affective responsibilities, altering the network flows and organization of transport systems through an ethics of care to make cities livable and workable for women. Digital technologies that reconfigure the mobility system to prioritize women's rights and safety extend gender awareness in infrastructure to enable women's participation in society. The gender dimensions of transport are well documented in reports by NGOs like Breakthrough, research institutes, and humanitarian agencies such as the World Bank, Civitas, UN-Habitat, the Institute for Transport and Development Policy, and others. These reports also stress the need for structural and cultural change, including policy and regulatory reform. Just as structural change is slow, behaviors toward women in public space are also slow to change. In the meantime, perhaps mobility services that remove men from the transport equation (e.g., women-only carriages, women-only rideshare) or women's active involvement in incident reporting and campaigning are needed and are the best that can be hoped for until feminist infrastructuring is sufficiently disruptive and impactful to trigger policy, legislative, and structural reform to eliminate their necessity.

REFERENCES

Amin, A. 2014. "Lively Infrastructure." *Theory, Culture and Society* 31 (7–8): 137–61, https://doi.org/10.1177/0263276414548490.

Australian Human Rights Commission. 2017. *Change the Course: National Report on Sexual Assault and Sexual Harassment at Australian Universities.* Australian Human Rights Commission. https://www.humanrights.gov.au/sites/default/files/document/publication/AHRC_2017_ChangeTheCourse_UniversityReport.pdf.

Bahrawi, N. 2014. "Why #illridewithyou Is an Ill Ride." *Al Jazeera*, December 19. https://www.aljazeera.com/indepth/opinion/2014/12/why-illridewithyou-an-ill-ride-2014121712402325335.html.

Banks, M., and K. Milestone. 2011. "Individualization, Gender, and Cultural Work." *Gender, Work, and Organization* 18 (1): 73–89, https://doi.org/10.1111/j.1468-0432.2010.00535.x.

BBC Trending. 2018. "Anna Dovgalyuk: Why Do People Think Her 'Manspreading' Video Is a Kremlin Hoax?" BBC, October 20. https://www.bbc.com/news/blogs-trending-45828060.

Beebeejaun, Y. 2017. "Gender, Urban Space, and the Right to Everyday Life." *Journal of Urban Affairs* 39 (3): 323–34, https://doi.org/10.1080/07352166.2016.1255526.

Bosman, C., D. Grant-Smith, and N. Osborne. 2017. "Women in Planning in the 21st Century." *Australian Planner* 54 (1): 1–5, https://doi.org/10.1080/07293682.2017.1297321.

Bowles Eagle, R. 2015. "Loitering, Lingering, Hashtagging: Women Reclaiming Public Space via #BoardtheBus,# StopStreetHarassment, and the #Everydaysexism Project." *Feminist Media Studies* 15 (2): 350–53, https://doi.org/10.1080/14680777.2015.1008748.

Buiten, D. 2007. "Gender, Transport, and the Feminist Agenda: Feminist Insights towards

Engendering Transport Research." *Transport and Communications Bulletin for Asia and the Pacific* 76: 21–33. https://epdf.tips/transport-and-communications-bulletin-for -asia-and-the-pacific-no76-gender-and-t.html.

Buksh, B., and C. M. Mouat. 2015. "Activating Smart Work Hubs for Urban Revitalisation: Evidence and Implications of Digital Urbanism for Planning and Policy from South-East Queensland." *Australian Planner* 52 (1): 16–26, https://doi.org/10.1080/0729368 2.2015.1019751.

Cameron, J., and D. Grant-Smith. 2005. "Building Citizens: Participatory Planning Practice and a Transformative Politics of Difference." *Urban Policy and Research* 23 (1): 21–36, https://doi.org/10.1080/0811114042000335296.

Caswell, M., and M. Cifor. 2016. "From Human Rights to Feminist Ethics: Radical Empathy in the Archives." *Archivaria* 81 (Spring): 23–43.

Clarsen, G. 2014. "Feminism and Gender." In *The Routledge Book of Mobilities*, edited by P. Ardey, D. Bissell, K. Hannam, P. Merriman, and M. Sheller, 94–102. Routledge.

Cloke, P. 2002. "Deliver Us from Evil? Prospects for Living Ethically and Acting Politically in Human Geography." *Progress in Human Geography* 26 (5): 587–604, https://doi.org /10.1191/0309132502ph391oa.

Dobbs, L. 2005. "Wedded to the Car: Women, Employment, and the Importance of Private Transport." *Transport Policy* 12 (3): 266–78, https://doi.org/10.1016/j.tranpol.2005 .02.004.

Elwood, S., and A. Leszczynski. 2018. "Feminist Digital Geographies." *Gender, Place, and Culture* 25 (5): 629–44, https://doi.org/10.1080/0966369X.2018.1465396.

Fenster, T. 2005. "The Right to the Gendered City: Different Formations of Belonging in Everyday Life." *Journal of Gender Studies* 14 (3): 217–31, https://doi.org/10.1080 /09589230500264109.

Fidge, D. 2016. "Why Women-Only Ride-Sharing Services Are Revolutionary." ABC News, August 26. https://www.abc.net.au/news/2016-08-26/women-share-why-women -only-ride-sharing-services-are-important/7787312.

Fileborn, B. 2017. "Why the 'Hands Off' Campaign Targeting Sexual Harassment on Public Transport Misses the Mark." *The Conversation*, October 25. https://theconversation. com/why-the-hands-off-campaign-targeting-sexual-harassment-on-public-transport -misses-the-mark-86213.

Fileborn, B., and F. Vera-Gray. 2017. "'I Want to Be Able to Walk the Street without Fear': Transforming Justice for Street Harassment." *Feminist Legal Studies* 25 (2): 203–27, https://doi.org/10.1007/s10691-017-9350-3.

Fisher, B., and J. Tronto. 1990. "Toward a feminist theory of caring." In *Circles of Care*, edited by E. Abe and M. Nelson, 36–54. SUNY Press.

Fritze, J. 2007. *"You Might as Well Just Stay at Home": Young Mums and Transport in Victoria.* Victorian Council of Social Services, Melbourne.

Gardner, N., J. Cui, and E. Coiacetto. 2017. "Harassment on Public Transport and Its Impacts on Women's Travel Behaviour." *Australian Planner* 54 (1): 8–15, https://doi.org /10.1080/07293682.2017.1299189.

Gilmore, J. 2017. "Shebah's a Ride Share for Women and by Women." *The Age*, March 8. https://www.theage.com.au/lifestyle/shebahs-a-ride-share-for-women-and-by -women-20170308-gutdlr.html.

Graham, S., and C. McFarlane. 2014. *Infrastructural Lives: Urban Infrastructure in Context.* Routledge.

Grant-Smith, D., N. Osborne, and L. Johnson. 2017. "Managing the Challenges of Combining Mobilities of Care and Commuting: An Australian Perspective." *Community, Work, and Family* 20 (2): 201–10, https://doi.org/10.1080/13668803.2016 .1202194.

Grant-Smith, D., N. Osborne, and P. Marinelli. 2016. "Transport and Workplace

Accessibility: Routes to Improved Equity." In *Overcoming Challenges to Gender Equality in the Workplace*, edited by P. F. Flynn, K. Haynes, and M. A. Kilgour, 107–23. Greenleaf Publishing.

Greed, C. 1994. *Women and Planning: Creating Gendered Realities*. Routledge.

Greed, C. 2008. "Are We There Yet: Women and Transport Revisited." In *Gendered Mobilities*, edited by T. Uteng and T. Cresswell, 243–53. Ashgate.

Hamilton, K., and J. Jenkins. 2000. "A Gender Audit for Public Transport: A New Policy Tool in the Tackling of Social Exclusion." *Urban Studies* 37: 1793–800, https://doi.org/10.1080/00420980020080411.

Hanlon, S. 1996. "Where Do Women Feature in Public Transport?" In *Women's Travel Issues: Proceedings from the Second National Conference*, US Department of Transportation, Federal Highway Administration, 648–62. http://www.fhwa.dot.gov/ohim/womens/chap35.pdf.

Haraway, D. 1985. "A Manifesto for Cyborgs: Science, Technology, and Socialist Feminism in the 1980s." *Socialist Review* 80: 65–108, https://doi.org/10.1080/08164649.1987.9961538.

Haraway, D. 1997. *Modest_Witness@Second_Millennium.FemaleMan©_Meets_OncoMouse™: Feminism and Technoscience*. Routledge.

Hindustan Times correspondent. 2017. "All-Women Police Units Take a Stand on the Streets of Jaipur." *Hindustan Times*, July 25. https://www.hindustantimes.com/india-news/all-women-police-units-take-a-stand-on-the-streets-of-jaipur/story-USzwDnRC6bFuvyX0j8BpVI.html.

Hjorthol, R. 2008. "Daily Mobility of Men and Women: A Barometer of Gender Equality?" In *Gendered Mobilities*, edited by T. Uteng and T. Cresswell, 193–212. Ashgate.

Jacobs, R. 2014. "How #illridewithyou Began with Rachael Jacobs' Experience on a Brisbane Train." *Brisbane Times*, December 16. http://www.brisbanetimes.com.au/queensland/how-illridewithyou-began-with-rachael-jacobs-experience-on-a-brisbane-train-2014 1216-128205.html.

Javed, Z. 2018. "All-Women Team at Kolkata Metro Station Focuses on Improving Passenger Amenities." *Times of India*, March 9. http://timesofindia.indiatimes.com/articleshow/63237048.cms.

Jha, S. 2018. "Gathering Online, Loitering Offline: Hashtag Activism and the Claim for Public Space by Women in India through the #whyloiter Campaign." In *New Feminisms in South Asia: Disrupting the Discourse through Social Media, Film and Literature*, edited by S. Jha and A. Kurian, 63–84. Routledge.

Johnson, L., F. Andrews, and E. Warner. 2017. "The Centrality of the Australian Suburb: Mobility Challenges and Responses by Outer Suburban Residents in Melbourne." *Urban Policy and Research* 35 (4): 1–15, https://doi.org/10.1080/08111146.2016.1221813.

Kalms, N., G. Bawden, G. Matthewson, P. Salen, A. Edwards, and H. Korsmeye. N.d. "Free to Be: Design Thinking Workshop." XYX Lab, Monash Space Gender Communication Lab, Monash University, Melbourne. https://www.monash.edu/mada/research/labs/xyx-lab-monash-space-gender-communication-lab/free-to-be-design-thinking.

Kipfer, S. 2009. "Why the Urban Question Still Matters." In *Leviathan Undone: Towards a Political Economic of Scale*, edited by R. Keil and R. Mahon, 67–85. University of British Columbia Press.

Lawson, V. 2007. "Geographies of Care and Responsibility." *Annals of the Association of American Geographers* 9 (1): 1–11, https://doi.org/10.1111/j.1467-8306.2007.00520.x.

le Dantec, C. A., and C. DiSalvo. 2013. "Infrastructure and the Formation of Publics in Participatory Design." *Social Studies of Science* 43 (2): 241–64, https://doi.org/10.1177/0306312712471581.

Levy, C. 2013. "Travel Choice Reframed: 'Deep Distribution' and Gender in Urban Transport."

Environment and Urbanization 25 (1): 47–63, https://doi.org/10.1177/0956247
813477810.

Marsh, S. 2017. "Reports of Sexual Assaults by Taxi Drivers Rise 20% in Three Years." *The Guardian*, December 28. https://www.theguardian.com/uk-news/2017/dec/28/reports-of-sexual-assaults-by-taxi-drivers-rise-20-in-three-years.

Martin, J. 2017. "The Rise of Ridesharing for Women Only." ABC News, February 18. https://www.abc.net.au/news/2017-02-18/shebah-rise-of-ridesharing-for-women-only/8271910.

Massey, D. 2005. *For Space.* Sage.

McDonald, N. 2006. "Exploratory Analysis of Children's Travel Patterns." *Transportation Research Record* 1977: 1–7, https://doi.org/10.3141/1977-03.

Mills, K. 2017. "'Hands Off' Campaign Aims to Track Down Pervs Who Molest Women on Trains, Trams." *The Age*, October 24. https://www.theage.com.au/national/victoria/hands-off-campaign-aims-to-track-down-pervs-who-molest-women-on-trains-trams-20171023-gz67ze.html.

Morris, J., S. Roddis, and F. Spiridonos. 2010. "Women's Changing Role: Implications for the Transport Task and for Modelling Personal Travel Patterns." *Australasian Transport Research Forum 2010 Proceedings* (September 29–October 1, 2010, Canberra). Australasian Transport Research Forum, https://australasiantransportresearchforum.org.au/wp-content/uploads/2022/03/2010_Morris_Roddis_Spiridonos.pdf.

Næss, P. 2008. "Gender Differences in the Influences of Urban Structure on Daily Travel." In *Gendered Mobilities*, edited by T. Uteng and T. Cresswell, 173–92. Ashgate.

O'Brien, S. A., N. Black, C. Devine, and D. Griffin. 2018. "CNN Investigation: 103 Uber Drivers Accused of Sexual Assault or Abuse." CNN Business, April 30. https://money.cnn.com/2018/04/30/technology/uber-driver-sexual-assault/index.html.

Osborne, N., and D. Grant-Smith. 2017. "Constructing the Cycling Citizen: A Critical Analysis of Policy Imagery in Brisbane, Australia." *Journal of Transport Geography* 64: 44–53, https://doi.org/10.1016/j.jtrangeo.2017.08.015.

Peake, L., and M. Rieker. 2013. *Rethinking Feminist Interventions into the Urban.* Routledge.

Plan International Australia. 2018a. *Free to Be.* https://bit.ly/2N0Hg1C.

Plan International Australia. 2018b. *Unsafe in the City.* https://www.plan.org.au/learn/who-we-are/blog/2018/10/11/unsafe-in-the-city.

Pocock, B., N. Skinner, and P. Williams. 2012. *Time Bomb: Work, Rest and Play in Australia Today.* New South.

QUT Urban Informatics/Smart Services CRC. 2015. *Queensland Government Flexible Work Centres Trial: Final Report.* Brisbane.

Rosenbloom, S. 2005. "Women's Travel Issues." In *Gender and Planning: A Reader*, edited by S. F. Fainstein and L. J. Servon, 235–55. Rutgers University Press.

Salter, M. 2013. "Justice and Revenge in Online Counter-Publics: Emerging Responses to Sexual Violence in the Age of Social Media." *Crime, Media, Culture* 9 (3): 225–42, https://doi.org/10.1177/1741659013493918.

Sánchez de Madariaga, I. 2013. "Mobility of Care: Introducing New Concepts in Urban Transport." In *Fair Shared Cities: The Impact of Gender Planning in Europe*, edited by I. Sánchez de Madariaga and M. Roberts, 33–48. Ashgate.

Scheiner, J. 2014. "Gendered Key Events in the Life Course: Effects on Changes in Travel Mode Choice over Time." *Journal of Transport Geography* 37: 47–60, https://doi.org/10.1016/j.jtrangeo.2014.04.007.

Simone, A. 2004. "People as Infrastructure: Intersecting Fragments in Johannesburg." *Public Culture* 16 (3): 407–29. https://muse.jhu.edu/article/173743.

Sniffer, C., J. Durnan, and J. Zwieg. 2018. *Helping Industries to Classify Reports of Sexual Harassment, Sexual Misconduct, and Sexual Assault.* National Sexual Violence Resource

Center. https://www.nsvrc.org/sites/default/files/publications/2018-11/NSVRC_
HelpingIndustries.pdf.

Soubelet-Fagoaga, I., M. Arnoso-Martínez, I. Guerendiain-Gabás, E. Martínez-Moreno, and
G. Ortiz. 2021. "(Tele)work and Care during Lockdown: Labour and Socio-Familial
Restructuring in Times of COVID-19." *International Journal of Environmental Research
and Public Health* 18 (22): 12087. https://doi.org/10.3390/ijerph182212087.

Star, S. L. 1999. "The Ethnography of Infrastructure." *American Behavioral Scientist* 43 (3):
377–91, https://doi.org/10.1177/00027649921955326.

Sweet, E. L., and S. O. Escalante. 2010. "Planning Responds to Gender Violence: Evidence
from Spain, Mexico and the United States." *Urban Studies* 47: 2129–47, https://doi
.org/10.1177/0042098009357353.

Tonkiss, F. 2005. *Space, the City, and Social Theory: Social Relations and Urban Forms*. Polity
Press.

Tonkiss, F. 2013. *Cities by Design*. Polity Press.

Tronto, J. 1993. *Moral Boundaries: A Political Argument for an Ethic of Care*. Routledge.

UN-Habitat, UNEP, and SLoCaT. 2015. Analysis of the Transport Relevance of Each of the 17
SDGs Draft Report. September UN-Habitat, UNEP, SLoCaT. https://sdgs.un.org/sites
/default/files/documents/8656Analysis%2520of%2520transport%2520relevance%252
0of%2520SDGs.pdf.

United Nations. 2017. *New Urban Agenda*. http://habitat3.org/wp-content/uploads/NUA
-English.pdf.

UN Women. N.d. *Women and Sustainable Development Goals*. https://sustainabledevelopment.
un.org/content/documents/2322UN%20Women%20Analysis%20on%20Women%20
and%20SDGs.pdf.

UN Women. 2014. *Ensuring Safe Public Transport for Women and Girls in Port Moresby*. https://
unwomen.org.au/wp-content/uploads/2017/05/UNW_safe_public_transport.pdf

UN Women. 2016. *Making Public Transport Safe for Women and Girls in Papua New Guinea*.
http://www.unwomen.org/en/news/stories/2016/11/making-public-transport-safe-for
-women-and-girls-in-papua-new-guinea.

Valentine, G. 1989. "The Geography of Women's Fear." *Area* 21: 385–90. https://www.jstor
.org/stable/20000063.

Wajcman, J. 1991. *Feminism Confronts Technology*. Pennsylvania State University Press.

Wajcman, J. 2004. *Technofeminism*. Polity Press.

Wekerle, G. R. 2005. "Gender Planning in Public Transit." In *Gender and Planning: A Reader*,
edited by S. F. Fainstein and L. J. Servon, 275–95. Rutgers University Press.

Wekerle, G. R. 2013. "Interrogating Gendered Silences in Urban Policy: Regionalism and
Alternative Visions of a Caring Region." In *Rethinking Feminist Interventions into the
Urban*, edited by L. Peake and M. Rieker, 142–58. Routledge.

Whitson, R. 2017. "Gendering the Right to the City." In *Feminist Spaces: Gender and Geography
in a Global Context*, edited by A. M. Oberhauser, J. L. Fluri, R. Whitson, and S. Mollett,
77–105. Routledge.

Whitzman, C. 2013. "Women's Safety and Everyday Mobility." In *Building Inclusive Cities:
Women's Safety and the Right to the City*, edited by C. Whitzman, C. Legacy, C. Andrew, F.
Klodawsky, M. Shaw, and K. Viswanath, 35–52. Earthscan.

Williams, P., K. Bridge, J. Edwards, N. Vujinovic, and B. Pocock. 2009. *Sustainable Lives in
Sustainable Communities: Living and Working in Ten Australian Communities*. Centre for
Work + Life, University of South Australia.

Wilson, A. 2016. "The Infrastructure of Intimacy." *Signs: Journal of Women in Culture and
Society* 41 (2): 247–80, https://doi.org/10.1086/682919.

Yon, A., and S. Nadimpalli. 2017. "Cities for Whom? Re-examining Identity to Reclaim the
Right to the City for Women." *Australian Planner* 54 (1): 33–40, https://doi.org/10.1080
/07293682.2017.1297317.

CHAPTER 6

TRAINS, TREES, AND TERRACES: INFRASTRUCTURES OF SETTLER COLONIALISM AND RESISTANCE IN THE REFAIM VALLEY, PALESTINE-ISRAEL

Gabi Kirk

INTRODUCTION

This chapter examines the Refaim Valley[1] in southern Jerusalem, Palestine-Israel. The internationally recognized border of the 1949 Armistice Line (the "Green Line") which runs along the valley floor puts the northern hillsides of the valley in Israel. The southern hillsides are in the West Bank, militarily occupied by Israel since June 1967 in contravention of international law. Israeli sites in the valley on both sides of the Green Line include settlements, the Jerusalem-Tel Aviv Railway, a national park, archaeological sites, and a zoo. The Palestinian villages of Battir and al-Walaja also straddle the Green Line. Israel has expanded its control and confiscation of Palestinian land in the valley not only through direct annexation to support the growth of the Gilo and Har Gilo West Bank settlements, but also under the guise of transit infrastructure, nature conservation, and tourism.

Israel has constructed itself as a modern state with technologically advanced infrastructures by burying Palestinian infrastructure, past and present, and relying on an imaginative geography of Palestine as unmodern, uncivilized, and uncultivated (Said 1978). Israel also builds on imperial infrastructures from the Ottoman and British Empires. I argue that Israeli settler colonialism and the attempted erasure of Palestinian landscapes and lifeways can be understood as an infrastructural process. Israel defines itself, and its place in a dominant hierarchy of modernity, through infrastructural violence. This infrastructural violence, I contend, is a form of gendered violence even when it does not directly target gendered bodies, because Israel aims to inhibit Palestinian social, economic, and biological reproduction through infrastructural control. However, rather than pure dominance, settler colonialism can be better understood as "a shifting and impossible assemblage" (Simpson 2016, 439–40), which can be understood, as Yaffa Truelove and Anu Sabhlok explain in this volume's introduction, as social and material collections "which make circulations in space possible and that coalesce uneven geographies." Within and against settler colonialism's assemblage, Palestinians manifest gendered infrastructures of resistance. Palestinian agricultural terraces on the hillsides in the Refaim Valley, internationally recognized by UNESCO as a World Heritage Site, rise above Israeli settler-colonial infrastructure. Israel has repeatedly tried to either destroy or appropriate these terraces to de facto annex the Gilo settlements to Israel proper. I take a feminist approach to understanding Palestinian social relationships of resistance within these two Palestinian villages, between the villages and international actors, and between the villages' farmers and their agroecosystems. Social infrastructures undergird *sumud*, or steadfastness, the Palestinian ethos of tenacity to stay with their land and homes despite ongoing settler-colonial dispossession.

I will first outline my contribution to conversations in infrastructural studies, particularly in Palestine-Israel and on feminist geographies of infrastructure. Then, I will reflect on my methodology—a series of field walks I took in the valley between 2013 and 2018—and the fraught nature of conducting embodied field research in the racially segregated landscape of Palestine-Israel. Finally, I will analyze my case study, meandering through historical and current settler-colonial infrastructures in the Refaim Valley. Using insights from infrastructural studies and feminist studies, I will both critique Israeli settler-colonial transit and tourist infrastructure and analyze Palestinian relationships and resistance in the valley as themselves infrastructural.

STRUCTURES OF POWER AND PLACE

Understanding Settler Colonial Infrastructure

If settler colonialism is "a structure, not an event" (Wolfe 2006), then to understand settler colonialism's organization of domination, we must examine its infrastructures. *Infrastructure* as a term first emerged from technical and planning documents about rail development in the late nineteenth century. It grew as both a concept and material reality after World War II, as "infra-structural development" became used as a tool and an ideology of Western neo-imperial geopolitical machinations in the "Third World" (Carse 2017).

Because "infrastructures are matter that enable the movement of other matter" (Larkin 2013, 329), it is no wonder that empires around the world—who rely on controlling and restricting movement of populations and re-sources—have long been concerned with infrastructure. European imperial powers in the long nineteenth century prioritized infrastructural development for military conquest, to move soldiers and resources across their holdings. Imperial infrastructures are not just a historical concept, though. Today, pri-vate and state interests in settler-colonial societies work together to main-tain constricted control over Indigenous populations, lands, and lifeways in the service of securing capitalist infrastructure to keep commodities moving (Pasternak and Dafnos 2018). Omar Jabary Salamanca argues that "settler infrastructures are normalized through their association with tropes of mo-dernity, progress, humanitarianism, and development," materially and discur-sively naturalizing state domination (Salamanca 2016, 65). Yet settler-colonial domination is never a complete project; indigenous resilience and resistance emerge and persist. Friction arises as infrastructure as a technopolitics of mo-dernity displaces or clashes with "other ways of knowing and governing the landscape" (Carse 2014, 7).

As Truelove and Sabhlok review in the introduction to this volume, analy-ses of infrastructural inequality have demonstrated how marginalized subjects are excluded through and from infrastructure, how the uneven distribution of infrastructure reinforces social hierarchy, and how infrastructural projects are often built for a dominant class at the expense of a subaltern group, fre-quently with their labor. However, too often these studies do not question the overarching framework embedded within infrastructure of development as desirable and necessary, even when they seek to do so. Relatedly, material infrastructure is often defined in a limited way to mean technological projects for distributing resources or people, almost always within an urban setting. A focus on the urban in infrastructural studies can reinforce notions of the rural as isolated, "underdeveloped" spaces, a notion challenged by understanding and centering the lived experiences of rural communities. Thus, many trends in infrastructural studies may unintentionally reify a framework of modernity that it explicitly wishes to unravel.

Finally, the lack of attention to settler colonialism in infrastructural stud-ies writ large is a missed opportunity. Colonialism justified violence under the

132 / Gabi Kirk

guise of development, claiming to bring infrastructure to "uncivilized" people and places, and such questions of the potential and problematics of infrastructure continue in postcolonial states (McFarlane and Silver 2017). Yet settler colonialism is not "post" colonialism, but ongoing. Settler states often do a double move of both claiming to improve the lives of the colonized through infrastructure as "humanitarian aid" while also using it to expropriate land (Salamanca 2016).

Infrastructures in Palestine-Israel

Infrastructural studies scholarship on Palestine-Israel has offered sustained attention to settler-colonial infrastructure, demonstrating how Israeli development projects have racialized Palestinians as inferior, dispossessed them of their land and resources, and prioritized Jewish settler mobility and the building of state capital. Infrastructural inequality in the pre-state period included Jewish-only settlements receiving the bulk of monetary aid and technology from the British Mandatory government (1922–1947). Palestinians were treated as objects in need of development, not as subjects capable of creating their own infrastructure (El-Eini 2006; Seikaly 2016). After Israel's establishment, Palestinians who found themselves within Israel's borders formed a second-class citizenship population, and Palestinian villages to this day face challenges and discriminatory treatment when seeking legal approval for master plans to develop and improve waste, water, agricultural, and road infrastructures (Humphries 2009; Yiftachel 2006). Similar issues occur in Palestinian neighborhoods and villages in East Jerusalem occupied by Israel after 1967, which will be detailed below in the case study of Battir and al-Walaja.

Israel has also targeted physical infrastructure for destruction in the numerous wars it has waged against Palestinians since 1948, particularly in the Gaza Strip. Since Israel's official withdrawal of settlements in 2005, Israel has bombed Gaza multiple times since Operation Cast Lead in 2008, leaving Gaza without adequate water sanitation and waste infrastructures (Abu Yahia, Westheimer, and Gilboa 2022). Furthermore, as Israel controls most of the land crossings into Gaza, new construction supplies to repair infrastructure are rarely allowed in, and Gazans face extreme difficulties in exporting their products, harming their economic growth.

Israel's racial segregation of infrastructure is perhaps most evident when it comes to mobility. For instance, transit infrastructure facilitates Israeli mobility and relationships across the land while severing Palestinian ones (Bishara 2015; Griffin 2020; Salamanca 2015). Highways, buses, and trains physically and seamlessly connect settlements in the Occupied West Bank with Israel, offering a "standardized solution" for Israelis to travel through a segregated landscape (Carse 2017, 28). Meanwhile, checkpoints, road closures, and maintenance neglect of Palestinian roads both in the West Bank and in Palestinian villages within Israel's borders inhibits reproduction in multiple forms: economic (e.g., Palestinian farmers carrying fresh produce to market can be stopped at a checkpoint for hours, losing product to spoilage), social (e.g., poor road conditions and segregated transit separates family members from each other within the West Bank or causes students to miss study time due to long delays), and even biological, as demonstrated by the harrowing stories of Palestinian women forced to give birth at checkpoints when stopped on their way to the hospital (Long 2006).

Eyal Weizman's *Hollow Land* (2007), a foundational text on Israel's infrastructural violence, argues that Israel has been able to control Palestinian territory and population even without direct military presence by keeping "Israelis and Palestinians separated vertically, occupying different spatial layers" (11). Israel's militarized architecture is on the "upper-land" while below is "the other, Palestine . . . inhabit[ing] the valleys between and underneath" (182). While Weizman does acknowledge contradictions to this framework, he still asserts that generally Israel builds itself on a vertical hierarchy above Palestine. Yet this cannot fully explain Palestinian infrastructural systems, nor does it necessarily challenge the ideas of modernity that undergird Israel's self-construction and justification for existence.

How can the persistence of Palestinian relationships challenge linear and hierarchical notions of infrastructure? I am interested in how resistance is enacted not just *to* settler-colonial infrastructure but also *through* infrastructure. Recent work on Palestinian transit and waste management infrastructure captures the multiplicities and contradictions of infrastructural development under apartheid (Griffin 2021; Stamatopoulou-Robbins 2019); I focus here on rural, agricultural examples. For instance, Muna Dajani and Michael Mason's work shows how Jawlani farmers (Syrians in the Occupied Golan Heights) build water "counter-infrastructures" to circumvent Israeli settlements overdrawing groundwater resources. Concurrently, Jawlani community cooperatives organize against the Israeli state water company Mekorot's high prices and discriminatory water distribution (Dajani and Mason 2018). Jawlani collective agricultural practices go beyond securing material resources for their livelihoods: counter-infrastructures contribute to new forms of collective subjectivity and identity (Mason and Dajani 2019).

I want to highlight the importance of social relationships to the Jawlani's counter-infrastructures. Much work has been done to understand subaltern material and social networks as themselves infrastructural (McFarlane and Silver 2017; Simone 2004). However, social infrastructures do not only exist "when material infrastructures fail to deliver" (Anand, Gupta, and Appel 2018, 11). The Jawlani explicitly *do not want* Israel's water delivered; they have built their own infrastructure instead of accepting Israel's occupation as sovereign and legitimate. Infrastructure has not "failed to deliver"—Jawlani are refusing settler-colonial deliverance (Simpson 2014). Therefore, studies of how material and social infrastructures work together can transcend both static ideas of linear development and hegemonic notions of domination/resistance. Much of this exciting work is being done in feminist infrastructural studies.

Feminist Relational Infrastructures

Recent scholarship on feminist relational infrastructures offers compelling theories to understand Palestinian infrastructural resistance. A feminist understanding of infrastructural "interconnection" calls attention to the micro-scale effects of infrastructural inequality across gendered difference (Truelove 2011). Ara Wilson's theory of "intimate infrastructures" animates how, within and across scales, a turn to infrastructure's relationships allows one to make messy the divides of material-social, private-public, and local-global (Wilson 2016). Relationships stretch across time to undergird infrastructural development, thus troubling linear notions of progress by instead illuminating how the past is always in continuous relationship with the present and the future. Finally, a turn to relationality challenges simply including all within infrastructure's draw as a political solution to issues of destruction, disrepair, or disadvantage (Berlant 2016). An "additive" framework of infrastructure can serve to reify settler states' claim to territory while assimilating colonized people as racialized minorities in multicultural liberalism (Daigle 2016).

Palestinians in Battir and al-Walaja do not want to be simply "added" to Israel's infrastructural development. Instead, it is important to use feminist critique to analyze how the entangled power network between material infrastructure and settler-colonial discourse has produced racialized and violent spaces in Palestine-Israel. This material and discursive violence against Palestinian bodies and lands is also always gendered, because national material infrastructure builds on and often relies on masculinist ideas of hierarchy and control (Sabhlok 2017; Siemiatycki, Enright, and Valverde 2020), and because settler-colonial dispossession of land relies on the propagation of violent heteropatriarchy (Arvin, Tuck, and Morrill 2013). Palestinian feminist scholars have shown how justice for Palestinians is always a feminist concern, even if it does not directly deal with issues of gendered subjectivity, identity, or oppression (Elia 2017). Thus, my project here follows Sharlene Mollett and Caroline Faria's (2013) call for feminist political ecology to move beyond a "particularly narrow reading of gender" (117) and see how Israel's racialized and colonial infrastructural violence serves as gendered violence, by trying to inhibit Palestinian reproduction of their homes, relationships, and ecosystems.

WALKING AS A METHOD

Field walks have a long history as masculinist and colonialist ways of objectively "seeing" the landscape (Rose 1993). I offer here instead a walking methodology rooted in Palestinian practices of walking to maintain relationships with the land despite Israeli violence (Shehadeh 2007).

My ability to walk on both sides of the Green Line is predicated on colonial transit infrastructures and legal geographies of Palestinian displacement, dispossession, and restriction. But Palestinians have worked hard to expose Israel's unjust infrastructure through their walking relationships, so that their stories of displacement and dispossession may travel farther. Jennifer Lynn Kelly has shown how Palestinians "use tourist mobility to highlight their own immobility under military occupation" (Kelly 2016a, 725), but like Kelly, I must "[sit] with the ambivalence of the practice" of walking in Palestine (Kelly 2016b, 101). My personal relationship to Palestine-Israel as a white American Jew is one of multiple intertwined legacies of violence. Walking cannot undo the infrastructures that facilitate my ease of movement. However, my embodied methodology—seeing and being close with trees, rocks, flowers, and critters; conversations with those I meet along the path; stopping to catch my breath; or falling due to a misstep—helps me to "explore how landscapes . . . are produced through colonial practice" (Robbins 2006, 316). So too does walking keep me connected to the political goals of my scholarship. The relational infrastructures of the Palestinian terraces and villages in Battir and al-Walaja inspire me to build toward binational futures of justice in Palestine-Israel, built on strong relationships of co-resistance with Palestinians, as well as with the natures and environments that we share.

Relationships of co-resistance must be built on trust, which is slow to build. Palestinians in Battir and al-Walaja have hosted international visitors for many years as their legal cases against Israel's wall gained international attention. Many in the villages have grown weary that Israel's violence has continued or even worsened despite media coverage and professions of solidarity. When I visited Battir in 2018, I spoke with some villagers who consented only to off-the-record interviews, performing an "ethnographic refusal" (Simpson 2014). Instead, they offered me an English-language book written by villagers on the history of community development in Battir. My field walks and analysis in this chapter, therefore, are methods that respect these villagers' requests.

ISRAELI SETTLER-COLONIAL INFRASTRUCTURES

Imperial Infrastructural History: The Jaffa-Jerusalem Railway

My first walk in 2013 began at the bottom of the Refaim Valley, on the train tracks (see figure 6.1). This route, the Jaffa-Jerusalem Railway, has an interesting history tied to both Ottoman and British imperialism. It opened in 1892, built and operated by private British entrepreneurs to bring religious tourists easily between Jaffa and Jerusalem. The Ottoman Empire greatly expanded the regional Palestine railways beginning in 1900, when Sultan Abdulhamid II built a railroad from Damascus to Mecca. The railroad increased the Ottomans' ability to export wheat and other agricultural products from Palestine and move their soldiers more quickly through the Levant. Early Zionists also supported the Ottoman project with zeal, seeing infrastructural improvement as crucial to bringing Palestine into a more civilized era (Pick 1990). A train station flourished in the valley at the Arab-Palestinian village of Battir at this time. Battiri produce—notably a unique variety of eggplant, in addition to other vegetables, stone fruit, olives, and almonds—was taken to all corners of the Ottoman empire by rail. Much of Battir's produce, however, stayed local, supplying the quickly growing Jerusalem population (Tamari 2002).

During World War I, the Ottomans expanded and improved railways in Palestine to ferry troops and supplies. In hegemonic historical narratives of this era, the Ottomans sacrificed nature for infrastructure, deforesting huge swaths of land for track ties and fuel (Cohen 1993, 46). This narrative conveniently justifies Zionist claims of finding a barren and degraded landscape in need of rehabilitation during the second *Aliyah*, or the large wave of Jewish Zionist settlement post World War I.

After the dissolution of the Ottoman Empire, the British Mandate government undertook huge infrastructure projects in Palestine from 1923 to 1947, expanding railways, constructing ports, and reorganizing city streets (Rotbard 2015; Rubin 2011). Military and security needs motivated infrastructural choices, as the British reorganized space to control local Arab populations who were agitating for national sovereignty. Infrastructure was therefore a logical target for Palestinian resistance efforts, from mass civil disobedience, such as

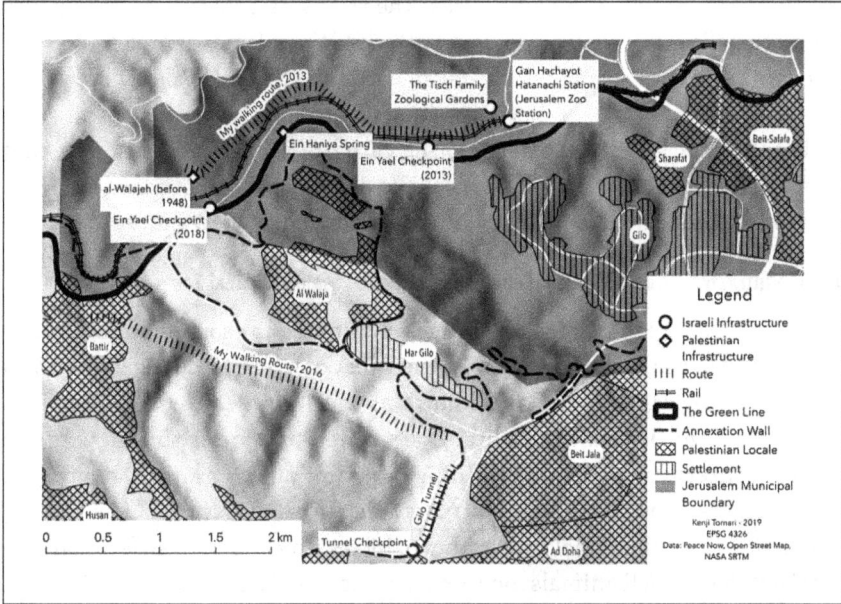

Fig. 6.1. A map of the Refaim Valley area, southern Jerusalem. (Map by Kenji Tomari)

general strikes, to armed guerilla attacks against railroads. During the Arab Revolt of 1936–1939, the British deputized Jewish Zionist settlers as security for the coastal rail line; these became part of the Zionist militias that would fight the War of Independence in 1947–1949 (Lockman 1996).

The State of Israel after 1948 benefitted greatly from the physical infrastructure built by the British, yet the link between British and Israeli infrastructure was more than material. As Ann Laura Stoler argues, contemporary nation-states "elaborate upon practices" of spatial violence and exclusion "long in imperial use" (2010, xiii). Israel continued the tautology conflating infrastructure and national security. When the 1949 armistice agreement was negotiated for Jerusalem, Battir's railway station was at a crucial crossroads between Israel and the Jordanian-controlled West Bank. Israel thus prioritized controlling the station, the tracks in the base of the valley, and most of Battir and al-Walaja's arable land. Infrastructural control for security was the pretense, but expanding land annexation while minimizing Palestinian population in the new state was the true goal. When the Green Line was finalized, the tracks, station, and agricultural land all ended up inside Israel.

Battir's village leader, Hassan Mustafa, negotiated directly for villagers to continue to access Battir's land across the tracks. Israel agreed but required Battir to police the railway to prevent attacks. When Israel occupied the West Bank in 1967, the agreement continued. Battir was the only Palestinian village in the West Bank that was allowed some access to their historic lands after the Nakba (Botmeh 2006).[2] The neighboring village of al-Walaja did not have that privilege. The train station was eventually demolished sometime after 1967, and today the location is marked with a sign only in Hebrew (not Arabic).

Leisure Infrastructures of "Jewish Indigeneity": The Jerusalem Biblical Zoo

Israel's settler-colonial infrastructure is not limited to economic and security purposes. On the northern slopes of the valley along the rail line is the Tisch Family Zoological Gardens, also known as the Jerusalem Biblical Zoo. Like other zoos, the Jerusalem Biblical Zoo's stated mission is to contribute to animal conservation through breeding programs and community education. However, the Jerusalem Zoo constructs a historical narrative of Jewish indigeneity to Palestine-Israel through its exhibits which "emphasiz[e] local species" notably "Israeli animals mentioned in the Bible" ("Biblical Animals" n.d.). It is among a series of Israeli tourism projects focused on a positive portrayal of Israel's environmental stewardship as a legacy stretching since Jewish residency during biblical times to the Israeli state today (Barnard and Muamer 2015). Infrastructures of leisure, tourism, and environmental conservation are a crucial part of Israel's claim of "Jewish indigeneity" to Palestine-Israel, justifying Israel's occupation.

I visited the zoo in July 2018, via a packed bus from West Jerusalem filled mostly with religious Jewish families. The zoo prides itself not only on being one of the most popular tourist attractions in Israel, but also in its efforts towards Jewish-Arab coexistence through recreation. All its informational signs are written in Hebrew, Arabic, and English. The zoo sells enjoyment of the environment as a politically neutral activity that all of Jerusalem's residents can partake in equally (Braverman 2013). Positioning the zoo as a mixed space where Jewish Israelis and Palestinians enjoy equality helps bolster the vision of Israel as a liberal, multicultural democracy—a vision that obscures the historic and ongoing dispossession the zoo is built upon (Cornellier and Griffiths 2016).

Rather awkwardly, this project of multiculturalism betrayed itself outside and within the zoo. No buses go to the zoo from Palestinian East Jerusalem or Palestinian neighborhoods in southern Jerusalem. Some of the Arabic exhibit signs have blatant typographic and spelling errors. Additionally, one sign had a conspicuous lack of Arabic translation: a memorial plaque written only in Hebrew and English was dedicated to an Israeli soldier who had been a volunteer zookeeper but was killed in the Second Intifada while serving in the Occupied Territories. The zoo seemed to assume that Palestinians would not be interested in a memorial to a soldier of the occupation. Finally, one could clearly see the wall surrounding the settlement and construction on new homes in Gilo and Har Gilo across the valley from every part of the zoo, a stark reminder that despite multiculturalism proclaimed within the zoo's walls, infrastructural violence continued right next door. The centerpiece of the zoo is the Bible Land Preserve. The opening plaque greets you: "Most of the animals included in this enclosure are mentioned in the Bible and lived in the land of Israel during biblical times . . . The Bible provides us with a valuable source of information documenting great zoological changes in the land of Israel from the days of the biblical fathers and continuing on up to the present day." Here, an intentional slippage occurs between the Hebrew Bible as historical and scientific evidence, as theological guidance, and as political manifesto. Other signs alternate between generalized notions of human stewardship for the earth ("The future of animals rests in the hands of mankind") and invoking Bible stories as the ancient ancestors of the zoo's conservation efforts ("Noah was the first nature conservationist in History"). This is not done subtly: a large wooden ark hosts an information center and café. Each plaque in the Bible Lands exhibit also contains a Hebrew Bible passage referring to the animal on display. Beyond the zoo's walls, a large herd of Persian fallow deer bred in the zoo have been released, in the hopes they will repopulate the Jerusalem hills after being hunted to near extinction in the nineteenth century. The zoo highlights their reintroduction not just as an ecological restoration project but also as restoration of a biblical landscape.

Settler states have long used infrastructures of tourism, particularly ecotourism, to erase colonial violence and dispossession (Williams and Gonzalez 2017). Thus, the Jerusalem Biblical Zoo promotes a discourse of Israel as a modern, scientific steward of the land and also of Jews as the ancient inhabitants, justifying Israel's claims over all of historic Palestine. This naturalization of settler indigeneity requires both material and discursive infrastructures at the zoo, all hidden in plain sight by the zoo's claims to being an apolitical tourist destination and environmental steward.

Settler-Colonial Dispossession: The Ongoing Nakba

In January 2013, I hiked past the zoo onto a designated trail in the Jerusalem Park, the railroad tracks below me. I tried to understand what I was seeing beyond the picturesque landscape of wildflowers and pine forests. Looking into the valley, I saw children playing in the crumbling remains of stone houses along the valley walls. While no signage indicated them as such, I knew these were houses of the village of al-Walaja destroyed during the *Nakba*, the Catastrophe. From 1947–1949, Zionist militias drove more than 750,000 Palestinians from their lands and homes throughout historic Palestine and into the West Bank, the Gaza Strip, Jordan, Lebanon, and Syria (Pappé 2006). The villages surrounding west Jerusalem were targeted with particular and cruel violence. On April 9, 1948, the Irgun and Lehi militias attacked civilians in the Palestinian village of Deir Yassin, only a few kilometers north of al-Walaja. The militias killed more than one hundred civilians, and there were widespread reports of rape and mutilation (Sa'di and Abu-Lughod 2007). As the story of Deir Yassin spread throughout Palestine (often disseminated by Zionist and Israeli forces), Palestinians fled their homes to avoid a similar fate.

At the war's end in 1949, the Armistice Line was drawn through al-Walaja, leaving 70 percent of the village land and 30 percent of the springs on the Israeli side (R. A. Davis 2011). The villagers were unable to return to their homes in what was now Israel, so they built "new" al-Walaja about two kilometers to the south, in the West Bank. Because Israel prevented al-Walaja residents from returning, their former homes and lands became state property under Israel's Absentee Property Law of 1950. Then, in June 1967, the new village of al-Walaja came under Israeli military occupation, along with the rest of the West Bank, East Jerusalem, Gaza Strip, and the Golan Heights (Syria). Israel annexed much of "new" al-Walaja's arable land and about half of al-Walaja's homes to the Jerusalem municipality. However, the villagers enjoy none of the benefits of municipal infrastructure, like trash, water, or electrical hookups, yet they are still subject to city regulations and control of their community's development. Israel has issued demolition orders for most of al-Walaja's homes in the Jerusalem municipality, claiming they are unpermitted, even though it is nearly impossible legally and financially for Palestinians to receive the necessary permissions to build or expand their homes (Joronen and Griffiths 2019). Palestinians traditionally live in multifamily households, with parents building additions in the form of small apartments or connecting houses for their adult children and their families. Permission to expand the infrastructure of the home in close proximity to existing homes in the village is necessary for the maintenance and health of social ties and social reproduction. However, in January 2021, the Jerusalem District Planning Committee, an office of the Jerusalem Municipality, rejected the master plan put forth by the village of al-Walaja for the sustainable development of the village. Instead, the committee declared that the village land, upon which many homes currently deemed "illegal" are sited, is sensitive agricultural land that should be included in a national park for environmental conservation. This decision unfroze the demolition orders against al-Walaja houses, and the Israeli army has demolished at least six homes in 2021—including, in at least one instance, the agricultural terraces.[3]

Israel's destruction of al-Walaja during the Nakba and subsequent reoccupation and annexation in 1967 is part of the settler-colonial desire to maximize land while minimizing indigenous population. In recent years, Israel has used infrastructural tools to perpetrate this ongoing process of "colonial accumulation" (Coulthard 2014). Israel has expanded the annexation wall in the area (detailed in the next section), expropriated village land to build more settlement housing in Gilo and Har Gilo, and built a new road and checkpoint only for settlers. While hiking in January 2013, I happened to be able to see the construction of the new Ein Yael checkpoint at the bottom of the valley before the road climbed up to the settlements (see figure 6.2). Checkpoints inhibit or prohibit Palestinian mobility by restricting where they can travel, by slowing down travel times, and through the identification systems at checkpoints,

Fig. 6.2. Viewing the construction of the checkpoint looking toward Gilo settlement, January 2013. (Photo by Gabi Kirk)

classifying Palestinians as a population in need of policing and surveillance (Griffiths and Repo 2018; Tawil-Souri 2012). The Ein Yael checkpoint can only be used by settlers. It is another part of the tautology of Israel's military-infrastructural complex: they need the checkpoint for security purposes to protect the road; they need the road for the broader security of a healthy state economy, to bring commuters from the settlements to work in Jerusalem and Tel Aviv. Additionally, the road serves to smoothly transport tourists to the new national park in the valley.

In November 2017, Israel announced it would be moving the checkpoint and Palestinians from al-Walaja without Israeli entrance permits would no longer be permitted to tend to their fields or draw water from the spring of Ein Hanya (Hasson 2017). In February 2018, a Jerusalem District Court judge issued an injunction to stop the checkpoint's construction as the city has moved forward without any proper permits, but construction continued and even quickened (Hasson 2018b). The checkpoint is operational today and closed to Palestinians with West Bank identification cards without special permits. However, despite the violence of the checkpoint, Palestinians have continued to cultivate their terraces on both sides of the Green Line.

PALESTINIAN INFRASTRUCTURAL RESISTANCE

The Battir Terraces

In July 2016, I walked through the valley again, this time starting from the east side of the annexation wall,[4] at the top of the valley overlooking the massive "tunnel checkpoint" between Jerusalem and the Gush Etzion settlement bloc (see figures 6.3 and 6.4). I hiked a route popularized by Palestinian eco-tourism efforts (Barnard and Muamer 2015; Sakhnini 2014), scraping between Palestine oak and scrambling down limestone hillsides lined with parallel terraces. The hill was steep, and the terraces alternated between easily navigable, almost staircase-like, to older piles of rock crumbling down the hillside.

Terracing is an infrastructure underlying the most common form of Palestinian dry farming agriculture. Terraces built from endemic limestone can be found on hillsides stretching from the northern border with Lebanon to the South Hebron Hills. The terraces prevent rainfall from sluicing straight into the valley, and as the water loses momentum it sinks deeper into the soil, building up a stable water table for crops to tap during the long, dry months of summer and fall. Communities maintain rainwater cisterns for supplemental irrigation (Tesdell, Othman, and Alkhoury 2019). Very little Palestinian agricultural land is irrigated. Over 98 percent of al-Walaja's biodiverse food system is rain-fed, from olives and nut orchards (80 percent of arable land), to peppers, cucumbers, eggplant, wheat, barley, and various legumes (Applied Research Institute— Jerusalem 2010). Dryland farming is not only pragmatic for the Mediterranean climate but also a form of infrastructural resistance to settler colonialism in Palestine, dating back to the earliest periods of Zionist settlement. Historically, Western imperialists have used scientific justifications to territorialize dryland and classify it as needing improvement, thus justifying its expropriation (D. K. Davis 2016). Using technoscientific justification to support settlement buildup, Zionist settlers under the British Mandate preferred intensive farming methods, requiring intense irrigation to produce more on less land and supporting rapid capital accumulation to fuel more settlement expansion.

In contrast, extensive dryland farming took advantage of existing Palestinian techniques, relied on rainfall instead of artificial irrigation—and used more land, keeping more under Palestinian cultivation and therefore control: "If tree planting and dryland cultivation helped to engineer a settler-colonial political order with control over land at its heart, then [Palestinians] may have thought that struggles against dispossession must also invest in and draw on the natural forces of plant life inherent to cultivation" (Tesdell 2015, 572). Terraces are common across Palestine, but many are in disrepair because Israel restricts farmers' ability to access them for maintenance. However, because of Battir's aforementioned special arrangement with Israel, their terraces have remained incredibly well maintained. Their terraces are an example of what Omar Imseeh Tesdell has termed Palestinian "infrastructures of recalcitrance" (Tesdell 2013), in which Palestinians' agricultural practices, rather than only resisting settler-colonial domination, "give form to the potential residing in the landscape and in history, thereby producing new political horizons" (167). Without downplaying Israel's material and legal suppression of Palestinian agriculture, Tesdell notes how Palestinian cultivation uses the settler state's legal and cultural definitions of property against itself. Since Hassan Mustafa negotiated with Moshe Dayan for Battir's continued access to their land across the Green Line in 1949, Battir has engaged ambivalently with Israeli state law, not necessarily to legitimate its sovereignty but to assert Palestinian continuous survival. It makes sense, therefore, that terraces would also play major role in the legal campaign to reroute Israel's annexation wall and gain UNESCO World Heritage designation for Battir.

The UNESCO World Heritage Campaign

Israel's original route for a thirty-foot-high cement annexation wall in southern Jerusalem would have destroyed Battir's terraced hillsides. Battir went

Fig. 6.3. Viewing the terraces from Battir, July 2018. (Photo by Gabi Kirk)

to Israel's High Court of Justice in 2007, arguing that the cultural and natural significance of the terraces needed to be protected. They then launched a campaign to name the terraces a UNESCO World Heritage Site (Joronen 2016; Sawafta 2014). Environmental groups also sued over the fence's route, and an uneasy coalition emerged against the wall, ranging from those sympathetic to the Palestinian cause to Israeli state agencies and pro-settler groups. The former included Friends of the Earth Middle East, an environmental NGO.

Fig. 6.4. Viewing the terraces from Battir, July 2018. (Photo by Gabi Kirk)

The latter included the Israeli National Parks Association, concerned about damage to the environment from the wall, and settler groups, who argued the wall would harm archaeological sites in the area that they felt prove a continuous Jewish inhabitance in the land (Barnard and Muamer 2015). Israel offered to build a chain link fence instead, arguing that some barrier was necessary as security for the train tracks. Battir won UNESCO World Heritage Site recognition in 2014, but Israel still built the fence (although closer to the train tracks than originally planned). The legal battle over the main stretch of the wall continued: in January 2015, Israel's High Court froze wall construction, but in April 2017, construction resumed. Instead of cutting through the terraces, it will surround al-Walaja, cutting the village off from their springs and farmland.

UNESCO's Limits: Cultivation, Conservation, and Settler Colonialism

The UNESCO designation acknowledges this natural landscape as a Palestinian cultural contribution to the world, but it may be because an agricultural site fits hegemonic ideals of a properly cultivated landscape. Under this ideal, if Palestinians neglected to tend to the terraces, they would need to be restored to a productive state (Fields 2017). Through both direct violence and the threat of more to come, Israel has curtailed Palestinian cultivation. This leaves the terraces, in Israel's eyes, as a wasteland in need of need of improvement. Israel then moved to annex the separated land under the auspices of environmental stewardship by declaring it the Refaim Stream National Park. States have frequently used environmental explanations to "justify coercion in the name of conservation, often by using violence" (Peluso 1993, 199). Israel first prohibited residents of Battir and al-Walaja from tending this land by attempting to extend the annexation wall, then by moving the checkpoint, and finally through harassing and arresting Palestinian farmers who do tend their land. Israel often accuses farmers of "harming a national park" if they attempt to build any agricultural infrastructure such as water catchment systems (Hasson 2018a).

Israel's material drive to claim Battir's land was linked with their discursive claim of exclusive Jewish stewardship of the environment. Like the Jerusalem Biblical Zoo, the new national park rewrites the landscape as one that has always been Jewish, allowing Israel to move towards a settler "indigeneity" and claiming Palestinians are harming "nature." However, against this positioning of Palestinian farmers as despoilers of nature, Battir and their supporters argue that their care is what helps the ecosystem to thrive (Weizman 2018, 126). Without ongoing Palestinian cultivation, the terraces would be unlikely to be in the healthy and beautiful form that allowed them to be turned into a national park at all.

However, Israel's court acknowledged only the environmentalists' claims that a cement wall would harm the ecosystem, rather than the Palestinians' sovereign relationship to the terraces. The ruling was a limited victory—the wall was moved, but the justification is an instance of contemporary settler-colonial liberalism (Coulthard 2014). Specifically, it is a contemporary form of "eco-liberalism," a pivot away from older Zionist narratives of conquering the land and "making the desert bloom," transforming it from a barren landscape into a productive and fruitful one. Earlier Zionist environmentalism was a form of "environmental Orientalism" (D. K. Davis 2011), portraying Palestinians as both natively part of the landscape and as degraders of its fertility. Today, Israel still claims to be the redeemer of the land, but through environmental conservation and sustainability, protecting an "unchanged" landscape.

This pivot to Israeli conservation ignores the history of Zionist ecological reshaping of the landscape to fit Eurocentric ideals. The Refaim Stream National Park is part of the "Jerusalem Ring Park" complex, which aims to circle Jerusalem with a "green belt." This green belt consists mostly of non-native pine trees first planted by the British to provide cover for the railroad from guerrilla attacks (El-Eini 2006). After 1948, the Jewish National Fund (JNF) undertook a massive afforestation project around Jerusalem to cover Palestinian villages destroyed in the Nakba, preventing Palestinian refugees from returning to their homes (Braverman 2009; Cohen 1993)—including the al-Walaja homes I saw during my hike. The constructed nature of the forest is erased now, as it is portrayed as an urban greening project, and the JNF does not acknowledge the possible ecological harms of afforestation with nonnative trees.

Palestinian Relationships as Infrastructure

Despite Israel's efforts to cut Palestinians off from their land, Palestinians still farm in Battir. The village's UNESCO World Heritage campaign is often told as a narrative of *sumud*, the Palestinian ethos of "steadfastness" in the face of Israeli oppression (Joronen 2016). Yet this narrative can sometimes reify ideas of Palestinians as unchanging, ancient people, farming and living in the same way as they always have. In fact, the UNESCO designation itself romanticizes Palestinian farming, noting the Battir terraces are worth conserving because "the irrigation system and the cultivation system have hardly changed in time" (UNESCO n.d.). In reality, Palestinians have evolved their agricultural practices significantly over time, even as they hold on to key relationships with certain agroecological species and places (Tesdell, Othman, and Alkhoury 2019). Turning to the history of community development in Battir illustrates both the continuances and the changes to Palestinian infrastructural relationships under Israeli settler-colonialism.

Battir published a short book focused on Hassan Mustafa's life, which details community development projects in the village launched just after the Nakba in the 1950s. These included rebuilding the communal spring, building a new road to Bethlehem as Israel blocked the old road after 1948, and opening a women's and girls' school (Harbuk 2016). These community infrastructure projects disrupt the idea of Battir as a village unchanged since time immemorial, showing in recent history the village's ongoing relationships of repair. Additionally, the book praises Mustafa not for his negotiation with Israel but for embodying the value of al-'awna, which Rochelle A. Davis translates as the "ideal of communal conduct" (2011, 72). It is through al-'awna that Battir "again had a link with the world" as the village collectively built the new Battir-Bethlehem road with little outside aid (Harbuk 2016, 31). Thus infrastructures that could otherwise be classified only as "modern," such as new roads and educational institutions, are for Battir rooted in older and distinctly Palestinian ethics and relationships.

Additionally, women's development is a major theme in Battir's village history. Mustafa "believed in the development of the ladies of Battir as mothers, educators and guardians of the future generations" and the village felt "women always held the key" to "society's advancement" (Harbuk 2016, 18). The village claims their girls' school built in 1952 was the first in the West Bank, and that Mustafa advocated for girls' schools to be opened in all refugee camps. The book contains multiple adages from Mustafa on women's roles in society, such as "He who teaches a man shall have taught a single individual or a number of individuals but he who teaches a woman shall have taught all people" (88). These examples are reminiscent of how, in development projects and discourses, the nascent Iraqi state post–World War II valorized women as the protectors of future generations, and therefore of state development and sovereignty, while at the same time aiming to quell civil discontent through women's development (Pursley 2019).

However, one key difference here is the expressly *political*, not depoliticizing, goals of women's development in Battir: women were not meant to be the protectors of a neutral future nation-state of Palestine, but resisters of Israeli occupation and dispossession. In their village history book, Battir tells a history of infrastructure to external visitors today in a way that emphasizes gendered relationships (al-'awna as a relationship of care, which is always gendered even if not explicitly feminine or performed by women). Palestinians in Battir call upon their own history of development outside of Israeli settler-colonialism to assert themselves as active agents without reifying a Western model of linear development or history. Understanding Palestinians' infrastructural relationships through the value of al-'awna turns the narrative away from Israel's "operations of biopolitical logic" and toward "the institutional structures that provision needs themselves" (Wilson 2016, 274).

This is not without its problematics; the centrality of women to reproducing Palestinian futures can be taken with a critical eye, primarily because development has so frequently been used as a depoliticizing project. As one resident of Battir put it, "today's artificial or fake development . . . is not more than a way of beautification of a poor status quo rather than actual improvement or development, [and] does not represent any values, change or real structural meaning that may affect the root of the conditions themselves" (Harbuk 2016, 21). Here the "root of the conditions" may refer both to Israel's occupation, which persists even when new infrastructure (usually built with international humanitarian donations) is added to the village, and social and economic inequality (including gendered inequality) within Palestinian society. Celebrating Battir's history of development, or women's development in particular, does not absolve the present of persistent infrastructural inequality, as villagers themselves note.

CONCLUSION

The examples detailed in this chapter first demonstrate how Israel uses infrastructure as a tool of racial and gendered violence against Palestinians, particularly in the southern Jerusalem area. This includes cutting them off from economic reproduction by restricting the movement of people and goods through checkpoints and walls, and restricting social reproduction by making it difficult for households to grow through denying building permits and demolishing homes. Israeli settler-colonialism also operates through seemingly neutral infrastructures of tourism and leisure, as shown with the Refaim Valley National Park and Jerusalem Biblical Zoo.

Battir's victory against the annexation wall should be celebrated, but as evidenced by the resumption of home demolitions in al-Walaja, the struggle continues. Furthermore, caution should be taken to avoid forms of international recognition of Palestinian infrastructures, places, and cultural practices that can reproduce ideas of Palestinians as ancient people stuck in the past, as well as apolitical ecotourism efforts that can erase the Palestinian sovereignty that has maintained the material and social health of the Refaim Valley. Therefore, any engagement with Palestinian social and material infrastructures must challenge the hierarchical notion of development and underdevelopment that undergird settler-colonial oppression.

The example of the Refaim Valley demonstrates how closer attention to settler colonialism in feminist infrastructural studies can reveal how states replicate gendered violence across time, building on older infrastructures of inequality to segregate colonized people and dispossess them of lands and resources. This happens both materially and discursively, and feminist geographies are well suited to continue to explore the joint material-discursive elements of settler-colonial infrastructures in multiple sites and time periods. Finally, even when not explicitly targeted at Palestinian women, Israeli settler-colonialism is always a form of gendered violence, because of its explicit targeting of Palestinians' ability to reproduce their families, communities, and social and political projects. Expanding our notion of gendered violence to encompass forms of racial and colonial exclusion that target relationships of care expands our analytic in productive ways; furthermore, understanding resistance to settler-colonialism as not just against but also through infrastructure undoes notions of infrastructure as always top-down or hierarchical.

ACKNOWLEDGMENTS

Thank you to Diana Davis; Caren Kaplan; Maryam Griffin; Mikko Joronen; the UC Davis Critical Militarization, Policing, and Security Studies Group; and the UC Davis Political Ecology Lab for your thoughtful feedback on various drafts of this piece. Thank you, Kenji Tomari, for making the map and Peace Now for spatial data.

NOTES

1. This is the English translation of the Hebrew name for the valley, which is the one most used in English-language literature. Wherever possible, I try to use the Arabic names for specific springs and sites within the valley. However, in Arabic, the valley itself is more often referred to by the names of the two major villages (Battir and al-Walaja); I use this English name to refer to the entire physical geography of the valley that encompasses both villages' lands.
2. Jawad Botmeh offers the best English-language history of Battir; however, his personal story is usually hidden. The grandson of Hassan Mustafa, Botmeh wrote his thesis while in prison after being convicted of the 1994 bombing of the Israeli embassy in London, despite his alibi and a lack of evidence. After decades of campaigning and protesting his lack of a fair trial, he was released from prison in 2008.
3. See Ir Amim, December 2, 2021, https://twitter.com/IrAmimAlerts/status/1466378270652481540.
4. Thanks to Fayrouz Sharqawi and Grassroots al-Quds for introducing me to this term, which draws attention to the wall as a settler-colonial infrastructure designed for land dispossession. See also Monaghan and Careccia (2012).

REFERENCES

Abu Yahia, Khalil, Natasha Westheimer, and Mor Gilboa. 2022. "Gaza's Race against Climate Breakdown." *972 Magazine*, January 13. https://www.972mag.com/gaza-climate-breakdown-siege.
Anand, Nikhil, Akhil Gupta, and Hannah Appel, eds. 2018. *The Promise of Infrastructure*. Duke University Press.
Applied Research Institute—Jerusalem. 2010. "Al Walaja Village Profile." Bethlehem.
Arvin, Maile, Eve Tuck, and Angie Morrill. 2013. "Decolonizing Feminism: Challenging

Connections between Settler Colonialism and Heteropatriarchy." *Feminist Formations* 25 (1): 8–34.

Barnard, Ryvka, and Hassan Muamer. 2015. "Ongoing Dispossession and a Heritage of Resistance: The Village of Battir vs. Israeli Settler-Colonialism." In *The Politics and Power of Tourism in Palestine*, edited by C. Michael Hall, Rami K. Isaac, and Freya Higgins-Desbiolles, 63–78. Routledge.

Berlant, Lauren. 2016. "The Commons: Infrastructures for Troubling Times." *Environment and Planning D: Society and Space* 34 (3): 393–419.

"Biblical Animals." N.d. Tisch Family Zoological Gardens in Jerusalem. https://www .jerusalemzoo.org/eng/biblical-animals.

Bishara, Amahl. 2015. "Driving while Palestinian in Israel and the West Bank: The Politics of Disorientation and the Routes of a Subaltern Knowledge." *American Ethnologist* 42 (1): 33–54.

Botmeh, Jawad. 2006. "Civil Resistance in Palestine: The Village of Battir in 1948." MA thesis. Coventry University.

Braverman, Irus. 2009. *Planted Flags: Trees, Land, and Law in Israel/Palestine*. Cambridge University Press.

Braverman, Irus. 2013. "Animal Frontiers: A Tale of Three Zoos in Israel/Palestine." *Cultural Critique*, no. 85: 122–62.

Carse, Ashley. 2014. *Beyond the Big Ditch: Politics, Ecology, and Infrastructure at the Panama Canal*. MIT Press.

Carse, Ashley. 2017. "Keyword: Infrastructure." In *Infrastructures and Social Complexity: A Companion*, edited by Penny Harvey, Casper Bruun Jensen, and Atsuro Morita, 27–39. Routledge.

Cohen, Shaul Ephraim. 1993. *The Politics of Planting: Israeli-Palestinian Competition for Control of Land in the Jerusalem Periphery*. University of Chicago Press.

Cornellier, Bruno, and Michael R. Griffiths. 2016. "Globalizing Unsettlement: An Introduction." *Settler Colonial Studies* 6 (4): 305–16.

Coulthard, Glen Sean. 2014. *Red Skin, White Masks: Rejecting the Colonial Politics of Recognition*. University of Minnesota Press.

Daigle, Michelle. 2016. "Awawanenitakik: The Spatial Politics of Recognition and Relational Geographies of Indigenous Self-Determination." *Canadian Geographer / Le Géographe Canadien* 60 (2): 259–69.

Dajani, Muna, and Michael Mason. 2018. "Counter-Infrastructure as Resistance in the Hydrosocial Territory of the Occupied Golan Heights." In *Water, Technology, and the Nation-State*, edited by Filippo Menga and Erik Swyngedouw, 131–46. Routledge.

Davis, Diana K. 2011. "Imperialism, Orientalism, and the Environment in the Middle East: History, Policy, Power, and Practice." In *Environmental Imaginaries of the Middle East and North Africa*, edited by Diana K. Davis and Edmund Burke III, 1–22. Ohio University Press.

Davis, Diana K. 2016. *The Arid Lands: History, Power, Knowledge*. MIT Press.

Davis, Rochelle A. 2011. *Palestinian Village Histories: Geographies of the Displaced*. Stanford University Press.

El-Eini, Roza I. M. 2006. *Mandated Landscape: British Imperial Rule in Palestine, 1929–1948*. Routledge.

Elia, Nada. 2017. "Justice Is Indivisible: Palestine as a Feminist Issue." *Decolonization: Indigeneity, Education, and Society* 6 (1): 45–63.

Fields, Gary. 2017. *Enclosure: Palestinian Landscapes in a Historical Mirror*. University of California Press.

Griffin, Maryam S. 2020. "Transcending Enclosures by Bus: Public Transit Protests, Frame Mobility, and the Many Facets of Colonial Occupation." *Critique of Anthropology* 40 (3): 298–322.

Griffin, Maryam S. 2021. *Vehicles of Decolonization: Public Transit in the Palestinian West Bank.* Temple University Press.

Griffiths, Mark, and Jemima Repo. 2018. "Biopolitics and Checkpoint 300 in Occupied Palestine: Bodies, Affect, Discipline." *Political Geography* 65: 17–25.

Harbuk, Shafiq, ed. 2016. *Hassan Mustafa (The Son of Battir Village), In Living Memory: Brief Biography of a Thinker and Community Development Pioneer.* Hassan Mustafa Cultural Center.

Hasson, Nir. 2017. "Renewed Work on Separation Barrier to Cut Palestinian Villagers from Their Lands." *Haaretz*, April 29.

Hasson, Nir. 2018a. "Israel Summons Palestinian Farmer over Scarecrows, Rain Shelter on His Land." *Haaretz*, January 24.

Hasson, Nir. 2018b. "Flouting Courts, Jerusalem Pushes Ahead with New West Bank Checkpoint to Keep Palestinians Out of Park." *Haaretz*, February 16.

Humphries, Isabelle. 2009. "Exile Within: Israeli Development and the Palestinians in Israel." *Development* 52 (4): 509–13.

Joronen, Mikko. 2016. "'Refusing to Be a Victim, Refusing to Be an Enemy': Form-of-Life as Resistance in the Palestinian Struggle against Settler Colonialism." *Political Geography* 56: 91–100.

Joronen, Mikko, and Mark Griffiths. 2019. "The Affective Politics of Precarity: Home Demolitions in Occupied Palestine." *Environment and Planning D: Society and Space*, 37 (3): 561–576.

Kelly, Jennifer Lynn. 2016a. "Asymmetrical Itineraries: Militarism, Tourism, and Solidarity in Occupied Palestine." *American Quarterly* 68 (3): 723–45.

Kelly, Jennifer Lynn. 2016b. "Locating Palestine within American Studies: Transitory Field Sites and Borrowed Methods." In *Theorizing Fieldwork in the Humanities: Methods, Reflections, and Approaches to the Global South*, edited by Shalini Puri and Debra A. Castillo, 95–107. Palgrave Macmillan.

Larkin, Brian. 2013. "The Politics and Poetics of Infrastructure." *Annual Review of Anthropology* 42: 327–43.

Lockman, Zachary. 1996. *Comrades and Enemies: Arab and Jewish Workers in Palestine, 1906–1948.* University of California Press.

Long, Joanna C. 2006. "Border Anxiety in Palestine-Israel." *Antipode* 38 (1): 107–27.

Mason, Michael, and Muna Dajani. 2019. "A Political Ontology of Land: Rooting Syrian Identity in the Occupied Golan Heights." *Antipode* 51 (1): 187–206.

McFarlane, Colin, and Jonathan Silver. 2017. "The Poolitical City: 'Seeing Sanitation' and Making the Urban Political in Cape Town." *Antipode* 49 (1): 125–48.

Mollett, Sharlene, and Caroline Faria. 2013. "Messing with Gender in Feminist Political Ecology." *Geoforum* 45: 116–25.

Monaghan, Lisa, and Grazia Careccia. 2012. *The Annexation Wall and Its Associated Regime.* Al-Haq.

Pappé, Ilan. 2006. *The Ethnic Cleansing of Palestine.* OneWorld.

Pasternak, Shiri, and Tia Dafnos. 2018. "How Does a Settler State Secure the Circuitry of Capital?" *Environment and Planning D: Society and Space* 36 (4): 739–57.

Peluso, Nancy Lee. 1993. "Coercing Conservation? The Politics of State Resource Control." *Global Environmental Change* 3 (2): 199–217.

Pick, Walter Pinhas. 1990. "Meissner Pasha and the Construction of Railways in Palestine and Neighboring Countries." In *Ottoman Palestine, 1800–1914: Studies in Economic and Social History*, edited by Gad G. Gilbar, 179–218. E. J. Brill.

Pursley, Sara. 2019. *Familiar Futures: Time, Selfhood, and Sovereignty in Iraq.* Stanford University Press.

Robbins, Paul. 2006. "Research Is Theft: Environmental Inquiry in a Postcolonial World." In

Approaches to Human Geography, edited by Stuart Aitken and Gill Valentine, 311–24. Sage Publications.

Rose, Gillian. 1993. *Feminism and Geography: The Limits of Geographical Knowledge*. Polity Press.

Rotbard, Sharon. 2015. *White City, Black City: Architecture and War in Tel Aviv and Jaffa*. MIT Press.

Rubin, Noah Hysler. 2011. "Geography, Colonialism, and Town Planning: Patrick Geddes' Plan for Mandatory Jerusalem." *Cultural Geographies* 18 (2): 231.

Sabhlok, Anu. 2017. "'Main Bhi to Hindostaan Hoon': Gender and Nation-State in India's Border Roads Organisation." *Gender, Place, and Culture* 24 (12): 1711–28.

Sa'di, Ahmad H., and Lila Abu-Lughod, eds. 2007. *Nakba: Palestine, 1948, and the Claims of Memory*. Columbia University Press.

Said, Edward W. 1978. *Orientalism*. Vintage Books.

Sakhnini, Mohammad. 2014. "Walking, Telling and Resisting in Raja Shehadeh's Palestinian Walks." *Settler Colonial Studies* 4 (2): 209–19.

Salamanca, Omar Jabary. 2015. "Road 443: Cementing Dispossession, Normalizing Segregation, and Disrupting Everyday Life in Palestine." In *Infrastructural Lives: Urban Infrastructure in Context*, edited by Stephen Graham and Colin McFarlane. Routledge.

Salamanca, Omar Jabary. 2016. "Assembling the Fabric of Life: When Settler Colonialism Becomes Development." *Journal of Palestine Studies* 45 (4): 64–80.

Sawafta, Ali. 2014. "UNESCO Recognizes Palestinian Village as World Heritage Site." *Haaretz*, June 20.

Seikaly, Sherene. 2016. *Men of Capital: Scarcity and Economy in Mandate Palestine*. Stanford University Press.

Shehadeh, Raja. 2007. *Palestinian Walks: Forays into a Vanishing Landscape*. Scribner.

Siemiatycki, Matti, Theresa Enright, and Mariana Valverde. 2020. "The Gendered Production of Infrastructure." *Progress in Human Geography* 44 (2): 297–314.

Simone, AbdouMaliq. 2004. "People as Infrastructure: Intersecting Fragments in Johannesburg." *Public Culture* 16 (3): 407–29.

Simpson, Audra. 2014. *Mohawk Interruptus: Political Life across the Borders of Settler States*. Duke University Press.

Simpson, Audra. 2016. "Whither Settler Colonialism?" *Settler Colonial Studies* 6 (4): 438–45.

Stamatopoulou-Robbins, Sophia. 2019. *Waste Siege: The Life of Infrastructure in Palestine*. Stanford University Press.

Stoler, Ann Laura. 2010. *Carnal Knowledge and Imperial Power: Race and the Intimate in Colonial Rule*. University of California Press.

Tamari, Salim, ed. 2002. *Jerusalem 1948: The Arab Neighbourhoods and Their Fate in the War*. 2nd ed. Institute of Jerusalem Studies and Badil Resource Center.

Tawil-Souri, Helga. 2012. "Uneven Borders, Coloured (Im)Mobilities: ID Cards in Palestine/Israel." *Geopolitics* 17 (1): 153–76.

Tesdell, Omar Imseeh. 2013. "Shadow Spaces: Territory, Sovereignty, and the Question of Palestinian Cultivation." PhD diss. University of Minnesota.

Tesdell, Omar Imseeh. 2015. "Territoriality and the Technics of Drylands Science in Palestine and North America." *International Journal of Middle East Studies* 47 (3): 570–73.

Tesdell, Omar Imseeh, Yusra Othman, and Saher Alkhoury. 2019. "Rainfed Agroecosystem Resilience in the Palestinian West Bank, 1918–2017." *Agroecology and Sustainable Food Systems* 43 (1): 21–39.

Truelove, Yaffa. 2011. "(Re-)Conceptualizing Water Inequality in Delhi, India through a Feminist Political Ecology Framework." *Geoforum* 42 (2): 143–52.

UNESCO. N.d. "Palestine: Land of Olives and Vines—Cultural Landscape of Southern Jerusalem, Battir." https://whc.unesco.org/en/list/1492.

Weizman, Eyal. 2007. *Hollow Land: Israel's Architecture of Occupation*. Verso.

Weizman, Eyal. 2018. *Forensic Architecture: Violence at the Threshold of Detectability*. Zone Books.

Williams, Liza Keānuenueokalani, and Vernadette Vicuña Gonzalez. 2017. "Indigeneity, Sovereignty, Sustainability and Cultural Tourism: Hosts and Hostages at ʻIolani Palace, Hawaiʻi." *Journal of Sustainable Tourism* 25 (5): 668–83.

Wilson, Ara. 2016. "The Infrastructure of Intimacy." *Signs: Journal of Women in Culture and Society* 41 (2): 247–80.

Wolfe, Patrick. 2006. "Settler Colonialism and the Elimination of the Native." *Journal of Genocide Research* 8 (4): 387–409.

Yiftachel, Oren. 2006. *Ethnocracy: Land and Identity Politics in Israel/Palestine*. University of Pennsylvania Press.

CHAPTER 7

INFORMAL TRANSPORT INFRASTRUCTURES: GENDERED EXPERIENCES OF MOVING AROUND THE PERIPHERIES OF QUITO, ECUADOR

Cristen Dávalos and Julie Gamble

INTRODUCTION

In the cold and dark early hours of the morning, four working women begin their commutes at 5:30 a.m. from different points of the south of Quito to the valley of Cumbaya. Their journeys involve a walk followed by multiple types of transportation: taxi, formal bus, or informal bus. In the case of Anabela—a twenty-nine-year-old mother of two children and part-time domestic worker—the journey begins by walking from her house down from Santa Barbara Alto on the hills of the Pichincha volcano to catch a taxi (informal or formal). Once in Chillogallo, Anabela then boards an informal bus to continue her journey to work. She explains her indignation of using overcrowded informal transport accompanied by a lack of behavioral rules. Such an experience demonstrates the daily undocumented difficulties that women face when riding informal transport in Quito.

Understood as a flexible, demand-responsive service, informal transport provides both a way in which people can move in cities and a sensible solution for "low-income" cities with transport needs (Cervero and Golub 2007). Only recently has literature brought to the fore the study of informal transport as a social and material system that draws on the field of infrastructural studies (Agbiboa 2018; Doherty 2017; Evans, O'Brien, and Ch Ng 2018). Infrastructural studies approaches consider the active arrangement of people and materials but have not been particularly attentive to the embodied and affective been categorized between the identifying processes of social actors needed to produce the infrastructure itself (Sabhlok 2017). How do informal transport riders activate the infrastructure? How are these processes gendered? What does focusing on gender reveal about mobility, infrastructure, and urban space?

Understanding mobility is undoubtedly enhanced when linked to feminist geography's discussions. The "new mobilities paradigm" in the social sciences has transformed the ways in which transport research is conducted through the study of subjects, movement, and space (Sheller and Urry 2006). The focus on different bodies of men and women traveling shows how people, ideas, and things move in interconnected ways, producing gendered mobilities (Uteng and Cresswell 2012). In this chapter, we bridge the fields of gender and mobility through the study of women's experiences on informal transport infrastructure. Here we also wish to look at the role of informal transport infrastructure in reproducing and challenging gendered spaces. We argue that informal transport infrastructure experiences are dependent on mobilities that not only are shaped by gendered spaces but also shape gendered spaces.

To think across these subjects, we draw from feminist geographic perspectives on mobility to inform our discussion on infrastructural studies. We discuss the context of Quito and the methods used to study the mobility practices of women who take informal transport daily in the city. Using GPS data, semi-structured interviews, and audio files, we discuss the experiences and motivations of women using informal transport. Subsequently, we reveal two concerns for the female riders amid the transport infrastructural changes occurring in the city. On the one hand, they challenge their traditional domestic role when moving on transport, which, in response, is met with insecurity (Chant, Moser, and McIlwaine 2015). On the other hand, when moving on transport that is outside the control of the state, there are scarce possibilities for changes to safety through public activism and policy. Female riders must therefore rely on private solutions to their insecurity that involve sharing their journeys on infrastructure with fellow women. As such, the riders' experiences show how transport infrastructural networks are spaces of both insecurity and intimacy (Wilson 2015).

GENDERED MOBILITIES, GENDERED SPACES, AND INFORMAL TRANSPORT INFRASTRUCTURE

This chapter uses a gendered mobilities approach to the study of informal transport infrastructure. Understanding mobility is undoubtedly enhanced when linked to feminist geography's discussions on space, place, and scale. Feminist studies have questioned the concept of space not as a neutral category but as a product of interrelations and interactions, as well as a non-harmonious, non-static place (Massey 2005). They have also challenged the public and private divisions of space, as well as the formal and informal dichotomies. While there are a vast number of studies on women's roles in private spaces (Hayden 1980), as well as in informal employment (Chant, Pedwell, and International Labor Office 2008), this research adds to these binaries by addressing the double exclusion of women in both public and informal infrastructural spaces of mobility. The research therefore acknowledges the connections between the public and private, but also its continuums with informality and infrastructure, as they are all entwined.

Feminist geography has a long tradition of examining women's activities in public spaces. Traditionally, literature assumed women's safe spaces to be the home, until awareness was made of how most violence toward women occurs in the home and is perpetrated by other family members (Oberhauser et al. 2017). In this vein feminist scholarship examines how private needs have been brought into public debates. Inversely, this study examines how violence in public spaces may be downscaled by adopting private safety strategies. On informal transport, for example, where there is an absence of public policing and surveillance, mobile women draw on private embodiment as a form of protection in public spaces. Building on the feminist work of Judith Butler, Fluri (2017) argues that corporeal geographies are socially constructed and influence power relations. For example, studies have observed dress, particularly on the use of the veil in public spaces in Islamic contexts, as reinforcing power over citizens' bodies and as an effort for women to be protected from public harassment (Raheja and Gold 1994). In order to examine the intersection of power relations on multiple scales, this chapter links the intimate scale of the woman's body, or of intimacy, to understand "identities as multiple and shaped through power relations, structural violence and unequal access to social, economic and political rights" (Fluri 2017, 28).

Literature from a postcolonial perspective resonates with women's subordination in public spaces. There are a growing number of studies from the Global South on women's oppression manifested through violence, including during their daily journey (Dunckel-Graglia 2013; Howard, Hume, and Oslender 2007; McIlwaine 2013; Whitzman, Andrew, and Viswanath 2014). A prominent theme has been women's experience of fear (see Dammert and Malone 2006 on Latin America). Building on Valentine's (1989) work on women's fear in terms of mobility, studies find that women employ a number of strategies out of this fear of violence. For example, transport can be situated in dark and isolated spaces, where women may face harassment, assault, and theft. Consequently, women avoid particular areas at certain times of the day as well as unaccompanied travel. They also seek protection from men when entering public spaces. Parikh (2018) describes how working women's mobility while working night shifts in India led to increased supervision. Similarly, Phadke (2005) in the same context describes how women's mobility is not surveilled by the police but by families and communities. This particular response to women's fear reinforces their oppression by familial males and male members of the community controlling public spaces. Subsequently, women who engage in urban public space with fear are increasingly vulnerable. In some contexts, such as Mexico City and Rio de Janeiro, governments and activists organize women-only transportation in order to promote safe ways of moving through the city (Dunckel-Graglia 2013). An innovative use of digital technology for mobile women are initiatives that provide reports of harassment or abuse via texts and emails (Chant and McIlwaine 2015). These initiatives provide immediate techno-infrastructural solutions to harassment to which women are exposed during their journeys, yet the authors also present its limitations for not transforming structural inequalities and violence.

Feminist geographers have long focused on urban public spaces as sites for examining social justice issues. From a perspective that involves women's right to the city, Fenster (2005) develops the concept of women's right to appropriate urban spaces. Activism against women's exclusion in public spaces is encouraged, related to the recent global movements to publicly disclose harassment and abuse. Consequently, Whitson argues that "women's presence in public spaces allows for different groups, including marginalized groups, to become visible and legitimate members of broader public" (Whitson 2017, 82). This chapter on gendered mobilities demonstrates that working-class women challenge and contest their traditional domestic role and space through embodied strategies when moving on informal transport. Starting from such a perspective is outside the control of the state and thus presents the limitations for change through public activism and policy. Women, instead, are further segregated within the marginal areas and populations tied to processes of informality found in the city and its infrastructures.

In the field of urban studies, informality emerges as a mode of urbanization (Roy and AlSayyad 2004). In Latin America it stems from how urban land itself is categorized by legal and illegal titling practices on the urban periphery (Holston 1991). Conceptualizations of informality are fundamentally concerned with the distinction between laws that are regulated and unregulated, which are ambiguously deployed and negotiated between people and the state (Doshi and Ranganathan 2018; Roy 2009). The existence of informal transport is also due to surplus labor that is employed in hyper-exploitative units in capitalist markets (Portes 1996). Yet, informality is also useful in considering the role of people as active agents who appropriate urban spaces (Fischer, McCann, and Auyero 2014; Goldstein 2016). Thus, instead of a fixed framework, informality offers an open-ended manner to interpret how these transport systems function and how they place claims on urban spaces that we argue are also gendered. Informal transport is an enduring form of movement in cities in the Global South (Simone 2011). These forms of infrastructure are still left outside of innovative, sustainable transport development that is in favor of modernizing and connecting the city (Evans, O'Brien, and Ch Ng 2018). Informal transport systems respond to the unmet needs of the modern infrastructural promise. It is well established that modern infrastructures like transport infrastructure produce fragmentation and inequality in cities across the world (Graham and Marvin 2001). The universality and uniformity of infrastructures have been challenged in the Global South.

As agents in the city, informal transport systems, then, must be conceptualized as an infrastructural arrangement that emerges due to the dynamic intersection of people in urban space (Simone 2004). Infrastructures offer an important way in which these technical systems offer insights into practices of government, religion, and sociality (Larkin 2013). Infrastructures are a political backdrop (McFarlane and Rutherford 2008) that have recently received attention from the vantage points of citizenship (Anand 2017). Thus, infrastructures, like informal transport, provide multiple opportunities to investigate entangled relationships in urban space. For example, if "infrastructures are the means by which a state proffers these representations to its citizens and asks them to take those representations as social facts" (Larkin 2013, 335), then informal transport systems emerge from their lack of representation by the state and gaps in transport's technical function. As a consequence, informal transport systems serve as an expression of poor people's politics and resistance by quietly encroaching on urban space (Bayat 2000). Mass mobilization in public spaces in Latin America has opened up space for popular participation and transformed traditional understandings of democratic politics (Avritzer 2009). As such, informal transport infrastructures provide an important intersection for the study of democratic politics and claims to public space. However, these studies place emphasis on the materials and connections to people, leaving outside the critical perspective how these heterogenous configurations are also gendered. Overall, research on informal transport shows that systems are laden with power dynamics that construct differentiated urban experiences, shape socio-spatial mobilities, and constitute gendered identities and spaces. Next, we bridge together the transport infrastructural changes and gendered realities of the informal transport service in Quito in order to think across these subjects.

INSECURE TRANSPORT INFRASTRUCTURAL TIMES IN QUITO

As an effort to mitigate sprawling urban development trends, Quito boasts a sustainable urban mobility plan that embraces notions of equity, environment, and economy, providing ecological transport options such as public bike share, three bus rapid transport (BRT) lines, a possible cable car system, and an underground metro rail currently under construction. However, these new sustainable transport trends cause new mobility cultures that are embedded in broader spatial patterns of uneven urban form (Sheller 2015). The city has an expanding vehicle ownership rate of 9.2 percent, and 4,565,000 trips are made daily, of which 3,850,000 are motorized (DMQ 2013). The city's densest urban areas continue to spread into the peripheries with an overall growth rate of 1.8 percent (DMQ 2012). Just between the years 2010 and 2011, suburban administrative zones such as the elite expansive valley of Tumbaco had growth rates of 0.5 percent, and the popular low-income zone of Calderón experienced a growth rate of 2.2 percent (DMQ 2012). Meanwhile, the city's urban core and consolidated city experienced *negative* growth of 2.5 percent. The increase in vehicle ownership surpasses the population growth rate (1.7 percent) by four times. Thus, the built environment trends indicate urban expansion in the periphery, the abandonment of the urban core, and a rise in preference for automobiles.

Such statistics are met equally with efforts to make Quito a place in which both women and men of all ages feel safe, but such efforts mainly require institutional changes and effective public policies that are burgeoning (Alfonso, del Pozo, and Ramírez 2016). In 2013 the United Nations Entity for Gender Equality, also known as UN Women, teamed up with the municipal administration to improve women's well-being in the city. This initiative was called Ciudades Seguras, or Safe Cities. As the first step in the collaboration, the initiative gathered data at the municipal level. For instance, in 2014 the municipality conducted an analysis showing that 34 percent of women entering one BRT line, the Trolebus, felt insecure (DMQ 2014b). In this same survey on sexual violence, 49 percent of women between the ages of fifteen and seventy had experienced uncomfortable looks or received verbal or obscene sexual gestures while riding the Trolebus. In addition, 66.6 percent of women felt fear of sexual assault or sexual abuse and 57.9 percent of women were touched inappropriately while on the BRT. Such statistics provided by the Municipality of the Metropolitan District of Quito (DMQ) indicate that women do not feel safe on transport.

DMQ attempted to take on and improve conditions for women and all transport users through innovative programming like Bájale al Acoso, or Get Rid of Assault, a monitoring and SMS-messaging reporting service for victims to denounce assault. More recently, a study titled *"Ella Se Mueve Segura"* (She Moves Safely) reported on a perception survey of insecurity on public transport in Quito that was expanded to all three BRT lines. The comparative report includes results from Quito, Buenos Aires, and Santiago and overwhelmingly shows that women experience higher levels of harassment while on public transport and lack trust in security responses (Allen et al. 2017, 23). Similarly, in this survey women reported that their perception of security was based on their experiences and the experiences of others in their immediate social circles. While important, these studies have little to do with the daily lived insecurity that women experience on informal transport that is not concessioned. What about the people who are not covered by public transport? How and what happens on informal and illegal networks that are unregulated? Our work takes up these questions by analyzing women's experiences using informal transport in Quito.

MOBILE AND FEMINIST METHODS

We started this collaborative research project from standpoint theory to render visible the narratives of subaltern or urban marginal women who take public transport daily (Haraway 1988). Our previous work on informal transport showed that people take this mode of transport for a variety of reasons, but in general because it is the best option for moving around (Gamble and Dávalos 2019). Starting from the infrastructural approach, we identified the materials and subjects necessary to discuss both informal transport and its users in Quito (Star 1999). This vantage point was necessary as it stems from carefully identifying elements in urban space that are both fixed and mobile. We identified various tools associated with informal transport, including cars, bus stations, the street, providers, and users. This assemblage of elements is complex due to its illicit and informally maintained relationship to municipal transport agents and the municipal administration. Thus, we drew on a variety of tools associated with an infrastructural tool box (Appel, Anand, and Gupta 2015), such as interviews and participant observation, and drew from mobility studies approaches because we could not "be there" or "see there" at all moments of the research (Spinney 2015).

Traditional methods to study mobility, such as transport studies, leave out the experience of the journey itself. Jirón, Imilan and Iturra argue that the "trajectory is a place of experience" (2016, 602). Thus, this research is based on ethnographic work in which four female travelers were accompanied during their daily journeys to gain an understanding of these trips. GPS devices facilitated tracking the participants' routes between the south of Quito, specifically Guamani and Chillogallo, and Cumbaya. Since our presence on the bus could influence what our informants reported in a context of risk and insecurity, we pulled again from mobility studies methods, providing a way to listen to what women experienced on their daily journeys. In addition to "go-alongs" (Merriman 2014), we gave women audio devices in order to avoid the idea that we as researchers knew more accurately what they were witnessing, giving rise to the ability to interpret the everyday situations of the emotional and rational reactions that women experienced. In mobile methods listening can create personal connection or empathy to the embodied mobile practice (Spinney 2015). We also were investigating how everyday situations on transport supported or contrasted with what women said in interviews. In total, four female participants used an audio device on informal transportation on a daily basis, two times a day with a recording time ranging from ninety minutes to four hours a day, over a period of one month between April and July 2018 (see table 7.1). In addition, the participants also produced travel diaries by orally accounting for their experiences and perceptions of their trips.

As the researcher is simultaneously an onlooker and a participant, this method places reflexivity at the forefront. Trust was fundamental during the research process. Access to participants was gained through trustworthy personal networks. We prioritized meeting female participants through a familiar person who also rode informal transportation. It is noted that it is easier for a female researcher to achieve a better rapport with female participants (Bhasin 1997). Indeed, during the research process, we built rapport with the participants by establishing frequent communication. As a result, we formed careful relationships with the four women we recruited from one informal transport

Table 7.1. Travel routes and participant profiles

Pseudonym	Months	Route	Type(s) of transport	Employ-ment	Profile
Anabela	April–May 2018	Santa Barbara Alto to Cumbaya	Walk, taxi (formal or informal), informal bus	Domestic worker, 2 days a week from 8 a.m. to 4 p.m.	29 years old, unmarried in domestic partnership, 2 children (ages 4 and 15)
Lourdes	April–June 2018	Quitumbe to Cumbaya	Walk, formal bus, informal bus	Domestic worker, 5 days a week from 7 a.m. to 5 p.m.	54 years old, divorced, 4 children (ages 15, 18, 19, and 28)
Fabiana	April–June 2018	Near Guamani to Cumbaya	Walk, formal bus, informal bus	Contract cleaner, 5 days a week from 6:30 a.m. to 3:30 p.m.	39 years old, widow, 4 children (ages 5, 15, 19, and 24); 1 grandchild
Kim	April–May 2018	Ferroviaria to Cumbaya	Walk, informal taxi, formal bus, informal bus	Contract cleaner, 5 days a week from 6:30 a.m. to 3:30 p.m.	34 years old, married, 3 children

line. However, gender does not always translate into complete commonality. For example, similarities and differences are never fixed between the researcher and the researched. In terms of our own background, being half Ecuadorian and foreigner, and decolonizing our research through a North-South collaboration, there are advantages to being raised in the same culture, although there were differences between the researchers and participants along the lines of social class (Fortier 2000).

Qualitative methods, such as interviews, are also crucial as they generate in-depth understanding of personal experiences on informal transport (Brunskell 2000). Feminist studies argue that interviews "draw on women's (purported) ability to listen, to empathize, and to validate personal experiences as part of the research process" (McDowell 1997, 107). Participant observation, another qualitative method, complements the information gathered through other methods in that the researcher observes the actors, or the group under study, in their natural setting (Fortier 2000). Thus, the researcher accounts for the actions of the participants by making observations of their activities, behaviors, actions, and conversations. During the complete research process, as well as after processing the ethnographic and audio data using NVivo software, we conducted five interviews to triangulate the information obtained from the different methods. In this sense, mobile methods were a useful entry point to gain understanding into the porosity of both the public and private spaces of women's daily mobility on informal transport.

Informed consent demands voluntary participation in a research process, with full knowledge of the purpose of the research, what participation will entail, and how the information will be used. Therefore, with the participants' consent and ensuring confidentiality, participants can also find a means to express themselves. Furthermore, it must be made clear that participants in our study answered only the questions with which they felt comfortable, and they had the option to withdraw at any time if they wished, thus allowing the option of "informed dissent" throughout the process. This understanding also gave the participants greater control over their roles in the process. In the next section we draw on the mobile and feminist methods to highlight the intersections between gender and transport infrastructural networks to emphasize spaces of both insecurity and intimacy.

MOBILE WOMEN CHALLENGING THE INSECURE CITY

The road we studied, with its informal transport services, is the main peripheral freeway, Simon Bolívar, which runs north-south between the nuclear urban core and suburban valleys. We studied this route because it connects the southern periphery of Quito with the elite valley, Cumbaya. During fieldwork from 2016 to 2018, we found that companies that operate on the route are part of an ongoing negotiation for a concession agreement with the municipality. As it stands, the freeway that connects these geographies does not have any public transport option. In what follows we discuss the daily realities of what it is like for women to use this infrastructural service as a means to move around. In this case, we start from the price of the trip and build up to the spaces that they occupy on transport itself. Each interaction contributes to the socio-material configuration of informal transport infrastructure, which is simultaneously presented from a gendered perspective.

The regular price of a trip via an informal bus between the south of Quito and Cumbaya is US$0.75 per trip, which is an economic burden for the participants, who earn the standard minimum wage of $386 per month as contract cleaners and domestic workers. (In contrast, formal transportation costs $0.25 per bus trip.) All our participants criticized the high price in relation to the poor conditions of the trip: "One pays fifty or seventy-five cents, that is, if you are going to be comfortable and relaxed, but not close-fitting against other people. There are people who do not bathe, they smell bad, sometimes they do not open the windows and you suffocate, and one wants to faint. It is horrible to travel so tight, it is like being tied up and squeezed between two people." During the months of the study, there was evidence of gender-based price discrimination. The majority of female participants explained that the *cobradores*, or bus money collectors, forced the women under study to pay $1 a trip (instead of $0.75). They had no option but to pay since there was no alternative transportation from their homes in the south of Quito to Cumbaya (and vice versa). In the words of Lourdes, a divorced woman aged fifty-six, a mother to four grown children, and also a domestic worker in Cumbaya, one has to "pay or get off [the bus]!" Kim, a contract cleaner and mother to three daughters, leaves her house in the Ferroviaria sector before her daughters wake up and then returns home in the evening to prepare dinner for her family. Kim describes that mobile women must bear the economic mistreatment on informal transport because "it is an obligation to take this type of transport, there is no other alternative to take other public transport."

Fabiana, a widowed mother to four children and a contract cleaner for over ten years in the area of Cumbaya, during an interview expressed her anger over the poor conditions and the economic extortions: "On the bus there are insults and many rude people, the passengers fight among themselves, they insult the driver, and the collector, above all the collectors, they are coarser. The *cobradores* sometimes want to collect more. On one occasion I was recording when he came over to charge me for a second time. I told him that I already paid, and he pretended not to remember." Fabiana ended up resolving the manner by talking with the *cobrador*. Such a statement suggests the level of precarity involved in just the daily interactions that are part of the infrastructure itself (Doherty 2017). But on a different occasion, there was an incident of outright scamming. During an interview Lourdes recounted an incident with a fellow female rider that she had also recorded:

> The cobrador stole from the lady [passenger]. She gave him a $10 bill, and since he didn't have change he continued to collect money from the other passengers. Later, he said no, you gave me $1. We all saw that she gave him a $10 bill. We asked the bus driver to stop at the police station [PAI in

Spanish for Puesto de Auxilio Inmediato] but he did not want to, instead he asked the lady to get off in the Ludoteca School [on the Simon Bolivar road, far before her final destination]. She only had $0.25 to get home.

When Lourdes queried the bus driver about why he did not stop at the police station, he replied, "that if it was not for him that they [women] would not work." Rather than ensuring safety, according to the participants, the *chofer*, or bus driver, and *cobradores* perpetuate injustices toward women. Thus, the informal workers who organize and manage the system might be in a hyper-exploited industry, but another element of this configuration is the rider, which carries multiple layers of invisibility that go unaccounted for in the study of infrastructure. These veins of injustices resonate with the work of Ganesh on Indian women titled "Travel as a Rite of Passage" (2017, 146), which explains, "'Going out to work,' that is, being employed outside of the immediate family domain, thus has spatial connotations that substantially define the 'public/private' divide. When the 'outside' is seen as 'male,' women are not as easily allowed as men." In agreement, female presence contested the association of public spaces for men only, and therefore working women's presence was accompanied by violence during their walks, at the bus stops, and while riding informal transport. During the months of the study, three out of the four participants had been victims of different types of violence. In April 2018, for example, Anabela was waiting at the bus stop at Chillogallo at the break of dawn, and in the dark she was a victim of theft by a man who held her at knifepoint. Among her personal belongings and identification, the voice recorder from this study was stolen, and during her interview she recounted another incident that she wanted to share: "On the recorder that you gave me to record I had how they insulted a woman on the bus. A black man starts insulting a woman, and she answers back, and then he wanted to hit the lady and the *cobrador* does nothing, he is supposed to ask the man to get off the bus because he is disrespecting the passengers, but no, he turns a blind eye, as if nothing happened. Here you have to defend yourself!"

Informal transportation is necessary for working women, yet their physical mobility is uncertain given verbal harassment, theft, and assault resulting in physical and economic harm when moving around the city. In another case Kim recounted the incident of theft on the bus on her way home from work:

Well, the day I was robbed someone stole my purse with the money to pay for my weekend nurse course that I am doing. So, I had my purse in

my zipped jacket pocket with my cell phone that my father gave me . . .
so when I got on the bus I took out the purse to pay the ticket, and then
when I got off the bus I checked my pocket and they were not there. I
went back to the bus to tell them [bus driver and the money collector]
that I didn't have my purse and phone. . . . I do not know, I only think of
the person sitting next to me, he took my phone and the purse.

Fabiana also shared an incident of when she was robbed while on the bus:
"On the bus at five thirty in the morning first a black man got on, then at
Quicentro two more, and after the bridge of Guajaló another one. I think the
driver was an accomplice it cannot be a coincidence during the early dark hours
of the morning. One man stood up and went to the front of the bus, another
one in the back, and the others started to steal. They took out a gun, and a
knife, and told me to give them everything that I had."

One of the most serious cases involved an attempted kidnapping. Anabela,
mother to a four-year-old daughter, was in a taxi from Santa Barbara Alto. That
day she was traveling to work with her daughter:

She [female taxi driver] wanted to steal my daughter. Usually when one
talks to the driver, one asks about basic things: about the weather, about
football, things like that, never about family. And the lady [driver] starts
to ask me where I live, my name, how many children I have, my work.
From there I was suspicious, it was not right. She then took me down
another road, and she put a gas that made us sleepy, and my daughter lays
down and says to me, 'Mom, I am not feeling right.' I opened the door and
I threw myself out of the car with my daughter, I threw the money at the
lady, and we ran!

Women's personal safety was at risk and the stress, anxiety, and fear of
moving around the city was echoed by all participants (Valentine 1989). This
emotional insecurity was closely associated with the lack of effective policing.
Inadequate policing was highlighted during various incidents on informal transport. Anabela described the lawlessness as a female passenger: "We pay for a
service, but we do not have the security and support that someone will watch
over us." For example, Anabela reported the robbery to the police, but she never
heard back. The other participants decided not to report the incidents because
of a lack of confidence in the police or out of fear that the bus drivers may
retaliate against them. Women's invisibility before the law was explained by

Anabela: "There is no one to assure us safety, there may be metropolitan police man standing there, but it is as if they were not there, this is no man's land." Across Latin American cities, women are more likely to suffer acts of violent aggression than their male counterparts, and the fear of violence or lack of access to justice can erode women's livelihoods and well-being (Moser 2004).

Women, however, are not passive in the face of violence during their journeys. There is vast evidence of public strategies being developed to address the problem, including the potential for using digital technologies (Chant, Moser, and McIlwaine 2015). Yet, in the illegal or informal context characterized by a lack of effective policies and policing, or absence of the state, women draw on private strategies to cope with violence on public transport. As mentioned above, private embodiment or dress has been observed as a way for women to be protected from public harassment (see Raheja and Gold 1994 in Islamic contexts), and along these lines in Quito, in the dark early mornings, women try to hide their feminine corporeal presence by not carrying a handbag and wearing heavy coats to protect their body, cellular phones, and bus fares. Once in Chillogallo, they avoid dark secluded areas, and women stand close together at the bus stop while they look out for familiar faces to huddle with. Also, when returning home from work, they leave work as early as possible and call one another so as to travel together before dark.

Above all, cordial and reliable bus drivers were scarce, but women quickly established preferences for *choferes*. A trustworthy bus driver, or *chofer de confianza*, was characterized as being punctual, honest, and concerned for the passengers' well-being and safety. Once women were on board with a trustworthy *chofer*, they seemed to experience autonomy in sharing their journey with other fellow female travelers. From the audio material, we reported on women sharing stories about themselves, their families, and their work, and information on the local and national contexts. Women seemed to engage with those they met during their journeys, between their homes and work, whether known women or strangers, and to generate relationships that went beyond neighborhood and family ties. Engaging with fellow female travelers seemed to help reduce the burdens of their long working hours in the home and at the workplace. Each leg of the journey meant that women had leisure time, untied from the surveillance of their families, the constraints of everyday domestic life, and their workplace, as an appealing part of the travel experience. Fabiana, for example, liked to find a seat to rest her legs, chat with a friend, and catch up on her sleep. These intimate practices on the buses seemed to reduce women's fears and anxieties toward "dealing with the outside" (see Sudarshan and

Bhattacharya 2008 on India). Sharing and engaging may not resolve the structural inequalities and insecurity problems, but mobility outside of a person's immediate area helps ease the oppressive practices in a masculine-dominated mobility in the city (Gamble and Dávalos 2019).

CONCLUSION

This chapter examines four women's audio recordings of mobility to give insight into how gender inequality and informality converge in the city, though simultaneously remaining understudied in global urban studies (Peake and Rieker 2013). Women's transport experiences are a critical component to the ways in which infrastructures are built up by people (Simone 2004). Gender, understood as a social construction, is a key element to the production of infrastructural networks (Sabhlok 2017). Gender and mobility practices are considered co-constitutive (Uteng and Cresswell 2012), which is evident when women move into traditionally male-dominated urban and public spaces (Fenster 2005). In the case of Quito, for example, working women's use of infrastructural networks like informal transport highlights these women's appropriation of public spaces, as well as the inequalities that inform male dominance of public spaces. For example, women's presence on transport is answered with violence from men. Women's coping strategies through travel include refraining from traveling alone, wearing appropriate clothing, and ignoring economic, physical, and verbal harassment. While gender violence and women's coping strategies have been examined across the Global South (Chant and McIlwaine 2015), this study found that practices of intimacy among female passengers was critical. Specifically, engaging and sharing private stories generated relations of trust. Thus, intimacy is a key component of infrastructural experiences (Wilson 2015). On informal transport infrastructure, spaces of the private and "public" go beyond women's families and neighborhoods, demonstrating that the boundaries of the dichotomy of spaces are fluid (Drummond 2000). Moreover, the shared moments on informal transport infrastructure challenge the domestic stereotypes of a poor working woman to one of resourcefulness and solidarity (Sudarshan and Bhattacharya 2008). While female sharing practices on transportation are a source of strength, the problem is that women's public needs are being privately resolved by the individual female passengers. Informal transport infrastructure presents serious structural limitations to improving women's mobility, denying them their right to work and to safely access their city (Beebeejaun 2017), which are not necessarily visible when the focus is limited to formal transport infrastructures.

ACKNOWLEDGMENTS

We are thankful to the School of Social Science and Humanities of the Universidad San Francisco de Quito for its support and funding; to Princeton University for offering their library and resources in 2018; and to Wendy Torres for her collaboration during fieldwork as an assistant researcher. We are especially thankful to the brave and resilient women who participated in our research project and who travel daily to provide a better future for their families.

REFERENCES

Agbiboa, D. E., ed. 2018. *Transport, Transgression and Politics in African Cities: The Rhythm of Chaos*. 1st ed. Routledge.

Alfonso, L. M., N. Q. del Pozo, and G. Ramírez. 2016. "Acoso Sexual en Lugares Públicos de Quito: Retos para una 'Ciudad Segura.'" *URVIO—Revista Latinoamericana de Estudios de Seguridad*, no. 19: 21–36. https://doi.org/10.17141/urvio.19.2016.2425.

Allen, H., L. Pereya, L. Sagaris, and G. Cardenas, G. 2017. *Ella Se Mueve Segura—She Moves Safely: A Study on Women's Personal Security and Public Transport in Three Latin American Cities*. Research Series No. 10. FIA Foundation. https://www.fiafoundation.org/media/461162/ella-se-mueve-segura-she-moves-safely.pdf.

Anand, N. 2017. *Hydraulic City: Water and the Infrastructures of Citizenship in Mumbai*. Duke University Press.

Appel, H., Anand, N., and Gupta, A. 2015. "Introduction: The Infrastructure Toolbox." Theorizing the Contemporary, September 24. Society for Cultural Anthropology. https://culanth.org/fieldsights/714-introduction-the-infrastructure-toolbox.

Avritzer, L. 2009. *Democracy and the Public Space in Latin America*. Princeton University Press.

Bayat, A. 2000. "From 'Dangerous Classes' to 'Quiet Rebels': Politics of the Urban Subaltern in the Global South." *International Sociology* 15 (3): 533–57. https://doi.org/10.1177/026858000015003005.

Beebeejaun, Y. 2017. "Gender, Urban Space, and the Right to Everyday Life." *Journal of Urban Affairs* 39 (3): 323–34. https://doi.org/10.1080/07352166.2016.1255526.

Bhasin, K. 1997. "Gender Workshops with Men: Experiences and Reflections." *Gender and Development* 5 (2): 55–61. https://doi.org/10.1080/741922356.

Brunskell, H. 2000. "Feminist Methodology." In *Researching Society and Culture*, edited by C. Seale, 37–47. Sage Publications.

Cervero, R., and A. Golub. 2007. "Informal Transport: A Global Perspective." *Transport Policy* 14 (6): 445–57. https://doi.org/10.1016/j.tranpol.2007.04.011.

Chant, S., and C. McIlwaine. 2015. *Cities, Slums, and Gender in the Global South: Towards a Feminised Urban Future*. Routledge.

Chant, S., C. Moser, and C. McIlwaine. 2015. *Cities, Slums, and Gender in the Global South: Towards a Feminised Urban Future*. Routledge.

Chant, S., C. Pedwell, and International Labor Office. 2008. *Women, Gender and the Informal Economy: An Assessment of ILO Research and Suggested Ways Forward*. Report. http://www.ilo.org/gender/Informationresources/WCMS_091605/lang--en/index.htm.

Dammert, L., and M. F. T. Malone. 2006. "Does It Take a Village? Policing Strategies and Fear of Crime in Latin America." *Latin American Politics and Society* 48 (4): 27–51.

DMQ (Municipality of the Metropolitan District of Quito). 2012. *Plan Metropolitano de Ordenamiento Territorial 2012–2022. Municipio del Distrito Metropolitano de Quito*. http://cite.flacsoandes.edu.ec/media/2016/01/Alcaldia-de-Quito_2012_Plan-metropolitano-de-ordenamiento-territorial-2012-2022.pdf.

DMQ (Municipality of the Metropolitan District of Quito). 2013. "La Movilidad en Quito: Un Proyecto Transformador." *Boletín Estadístico Mensual ICQ*, no. 21: 2.

DMQ (Municipality of the Metropolitan District of Quito). 2014. *Encuesta de Percepción sobre Violencia Sexual contra las Mujeres en el Sistema Trolebús*. Municipality of the Metropolitan District of Quito.

Doherty, J. 2017. "Life (and Limb) in the Fast-Lane: Disposable People as Infrastructure in Kampala's Boda Boda Industry." *Critical African Studies* 9 (2): 192–209. https://doi.org/10.1080/21681392.2017.1317457.

Doshi, S., and M. Ranganathan. 2018. "Towards a Critical Geography of Corruption and Power in Late Capitalism." *Progress in Human Geography* 43 (3). https://doi.org/10.1177/0309132517753070.

Drummond, L. B. W. 2000. "Street Scenes: Practices of Public and Private Space in Urban Vietnam." *Urban Studies* 37 (12): 2377–91. https://doi.org/10.1080/00420980020002850.

Dunckel-Graglia, A. 2013. "Women-Only Transportation: How 'Pink' Public Transportation Changes Public Perception of Women's Mobility." *Journal of Public Transportation* 16 (2). https://doi.org/10.5038/2375-0901.16.2.5.

Evans, J., J. O'Brien, and B. Ch Ng. 2018. "Towards a Geography of Informal Transport: Mobility, Infrastructure, and Urban Sustainability from the Back of a Motorbike." *Transactions of the Institute of British Geographers* 43 (4): 674–88.

Fenster, T. 2005. "The Right to the Gendered City: Different Formations of Belonging in Everyday Life." *Journal of Gender Studies* 14 (3): 217–31. https://doi.org/10.1080/09589230500264109.

Fischer, B., B. McCann, and J. Auyero. 2014. *Cities from Scratch: Poverty and Informality in Urban Latin America*. Duke University Press.

Fluri, J. L. 2017. "The Body Performance and Space." In *Feminist Spaces: Gender and Geography in a Global Context*, edited by A. M. Oberhauser, R. Whitson, J. L. Fluri, and S. Mollett, 25–46. Routledge.

Fortier, A. M. 2000. "Gender, Ethnicity, and Fieldwork: A Case Study." In *Researching Society and Culture*, edited by C. Seale, 48–57. Sage Publications.

Gamble, J., and C. Dávalos. 2019. "Moving with Masculine Care in the City: Informal Transit in Quito, Ecuador." *City* 23 (2): 189–204. https://doi.org/10.1080/13604813.2019.1615796.

Ganesh, L. 2017. "Gendered Mobility: Travel as a Rite of Passage." *Indian Journal of Gender Studies* 24 (2): 145–70. https://doi.org/10.1177/0971521517697877.

Goldstein, D. M. 2016. *Owners of the Sidewalk: Security and Survival in the Informal City*. Duke University Press.

Graham, S., and S. Marvin. 2001. *Splintering Urbanism: Networked Infrastructures, Technological Mobilities and the Urban Condition*. Psychology Press.

Haraway, D. 1988. "Situated Knowledges: The Science Question in Feminism and the Privilege of Partial Perspective." *Feminist Studies* 14 (3): 575–99. https://doi.org/10.2307/3178066.

Hayden, D. 1980. "What Would a Non-Sexist City Be Like? Speculations on Housing, Urban Design, and Human Work." *Signs: Journal of Women in Culture and Society* 5 (S3): S170–S187. https://doi.org/10.1086/495718.

Holston, J. 1991. "The Misrule of Law: Land and Usurpation in Brazil." *Comparative Studies in Society and History* 33 (4): 695–725. https://doi.org/10.2307/179087.

Howard, D., M. Hume, and U. Oslender. 2007. "Violence, Fear, and Development in Latin America: A Critical Overview." *Development in Practice* 17 (6): 713–24.

Jirón, P. A., W. A. Imilan, and L. Iturra. 2016. "Relearning to Travel in Santiago: The Importance of Mobile Place-Making and Travelling Know-How." *Cultural Geographies* 23 (4): 599–614. https://doi.org/10.1177/1474474015622141.

Larkin, B. 2013. "The Politics and Poetics of Infrastructure." *Annual Review of Anthropology* 42 (1): 327–43. https://doi.org/10.1146/annurev-anthro-092412-155522.

Massey, D. 2005. *For Space*. 1st ed. Sage Publications.

McDowell, L. 1997. "Doing Gender: Feminism, Feminists, and Research Methods in Human Geography." In *Space, Gender, Knowledge*, edited by L. McDowell and J. Sharp, 105–14. Arnold.

McFarlane, C., and J. Rutherford. 2008. "Political Infrastructures: Governing and Experiencing the Fabric of the City." *International Journal of Urban and Regional Research* 32 (2): 363–74. https://doi.org/10.1111/j.1468-2427.2008.00792.x.

McIlwaine, C. 2013. "Urbanization and Gender-Based Violence: Exploring the Paradoxes in the Global South." *Environment and Urbanization* 25 (1): 65–79. https://doi.org/10.1177/0956247813477359.

Merriman, P. 2014. "Rethinking Mobile Methods." *Mobilities* 9 (2): 167–87. https://doi.org/10.1080/17450101.2013.784540.

Moser, C. O. N. 2004. "Urban Violence and Insecurity: An Introductory Roadmap." *Environment and Urbanization* 16 (2): 3–16. https://doi.org/10.1177/095624780401600220.

Oberhauser, A. M., J. L. Fluri, R. Whitson, and S. Mollett. 2017. *Feminist Spaces: Gender and Geography in a Global Context*. 1st ed. Routledge.

Parikh, A. 2018. "Politics of Presence: Women's Safety and Respectability at Night in Mumbai, India." *Gender, Place, and Culture* 25 (5): 695–710. https://doi.org/10.1080/0966369X.2017.1400951.

Peake, L., and M. Rieker. 2013. *Interrogating Feminist Understandings of the Urban*. Routledge.

Phadke, S. 2005. "'You Can Be Lonely in a Crowd': The Production of Safety in Mumbai." *Indian Journal of Gender Studies* 12 (1): 41–62. https://doi.org/10.1177/097152150401200102.

Portes, A. 1996. "The Informal Economy: Perspectives from Latin America." In *Exploring the Underground Economy*, edited by Susan Pozo, 147–65. Upjohn Institute for Employment Research. https://doi.org/10.17848/9780880994279.ch7.

Raheja, G. G., and A. G. Gold. 1994. *Listen to the Heron's Words: Reimagining Gender and Kinship in North India*. University of California Press.

Roy, A. 2009. "Why India Cannot Plan Its Cities: Informality, Insurgence and the Idiom of Urbanization." *Planning Theory* 8 (1): 76–87. https://doi.org/10.1177/1473095208099299.

Roy, A., and N. AlSayyad. 2004. *Urban Informality: Transnational Perspectives from the Middle East, Latin America, and South Asia*. Lexington Books.

Sabhlok, A. 2017. "'Main Bhi to Hindostaan Hoon': Gender and Nation-State in India's Border Roads Organisation." *Gender, Place, and Culture* 24 (12): 1711–28. https://doi.org/10.1080/0966369X.2017.1384365.

Sheller, M. 2015. "Racialized Mobility Transitions in Philadelphia: Connecting Urban Sustainability and Transport Justice." *City and Society* 27 (1): 70–91. https://doi.org/10.1111/ciso.12049.

Sheller, M., and J. Urry. 2006. "The New Mobilities Paradigm." *Environment and Planning A: Economy and Space* 38 (2): 207–26. https://doi.org/10.1068/a37268.

Simone, A. M. 2004. "People as Infrastructure: Intersecting Fragments in Johannesburg." *Public Culture* 16 (3): 407–29.

Simone, A. M. 2011. "The Urbanity of Movement: Dynamic Frontiers in Contemporary Africa." *Journal of Planning Education and Research* 31 (4): 379–91. https://doi.org/10.1177/0739456X11416366.

Spinney, J. 2015. "Close Encounters? Mobile Methods, (Post)Phenomenology, and Affect." *Cultural Geographies* 22 (2): 231–46. https://doi.org/10.1177/1474474014558988.

Star, S. L. 1999. "The Ethnography of Infrastructure." *American Behavioral Scientist* 43 (3): 377–91. https://doi.org/10.1177/00027649921955326.

Sudarshan, R. M., and S. Bhattacharya. 2008. *Through the Magnifying Glass: Women's Work and Labour Force Participation in Urban Delhi*. Working paper. http://www.ilo.org/asia/publications/WCMS_098839/lang--en/index.htm.

Uteng, M. T. P., and P. T. Cresswell. 2012. *Gendered Mobilities*. Ashgate Publishing.

Valentine, G. 1989. "The Geography of Women's Fear." *Area* 21 (4): 385–90.

Whitson, R. 2017. "Gendering the Right to the City." In *Feminist Spaces: Gender and Geography in a Global Context*, edited by A. M. Oberhauser, J. L. Fluri, R. Whitson, and S. Mollett, 77–105. Routledge.

Whitzman, C., C. Andrew, and K. Viswanath. 2014. "Partnerships for Women's Safety in the City: 'Four Legs for a Good Table.'" *Environment and Urbanization* 26 (2): 443–56. https://doi.org/10.1177/0956247814537580.

Wilson, A. 2015. "The Infrastructure of Intimacy." *Signs: Journal of Women in Culture and Society* 41 (2): 247–80. https://doi.org/10.1086/682919.

CHAPTER 8

"DIRTY PHONE": INFRASTRUCTURES OF VIOLENCE AGAINST WOMEN IN URBAN KERALA

Nabeela Ahmed and Ayona Datta

I don't know anything about mobiles. The small one—you saw it right?—that dirty one, is mine. Sometimes even I feel like breaking it apart when one can't hear what is being said. I go mad.

> —Shalini, a woman in her late fifties, a grandmother living in Thiruvananthapuram

Phones are being misused. The boys are using phones to view sex. They watch it and get wrong ideas. Under the influence of drugs, they do not even spare young girls. That needs to be stopped somehow.

> —Swati, married woman in her twenties, an Ayurvedic therapist living in Thiruvanthapuram

The women quoted above both reside in a low-income neighborhood, known as NTL Colony,[1] located in the periphery of the city of Thiruvananthapuram in Kerala, southern India. These are two very different narratives of the mobile phone—one in which the mobile phone is an object of frustration because of its technological limitations, and the other in which the mobile phone becomes a tool of "moral corruption" for men seen as a cause of violence against women. The diverse associations that women make with the mobile phone are complex and ambiguous and span across social, cultural, political, and technological contexts. The mobile phone as an infrastructure of information is far from neutral; it is a political technology vested with gendered capacities of violence. Everyday violence against women is mediated and enacted through the use, nonuse, and misuse of the mobile phone and its technologies. The lack of access to functioning telecommunications—exemplified by Shalini's "dirty" phone—itself inspires a violent reaction, evoking Star's claim that infrastructures become visible (and obstructive) when they become broken and exclusionary (1999).

In this chapter, we take on an expanded notion of the mobile phone as a relational, intersectional, and social infrastructure (Star 1999; Simone 2004), constituting and constituted by gender-based relations of power and violence. Developing Rodgers and O'Neill's conceptualization of infrastructural violence as continuous "processes of marginalization, discrimination and exclusion" through and sustained by infrastructure (2012, 401), we focus on the mobile phone as a political technology of violence. This violence is undeniably infrastructural in that a lack of access to mobile phones can deny women access to crucial means of communication, knowledge, and information about living and thriving in the city. While information and communications infrastructures have given greater agency to women and marginal groups, barriers to the meaningful use of and access to mobile technologies and information remain, which overlap with ongoing restrictions on women's bodies and mobility due to disconnected and absent physical infrastructures. Women face all forms of physical and sexual violence during access to and use of water, toilets, telecommunications, public transport, energy sources, and walkways (Datta 2016). But we conceptualize violence beyond a mere lack, arguing that the phone can channel other social, symbolic, and cultural forms of violence, furthered through access to (mis)information. Scholarship in this area (Gurumurthy and Chami 2014; O'Neill 2003) shows that phone ownership is not necessarily a pathway to empowerment; rather it is the capacity to reflect on information and develop critical consciousness that has transformative potential. Women, particularly in low-income neighborhoods, are often confined to the "premium networked spaces" (S. Graham and Marvin 2001) of mobile apps pushed through smartphones, while being unaware of services and schemes available through internet browsers. This extends debates in feminist critical geography that critique binary constructions of gender-based violence as intimate/structural, public/domestic, political/private, spectacular/everyday (Katz 2006; Brickell 2008; Datta 2012; Pain 2014). In this way we move beyond mere claims of "blurring" the "boundaries between the body and the city" (Gandy 2005, 33) to examine the mobile phone as a continuum between the physical (and digital and social) terrain of the body and the spaces that service its everyday corporeal needs.

Focusing on the mobile phone as an information infrastructure and a political technology of gender-based violence engages with the "digital turn" in human geography (Ash, Kitchin, and Leszczynski 2018) through a gendered intersectional lens. Although there is now a rich scholarship on other aspects of urban infrastructure, such as water, sanitation, energy, and electricity, there is little understanding of the digital as another form of infrastructure that is increasingly shaping gendered experiences of the city. Drawing from a two-year project in a low-income slum resettlement colony in Thiruvananthapuram, Kerala, we argue that despite the "quotidian" (Ash, Kitchin, and Leszczynski 2018) spread of mobile phones in the lives of women in low-income urban neighborhoods, significant divides still persist across gender (Datta 2020; Thi Hoan, Chib, and Mahalingam 2016), generation (Rangaswamy 2013), caste (Kamath 2018), religion (Sarkar 2016), and class (Gilbert 2010). In mapping available digital infrastructures and testing mobile applications and software to understand their relationship to women's safety in the city, we found that access, empowerment, connectivity, and understanding among women in low-income communities is largely neglected in policy, despite new investments and projects encouraging smart cities and municipal digitalization of citizen services. While mobile phones and data connectivity can offer pathways to information that help women navigate cities safely—either through GPS mapping or through instant access to emergency services and helplines and other forms of specific safety applications—the same phones can also be weaponized as tools of violence against women across digital and material spaces in the home, neighborhood, and city. This chapter then offers a small intervention in thinking through the simultaneously transformative potential and debilitating violence of the dirty, messy, and indispensable mobile phone in the lives of women in low-income neighborhoods of Indian cities.

BEYOND THE DIGITAL DIVIDE

The digital divide in India, as with other postcolonial contexts, denotes the "uneven geographies of underlying infrastructures" (Ash, Kitchin, and Leszczynski 2018, 30). Despite a widespread digital and information revolution, it remains fragmented and dispersed and overlaps closely with socioeconomic disadvantages. In addition to infrastructural disconnections in terms of signal towers and broadband availability and the availability of only low-tech, low-cost phones to women in low-income settlements, economic barriers and gender norms and subjectivities deepen uneven access and usage to digital technologies, even within cities and among women, furthering divisions of class, caste, generation, and religion. The literature on gendered digital divides (Chary 2010; Gurumurthy, Chami, and Thomas 2016; Rao 2005) primarily focuses on developmental outcomes and economic impacts but attends less to the ways in which women actually *use* and consider mobile phones, their symbolic and cultural associations with phones, and how mobile phones impact their daily experiences with violence in all its forms.

Urban studies is only now addressing the complex infrastructural issues that relate to digital access and exclusions, distinguishing between the systems elements of the internet as an infrastructure characterized by "ubiquity, reliability, invisibility, gateways, and breakdown" (Plantin et al. 2018) and the content elements of internet as media platforms, focusing on software devices and environments in relation to programmability, access and logics of data, and user interfaces (Kitchin 2014; Kitchin, Lauriault, and McArdle 2015; Longley 1998; Luque-Ayala and Neves Maia 2018; Warf 2018). Finally, we seek to extend the elision of public/private binaries regarding violence against women (Katz 2006; Brickell 2008; Datta 2012) in the digital terrain, reconciling the discursive break between offline and online spheres (Willems 2019) and top-down urban (infra)structural violence of digital disconnection from urban resources and rights, and multiple forms of intimate violence enabled through mobile phones.

Seeing the digital as a form of infrastructure, in our expanded relational and gendered notion, can enable a relational understanding of infrastructures—an invisible and sometimes immaterial infrastructure, where ruptures wield material as well as social impacts (Star 1999; Sandvig 2013). Thus, digital biases in the city can be shaped both by material and social infrastructures, as well as by the content carried by digital mediums (M. Graham et al. 2014). Beyond barriers to communication itself, as articulated by Shalini at the outset of this chapter, access to everyday digital hardware (mobile phone devices) is linked with access to digital software (that is, social media, apps that navigate the city or alert emergency services, e-governance, or employment services). The development literatures represent such barriers to access as inhibiting factors in gendered capabilities to exercise agency and choice (Kleine 2011; Poveda and Roberts 2018).

The heralding of top-down technology *as* intrinsic development and feminist empowerment narratives can be problematic in their normative trappings (Gajjala 2003); these narratives are often aligned with market-based rather than social and distributional interests (M. Graham 2011). The digital turn in urbanization in postcolonial contexts—such as the "smart city" trend—has evolved to center around neoliberal agendas that reintroduce coloniality and reinforce existing intersectional divides and fragmented access to infrastructures

(Datta 2015). Engaging with the digital divide—as with access to other forms of infrastructures—can also demarcate the boundaries of urban citizenship hierarchies and concomitant rights (Lemanski 2019; Datta 2018).

Mobile phones are marked by ambivalence—they are seen as an important medium for communication and social ties yet are also identified as attributes of violence against women and other social ills. In India's post-Nirbhaya era, a gendered right to the city has, at least superficially, been incorporated into urban infrastructure policy and thinking (Datta and Thomas 2021; Viswanath and Basu 2015). A nationwide Safe City program was launched in 2017, after the UN Safe Cities and Safe Public Spaces project was piloted in New Delhi in 2013 in the immediate aftermath of the Delhi Nirbhaya case, aiming to increase female representation in the police (an example in Kerala is the Pink Police initiative), CCTV surveillance, and infrastructure development such as the improvement of street lighting (IANS 2017). However, the focus remains narrowly on security and surveillance rather than a substantive approach to addressing the lived realities of how women access, navigate, and experience public infrastructures—and how safety is "dynamically produced through space and negotiated in tandem with other people" (Beebeejaun 2018). Patriarchal norms around notions of safety can restrict and perpetuate "forbidden spaces" and times of the day in which women can be mobile in the city (Fenster 2005) and these norms still determine contemporary and digitalized approaches to developing "smart safe cities."

Going beyond the developmental rationale for overcoming the digital divide paradigm, feminist digital geographers have redirected focus toward the patriarchal impetus of digital infrastructures, highlighting the masculinist positioning "encoded" into the very design of digital devices and software apps (Leszczynski and Elwood 2015). Gendered politics are embedded within digital modes of collecting spatial data and enabling privacy, privileging "masculinist ways of knowing and seeing." The gendering of digital spaces has been largely confined to reinforcing gendered norms and praxis such as care networks and waged labor (Elwood and Leszczynski 2018).

The divide is more entrenched, however, when it comes to modes of agency in overcoming the structural violence embodied by other forms of urban infra-structures. Many of the women residing in NTL Colony, across all age groups, are politically active, routinely vocalizing their grievances regarding broken urban infrastructures such as inadequate sanitation and waste management systems—the burden of which is faced explicitly by women—in civic fora such as the SEWA women's group, and through political party platforms. However, these "analog" forms of civic agency seem redundant—for example, drainage systems are blocked for entire generations, despite promises from electioneering officials and demands made of the municipality. The scope of protest and community mobilization is restricted to offline/material spaces, and many of the women are unaware of online platforms for public grievances, or do not use social media platforms for infrastructural activism. Despite clear manifestations of political activism—denoted by banners, posters, and signs proudly placed within and in front of individual households—and civil society activity, this consciousness is comparatively muted in terms of addressing public and private violence.

THIRUVANANTHAPURAM'S INFRASTRUCTURAL MARGINS

Kerala was the first state in India to declare internet access as a basic human right in 2017. While the state's internet coverage is among the highest in India—including 62 percent smartphone penetration (Ummer et al. 2021), a gender gap persists (Barboni et al. 2018), particularly in low-income neighborhoods.

The Kerala state government has spearheaded "digital inclusion" through top-down interventions in infrastructure, such as the Kerala Fibre Optic Network, which seeks to provide free Wi-Fi access to all below-poverty-line households, but with little attention on their gendered and socioeconomic impacts (Government of Kerala 2022). The state has overseen a proliferation of IT parks, investing in the upgrade of existing IT parks, including Technopark in Thiruvananthapuram. However, these sites have also attracted media attention for incidents and risks of violence against women for women employees, already marginalized in such masculinized sectors,[2] further highlighting the depth of the gendered divide, embedded in the engineering and design stages through to the top-down implementation of digital inclusion programs.

The Thiruvananthapuram Smart City Mission (SCM) was in its introductory phase at the time of our project in 2018. The proposal states its commitment to improvements in basic infrastructure (drainage, water supply, solid waste, public toilets), mobility, connectivity, and ease of navigating the city. Of particular relevance to our project are themes of safety in the city, gender inclusion, and disconnected infrastructures, including digital infrastructure; the proposal recognizes the need for "Providing safe and comfortable transportation for people of all ages and abilities" and "improving street-scapes by incorporating better lighting. Improving mobility and connectivity through actions that will contribute to a safe, accessible and convenient transportation network."[3] Significantly, the Thiruvananthapuram SCM proposal also recognizes the digital divide at large and how access to technology is crucial to enable inclusion in the smart city. The proposal also recognizes how the digital divide and lack of capacity can potentially affect governance infrastructures and includes provisions for training, capacity building, and awareness of digital infrastructure for SCM staff and implementing agencies. The mayor of Thiruvananthapuram says, "Our primary objective is to make this a woman friendly city."[4] The Thiruvananthapuram SCM converges with other key national and regional urban policies to envision a connected city where digital technology is harnessed to improve, speed up, and enable access to infrastructure. Yet simultaneously, an inherent (dis)connectedness of underlying basic infrastructure that could bring visions for a smart and safe city to life. The Safe City approach assumes that safety is a law-and-order issue and that it can be "fixed" through the increased monitoring, control, and surveillance of city spaces (Datta 2020).

The settlement we focused on forms part of this mobile and infrastructural margins in Thiruvananthapuram. The fieldwork was conducted in NTL Colony, a resettlement colony within a ward located south of the city center of Thiruvananthapuram, the capital of Kerala. NTL Colony consists of approximately 325 households—a combination of *pukka*, semi-*pukka*, and *kacha*[5] houses predominantly owned or occupied by Hindu households (the neighborhood is located next to a significant temple) and a small minority of Christian households. While there is little in the way of available official documentation regarding its origins, according to local stakeholders and resident interviews, we established that the neighborhood originated in the 1970s as a resettlement colony for Dalits developed by the municipal government. However, over time, new households belonging to different, historically more privileged caste groups, have encroached on the settlement. In terms of physical infrastructure, the original colony lacked built houses, providing only unserviced plots with no private household connections to urban basic services: water, sewage, sanitation, or energy. After three decades, households in the colony still have varying access to private piped water, or public water taps and pumps.

We conducted ethnographic fieldwork as part of a broader multiscalar and multimethod project. In addition to stakeholder interviews (with state government officials, urban planners, local advocacy groups) and visual data collected via GPS software, we conducted a series of transect walks, participatory mapping exercises, digital training sessions, and in-depth interviews with sixteen women across diverse age groups (twenties through to sixties) over four months in 2018. These women were engaged in unwaged and/or waged labor; most were married, but some were also separated, divorced, or widowed. This research was supported by a local partner NGO, a well-established feminist advocacy group based in Thiruvananthapuram, as well as a Delhi-based NGO focusing specifically on safe cities for women.

INTIMATE DIGITAL INFRASTRUCTURES OF VIOLENCE

For women in NTL Colony, mobile phone devices are a primary means of access to communications and online spaces. This access is limited in terms of both gender and generation within households that possess mobile phone devices, as shown in table 8.1. This sample data aligns with the broader context of the gendered digital divide in India—in the absence of reliable gender-disaggregated data on internet usage, estimates suggest the ratio of male to female internet users is 75:25 in rural areas, while it is 60:40 in urban areas (Jain 2017, as cited in Gurumurthy and Chami 2018). Sixty-five percent of the female adult population possessed mobile phones, versus 84 percent of men, and when it comes to mobile internet usage, the gender gap is even wider, with 26 percent of men using mobile internet versus 8 percent of women (Rowntree 2018).

Table 8.1. Mobile phone ownership among women in NTL Colony

Type of mobile device in the household	Percentage
Smart phones (3G and 4G)	37.5
Feature phone (basic handset)	50
None	12.5

Source: Neighborhood study based on sample of 16 households

Variations among household access to mobile and smartphones are not necessarily linked to incomes, but rather to generational composition. Households with youth (teenage and young adult) members were more likely to use mobile internet and/or smartphones than those without. The use of smartphones was typically associated with male members of the household, particularly younger male members. Older women also showed a lack of awareness regarding the potential role of mobile phones in enabling civic engagement, grievance redressal, or safety against violence against women in cities. While they expressed a need to access smartphones for online and telecommunications on the one hand, on the other hand they shared a keen sense of the risks associated with the fact that mobile phones are prominently used by men. The women of NTL Colony routinely cited smartphones as a source of violent gendered behaviors that extends across both intimate and public spaces and infrastructures. "There are so many problems with mobiles, but some good things also. I have read in the paper, that it is because of chatting on mobile, [youth] fall in love and then get pregnant and so on. I read a lot about it. It's bad. It shouldn't be in excess, use as much as it is needed. . . . It can also be useful. If something happens to a woman, you can call from anywhere and inform the family or the police" (Mary, early thirties, canteen staff). The ambivalence regarding mobile phones is represented here. Mary reveals the influence of analog (print) media on her subjectivities regarding the immoral influence of mobile phones though empirically it has been of use to her in terms of communication and mobility within the city. The impact of social norms and offline spaces of information on shaping attitudes toward mobile phone technology among women in low-income neighborhoods highlights factors in addition to literacy, capacity, and material access in connecting digital infrastructures with excluded groups.

Understanding of digital infrastructures among the older women (age thirty and above) are linked with fears, taboos, and suspicion toward mobile phones and broadband internet, enabling an extension of bodily and other forms of violence against women through immaterial yet more widespread infrastructural capacities. While education, entertainment, communication, and maintaining social networks were all listed as "positive" functions of mobile phones—and internet connections—many of the working adult women lacked access to smartphones at all or within their households. The role of mobile phones and CCTV surveillance in ensuring safety against violence against women was not seen as relevant by any of the women. "There is an increase of incidents every five minutes, an incident every hour. It's not decreasing. No matter what laws you bring or how many CCTVs you install, this is not decreasing" (Veena, early twenties, canteen staff). The normalization of continuous crimes against women and the redundancy of "security" infrastructure, according to the community in NTL Colony, is encapsulated here. "Smart" physical infrastructures can only go so far in monitoring and ensuring safety in the city. The alarmist impressions of the rate and frequency of crimes of violence against women in public space from one interviewee belie a casual, offhand tone, characteristic of many of the references to public violence against women—normalized in the city among the neighborhood women. Smart city interventions that foreground the smartphone as a solution are also seen as fallible and thus indicative of deeply embedded barriers to accessing and understanding digital infrastructures among women in low-income communities. The older generation of women in NTL Colony see mobile phones themselves as driver of violence against women—describing how intimate relations and geographies are recalibrated (and corrupted) by digital technology. "In fact it is after the camera phone that women are subject to more [violence] isn't it? People take photos, it is because it is seen as sexual, through social media, and things like that. After the arrival of the camera phone, women are not secure. Earlier women would bathe near river—now they wouldn't, they are scared it will come on Whatsapp" (Revathi, woman in her forties). Intimate spaces—such as those used for bathing in the absence of connected sanitation infrastructures—are made further unsafe through the gendered use of digital technology. The subjectivities shift according to intersections of age, class, region (urban/rural), and caste, in addition to gender and social attitudes, fears, and taboos. While education, entertainment, communication, and maintaining social networks were all listed as "positive" functions of mobile phones, many of the working adult women lacked access to smartphones at all or within their households. Men, on the other hand, often used mobile phones in public places to constantly violate the women's intimate personal spaces. "When the woman was leaving the bus, the man took a video of the woman on her mobile, of her backside while she was walking towards the exit" (Anu, early twenties, training to be a beautician). The violation of intimate space is embodied here not only through unsafe public transport (the Kerala state bus) but further enabled through the medium of digital and surveillance technologies. Returning to Swathi's description earlier of the nefarious influence of mobile phones on young men and the link between technology and immorality, typified in representations of pornography, reveals a confluence of paternalistic top-down restrictions (Gurumurthy and Chami 2018) and pervasive norms that define moral transgressions. The prevalence of pornography on digital devices echoes in the narratives shared by most of the women in NTL Colony. According to Swathi, the online content directly informs the offline behaviors, further fueled by substance abuse (framed here as immoral rather than a health hazard or social disenfranchisement). The co-constitutive role of both offline and online spaces (Willems 2019) in shaping violence against women further elides the boundaries of public/intimate forms and spaces of gendered violence.

Public spaces across the city at large and within the neighborhood of NTL Colony were frequently mapped as "unsafe" areas for women, due to the male occupancy of such spaces at particular times of the day. Such spaces become pronounced after dark as the site of alcohol and substance abuse, mobile phones are often used for entertainment, and both behaviors are cited as drivers of public forms of violence against women, ranging from harassment to bodily violence, as well as domestic abuse when women return home in the evening. Thus "outside" infrastructures, such as the social infrastructure of public spaces and transport infrastructures of public buses, are rendered intimate through the spatialized and temporal narratives of fear.

CONCLUSIONS

Much of recent research on addressing violence against women through digital technology suggests that mobile phones are not a silver bullet solution. Our aim in this chapter has been to add to that argument by showing how women's experiences and perceptions of the mobile phone are relative to the location of the mobile phone between physical and social infrastructures. This means that we cannot understand gendered use of the mobile phone through a reductive binary lens of solution/problem, but rather as a social technology that reinforces as well as challenges existing structural and gendered inequalities within the context of women's lives. Reflecting upon the "dirty phone" in the title of this chapter, we argue that the mobile phone is more than just digital infrastructure or handheld technology—it is tied to a network of social and cultural geographies that lend significance to its use and misuse among men and women.

The mobile phone maps and encodes a moral geography of both fear and safety among women. Their narratives in this chapter highlight how digital, material, and social infrastructures intersect to extend and embody violence against women. Importantly, the narratives and everyday experiences of women in low-income neighborhoods further complicate digital divide paradigms by broadening the scope of exclusionary metrics to include affect and agency, subjectivities and corporeality, knowing and unknowing, and use and misuse of digital infrastructures. Incredibly, then, the mobile phone is also an "intimate infrastructure" (Datta and Ahmed 2020) of fear and violence across public and private spaces in the hands of men directed toward women.

The discursive and developmental norms regarding the urban digital divide in terms of access and gender empowerment, as well as much celebrated movements such as Smart Cities Mission in India and advancing digital inclusion in Thiruvananthapuram, are starkly in contrast with our findings around the infrastructures of violence within which the mobile phone is located. While the mobile phone is largely celebrated in policy and governance, it is a far more political and moral instrument of technology, particularly among women in lower-income neighborhoods. Any policy on digital infrastructure or smart city governance that does not take into account the contested and ambivalent ways that the phone is used and perceived as a gendered technology will be unable to respond to the challenges faced by these women in public and private spaces, as well across a diversity of physical and social infrastructures.

ACKNOWLEDGMENTS

This paper has been facilitated by funding from the British Academy GCRF Cities and Infrastructure Programme (PI ref: CI170047). We are grateful to the participants for sharing their time and experiences with us, to Susan Sukanya for local research assistance, as well as to partners Safetipin and Sakhi for their collaboration and fieldwork support.

NOTES

1. Name changed.
2. From: http://www.technoparktoday.com/stop-violence-women-technopark-signature-campaign.
3. See Thiruvananthapuram Indian Smart Cities Mission application report: http://smart cities.gov.in/upload/uploadfiles/files/KL%2002%20%20TVM%20-%20%20MAIN%20 REPORT.pdf.
4. See Thiruvananthapuram Indian Smart Cities Mission application report.
5. *pukka* = permanent; semi-*pukka* = semi-permanent; *kacha* = temporary, referring usually to informal housing.

REFERENCES

Ash, James, Rob Kitchin, and Agnieszka Leszczynski. 2018. "Digital Turn, Digital Geographies?" *Progress in Human Geography* 42 (1): 25–43.

Barboni, G., E. Field, R. Pande, N. Rigol, S. Schaner, and C. T. Moore. 2018. "A Tough Call: Understanding Barriers to and Impacts of Women's Mobile Phone Adoption in India." Harvard Kenney School Policy Report: Evidence for Policy Design. October.

Beebeejaun, Y. 2017. "Gender, Urban Space, and the Right to Everyday Life." *Journal of Urban Affairs* 39 (3): 323–34, https://doi.org/10.1080/07352166.2016.1255526.

Brickell, K. 2008. "'Fire in the House': Gendered Experiences of Drunkenness and Violence in Siem Reap, Cambodia." *Geoforum* 39(5): 1667–75. https://doi.org/10.1016/j.geo forum.2008.04.002.

Chary, Meena. 2010. "Social Equity, the Digital Divide and E-Governance: An Analysis of e-Governance Initiatives in India." In *E-Government Website Development: Future Trends and Strategic Models: Future Trends and Strategic Models*, edited by Ed Downey, Carl D. Ekstrom, and Matthew A. Jones, 87–147. IGI Global.

Datta, Ayona. 2012. *The Illegal City: Space, Law and Gender in a Delhi Squatter Settlement*. Routledge.

Datta, Ayona. 2015. "A 100 Smart Cities, a 100 Utopias." *Dialogues in Human Geography* 5 (1): 49–53.

Datta, Ayona. 2016. "Another Rape? The Persistence of Public/Private Divides in Sexual Violence Debates in India." *Dialogues in Human Geography* 6 (2): 173–77.

Datta, Ayona. 2018. "The Digital Turn in Postcolonial Urbanism: Smart Citizenship in the Making of India's 100 Smart Cities." *Transactions of the Institute of British Geographers* 43 (3): 405–19.

Datta, Ayona. 2020. "The 'Smart Safe City': Gendered Time, Speed, and Violence in the Margins of India's Urban Age." *Annals of the American Association of Geographers* 110 (5): 1318–34.

Datta, Ayona, and Nabeela Ahmed. 2020. "Intimate Infrastructures: The Rubrics of Gendered Safety and Urban Violence in Kerala, India." *Geoforum* 110: 67–76.

Datta, Ayona, and Arya Thomas. 2021. "Curating #AanaJaana [#ComingGoing]: Gendered Authorship in the 'Contact Zone' of Delhi's Digital and Urban Margins." *Cultural Geographies* 29 (2): 233–52.

Elwood, Sarah, and Agnieszka Leszczynski. 2018. "Feminist Digital Geographies." *Gender, Place, and Culture* 25 (5): 629–44.

Fenster, T. 2005. "The Right to the Gendered City: Different Formations of Belonging in Everyday Life." *Journal of Gender Studies* 14 (3): 217–31, https://doi.org/10.1080/09589230500264109.

Gajjala, Radhika. 2003. "South Asian Digital Diasporas and Cyberfeminist Webs: Negotiating Globalization, Nation, Gender and Information Technology Design." *Contemporary South Asia* 12 (1): 41–56.

Gandy, M. 2005. "Cyborg Urbanization: Complexity and Monstrosity in the Contemporary City." *International Journal of Urban and Regional Research* 29: 26–49. https://doi.org/10.1111/j.1468-2427.2005.00568.x.

Gilbert, Melissa. 2010. "Theorizing Digital and Urban Inequalities." *Information, Communication & Society* 13 (7): 1000–1018.

Government of Kerala. 2022. "Internet—a Basic Right." https://kfon.kerala.gov.in.

Graham, Mark. 2011. "Time Machines and Virtual Portals: The Spatialities of the Digital Divide." *Progress in Development Studies* 11 (3): 211–27.

Graham, Mark, Bernie Hogan, Ralph K. Straumann, and Ahmed Medhat. 2014. "Uneven Geographies of User-Generated Information: Patterns of Increasing Informational Poverty." *Annals of the Association of American Geographers* 104 (4): 746–64.

Graham, Stephen, and Simon Marvin. 2001. *Splintering Urbanism: Networked Infrastructures, Technological Mobilities*. Routledge.

Gurumurthy, Anita, and Nandini Chami. 2014. *Digital Technologies and Gender Justice in India—An Analysis of Key Policy and Programming Concerns*. IT for Change. August 9. http://www.itforchange.net/sites/default/files/IT%20for%20Change%20-%20HLPC%20Submission%20-%2016%20April%202014-1.pdf.

Gurumurthy, Anita, and Nandini Chami. 2018. "Digital India through a Gender Lens." IT for Change and the Heinrich Böll Foundation, https://in.boell.org/sites/default/files/digital_india_through_a_gender_lens.pdf.

Gurumurthy, Anita, Nandini Chami, and Sanjana Thomas. 2016. "Unpacking Digital India: A Feminist Commentary on Policy Agendas in the Digital Moment." *Journal of Information Policy* 6: 371–402.

IANS. 2017. "Safe City Plans for Women in Eight Metropolitan Cities Initiated—The Financial Express." *Financial Express*, July 26. https://www.financialexpress.com/india-news/safe-city-plans-for-women-in-eight-metropolitan-cities-initiated/943981.

Jain, S. 2017. "Rural India to Drive Next Phase of Growth in Internet Usage: IMAI-IMRB Report." VC Circle, March 2. https://www.vccircle.com/rural-india-drive-next-phase-growth-internet-usage-imai-imrb-report.

Kamath, Anant. 2018. "'Untouchable' Cellphones? Old Caste Exclusions and New Digital Divides in Peri-Urban Bangalore." *Critical Asian Studies* 50 (3): 375–94.

Katz, C. 2006. "Power, Space, and Terror: Social Reproduction and the Public Environment." In *The Politics of Public Space*, edited by S. Low and N. Smith, 105–21. Routledge.

Kitchin, Rob. 2014. *The Data Revolution: Big Data, Open Data, Data Infrastructures, and Their Consequences*. Sage.

Kitchin, Rob, Tracey P. Lauriault, and Gavin McArdle. 2015. "Knowing and Governing Cities through Urban Indicators, City Benchmarking, and Real-Time Dashboards." *Regional Studies, Regional Science* 2 (1): 6–28.

Kleine, Dorothea. 2011. "The Capability Approach and the 'Medium of Choice': Steps towards Conceptualising Information and Communication Technologies for Development." *Ethics and Information Technology* 13 (2): 119–30.

Lemanski, C. 2020. "Infrastructural Citizenship: The Everyday Citizenships of Adapting and/or Destroying Public Infrastructure in Cape Town, South Africa." *Transactions of the Institute of British Geographers* 45 (3): 589–605.

Leszczynski, Agnieszka, and Sarah Elwood. 2015. "Feminist Geographies of New Spatial Media." *Canadian Geographer* 59 (1): 12–28.

Longley, P A. 1998. "GIS and the Development of Digital Urban Infrastructure." *Environment and Planning B: Planning and Design* 25 (7): 53–56.

Luque-Ayala, Andrés, and Flávia Neves Maia. 2018. "Digital Territories: Google Maps as a Political Technique in the Re-Making of Urban Informality." *Environment and Planning D: Society and Space* 37 (3): 449–67.

O'Neill, Peter D. 2003. "The 'Poor Man's Mobile Telephone': Access versus Possession to Control the Information Gap in India." *Contemporary South Asia* 12 (1): 85–102.

Pain, R. 2014. "Everyday Terrorism: Connecting Domestic Violence and Global Terrorism." *Progress in Human Geography* 38 (4): 531–50. https://doi-org.hallam.idm.oclc.org/10.1177/0309132513512231.

Plantin, Jean-Christophe, Carl Lagoze, Paul N. Edwards, and Christian Sandvig. 2018. "Infrastructure Studies Meet Platform Studies in the Age of Google and Facebook." *New Media and Society* 20 (1): 293–310.

Poveda, Sammia, and Tony Roberts. 2018. "Critical Agency and Development: Applying Freire and Sen to ICT4D in Zambia and Brazil." *Information Technology for Development* 24 (1): 1–19.

Rangaswamy, Nimmi. 2013. "Digital Life of the Youth in India—What Is the Current Scenario and Where Are We Headed?" *Digital Equality* (blog). https://digitalequality.in/internet-magic-in-indian-slums.

Rao, Siriginidi Subba. 2005. "Bridging Digital Divide: Efforts in India." *Telematics and Informatics* 22 (4): 361–75.

Rodgers, Dennis, and Bruce O'Neill. 2012. "Introduction: Infrastructural Violence: Introduction to the Special Issue." *Ethnography* 13 (4): 401–12. http://www.jstor.org/stable/43497506.

Rowntree, O. 2018. "Connected Women: The Mobile Gender Gap Report." Global Systems for Mobile Communications Association and UK Department for International Development. https://www.gsma.com/mobilefordevelopment/wp-content/uploads/2018/04/GSMA_The_Mobile_Gender_Gap_Report_2018_32pp_WEBv7.pdf.

Sandvig, Christian. 2013. "The Internet as Infrastructure." In *The Oxford Handbook of Internet Studies*, edited by William H. Dutton, 86–106. Oxford University Press.

Sarkar, Sreela. 2016. "Beyond the 'Digital Divide': The 'Computer Girls' of Seelampur." *Feminist Media Studies* 16 (6): 968–83.

Simone, A. M. 2004. "People as Infrastructure: Intersecting Fragments in Johannesburg." *Public Culture* 16 (3): 407–29. https://muse.jhu.edu/article/173743.

Star, Susan Leigh. 1999. "The Ethnography of Infrastructure." *American Behavioral Scientist* 43 (3): 377–91.

Thi Hoan, Nguyen, Arul Chib, and Ram Mahalingam. 2016. "Mobile Phones and Gender Empowerment: Enactment of 'Restricted Agency.'" In *ICTD '16: Proceedings of the 8th International Conference on Information and Communication Technologies and Development*, 1–10. Association for Computing Machinery.

Ummer, Osama, Kerry Scott, Diwaker Mohan, Arpita Chakraborty, and Amnesty Elizabeth LeFevre. 2021. "Connecting the Dots: Kerala's Use of Digital Technology during the COVID-19 Response." *British Medical Journal: Global Health* 6: e005355.

Viswanath, K., and A. Basu. 2015. "SafetiPin: An Innovative Mobile App to Collect Data on Women's Safety in Indian Cities." *Gender and Development* 23 (1): 45–60, https://doi.org /10.1080/13552074.2015.1013669.

Warf, Barney. 2018. "Digital Technologies and Reconfiguration of Urban Space." In *The Routledge Handbook on Spaces of Urban Politics*. Routledge.

Willems, Wendy. 2019. "'The Politics of Things': Digital Media, Urban Space, and the Materiality of Publics." *Media, Culture & Society*: 016344371983159.

INFRASTRUCTURE OF RECYCLABLE WASTE AS ASSEMBLAGES: FROM SCAVENGERS ON THE GROUND TO RECYCLING WORKERS IN COLLECTIVES

Margarida Queirós, Antonio Cezar Leal, Fernanda Regina Fuzzi, and Mário Vale

INTRODUCTION

In Brazil, recyclable waste scavengers, waste pickers, or waste collectors informally collect, transport, separate, pack, negotiate, and sell those materials to intermediaries or to recycling centers for processing and resale for further use in the manufacturing sector (Rutkowski and Rutkowski 2015). Today in Brazil they are commonly known as *catador de lixo*. Waste is produced, then picked by this informal sector and goes again into the commodity chains in its production process and later reuse. In most of the cases, these activities are traditionally fulfilled in dump sites or collected directly from waste bins.

Recent studies identify around 400,000–600,000 *catador de lixo* in big and small cities around Brazil (Paiva 2016; www.mma.gov.br). According to Paiva (2016), the majority of these are informal/autonomous pickers in dump sites selling the recyclable waste they collect each day to intermediaries known as scrap dealers (*sucateiros* or *atravessadores*), and only around 10 percent are organized in collective working groups, formal associations, and/or cooperatives. As a response to their exclusion from the formal labor market, it is increasingly common for many unemployed to resort to informal activities as it happens with the waste sector, often combined with poor working conditions (Fuzzi 2016).

Waste recycling activity is a fundamental strategy for environmental sustainability in the global capitalist economy. Recyclable waste (paper, glass, metal, plastics) is a disposable material resulting typically from manufacturing, construction, and individual consumption. An ever-increasing urban population and the associated rise in consumption mean that potential recycling waste will continue to increase in the future (Whitson 2011; Santos and Lane 2017). However, waste recycling infrastructures materialize in different assemblages and recycling processes unfold in variegated ways across the globe. In the Global South, waste recycling has revolved around formal and informal practices involving public, private, and quasi-public organizations in the setting up of waste recycling infrastructures.

The informal activity that the waste pickers perform is particularly relevant to urban sustainability at least in two ways (Gutberlet 2015): (1) it gives a way of living to those who are marginalized by the formal economy, and (2) it provides an environmental service to the community, as resources are recovered and redirected to productive cycles. In Millington and Lawhon's (2018, 5) point of view, these workers create value as ecological actors and help municipal governments, which usually deal with scarce budgets, to manage material recovery and landfill reduction.

In Brazil, waste pickers' organizations are predominantly formed and run by women who survived for years as pickers of recyclable materials in waste dumps, until they organized into networks of workers assembled in associations or cooperatives that organize circuits of waste collection, sorting, batching, and exchange. With the support of other institutions (e.g., universities) and local governments, they have put in place infrastructures (for sorting and batching waste to be sold in the market) that have economic, social, environmental, and symbolic meaning. Infrastructures provide better working conditions, enable connectivity, and give meaning to the work and effort performed by the waste pickers, providing a symbolic home. In this perspective, the waste recycling infrastructures such as landfill sites and related hangars, trucks, squeezers, metal hoppers, freight elevators, conveyor belts, and so on, which are traditionally operated by men, are very much a result of some women's aspirations and their persistence in those collectivities (Siemiatycky, Enright, and Valverde 2019).

The study of infrastructure is an emerging field in the social sciences, with Boyer (2018) considering it as a conceptual New Deal for the humanities.

Moving away from traditional inquiry on infrastructures engineering, feasibility, and accessibility, Larkin (2013) points out that "infrastructure can offer insights into other domains such as practices of government, religion, or sociality" (328). Infrastructures reveal the contested terrains of power, sustaining economic, social, and political relations (Appel, Anand, and Gupta 2018). As with other infrastructures, waste recycling infrastructure gained support from public authorities since it is fundamental to achieve urban sustainability. The investment in waste recycling infrastructure can take different forms, producing uneven spatialities of waste recycling. We are interested in the study of infrastructure and community empowerment, particularly the ways certain communities organized to form waste recycling cooperatives and associations and thus avoid the extremely poor working conditions in landfill waste sites. Nevertheless, these territory-based social organizations are unstable and subject to the penetration of the neoliberal agenda in the environmental and waste treatment sector. As the neoliberal model advances in the waste recycling sector, cooperatives and associations struggle to survive in competition with private companies. In addition, infrastructure ruination issues are an important element in the everyday life of waste recycling co-op boards.

Assuming that human agency is always attached with the specific sociomaterial arrangements of which humans are part (Suchman 2009), we have a commitment to feminist research for two reasons. First, feminist research moves beyond traditional concerns with abstracted and decontextualized forms of knowledge in favor of specifically situated practices of knowing in action, thus this research takes a feminist perspective as it departs from the experiences of women in their reality and clearly assuming them as producers of knowledge (Baylina et al. 2019). Second, feminist research puts the focus on the arrangements (often ignored) that are an ongoing feature of socio-material assemblages and the capacities for action that they enable, and points to relations and symmetries among individuals and things, and to the politics of difference.

To take on board the study of the waste recycling infrastructure in Brazil, we understand that each woman is a component of multiple assemblages—familiar, cooperative, environmental—operating at different scales, not supposing any unity or totality, but referring to a plurality of assemblages, a "cartography of multiplicity" subject to multiple and coexisting relations and changes (Haesbaert and Bruce 2002; DeLanda 2006). Following McFarlane (2011), assemblage can be framed as an approach, operating as "a way of thinking the social, political, economic, or cultural as a relational processuality of composition and as a methodology attuned to practice, materiality, and emergence" (652). Accordingly, we work with assemblage as a concept and as an orientation to study the infrastructure and socio-material transformation of waste recycling.

In this chapter we pay attention to the process of recycling waste infrastructure development, focusing on women working in this sector in the west of the state of São Paulo, Brazil. We analyze the transition processes from which those pickers (especially women) who were "on the ground" randomly picking waste from sunrise to sunset, until they became recyclable waste workers organized in formal groups. These groups are either associations (for promoting assistance and class interests) or cooperatives (for economic or market purposes), and we follow them until they consolidate in networks of associations and cooperatives to strengthen their negotiation positions. According to Simas and Perez (2016), the associations and cooperatives of recyclable materials encapsulate strategies not only to support class benefits but also to facilitate direct sales to the recycling industries, reducing the interference of intermediaries in the recycling chain. This transition presupposes infrastructure investment supporting formal recognition, collective empowering to negotiate with public and private stakeholders, better income, class solidarity, and self-esteem building.

We claim, on the one hand, that in a context of masculine values and regulations concerning the waste sector, the rationalities, functions, and roles that women assume in the collaborative projects stabilize the assemblages' identity. On the other hand, when internal or external forces destabilize the assemblage boundaries—for example, a fire and destruction of the sorting/recycling infrastructure, enforcement of new waste sector regulations, or efforts to create networks for stronger negotiation capacity—new kinds of assemblages arise.

The methodology is qualitative, after in-depth voluntary interviews in the spaces studied (with the authors of this chapter), in order to display coherence between the theoretical framework and the ways people, mainly women, give meaning to their own experiences in spatial and temporal contexts of life (Valentine 1997). For ethical reasons the identity of the women interviewed is not disclosed, thus the names associated are our invention, and the specific places where they work are not revealed.

The chapter advances as follows. First, we explore some of the concepts of assemblage theory as formulated by DeLanda (2006) in articulation with the recent contributions from anthropology and geography on the study of infrastructures. Then we present a brief review of the extant literature on recycling waste collection in Brazil, followed by a discussion of the waste pickers' situation in the west of São Paulo state, based on visits to the wastescapes, interviews, previous academic research from the State University of São Paulo, official documents, and documents and news available on the internet. Then, departing from Deleuze and Guattari (2002), Haesbaert and Bruce (2004), and DeLanda (2006), with the support of interviews, we use assemblage theory to explain significant processes of change and stabilization of identities in the waste recycling infrastructure.

INFRASTRUCTURE AS ASSEMBLAGE

In the 1980s, the philosophers Deleuze and Guattari (1987) outlined what would be known as assemblage theory, a reasoning that proceeds from causal thinking that denies dichotomist thoughts and totalities (the tree) to embrace the multiple connections that shape the social phenomena (the rhizome). Later, Manuel DeLanda (2006) developed this way of thinking and proposed a theory of assemblages as an alternative framework to understand the world in which we live.

Assemblages are "wholes whose properties emerge from the interactions between parts," and they can be used to "model interpersonal networks and institutional organizations as assemblages of people," as well as a variety of infrastructural components, "from buildings and streets to conduits for matter and energy flows" (DeLanda 2006, 5–6). So, societal phenomena are in permanent change, and as assemblages, their components, materialities and infrastructures, regulations and policies, and communities and stakeholders are interrelated in a multitude of connections (Grossmann and Haase 2016). Furthermore, the wholes (assemblages) are "characterized by relations of exteriority," implying "that a component part of an assemblage can be detached from it and plugged into a different assemblage in which interactions are different." These processes either stabilize the identity of an assemblage, increasing its internal homogeneity, or destabilize it by increasing the sharpness of its boundaries and increasing its internal heterogeneity. These are known, respectively, as the processes of territorialization and deterritorialization. An assemblage can have both components that stabilize its identity as well as components forcing it to change, and the same component can participate in both processes (DeLanda 2006, 12–13).

A central idea is that complexity is more than simply the coming together of multiple entities or systems (Queirós 2018). The relationship between their parts constitutes new entities that make up a whole that is more than the sum of the parts (Thrift 1999; Urry 2005; James 2007). It is also the process through which new hybrids emerge from this assemblage of previously separate entities. Assemblage theory has therefore much in common with complexity theories, despite the differences, at least the focus on the dynamics of feedback loops (territorialization-deterritorialization), emergence, nonlinear developments, and context/path dependence.

Assemblage is used in different ways to understand and explain the socio-materiality of phenomena and as a "term for transgressing modernist dualisms like nature-culture, body-technology, or physical-political" (McFarlane 2011, 653). According to the author, actors, forms, and processes are defined primarily by the assemblages they enter and reconstitute, and such assemblages can be stabilized (territorialized) or destabilized (deterritorialized) through their cofunctioning and mutual constitution. Only the interactions between different elements establish the assemblage. Still, the agency of individual actors and of the interactive whole can change over time to form spatial relationalities (DeLanda 2006).

Transposing McFarlane's (2011) contribution to the understanding of city as assemblage, studying infrastructure as an assemblage points toward the understanding of how forms of power and rationality territorialize and deterritorialize. Thus, to study how waste recycling infrastructure as a socio-material assemblage is produced implies the mobilization of concepts of power, political economy, and sociocultural elements (McFarlane 2011), bringing together different actors—engineers, technical staff, academics, politicians, activists, and waste pickers—operating a specific technical operation (Gandy 2008; Larkin 2013; Appel, Anand, and Gupta 2018).

RECYCLING WASTE IN BRAZIL: A BRIEF OVERVIEW

According to a study conducted by the Instituto de Pesquisa Econômica Aplicada (IPEA 2013), 93 percent of the waste pickers in Brazil inhabit urban areas, and 66 percent of them are Black; education levels are low and a high percentage of them are women (Carvalho and Rondini 2017), suggesting that waste, gender, and race are intertwined to make waste materials valuable (Vasudevan 2019). Waste recycling begins as a way of survival, as the formal market and society marginalize these people. The work they do is socially disregarded, and it is vulnerable and precarious, as the value of recyclable waste is heavily dependent on market variations (Whitson 2011). Historically this is an activity of disadvantaged workers. Waste pickers are exposed to multiple risks, including extreme weather conditions, animal bites, contamination, accidents, and so on. These wastescapes or riskscapes are "environments of corporeal insecurity" as they expose workers (most of them Black women) to hazards (Vasudevan 2019, 3; Fuzzi 2016).

As a way to respond to the adversities of the waste collection activity, waste pickers in Brazil organized the Movimento Nacional de Catadores de Materiais Recicláveis (National Movement of Collectors of Recyclable Materials) in 2001. In 2002, the Ministry of Labor and Employment (MTE) recognized the recyclable material collector occupation (Brasil 2002), including recyclable and reusable material collection, selection and preparation of material for shipment and selling, and managing and dissemination of the recycling work. These activities are recognized by regulations on work conditions (Regulatory Standard 15, MTE). The National Policy on Solid Waste (PNRS) identifies the necessity of the social inclusion of the waste pickers (Law 12.3015, 2010, August 2). Since the early 2000s there has been an intensification of municipal programs and actions to support the waste collectors in Brazil, such as the PNRS.

Another significant action for the improvement of waste pickers' working conditions, known as the Programa Pró-Catador (Pro-Picker Program), was launched in 2010 by the Decree Law 7.405/2010 of December 23. Through this program, the Comité Interministerial para Inclusão Social e Econômica dos Catadores de Materiais Reutilizáveis e Recicláveis (Inter-Ministerial Committee for Social and Economic Inclusion of Reusable and Recyclable Waste Disposal) is tasked with establishing public policies regarding waste pickers (Carvalho and Rondini 2017). The Pro-Picker Program articulates the actions of the federal government to give support to the organization of the recyclable materials collectors, improve their working conditions, expand their opportunities for social and economic inclusion, and develop in partnership with the collectors the selective collection of solid waste, reuse, and recycling.

Under Law 12.305/2010, waste collection activities cannot be carried out in dump sites. Nevertheless, most of the waste collectors are still in public dump sites—a high proportion even live there—or in landfills scattered throughout Brazil (IPEA 2013). After the law was passed, it was necessary to integrate the waste pickers into the formal recycling chain, including actions for social inclusion and income protection to promote the full citizenship of these workers. In the initial phases of the process, it was a difficult task to organize into collectivities individuals who were isolated, individualistic, and suspicious (Leal 2002–2004). The increasing degree of organization of waste pickers comes with some caveats, however. Millington and Lawhon (2018) alert us to the risks of incremental "formalization" in wastescapes, resulting from uneven distribution of benefits, and encapsulating low labor costs. Moreover, opponents of waste facilities (e.g., landfills, recyclable storage sheds, waste sorting stations, etc.) complain about the burdens of smell, the visual landscape, pathogen infestation risks, and property value depreciation. They also view the poor people working in waste facilities through the lenses of criminality and marginalization (Millington and Lawhon 2018).

FROM "WASTE PICKERS" TO "COLLECTORS OF RECYCLABLE MATERIALS": INFRASTRUCTURE AND ORGANIZATION OF WASTE RECYCLING IN THE WEST OF SÃO PAULO STATE

In this section we briefly describe the development of waste recycling infrastructure in three collectives of recyclable waste workers (namely, ACMRR, ARPE/COOPERARPE, and COOPERLIX) operating in different small municipalities in the western part of São Paulo state (Regente Feijó, Presidente Epitácio, and Presidente Prudente). These collectives have distinctive levels of organization and infrastructure development, but they all began when the waste pickers joined efforts, with the support of public policies, to create organized structures of associations and cooperatives.

ACMRR, Regente Feijó, SP

The rural municipality of Regente Feijó did not control the landfill until 1999 (Kawatoko, Rizk, and Leal 2010). Prior to this, solid waste was left in a dump, but also in gullies, in valley bottoms, and on rural roadsides. Currently, the Regente Feijó landfill receives all of the municipality's household waste. In 2010, there were sixteen collectors of recyclable materials in the municipality, the majority being illiterate or with some elementary school education, with an average age of forty-eight. For most, the collection of recyclable waste is their only source of income (Kawatoko, Rizk, and Leal 2010).

For years, the scavengers carried out their activities in the municipal dump, under precarious working conditions. However, the municipal government acquired equipment (a press and a treadmill) and built a covered shelter for sorting the collected materials, with a mess room and an office. Nevertheless, due to the difficulties of articulation and operationalization of the actions between the waste pickers and the local government, this infrastructure has become unused and deteriorated, and the scavengers continue to develop their activities in the dump (Martins 2011).

It was only with the National Policy on Solid Waste, in 2010, that this situation was modified with the participation of the municipality of Regente Feijó in the state program called Programa Estadual Município Verde Azul (Blue Green Municipality), developed by the secretary of state of the environment, which proposed the insertion of collectors of recyclable materials in associations or cooperatives.

Fig. 9.1. Recyclable waste collection truck, ACMRR, Regente Feijó, SP. (Photo by Margarida Queirós)

Located near a municipal road in a rural area, the association known as Associação de Catadores de Materiais Recicláveis Rocha (ACMRR) was formalized in 2010, after two years of negotiations and planning, in partnership between city hall and the Universidade Estadual Paulista (UNESP). A dialogue was held with all recyclable waste pickers scattered in the city of Regente Feijó, all of whom (twenty-two scavengers) were working in poor conditions. However, only ten scavengers (four men and six women) working in the landfill area agreed to join the association (Martins 2011). By December 2018 they were only eight scavengers (five women and three men), with three women on the board of directors.

There was no organizational structure of the collectors prior to the formalization of the ACMRR. Nowadays the activities developed in the ACMRR are organized as follows: two women and one man work as collectors of the recyclable materials in the city, along with the truck driver (a man, who is an employee of the city hall); three women work in the sorting of recyclable materials; and two men work in the pressing of the sorted materials.

In 2010, the infrastructure and equipment of the association consisted of a covered area for the materials' organization, but without walls, it was exposed to rain, wind, and animals, and there was not adequate storage security. For this reason, the association has suffered several times from theft of materials ready to be dispatched. The ACMRR also has locker rooms with bathrooms; a meal room equipped with a stove, a refrigerator, a table, and benches; an office with closet and computer; a weighing scale for loading materials and a digital scale for the quantification of recyclable materials sorted and pressed; a bench for sorting the materials; and a press. The bench had never been used, as the collectors considerate it inadequate for the activity. The truck for selective collection is owned by the municipality (figure 9.1). Since then, the overall infrastructure has become degraded and therefore the working conditions are worsening.

Currently, the ACMRR has a contract with the municipality of Regente Feijó for collecting recyclable waste. A monthly amount is transferred to the association members to cover expenses, and the rest is divided among them. The commercialization of the materials is done through intermediaries, mainly with two private companies based in Presidente Prudente.

ARPE/COOPERARPE, Presidente Epitácio, SP

Presidente Epitácio county is considered a tourist resort due to its beautiful waterfront on the Paraná River. The old dump in Presidente Epitácio was closed in 1999. With the implementation of the new landfill (and the deactivation of the dump), the municipality solved its environmental problem, but soon after a social one arose. In the former dump, people used to make a living collecting recyclable materials—some of them developed this activity for more than twenty years.

According to the Plano de Gestão Integrada de Resíduos Sólidos de Presidente Epitácio (Solid Waste Management Plan for *Presidente Epitácio*), attempts were made to employ the waste pickers in other activities, most of the time unsuccessfully, because they were not qualified for other functions or because they were rejected by certain entrepreneurs who refused to hire them due to their past (criminal record, alcoholism, drugs, and other issues) or because they were living in slums (PGIRSPE 2014). To solve the problem, the municipality made an inventory of the collectors, including people who pick up garbage on the streets of the urban areas, known as *carrinheiros* as they use a handcart as a container for the material collected in the street. The initial register counted forty-eight people doing this activity.

City hall has now replaced the dump with a landfill and provided a building for sorting the recyclable materials, plus other related infrastructures (e.g., reception and storage areas, office, kitchen, and bathroom). Through an agreement with the Pontal of Paranapanema Hydrographic Catchment Area Committee (CBH-PP), a four-hundred-square-meter shed was built in the public area of the landfill, two presses and a mobile crawler were purchased, and a semi-artesian water well was dug. An extensive environmental education plan was developed with the workers. A grant from the Social Solidarity Fund of the state of São Paulo allowed the construction of the canteen and the acquisition of related equipment (cabinets, stove, water freezer, refrigerator, and a stainless steel dining table) for the members of the Associação de Recicladores de Presidente Epitácio (Association of Recyclers of Presidente Epitácio, ARPE). All the workers have personal protective equipment (gloves, masks, and boots).

ARPE was created in 2003, initially with thirty waste workers, and in 2014 it had around forty members. ARPE activity covers the whole municipality, using a door-to-door system of waste collection with a truck (PGIRSPE 2014). Initially, collection of door-to-door recyclable waste was carried out by ARPE members, who were properly uniformed, handing out green bags along with an explanatory brochure and asking people to sort out the recyclable waste for collection and further selection (figure 9.2). Residents deliver the recyclables and receive new bags. The purpose of exchanging the empty bag is the contact and trust building between the association members and the residents.

ARPE is funded through sales of processed recyclable materials that are divided in equal shares between the associates. Cooperative members receive a monthly payment depending on the volume of the recyclable waste collected. However, under Law 2.305 of 2010, there was a need to transform the association into a cooperative—as an association, ARPE could not issue invoices. In 2015 ARPE signed a yearly renewable contract with the city hall to create the Cooperative of Collectors of Recyclable Materials of Presidente Epitácio (COOPERARPE). With a cooperative structure, the group can sign a service contract with the municipality, a positive change for the recyclable materials workers, as they are formally able to perform a service to the public authority. The legal change from cooperation to association has not changed the basic nature of the group's work: it still operates in the same place and with the same infrastructures, equipment, and truck. The material gathering continues to be

Fig. 9.2. Bags with sorted recyclable paper, ARPE/COOPERARPE, Presidente Epitácio, SP. (Photo by Margarida Queirós)

carried out in all urban areas on specific days according to each neighborhood, with 80 percent adherence from the population of Presidente Epitácio.

ARPE gathered important equipment, such as a conveyor belt, a hand scale, a wheelbarrow, and two presses, provided by city hall. City hall also assisted with the supply of materials such as posters and leaflets distributed in public places, schools, and door to door in support of the door-to-door collection program. Recently, ARPE gained cooperative status, and it has about forty members (nine men and thirty-one women). Each member works about eight hours a day and receives a monthly income (not counting other payments, such as a reserve fund or payment for a selective collection service by the city hall). The division of work in this association is similar to the ACMRR in municipality of Regente Feijó (discussed above): the majority of the women work in the material selection process, and men work with the presses and forklifts and drive the trucks.

Now, COOPERARPE gained a forklift (obtained through a project) to streamline all services previously done by hand (to stack materials, load trucks, and perform other services that require the work of several people). COOPERARPE continues at the old address, the Epitacio/Caiuá road; its

members are developing their negotiation skills; and the cooperative continues to improve its infrastructure and equipment (the cooperative added a new
shed, enlarged the current shed by adding a kitchen, and purchased two new
trucks and three presses for cardboard and other materials).

COOPERLIX, Presidente Prudente, SP

In 2001, Presidente Prudente waste pickers were divided into two large
groups: those who used to collect recyclable material randomly deposited in
the urban area—the *carrinheiros*—and another group that collected recyclable
waste directly at the dump site. According to Gonçalves (2006) it was in this
sector of recycling that several scavengers found shelter against the exclusions of the formal labor market and found the means to ensure their survival
in recyclable materials. These people had journeys that exceed twelve hours a
day. In any case, the working conditions and the income obtained show how
much the waste pickers were exploited, since they did not have any type of
formal contract of work with the buyers, worked on their own rather than
cooperatively, and, most of the time, were linked to a purchaser (connected
with the recycling companies) who used a variety of resources to always keep
them linked to his services. This way those collectors are exploited by the
recycling companies, which pay low prices for the selected waste materials
(Leal 2002–2004; Gonçalves 2006; Fuzzi 2016; Carvalho and Rondini 2017).

Located in the industrial district of Presidente Prudente, within the municipal landfill area, Cooperativa dos Trabalhadores de Produtos Recicláveis
de Presidente Prudente (COOPERLIX) is a collective formally founded in
2002. The cooperative facilities were yielded by the city hall and the equipment acquired through projects developed in partnership, for example, with
the Foundation Bank of Brazil, Foundation for Research Support of the State
of São Paulo (FAPESP), and the Universidade Estadual Paulista (UNESP) (Leal
2002–2004).

To organize COOPERLIX, city hall sponsored a strategic diagnostic study of
the solid waste situation and the waste pickers' situation in January 2002. The
study identified 101 waste pickers (fifty-eight men and forty-three women),
all working in the municipal dump. Several meetings were held with the waste
pickers, and a series of university extension events was held where the waste
pickers were invited to be part of the round tables (to have voice and visibility), alongside researchers, students, managers, technicians, NGOs, and the
community at large. Several technical visits were made to other cooperatives
in the region, and meetings with the school community and the general population were organized to obtain the necessary support for the organization of

the collectors and to implement a program of selective collection of recyclable materials from waste.

In 2002, only thirty-seven waste pickers (twenty-one men and sixteen women) agreed to participate in the formal creation of COOPERLIX. The reasons explaining such low adherence could be that (1) waste pickers' lack of confidence in the teams of UNESP and city hall that were developing the initiative; (2) some, especially young men, considered that they would have greater earnings by continuing to work in isolation (it was common to hear "every person for himself and God for all") or working in small groups, usually with family; (3) anti-cooperative movements encouraged by other collectors and purchasers of recyclable materials who had no interest in the organization of the collectors. Between 2004 and 2015, the cooperative attracted less than half of the city's waste pickers due to the relatively low income it provided to its members. It remained a small group; women took the main leadership roles, but since its inception, COOPERLIX has struggled to complete construction and build strength and continuity. In this process, there was a change in the composition of the board of directors, with an increase in the number of women and a woman assuming the presidency of COOPERLIX.

COOPERLIX began to gain financial stability in 2015, when it was given a contract by city hall to carry out selective materials collection. This allowed a fixed monthly income for the members, complemented by sales of the collected recyclable waste. In 2016, waste pickers were prevented from accessing the municipal dump, so those still working on the site were voluntarily incorporated into COOPERLIX. The increasing empowerment and gains of the cooperative, and the impossibility of continuing to work on the closed dump, increased its membership: in December 2018, COOPERLIX had more than doubled its members, reaching eighty-eight people (forty-one women and forty-seven men), most of them Black.

When it was inaugurated in December 2003, COOPERLIX had a five-hundred-square-meter shed containing a mat and a press, and one administrative building with an office, a kitchen, dispensary, dining room, and bathrooms. These were built with resources from city hall, and the following items were purchased with FAPESP resources: a metal hopper; a complete conveyor belt with platform; a hydraulic press; a metal container cart; a gas cylinder with gauge, hose, and clamp; a stove with oven; a refrigerator; and other equipment (figure 9.3). Later the church and the Rotary Club donated trucks. With support from banks and other entities, COOPERLIX has been gaining more equipment and expanding its infrastructure, adding a secondhand bus to carry its members from their homes to the workplace. After a fire in July 2018 that

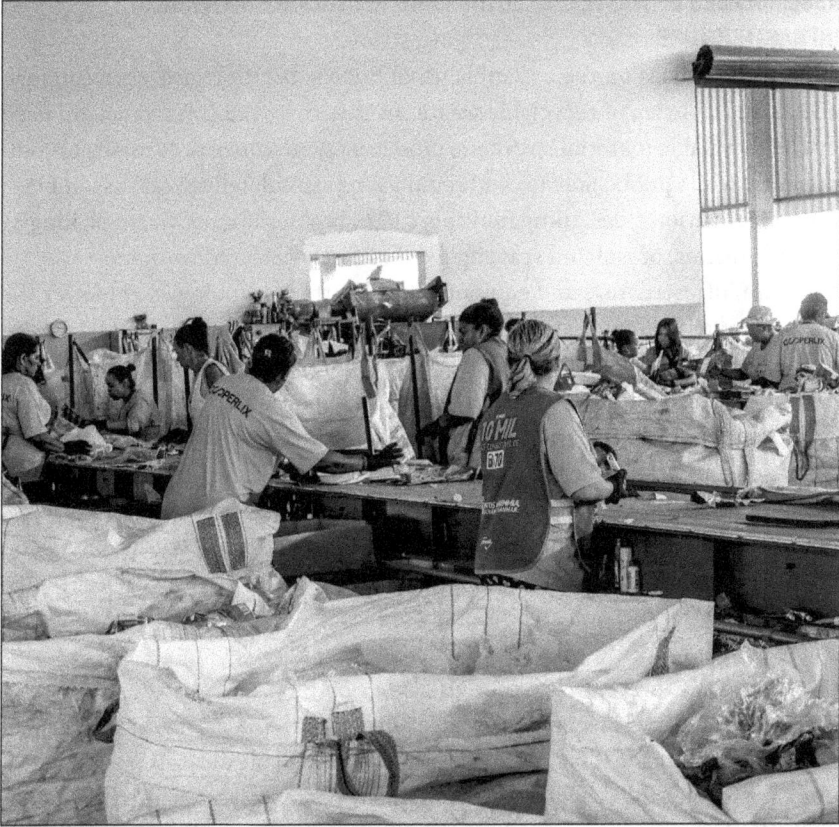

Fig. 9.3. Women sorting recyclable waste on the conveyor belt, COOPERLIX, Presidente Prudente, SP. (Photo by Margarida Queirós)

destroyed the COOPERLIX premises, city hall provided the cooperative with a new shed to host the selective center, with a covered space to unload the collected material for sorting, baling, and storage, and an office and a room for environmental education and training. The new headquarters also has a separate building with an office, a canteen, bathrooms, locker rooms, and other small rooms. Except for glass, the collected materials are pressed and commercialized in network with other cooperative organizations. Network commercialization began in 2015 through the Regional Cooperative of Collectors of Recyclable Materials of the Western Region of São Paulo (COOPERCOP), which was established in 2012 to gain negotiation power and increase the income of the recyclable waste workers.

ASSEMBLAGES OF WASTE COLLECTORS AND RECYCLABLE MATERIALS INFRASTRUCTURE

Our study focuses on the assemblages of bodies, technologies, socio-materialities and policies of recyclable waste. In this case, the infrastructure used by the recyclable materials workers, mostly women, consists of material components, while public policies and regulations stimulated several assemblage territorializations, designing multiple cartographies (e.g., of waste picking or formal entities, of isolated scavengers or groups of related workers).

More infrastructure and equipment and better technologies empower the waste workers, allow them to collect, package, and sell more materials and to make higher earnings. Bounded by rules and regulations, the buildings, machines, and technologies required for the operation of the recycling waste collectives are material and relational entities as they enable better working conditions, increase efficiency, and improve quality of life: "This place allows a closer approximation between the members, an environment with a place of rest" (Tina, interview, June 2018). The waste, sheds, tools, trucks, and so on are nonhuman materialities (what DeLanda would call "physical locales" [2006, 12]) interacting with human bodies to produce and reproduce the collectives of waste workers as socio-material assemblages.

Among the interviewees, there is also a common idea that the infrastructure, equipment, and technologies have relieved some of the physical burden of their work and made it more efficient. The decreased physical effort and better body posture enabled by the new equipment have positive health benefits as well. Workplace improvements to infrastructure, technologies, and equipment allow the work to be of higher quality, efficiency, and security, improving worker well-being and the dynamics of greater approximation between the cooperative members.

Regarding the infrastructure and processing facilities of one of the collectives, one of the respondents stated that the actual workplace is better than working in the middle of the garbage (referring to the landfill), but it is still not adequate. The workers are not totally happy with the buildings they currently have and complain about issues such as the site's security, as the bales of pressed materials are occasionally stolen. The workers stated that they have better clothes for protection (boots and gloves), but the workplace would be much better if they had a shed to carry out the activity of sorting the recyclables and more sophisticated equipment or recycling technologies. In fact, when the truck with waste collected in town gets to the premises, the unloading and the selection of waste (paper, metal, and different kinds of plastics) are done partially outdoors, sometimes in suffocating heat.

Infrastructure improved the quality of life of deprived populations that lived in deplorable conditions by the landfill and open waste dumps. Even simple tools and the most rudimentary machines can make a difference in the quality of work, not to mention in work efficiency and income generation. The storage and separation shed, truck, truck jibs, mechanical loaders, conveyor belts, mechanical waste press, and other equipment such as gloves, boots, eyewear, technical clothes, and so on have made an enormous change in the waste collection, sorting, and dispatching work. As one member declared, "We permanently fight to have all these equipments and this place to perform our job. The working conditions are far better than the previous ones but are far away of what it could be" (Elsa, interview, June 2018). According to another waste picker, "Another and better press, with more technology, would speed up the work, as it would be possible, for example, to press the plastic and the paper simultaneously" (Julia, interview, June 2018).

Due to its relevance, the infrastructure is permanently discussed, narrated, and negotiated among the different actors involved (Larkin 2013; Anand, Gupta, and Appel 2018), including among the recycling workers, municipal technicians, academics, activists, and politicians. Maintaining infrastructure is a constant concern among recyclers, as often the degradation of equipment affects activity, even stopping the process of collecting and separating waste for recycling. As discussed by Gupta (2018), the ruination of infrastructure is therefore a permanent risk and a major concern of communities not always shared with policymakers, who tend to regard the completion of infrastructure as the last necessary step, rather than a first step, in the project.

The axes of territorialization/stabilization–deterritorialization/destabilization enable us to understand the internal uniformity and stability of the waste collectives, as well as the forces that instigate heterogeneity and instability, sometimes leading to new arrangements. A change in the national policy such as the Pro-Picker Program and the National Policy on Solid Waste, both launched in 2010, can be seen as a process of deterritorialization. However, when these sites are forcibly closed, some of their users organized into collectives, as associations or cooperatives, located in well-defined places and with known boundaries, while others continued to work independently in other dump sites. Thus, waste picking processes unfold in different directions, as new and different assemblages emerge (territorialization), while others are restructured and changed—reterritorialization—or simply ceased to exist as we know it—deterritorialization).

The division of labor is another force of stabilization. Nevertheless, there are signs of changing roles. Highlighting changes in power relations in these collectives, Vasconcellos and Dias (2017) refer to reports on the ways in which women appropriate the technologies that are socially perceived to be men's work, and the proactive role must take to make this happen. In our cases, signaling a rupture from socially expected behavioral patterns, a woman stated, "Here I do everything a man does (use mechanical press, drive a truck), I am what I want to be" (Tina, interview, June 2018).

There are nonspatial processes increasing the internal homogeneity of the recycling waste collectives, as they are formed by people who used to be marginalized from the formal labor market and exposed to environments of corporeal insecurity. Moreover, many of them were objectified: "My father compared my worth to a wardrobe, it was how much I was worth at the time [. . .] I married and soon after with two daughters he left me, so I had to survive through the picking" (Sílvia, interview, June 2018). "My ex-husband and, earlier, my father said that the place of a woman was at home, being a mother and serving her man" (Tina, interview, June 2018). The collectives or assemblages stabilize by connectivity rebuilding processes, providing self-esteem, empowering women—"a woman's place is where she wants" (Elsa, interview, June 2018). Of course, identical strategies can produce different outcomes, as the national public policy toward the recycling sector had different outcomes in the three cases. Contrasting with COOPERLIX and ARPE/COOPERARPE, in Regente Feijó the waste recycling infrastructure assemblage did not stabilize, and the association is suffering decay.

Larkin's (2013) observation about the symbolism of infrastructure is exemplified in the affective quality of places where associations/cooperatives materialize, and in which women workers move. This is a product of a complex human/nonhuman relation. The infrastructure (the machinery/technologic apparatus for separation and compilation of the recycled materials, the storage warehouses, the spaces for cooking, meeting, etc.), the fauna and flora, the light, the heat, and the cold underpin feelings of hope, union, protection, and emotion. Despite the poor physical conditions of the sites, it feels familiar, as one waste picker said, "Nonetheless here I am with friends, I share with them my problems and we find solutions together" (Elsa, interview, June 2018).

In the three collectives it is important to note the pathways of the human, especially women components. Taking into account the external influencing factors, in all three municipalities we analyzed, women are in charge and are aware of their accomplishments, in spite of the fact that all of them were raised in and inhabit unfavorable masculine environments: "I was not born scavenger nor in the dump. I do not want to be discriminated against for the work I do. It is a status I won and I want to see it recognized. I want the respect I've earned; after all, I work for the sake of the environment and the public health" (Sílvia, interview June 2018). Thus, from their conscience, will, and actions emerged the unexpected: the collectivities' leadership, the empowered narrative on the environmental service they provide, and the sense of the association /cooperative as the real and united family they never had: "I could have been displeased with my husband, but at bath time the towel had to be at the bathroom door [. . .]. When he left me, it was my release, but I was afraid of everything. The collective gave me freedom, financial ability, social protection, respect [. . .] it is my second family, because my first are my children" (Tina, interview, June 2018). "We women want to have a voice, learn, seek equality, earn respect, fight against prejudice, occupy spaces, take leadership [. . .] discussing this in our meetings and doing this together, we find better solutions to our problems" (Julia, interview, June 2018). Expressive elements of these places distinguish themselves from others ("With the help of the municipality and above all, the university, we built all of this, it is not a luxury place but is our territory" [Elsa, interview, June 2018]). The confidence is given by the presence of other people sharing the same circumstances, not specifically from the "ornamentation." As one worker said, "I now see the value of the cooperative: once I had a dog disease and I stayed hospitalized for two months but I did not lose my job or earnings" (Rita, interview, June 2018). These are (feedback) processes that stabilize the identity of these assemblages.

Nevertheless, destabilization can arise from the conflicting interests of the industrial waste sector. "We fight against the industry that now sees the value we create [. . .] and some of our colleagues give up this job and return to the life in dumps" (Elsa, interview, June 2018). This is a powerful force of destabilization. Other are changing and reterritorializing forces, building relational capacities (being affected-affecting), producing wholes emerging from its parts that express a new identity: "We hold meetings between women, many with the support of the State Secretariat for Women, to overcome prejudice, verbal, psychological and physical aggression (at home and on the streets) [. . .] With them we share experiences, learn to share leadership" (Elsa, interview June 2018). Assemblages of recyclable waste infrastructures shape, and are shaped by, bodies, technologies, socio-materialities, and policies. Through time and space, infrastructure is always evolving, and the recyclable waste assemblages are in a continuous (de)(re)territorialization process, subjecting and being subject to diverging/converging actors' intentions, narratives, and actions.

CLOSING REMARKS

This chapter is about how waste enables the recyclable materials collectors to redefine their roles in society and recognition as equal members, and how infrastructure and social relations are mutually constituted. Assemblages of bodies, technologies, socio-materialities, and policies (de)(re)territorialize, shape, and are shaped by the struggle of deprived social groups, mostly Black women collecting and selecting recyclable waste in small urban agglomerations in the west of the state of São Paulo, Brazil.

In a fluid framework we have tried to build a narrative on recyclable waste pickers living in western São Paulo state, each one building their lives around assemblages of wastescapes, on dump sites (environments of extreme corporeal insecurity and fragile identities), or in organized collectives and the processes that preferably encourage or retract the stability of the existing assemblages. The line between staying in a collective or returning to the dump is tenuous and fluid. It requires persistence, believing in the strength of the group, and the emergence of a sense of home and protection. The materialities of the wastescapes (infrastructures, equipment, and related technologies acquired) are also symbols of belonging and achievement.

The process of moving from assemblages in waste dumps to assemblages of organized collectives in landfills shapes multiple cartographies and is subject to a constellation of relations and coexisting changes. In this process women move from invisibility, subordination, and lack of choice to visibility, leadership, and respect. Their major achievement is the consciousness or sense of providing value to society through the environmental service they deliver and the knowledge of their empowerment. This was possible since they understood the shared vulnerability, the power of bonding in collectives, the meaning of sharing knowledge, and the struggle for equality in the masculinized world of dumps, landfills, trucks, metal hoppers, conveyor belts, hydraulic presses, metal container carts, and so on. They were not alone; they had support mostly from the university and the municipalities, but above all they had each other.

ACKNOWLEDGMENTS

The authors would like to thank all the interviewees for their generosity in sharing so many things about their personal lives. We are also grateful to the colleagues of the Research Group on Environmental Management and Socio-Spatial Dynamics, GADIS, from UNESP Presidente Prudente–SP, for all the support given to us along this research. Special thanks to Jennifer McGarrigle for the revision of the English language.

REFERENCES

Anand, Nikhil, Akhil Gupta, and Hannah Appel, eds. 2018. *The Promise of Infrastructure*. Duke University Press.

Appel, Hannah, Nikhil Anand, and Akhil Gupta. 2018. "Temporality, Politics, and the Promise of Infrastructure." In *The Promise of Infrastructure*, edited N. Anand, A. Gupta, and H. Appel, 1–38. Duke University Press.

Baylina, Mireia, Montserrat Villarino, Maria Dolors Garcia Ramon, Maria Josefa Mosteiro, Ana Maria Porto, and Isabel Salamaña. 2019. "Género e innovación en los nuevos procesos de re-ruralización en España" [Gender and innovation in the new processes of re-ruralization in Spain]. *Finisterra, Revista Portuguesa de Geografía*, 54 (110): 75–91.

Boyer, Dominic. 2018. "Infrastructure, Potential Energy, Revolution." In *The Promise of Infrastructure*, edited N. Anand, A. Gupta, and H. Appel, 223–43. Duke University Press.

Brasil. 2002. Ministério do Trabalho e Emprego. *Portaria no 397, de 09 de outubro de 2002. Aprova a Classificação Brasileira de Ocupações—CBO/2002, para uso em todo território nacional.* Portal do Trabalho e Emprego, 2002 [Ordinance 397, which approves the Brazilian Classification of Occupations—CBO/2002, for use throughout the national territory. Labor and Employment Portal, 2002].

Carvalho, Ana Maria Rodrigues, and C. A. Rondini. 2017. "Perfil Socioprofissional de catadoras e catadores em associações e cooperativas do Oeste Paulista" [Socioprofessional profile of scavengers in associations and cooperatives of Oeste Paulista]. In *A Economia Solidária e os Desafios Globais do Trabalho* [The Solidarity Economy and the Global Challenges of Labor], 1st ed., edited by A. R. de Souza and M. Zanin, vol. 1, 251–61. EdUFSCar.

DeLanda, Manuel. 2006. *A New Philosophy of Society: Assemblage Theory and Social Complexity*. Bloomsbury Academic.

Deleuze, Gilles, and Félix Guattari. 1987. *A Thousand Plateaus*. University of Minnesota Press.

Deleuze, Gilles, and Félix Guattari, F. 2004. *O Anti-Édipo. Capitalismo e Esquizofrenia* [The anti-Oedipus: Capitalism and schizophrenia]. Assírio & Alvim. First published 1972.

Fuzzi, Fernanda Regina. 2016. *Organização de cooperativas e associações de catadores de materiais recicláveis em rede: Um estudo de caso da Rede Cataoeste com polo em Assis—São Paulo—Brasil* [Organization of cooperatives and associations of collectors of recyclable materials in a network: A case study of the Cataoeste Network in Assis—São Paulo—Brazil]. Master thesis in geography, Faculdade de Ciências e Tecnologia. Universidade Estadual Paulista.

Gandy, M. 2008. "Landscapes of Disaster: Water, Modernity, and Urban Fragmentation in Mumbai." *Environment and Planning* A, 40 (1): 108–30.

Gonçalves, Marcelino A. 2006. *O Trabalho no Lixo* [Work in the trash]. Doctoral thesis in geography. Faculdade de Ciências e Tecnologia. Universidade Estadual Paulista.

Grossmann, Katrin, and Annegret Haase. 2016. "Neighborhood Change beyond Clear Storylines: What Can Assemblage and Complexity Theories Contribute to Understandings of Seemingly Paradoxical Neighborhood Development?" *Urban Geography* 37 (5): 727–47.

Gupta, Akhil. 2018. "The Future in Ruins: Thoughts on the Temporality of Infrastructure." In *The Promise of Infrastructure*, edited by N. Anand, A. Gupta, and H. Appel, 62–79. Duke University Press.

Gutberlet, J. 2015. "Cooperative Urban Mining in Brazil: Collective Practices in Selective Household Waste Collection and Recycling." *Waste Management* 45 (2015): 22–31.

Haesbaert, Rogério, and Glauco Bruce. 2002. "A Desterritorialização na Obra de Deleuze e Guattari" [The deterritorialization in the work of Deleuze and Guattari]. *GEOgraphia* 4 (7): 7–22.

IPEA. 2013. *Situação Social das Catadoras e dos Catadores de Material Reciclável e Reutilizável—Brasil* [Social situation of recyclable and reusable waste pickers—Brazil]. Brasília: Instituto de Pesquisa Econômica Aplicada.

James, Sarah. 2007. "Culture and Complexity: Graffiti on a San Francisco Streetscape." *M/C Journal* 10 (3).

Kawatoko, Ivie Emi S., Maria Cristina Rizk, and Antonio Cezar Leal. 2010. "Estudo para a implantação de uma associação de catadores no município de Regente Feijó" [Study for the implementation of an association of waste pickers in the municipality of Regente Feijó]. *Tópos* 4 (1): 10–31.

Larkin, B. 2013. "The Politics and Poetics of Infrastructure." *Annual Review of Anthropology* 42: 327–43.

Leal, Antonio Cezar, ed. 2002–2004. *Educação Ambiental e o gerenciamento integrado de resíduos sólidos em Presidente Prudente–SP: Desenvolvimento de metodologias para a coleta seletiva, beneficiamento do lixo e organização do trabalho. Relatório Científico, Fase I (2002) e Fase II (2004)* [Environmental education and integrated solid waste management in Presidente Prudente–SP: Development of methodologies for selective collection, waste processing, and work organization. Scientific Report, Phase I (2002) and Phase II (2004)]. UNESP/FAPESP.

Martins, F. G. 2011. *Políticas públicas de resíduos sólidos e a coleta seletiva em Regente Feijó–SP* [Public policies of solid waste and selective collection in Regente Feijó–SP]. Graduação em Geografia. Faculdade de Ciências e Tecnologia, Universidade Estadual Paulista.

McFarlane, Colin. 2011. "Assemblage and Critical Urbanism." *City* 15 (2): 204–24.

Millington, Nate, and Mary Lawhon. 2018. "Geographies of Waste: Conceptual Vectors from the Global South." *Progress in Human Geography* 43 (6): 1044–63.

Paiva, Camila C. 2016. "Mulheres catadoras: Articulação política e ressignificação social através do trabalho." *Idéias* 7 (2): 151–74.

PGIRSPE. 2014. *Plano de gestão integrada de resíduos sólidos de Presidente Epitácio–SP. Versão consulta. Set. 2014* [Integrated solid waste management plan of Presidente Epitácio–SP. Consultation version].

Queirós, Margarida. 2018. "Cities and Regions as Complex Systems: Impact on Spatial Planning." In *Territorio y Estados. Elementos para la coordinación de las Políticas de Ordenación del Territorio en el Siglo XXI* [Territory and states: Essentials for the coordination of spatial planning policies in the 21st century], edited by Joaquin Farinos Dasí, 49–70. Tirant Humanidades.

Rutkowski, Jaqueline E., and Emilia W. Rutkowski. 2015. "Expanding Worldwide Urban Solid Waste Recycling: The Brazilian Social Technology in Waste Pickers Inclusion." *Waste Management and Research* 33 (2): 1084–93.

Santos, Dan, and Ruth Lane. 2017. "A Material Lens on Socio-Technical Transitions: The Case of Steel in Australian Buildings." *Geoforum* 82: 40–50.

Siemiatycki, Matti, Theresa Enright, and Mariana Valverde. 2019. "The Gendered Production of Infrastructure." *Progress in Human Geography* 44 (2): 297–314.

Simas, A. L. F. and Z. M. L. Perez, eds. 2016. *Plano de Resíduos Sólidos do Estado de São Paulo* [Solid waste plan of the state of São Paulo]. SMA.

Suchman, Lucy. 2009. *Agencies in Technology Design: Feminist Reconfigurations.* http://www.lancaster.ac.uk/fass/resources/sociology-online-papers/papers/suchman-agencies technodesign.pdf.

Thrift, Nigel. 1999. "The Place of Complexity." *Theory, Culture, and Society* 16 (3): 31–69.

Urry, John. 2005. "The Complexities of the Global." *Theory, Culture, and Society* 22 (5): 235–54.

Valentine, Gill. 1997. "Tell Me about Using Interviews as a Research Methodology." In *Methods in Human Geography: A Guide for Students Doing a Research Project*, edited by E. Flowerdew and D. Martin, 110–253. Longman.

Vasconcellos, Bruna M., and Rafael Dias. 2017. "Trabalho associado, mulheres, e tecnologia" [Associated work, women, and technology]. In *A Economia Solidária e os Desafios Globais do Trabalho*. [The Solidarity Economy and the Global Challenges of Labor], 1st ed., edited by A. R. de Souza and M. Zanin, vol. 1, 233–42. EdUFSCar.

Vasudevan, Pavithra. 2019. "An Intimate Inventory of Race and Waste." *Antipode* 53 (3): 770–90.

Whitson, Risa. 2011. "Negotiating Place and Value: Geographies of Waste and Scavenging in Buenos Aires." *Antipode* 43 (4): 1404–33.

CHAPTER 10

CONCEPTUALIZING BODIES AS URBAN INFRASTRUCTURE: GENDER, INTIMATE INFRASTRUCTURES, AND SLOW INFRASTRUCTURAL VIOLENCE IN URBAN NEPAL AND INDIA

Yaffa Truelove and Hanna A. Ruszczyk

INTRODUCTION

Critical urban scholars and geographers focusing on southern urbanism have created an impressive and growing literature on infrastructure. From the necessity to consider comparison between the north and the south (McFarlane and Robinson 2012; Ranganathan and Balazs 2015) and heterogeneous infrastructural configurations within cities themselves (Lawhon et al. 2018; McFarlane, Silver, and Truelove 2017), to understandings of infrastructure as hybrid (Larkin 2008), incremental (Silver 2014), visible/invisible (Star 1999; Amin 2014), lived (Graham and McFarlane 2015, and peopled (Simone 2004). This body of work has not only "importantly expanded meanings and understandings of infrastructure" (Lawhon et al. 2018, 722) that acknowledge both the social and material dimensions of infrastructure; it has also opened up multidisciplinary approaches that go beyond understanding infrastructure as being primarily rooted in nonliving material systems and structures. Furthermore, it highlighted the simultaneous social, cultural, and peopled dimensions of infrastructural networks that make infrastructure "living" (Berlant 2016). In Berlant's words, "infrastructure is not identical to system or structure, as we currently see them, because infrastructure is defined by the movement or patterning of social form. It is the living mediation of what organizes life: the lifeworld of structure" (393). Such understandings have led to a growing number of new studies that consider how infrastructures are forged, maintained, and eroded through changing relations that pattern social and material form—and in the case of the urban, structure the ways that life is made and unmade in cities (Simone 2004; Elyachar 2010; Lancione and McFarlane 2016; Ruszczyk 2017; Millington 2018). The everyday making (and unmaking) of infrastructures is thus inclusive of—and just as much about—the social, peopled, and financial infrastructures that enable life to take place, as it is about more conventional associations of infrastructures comprising roads, pipes, and sewer networks.

This chapter is based on a previously published article in *Political Geography* (Truelove and Ruszczyk 2022) and builds on geographic and interdisciplinary approaches to urban infrastructure that highlight their social, material, and "living" components and forms. While acknowledging the tremendous and varied scholarship in urban studies on the multiplicity of infrastructure, there continues to be a need to further interrogate how living social and material infrastructures shape, maintain, and enable urban life, politics, and distinctly unequal lived experiences of the city. As scholars such as Simone (2004) demonstrate that "people are infrastructure" through flows of information and networks of collaboration in cities like Johannesburg, and Elyachar (2010) demonstrates the social infrastructure she calls "phatic labor" that women use to bolster financial networks and resilience in cities like Cairo, we build on this body of work in several distinct ways. Specifically, this chapter pushes the concept of infrastructure further into the sphere and scale of the body, drawing on feminist theory and feminist political geography more specifically to do so. By exploring the body as infrastructure in three highly differing cities of South Asia, we argue that there is a consistency of this phenomenon. The embodied and gendered dimensions of infrastructure constitute integral forms of living infrastructure that enable critical networks in the city to function, while profoundly shaping urban life and the politics of inclusion and exclusion. Yet, gendered and embodied dimensions of infrastructure have been rather lightly interrogated in the literature thus far. In demonstrating the ways that gendered bodies act as critical urban infrastructure, we follow Star's (1999, 379) assertion that studying the unstudied with regard to infrastructure offers an enriched understanding of cities that brings infrastructural visibility through "a social justice agenda by valorizing previously neglected people and things."

In interrogating the relationships between bodies, gender and infrastructure, and specifically the making of cities such as Bharatpur and Dhangadhi in

Nepal and Delhi, India, this chapter seeks to make two primary contributions. First, we show how conceptualizing bodies as infrastructure reveals important dimensions of the social and material forms that enable critical resources to flow and integral networks to be built in cities. We explore this in relation to intimate infrastructures, referring to how the social and material work of the body helps to build, develop, and maintain cities through gendered infrastructures in the everyday. Second, we show from our comparative case studies the ways that gendered "slow infrastructural violence" accrues through patterns of infrastructural invisibility. Particular bodies act as urban infrastructure in everyday and unremarkable ways, and attention to embodied infrastructural configurations reveals important social and political dimensions of the consequences of infrastructure on everyday urban life. This chapter thus raises a simultaneous call for theoretical engagement with the socio-materiality of infrastructure and the body, an increased regard for the multiplicity of urban infrastructures, and an interrogation of gender and infrastructural politics in the city.

EXPERIENCING CITIES

Empirically, this chapter draws from long-term ethnographic research in two tier-two cities in Nepal, Bharatpur and Dhangadhi, as well as the megacity and capital of India, Delhi. Our ethnographic work is not intended to provide an exhaustive qualitative analysis of bodies as infrastructure in each field site, but rather demonstrate some of the key processes, mechanisms, and practices by which bodies act as urban infrastructure in the cities and sites of our long-time research. Specifically, Ruszczyk draws from research in second-tier cities of Nepal from November 2014 to April 2019 through four fieldwork trips to Bharatpur in which 120 people were interviewed, the majority of whom were women. Several focus group discussions with community groups (especially mothers' groups) took place, and some of the interviewees were repeatedly visited. Aims of the fieldwork included analyzing how urban governance was evolving and changing in an academically underresearched yet rapidly urbanizing second-tier city. One trip to Dhangadhi in November 2017 took place in order to compare how second-tier cities were developing and the role of women's bodies as infrastructure was specifically investigated. More than twenty interviews took place with community groups, government officials, health officials, and nongovernmental organizations in Dhangadhi. Truelove draws on ethnographic research on planned and informal settlements of Delhi, India during 2011–2012, as well as follow-up fieldwork in 2016 and 2017, including interviews and/or focus groups with more than sixty residents. This research was primarily aimed at tracking the differing gendered infrastructures by which water is accessed "beyond the network" in both formal and informal settlements.

By considering how bodies act as both social and material infrastructure in a set of cities that have distinct features and are of varying sizes, we hope to demonstrate how intimate infrastructures, their visibility and invisibility, and their consequent "slow violence" are forged, maintained, and navigated in highly situated ways. Further, by drawing from data sets across differing cities, we consider the differing types of intersectional caste, class, and gender politics that both produce intimate infrastructures, as well as their uneven social and political consequences in the cities of study. The chapter proceeds as follows. First, we draw from feminist political geography and other gendered approaches to infrastructure to conceptualize bodies as infrastructure. We then propose the frame of slow infrastructural violence for understanding the consequences of bodies as infrastructure, which brings attention to mundane and slowly accruing forms of violence that accompany gendered infrastructural practices in cities that are rapidly transforming or developing. The chapter then turns to an elaboration of empirical qualitative evidence of how the body as infrastructure, and slow infrastructural violence, manifests itself in two urbanizing cities of Nepal and in Delhi. We conclude by arguing for further theoretical engagement with the socio-materiality of infrastructure and the body, an openness to the multiplicity of urban infrastructures, and an interrogation of gender and infrastructural politics in cities where more people will be living in the future and where politics and infrastructure are being actively created. These cities warrant exploration.

BODIES AS INFRASTRUCTURE

This chapter puts forward the conceptualization of bodies as infrastructure. We specifically show how the body acts as both a material and social form of infrastructure not only in megacities like Delhi but, as importantly, in urbanizing spaces, such as Bharatpur and Dhangadhi, Nepal, that warrant critical analysis. Cities such as Delhi, Bharatpur, and Dhangadhi are important to reflect upon because it is in such places that urban dwellers of the world reside (United Cities and Local Governments 2020). These cities represent the lived experience of cities throughout the world. Although megacities and regional urbanizing cities may have many differences (including population size, geographic size, levels of inward and outward migration, density, and financial resources under the management of local authorities), there are similarities in the way infrastructure is evolving, the role of gendered bodies as socio-material infrastructure, and the power involved in these evolving dynamics. This is an important contribution to political geography.

Conceptualizing the body as infrastructure firstly seeks to build on and extend a growing scholarship that examines infrastructure across scales (global, regional, urban, intraurban) and spheres (social, cultural, political, economic, material, and ecological). As *infrastructure* is a collective term that has been reworked through recent social science studies that give attention to both its human and nonhuman agencies and associations, infrastructures consist of a plurality of integrated parts that are understood to support some higher-order project taking place (Carse 2017). Rather than what constitutes an infrastructure being predetermined and intuitive, Larkin (2013) argues that the act of defining something as an infrastructure is a categorizing moment that brings particular aspects of an infrastructure into view, while potentially obviating others. For Harvey, Jensen, and Morita (2017, 7), while "anything can be called into being as an infrastructure," it is important to consider that once something is defined as infrastructure, there are implications related to sites of governance. As infrastructure can be found on multiple scales in the city, we understand that defining an infrastructure is a political act that focuses attention on certain aspects of infrastructure while ignoring others. It is precisely because bodies are not conventionally understood to comprise infrastructure—that their roles in mundane tasks such as hauling water, providing social networks of support in neighborhoods, and even aiding in financial networks of exchange do not surface in policy, planning, and mainstream narratives of how resources and networks function to build cities—that the role of the body in critical urban networks is often made invisible and overlooked.

Second, in our case studies of bodies as infrastructure across South Asian cities, we also build on feminist political geographers' long-standing work on the intimate and the body. This scholarship has "long centered the body as subject and object of analysis through which to understand how power acts spatially in the world to control" (Mountz 2018, 759). Feminist political geography expands the realm of the political to untangle and attempt to understand the relationships between space, power, and politics (Staeheli, Kofman, and Peake 2004; Fluri 2009; Fluri and Piedalue 2017; Hyndman 2019). Through these relationships, the intimate sphere of life, which includes bodies and the body, becomes key. In the words of Mountz, the body "becomes analytical tool, scale, site, . . . that is subjected to other processes" (2018, 761). Thus, feminist geographic thought has reformulated the body as an active site by which wider processes become collapsed and experienced in the everyday, and by which differing forms of political engagement occur (Pain and Staeheli 2014; Fluri and

Piedalue 2017). We thus understand the intimate not to be disconnected from the structural but, as feminist political geographers and others have shown, to constitute a sphere of life and everyday practice by which wider political, economic, and social relations are experienced and lived. For example, Pain and Staeheli (2014) suggest that intimacy consists of both proximate and distant spatial relations that span interpersonal, institutional, and national realms. This also includes a consideration of how emotion, affect, and embodiment are tied to a range of differing spatial relations.

This work is particularly useful in embodying infrastructure studies through our framing of how bodies become a critical urban infrastructure. Considering bodies as an important dimension of intimate infrastructures provides insight into the multiscalar spatial relations that are connected to the body's infrastructural practices (Pain and Staeheli 2014). From the work of women's bodies that maintain waste infrastructure in Dakar (Fredericks 2018), to gendered social labor that bolsters financial networks in Cairo (Elyachar 2010), to networks of care by which water is secured by women for the benefit of other household members in Delhi (Truelove 2019)—all are connected to wider political, economic, ecological, and social relations. As the Collective (2019, 21) state, bringing feminist perspectives on the body into understandings of urban infrastructure "opens up avenues for exploring how bodies—in their racialized, classed, gendered, aged forms—constitute infrastructural systems. Such an approach challenges the prefigurative and performative role of people in / as infrastructure by revealing the ways embodied labour is embedded in large infrastructures, knowledge practices, urban lives." Ultimately, we show how the infrastructures maintained through the body's social, affective, and material practices disclose important dimensions of how infrastructures are made in the everyday, how networks across the city work, and how the city (and patterns of belonging, exclusion, and violence) are unevenly experienced. Bringing an intimate perspective to analyzing infrastructure is critical to uncovering important and unpredictable dimensions of infrastructure in daily life. As Wilson (2016) notes, "Tracing circuits of pipes and cables embeds intimate relations in unpredictable junctures of material and symbolic power."

Thus, thinking about infrastructures in urban Nepal and India through this lens opens up analytical space to consider the politics at hand in the mundane practices of the body as it engages in infrastructural labor, care, and social work and is connected to wider social, political, and economic processes at the neighborhood, city, and regional scales. We show how intimate and embodied activities of daily life, from forming social networks in neighborhoods to enacting gendered household labor of hauling and distributing water, form key infrastructures by which urban dwellers access and circulate resources and knowledge, while also disclosing how neighborhoods and cities are unequally experienced at the bodily scale. This analysis thus contributes an urban and infrastructural focus to "feminists' ongoing interrogations of the everyday, the intimate, and the mundane as vital spaces from which to theorize in/equality and to map the workings of power" (Piedalue 2019, 4; see also Nelson and Seager 2005 as well as De Leeuw 2016).

Finally, in understanding the body as infrastructure, we draw from the nuanced work of anthropologist Julia Elyachar (2010), who expands on the gendered social and financial infrastructure of Cairo. She delves into how women who live lives apart from the male world provide essential social and financial infrastructure. This, in turn, allows their communities and male family members to be successful. Elyachar utilizes the concept of phatic labor to make visible social infrastructure. She argues that women create key social infrastructures through maintaining relationships and extended contacts that can be mobilized not only in a time of need but to achieve long-term familial goals (e.g., marriage for children, establishing businesses). The gendered infrastructures of women's social networks, viewed as a form of "essential infrastructure" (456), allow the city to function. While the social labor of such networks may not create conditions for women or their families to thrive, women's bodies buttress against the city crumbling or collapsing and actively create conditions for male family members to be more successful and resilient in Cairo. Although Berlant (2016, 393), following Edwards (2003), proposes that "failure of an infrastructure is ordinary in poor countries and countries at war," our research draws on Elyachar and others to argue a different position. If we broaden the understanding of infrastructure to the social and material practices of bodies, then people as infrastructure (Simone 2004) do more than prevent the city from failing. They can actually help the city to develop, enable critical resources to reach households, and often support particular household members to have economic resilience and life opportunities in cities, albeit often reifying particular types of gender/class/race inequities in the process.

Fredericks's (2018) work demonstrates how such intersectional gender inequities become reified as gendered and classed bodies labor unequally in waste infrastructural networks in Dakar, Senegal. She provides essential signposting for this chapter by paying particular attention to overly burdened female bodies that comprise the materiality of rubbish collection in the city. Fredericks utilizes a materialist reading of infrastructure through which the definition of infrastructure is expanded to recalibrate how we think through material and social aspects of labor and working bodies. Here, the infrastructures of waste in the city become devolved onto the gendered, laboring body, which is further marked as disposable within wider urban and gender politics.

SLOW INFRASTRUCTURAL VIOLENCE

The second main conceptual contribution we seek to make in this chapter relates to what we call "slow infrastructural violence," which we argue often accompanies, and is a consequence of, bodies as urban infrastructure. In particular, we show in separate case studies in urban Nepal and India the *intersectional* (Crenshaw 1989) gendered dimensions of everyday infrastructural violence that emerge as bodies act as urban infrastructure. While a great deal of historical writing about women in the city has been concerned with safety and security (Bondi and Rose 2003), and literature on urban violence has tended to focus on geopolitical warfare and spectacular violence (Gregory 2011; Graham 2008), we use the framing of slow infrastructural violence to bring attention to mundane and slowly accruing forms of violence that accompany gendered infrastructural practices in the everyday city. Here we bring together literature that conceptualizes slow violence (Nixon 2011), infrastructural violence (Rodgers and O'Neill 2012), and feminist approaches to violence (Pain and Staeheli 2014; Datta and Ahmed 2020) in order to theorize the ways slow infrastructural violence results from embodied infrastructural practices.

Slow violence has been utilized as a conceptual device in the environmental and domestic spheres of life. In reference to the environment, Nixon's (2011, 2) foundational work defines slow violence as "a violence that occurs gradually and out of sight, a violence of delayed destruction that is dispersed across time and space, an attritional violence that is typically not viewed as violence at all." This concept can gain further nuance in relation to cities when tied to scholarly conceptualizations of "infrastructural violence" (Rodgers and O'Neill 2012, 403), which understand infrastructural violence to be both active and passive and recognize first and foremost that "the workings of infrastructure can be substantially deleterious." While not taking an explicitly gendered lens, Rodgers and O'Neill assert that, as infrastructures rework relations between people and things in daily life, these relationalities are often "to the detriment of marginalized actors" (404), but can receive little visibility since their deleterious effects often accrue slowly over time, rather than simply through spectacular events. Thus, while infrastructures can be the material embodiment of structural violence, revealing how networks of water, waste, and energy operate through political economic structures that exclude working class urbanites from equitable access, for example, infrastructures can also be what Rodgers and O'Neill call "the instrumental medium" of a violence more akin to Nixon's conceptualization that takes place slowly over time. Here, understanding the violence of infrastructure means investigating how "the material organization and form of a landscape not only reflect but also reinforce social orders, thereby becoming a contributing factor to reoccurring forms of harm" (303). As bodies provide often invisible forms of infrastructure in daily practice, we bring a gendered and embodied lens to understanding the workings of "slow infrastructural violence": a violence of gendered (and intersectional) social orders that organizes urban landscapes, helps distribute and circulate resources, and often leads to recurring forms of harm for particular gendered/classed/casted/racialized bodies in the city. Here, we also respond to feminist political geographers who advocate for further scholarship on the ways that slow violence "has clear though [until now] largely unexplored relevance for urban studies" (Pain 2019, 387).

We thus see the gradual accretion of slow infrastructural violence over time as part of infrastructural invisibility. Because bodies acting as infrastructures tend to be invisible, slow violence is a quality of this invisibility. In other words, we show that slow violence accretes over time as an unrecognized and unseen aspect of everyday intimate infrastructures: the waiting for water that prevents women from pursuing other income opportunities or the physically taxing processes of hauling cumbersome buckets to provide water for drinking, washing, and cooking in Delhi, and the social labor and networks of care that provide resilience in urbanizing Nepal but yield unequal effects for men and women. As indicated by Elyachar (2010), this type of infrastructure does not leave easily visible traces on the ground for researchers to follow or data for algorithms for engineers to reproduce. Its invisibility is part of its power to keep things the same. While not widely recognized or perceived, public visibility of these infrastructures and their violences occasionally happens at moments of rupture. For example, in the case study on Delhi, we will show how rupture occurs when Muslim men take over the typically feminized labor of finding water, with the result of disrupting patriarchal discourses and norms. As such practices stand out as against the norm, they thus reveal a visibility of relations that have otherwise remained normalized and status quo and present new openings for reworking and denaturalizing gendered infrastructural labor.

Finally, while few studies have taken a gendered lens to infrastructural violence (see Truelove and O'Reilly [2020] and Datta and Ahmed [2020] for exceptions), our chapter draws from Datta and Ahmed's (2020) recent writing on gendered and intimate violence in relation to urban infrastructures. In studying violence against women in Thiruvanathapuram, Kerala, Datta and

Ahmed importantly demonstrate that an *absence* of infrastructures such as water, toilets, and public transport constitutes a form of gendered and intimate violence. These scholars show how intimate infrastructures in the everyday—and particularly their absence or malfunction—not only spatialize structural violence but also critically reveal an "intimate and corporeal experience of this violence from the city to the household" (Datta and Ahmed 2020, 68). While our work draws from Datta and Ahmed's approach to intimate infrastructures and focuses on the slow violence of the everyday, we diverge from this research in looking at the making of infrastructures (rather than their absence) through our conceptualization of bodies as infrastructure. We show how gendered bodies acting as urban infrastructure constitute a slow violence that reinforces patterns of harm that are experienced by the body as simultaneously affective, structural, intimate, and ongoing. This includes the hidden violences of gendered social orders that shape unequal infrastructural practices in the first place or, additionally, the long-term, chronic physical and emotional tolls associated with finding and transporting resources like water, as well as lost life and income opportunities that can result for time devoted to the everyday labor surrounding infrastructure. In the following sections we show how the body works as an intimate (and thus often invisible) infrastructure of city life that circulates and enables resources to reach city dwellers, revealing the actually existing infrastructures by which fragments are pieced together and made into social and material systems that keep resources circulating. Thus, conceptualizing bodies as infrastructure helps to reveal important patterns of invisibility related to how infrastructures are made in the everyday, how the city works, and how the city is unevenly and often violently experienced.

THE BODY AS INFRASTRUCTURE IN NEPAL'S CITIES

Bharatpur is located in the south-central part of Nepal, bordering India. From 2014 to 2018, its population increased from 150,000 to 270,000 and its geographic area doubled. It is visually transforming from rural agricultural land to settled neighborhoods throughout the city. Many of its male residents are international migrants working in Malaysia or other more affluent countries. Dhangadhi is located in the far west of Nepal and shares a border crossing with India. It has a population of 170,000 and is the provincial hub for government. Many of Dhangadhi's residents work in India for very low wages compared to migrants working in Malaysia.

By looking at increasingly urbanizing Nepal we can see intimate social infrastructure in cities via a gendered lens. In some cities of Nepal, such as Bharatpur, it is the social infrastructure of mothers' groups that allows members to transmit meaning and economic value through an exchange, while in other cities, such as Dhangadhi, it is not a group but rather individual bodies that provide infrastructure. In Simone's discussion of infrastructure (2004, 419) he suggests: "Such infrastructure remains largely invisible unless we reconceptualize the notion of belonging in terms other than those of a logic of group or territorial representation. People as infrastructure indicates residents' needs to generate concrete acts and contexts of social collaboration inscribed with *multiple identities* rather than in overseeing and enforcing mod-ulated transactions among discrete population groups." It is this weaving of diverse people with multiple identities as urban infrastructure that is useful as an analogy to Bharatpur, Nepal. People's maneuvering in mothers' groups, for example, is represented as a geographical bound to the neighborhood be-cause this is the form of urban infrastructure that is being made visible from this city. Through action in informal collectives, people are able to function as infrastructure in the manner Simone describes. Women organize themselves into mothers' groups with sixty to one hundred members, on a neighborhood scale. The groups are between one and ten years old. The women interviewed explained that they established groups because they worried about basic infra-structural issues that were not being addressed by the local authorities. Often times, these mothers' groups are organized by caste, level of income, and ex-tended family networks, meanwhile excluding tenants as members. These in-tersections come to matter in the politics of infrastructure as bodies because there is always a hierarchy and a differentiation being made through different markers.

The mothers' groups provide a range of services: social support to one another as well as to vulnerable individuals in the neighborhood (who are not members), access to a group savings and credit scheme, and government initiated "environmental cleanliness campaigns" (the women clean and tidy the streets) in their neighborhood. In Bharatpur ward 4, the mothers' group members, led by Rita Devi, explain the range of activities during a focus group discussion in 2015: "This mothers' group helps the poor women in the group when they have problems such as the death of a family member. We also work for health and sanitation in the community. We also manage problems in some households. We help children in poor families with stationery [for school]. We also provide food to old-age people. We also do [a] savings [scheme] and the people in need can use the money on a rotation basis." With the help of a female community leader, Ruszczyk held a focus group discussion with the Little Flower mothers' group two hours after the Gorkha earthquake of April

2015 started. To her surprise, the members of the group stayed with her, while the ground beneath us shook and told her about their lives and their group. They explained that they wanted her to tell others about their efforts for the city that are unacknowledged by the government, indicating how visible work in local areas is rendered invisible at the city scale and within wider patriarchal social orderings. The women were proud of their activities and wanted respect from city dwellers and political actors embedded in patriarchal structures. The members of the Little Flower mothers' group overwhelmingly included high-caste Brahmin women whose families owned land. The women were housewives or teachers or had other paid employment. During the focus group discussion, they explained that the purpose of the mothers' group is to provide essential support to the community that is lacking, whether it be infrastructures that bolster financial security or the cleaning of streets. As a personal benefit, through participation in the Little Flower mothers' group, they can interact with other women. Otherwise they are physically restricted to their houses if they are not employed. These societal norms manage the mobility and actions of high-caste Brahmin women.

During November 2017, in the city of Dhangadhi, women express pride in their infrastructural labor as volunteer municipal health and community liaison officers. While unpaid and voluntary, their responsibilities include guiding women through safe pregnancies, providing early childhood care, health and family planning, and immunization services. Often times the volunteer health officers treat cases of lower respiratory tract infections. The women work irregular and long hours, but they do not receive a salary and are not valued sufficiently to be paid by the local authority, as these infrastructures of care become naturalized as unpaid gendered labor of women. However, women's work as health infrastructure for the city provides the essential link between vulnerable populations in rural, semiurban, and urban communities and the formal health system (Public Services International 2018). But they (and their husbands whom Ruszczyk also interviewed) are angry that it is not only their labor that is unpaid: they must also pay for their own public transportation. The municipality trains the health workers and relies on their essential labor but is unwilling to compensate them or to reimburse them for expenses. Instead the municipality saves municipal funds for other more visible infrastructure projects, such as the provision of roads or street lighting. These social and material practices in cities that are rapidly growing show the politics of this bodily work at the intimate scale (both through groups and an individual basis) and how political dimensions of the city are played out in gendered bodies. The ways that bodies are utilized as everyday socio-technical infrastructure to serve the city is often invisible but continues with the acknowledgment and support of the patriarchal society and government structures.

THE BODY AS INFRASTRUCTURE IN DELHI

Across Delhi's diverse neighborhoods, the everyday lives and routines of women are often shaped by both social and material practices to access household water. Due to patriarchal discourses and gender norms that relegate household water management to women's domestic labor, responsibility for water procurement across class groups predominately falls onto the bodies of female household members. It is through women's bodies, specifically women's gendered social and material practices, that an intimate infrastructure is made that actively subsidizes and enables water from (and beyond) the network to reach city dwellers. This all-too-invisible infrastructure is absent in dominant narratives of how water is circulated in India's capital. Yet the stress, strain, sacrifices, and physical and emotional care that makes water flow reveals a critical and overlooked dimension of both how the urban metabolism of the city's waterworks come to function and how the politics and infra-making (Lancione and McFarlane 2016) of the city itself is unevenly experienced.

While Delhi provides an average of two to four hours per day of centralized piped water to planned neighborhoods, excluding centralized water connections altogether from unplanned areas, the public water supply is often unreliable due to unequal allotments to differing districts, interruptions, lack of pressure, and leakages, each of which require social and material practices and negotiations of predominately middle-class women to overcome and circumvent. As women are primarily responsible for procuring and managing household water, it is common for middle-class women living in planned areas of the city to approach local resident welfare associations (RWAs) to try to rectify water inadequacies to their homes. In addition, a water board (Delhi Jal Board) office might be visited to issue a complaint of sporadic water timings or faulty pipes, or neighbors might need to be persuaded to stop letting water overflow in their own household water storage tanks through (often illegal) pumps, preventing those down the line from filling their own. Women often compensate for insufficient water through the gendered time and labor of calling a private water tanker, buying bottled water, or negotiating and managing water sharing with a neighbor who has an illegal tube well (personal communication, 2017).

Even if piped water arrives in adequate quantity to the planned city, it must be actively managed in real time: pumps must be turned on when water is flowing, and rooftop storage tanks must be filled to keep water so it can last the duration of the day or for days at a time for the household. Sometimes reverse osmosis machines are installed and utilized to filter the water so it will be potable. Women's social and material labor provides the "bridge" between these infrastructural fragments (McFarlane 2018) to enable and manage the city's water supply so that men and children in Delhi's households have safer and accessible water. However, waiting for, finding, and timing water's arrival must be negotiated in tandem with (or at the expense of) women's other plans and opportunities. Furthermore, as women pump water, often with illegal motors, to store as much as possible in overhead tanks during the hours it is running, the rush for water is often fraught with conflict among women neighbors who cooperate with each other at other times of day. For example, as one middle-class woman (who works in the water sector herself) summarized her own neighborhood's gendered water labor and conflicts: "The same women who used to go together to drop their children to school in the morning would be fighting in the afternoon for that maybe 200 litres of extra [piped] water [to store in overhead tankers]" (BBC 2012). As shown elsewhere (Truelove 2019), the water security of women household members is often curtailed through the risks, time, hazards, and sacrifices made to patch together fragmented infrastructural networks. Using their bodies as infrastructure enables not only their household members but the city itself to achieve higher levels of water security.

Thus, the politics of this bodily work, though highly normalized and thus invisible and taken for granted, is absolutely crucial to water politics at the city scale. This is a politics of how "actually existing" infrastructures, often invisible as they are relegated to the intimate sphere of everyday life, are pieced together and made into socio-technical systems that service the city. Zerah (1998, 2000) referred to this water labor as "compensation practices," estimating in the year 2000 that their worth totaled around 3 billion rupees each year, which was about twice the municipality's expenditure on its water supply during the same period of time. Here, the city's public network is able to render invisible many of its disruptions, gaps, and inadequacies through the embodied gendered labor that works on a daily basis to fill those gaps and ensure water is secured for households. Conversely, the gendered laboring bodies that pump, store, distribute, and negotiate neighborhood water distribution do not come to count or be seen in dominant understandings of the infrastructure by which water reaches city dwellers in the everyday. This not only represents a devaluing of labor that subsidizes the city's low costs and charges associated with distributing household water, but also demonstrates how the politics of water infrastructure at the city scale is ever-reliant and intimately connected to the gender politics of water at the household and bodily scale.

BETWEEN EMPOWERMENT AND SLOW VIOLENCE: INFORMAL FINANCIAL INFRASTRUCTURE

Informal community groups in Nepal often develop an urban financial infrastructural function through group savings schemes. Some groups such as the male-led neighborhood groups collect 100 or 200 Nepalese rupees from each member (equivalent of US$1–2 in April 2015) per month and annually they redistribute some of the funds to each participant (retaining 1,000 Nepalese rupees from each person in the financial scheme). The group members view the financial schemes as a fundamental part of the neighborhood group service provision. This new form of urban organization is rupturing historically unequal and destructive lending practices impacting the most vulnerable in the community. This informal, intimate infrastructure has somewhat relieved economic pressure on the very poor in Bharatpur and is changing social dynamics on multiple scales (individual and community level) for men. These new changing urban practices are mitigating slow violence of poverty and deprivation for men but, importantly, not for women, irrespective of intersectional markers including ethnicity, caste, and class. The rigid patriarchal society is not motivated to better the situation of women.

The financial infrastructure of savings and credit schemes is also viewed as essential by all of the mothers' groups interviewed. The Little Flower mothers' group in ward 4 explains that all members contribute 200 Nepalese rupees monthly. Any woman can access the funds (if necessary)—up to 30,000 Nepalese rupees with minimal interest. The most common uses for the money include medical treatment, private school tuition fees and materials, and, less frequently, construction of a house. The savings schemes provide women with economic empowerment, a financial safety net, and the psychological empowerment of "having a voice" in their community. Every member of a mothers' group mentions personal empowerment through finances. In Bharatpur, the women's saving and credit schemes do not provide income-generating loans; rather, the group approach enables women to ensure household subsistence and survival and, at times, planning for the future. Through the management of funds, the women have control and the power to support themselves and other women in a time of need without asking for approval from husbands. Through the provision of informal financial infrastructure in the form of the group saving and credit schemes, both the neighborhood groups and mothers' groups are addressing their perceived most important everyday risk in the city—economic security. The schemes are a safety net if a family faces extreme difficulty in their livelihoods strategy, if health deteriorates, in case of death, or in other everyday crises.

Tensions arise in cities when mothers' groups become too visible in terms of their labored infrastructure provision within rigid social orderings or when their requests for changes in neighborhoods and cities become too loud for men to bear. Tensions also arise when mothers' groups become too powerful in terms of the amount of money they have under management. On a local level, there are tensions between mothers' groups who control their own financial schemes and other financial groups. The Little Flower mothers' group explains that the local financial cooperative is not pleased with the power afforded to the Little Flower mothers' group by managing their own funds. The financial cooperative has high expenses related to managing their funds, while the mothers' group has minimal expenses due to free labor within the group. The financial cooperative wants "this mothers' group to be dissolved" and the money deposited directly into the financial cooperative instead to gain political power over the group's assets, according to the president of the mothers' group. On a municipal aggregated basis, the financial value of mothers' groups financial schemes in circulation could be in the range of $100,000–350,000.[1] Given the amount of money under informal management, it is not a surprise there is envy toward mothers' groups.

Slow violence and exploitation of gendered invisible infrastructure take place in audacious yet common place ways. In another part of ward 4, the new male neighborhood group president earnestly explained that his management team would not "take" the mothers' group funds and distribute to the neighborhood group's members as grants (unlike his predecessor, who had no qualms about stealing from the local mothers' group). When I asked the mothers' group about this theft, they responded with despair and anger toward the neighborhood group. Women felt humiliated and powerless. They were not allowed to control their own money and, simultaneously, they unwillingly continued to implement the dictates of the neighborhood group. The women continued to clean the streets and complete other tasks the neighborhood group (and local authority) "asked" of them; they did not have a choice. The threat that the neighborhood group could steal their money without any repercussions was always there. The slow violence placed upon women and their bodies, and even their hopes and aspirations for a future of their imagining, was rendered invisible to those not in the local area. There was no way for the women's groups to stake a larger claim. They were isolated in their neighborhoods and did not know how to connect with other women's groups in the city.

In this situation, the women were mindful of the patriarchal societal limitations in place that constrict their options for maneuvering. Several mothers' groups highlighted limitations of the mothers' group due to social constraints imposed by men (for example, wives need permission from husbands to join mothers' groups) and the government (who is not interested in engaging with urban concerns as articulated by women). The informal financial infrastructure can be considered empowerment and also slow violence that is affective with elements of shame, helplessness and anger, while also being intimate, elusive, and ongoing. There are promises and perils of financial infrastructure.

In the case of Dhangadhi, the local authority was keen to utilize women as core municipal (but unpaid) staff who provided essential health services to the city's residents. Furthermore, they expected the women and their families to subsidize expenses such as travel and materials needed to give to poor health clients. Nixon argues that the impacts of slow violence are "pervasive but elusive" (2011, 3). This type of violence "quietly accumulate[s] and defer[s] their damage over time" (Davies 2019, 2) leaving women devastated and angry yet simultaneously proud of their contribution to their communities and cities.

SLOW VIOLENCE AND FRAGMENTED WATER IN UNPLANNED DELHI

In the unplanned *bastis* (small informal settlements) of Delhi such as Rampur Camp, slow violence constitutes a particular quality and outcome of the invisible and intimate infrastructures that make water flow. Slow infrastructural violence appears in the social orderings by which particular bodies experience chronic and accruing harms from a systematic exclusion from the public water network; the social reproduction and care that structure gendered water practices; the hazards of finding, negotiating, and transporting water; and lost income, life opportunities, and even potentially life years due to the experience of mitigating a contaminated, insufficient, and irregular water supply.

Specifically, residents of Delhi's *bastis* are excluded from accessing centralized, in-house water connections from the public utility. The social and material labor of piecing together fragmented infrastructures beyond the network—including attempts to track, coax, and store water from inadequate and unreliable local tube wells and erratic and insufficient tanker deliveries—relies on specific bodies. While patriarchal discourses position women across class groups as household water managers, intersections of class, caste, and religion work to compound infrastructural violence over time for particular urbanites. First, working-class groups in Delhi face significantly more severe water problems and inadequacies as compared to middle and upper classes since the working class by and large lack centralized water connections due to the "illegality" of their housing, while often having less money and resources to circumvent water problems (Truelove 2019; Zerah 2000; Comptroller and Auditor General of India 2013). Their reliance on partial and fragmented infrastructures like tankers, tube wells, and privately purchased water often falls below baseline water levels of what the World Health Organization deems necessary for meeting even basic needs (Comptroller and Auditor General of India 2013; World Health Organization 2003). Apart from the substantial struggles to find water in the wake of supply inadequacies, shortages of potable water in and of themselves are associated with dehydration, an inability to cook food if there is not sufficient water for cooking, and reliance on nonpotable sources that lead to illness through contamination. Second, for nondominant-caste groups and Muslims among the working class, previous studies indicate that systems of ethno-religious discrimination can further erode access to and control over water infrastructures in Delhi's neighborhoods (Truelove 2019, 2016). These groups might be excluded altogether from local NGO development initiatives (Truelove 2016), be the last to receive access (at the highest price) when tube wells do service an area, and face other structural constraints (such as having no other family members in the city, or working as construction laborers) that further confine how they will problem-solve inadequate water flows during daylight hours. In Rampur Camp, it is the bodies of nondominant-caste and working-class women, as well as Muslim working-class men (who live without female family members), who bear the brunt of the slow violence of procuring and managing water beyond the piped network. This includes the labor, time, and social networking required to negotiate access and piece together fragmented networks. This might entail sharing water with a neighbor, negotiating with politicians for closer access to tanker deliveries, or the everyday practices of waiting for, hauling, and managing water and its various uses, storage, and circulation for household members. Women in particular reported shoulder and back injuries, lost time and income-generating opportunities, exposure to increased harassment from men, and ongoing stress. Piecing infrastructural networks together forms a politics of care and social reproduction that levels compounded yet often all too invisible tolls on the city dwellers who undertake this work.

Thinking through these intimate infrastructures thus opens up analytical space to consider the politics at hand in the mundane practices of the body as it engages in infrastructural labor, care, and the everyday maintenance of water flows that are connected to wider social, political, and economic processes at the neighborhood, city, and regional scales. Despite Delhi boasting more than two hundred liters per person per day of water in the city, largely drawn from regional areas and dams, specific social groups face intersectional inequalities that produce unequal burdens of both water procurement and insecurity. The slow violence of bodies working as a replacement for absent or defunct infrastructure is shaped by intersecting gender, class, caste, and ethnoreligious power relations. As particular (gendered, classed, and casted) bodies are unevenly tasked with supplementing and compensating for infrastructural inadequacies, other urban residents experience the benefits of increased water access and security that results.

For example, while dominant-caste women in Rampur Camp had stronger ties to the local leader and local water vendors, and could often use these social connections to press for increasing allotments of tube well water, nondominant-caste women had to find alternate and more laborious water solutions. This includes negotiating water access from places of work, for example, when tube well water in the settlement was not sufficient or had been disproportionately distributed to dominant-caste groups. Women reported that "borrowing" water from their employers in the form of a few buckets a day when other water sources were scarce diminished their negotiating power and even work incomes, sometimes leading to not receiving their full wages. On the flip side, Muslim women and men in Rampur Camp experienced ethno-religious discrimination at the neighborhood and city scale that curtailed their access to local water sources. For example, a local NGO initiative had not extended tube well water pipes to their side of the settlement to the degree granted to Hindu residents, which Muslim residents attributed to patterns of long-term discrimination they encountered in Delhi. As a whole, infrastructures for Muslim residents were visibly lagging behind in the settlement, including drainage, concrete lanes, and electricity, placing higher burdens on these residents to problem-solve the basics of water and cooking, a marked difference from their Hindu neighbors (Truelove 2016). The Muslim community's exclusion from equitable tube well water caused residents to resort to alternate water sources, including buying small packets of water or walking to another settlement with a tube well, in which the neighboring community was more willing to partly share the water. These situated material and structural forms of infrastructural deprivation show how slow violence accretes over time through both the limits of infrastructural access, and the body's work to compensate for absent, fragile, and defunct networks.

For local, predominately Dalit women in Rampur Camp, time given to water also plays a key role in the nature and toll of slow infrastructural violence. Some women give up jobs and life opportunities and even take girl children out of school just to devote the time needed to find and secure critical water sources. This includes waiting for unpredictable state tanker deliveries to come on any given day, and filling and transporting as much water as possible in the few minutes water is available after a tanker's arrival. Others face harassment and even violence when they seek out water sources outside their own communities, such as using water from another neighborhood's tube well, buying temporary stores of water packets or sachets, or visiting local government (Delhi Jal Board) offices to speak with engineers and even politicians about improving water deliveries (through more regular tankers). Most women Truelove interviewed expressed, for example, that it was not safe to walk the streets to neighboring areas to seek out water (and sanitation), and thus women often tried to coordinate so they could go in groups. Such experiences compound the emotional stress experienced due to a lack of water with the risks of facing harassment from men on the streets, and even within shops and offices, as women seek out alternate water sources.

While the robbing of life hours (and accompanied physical and mental strain) that are given to managing water—that for some accrues into years that could be devoted to other life purposes and opportunities—remains a source of unrecognized, invisible, and slow infrastructural violence, moments of rupture do occasionally occur. Such ruptures help disclose both the highly gendered and intersectional dimensions of this slow violence and bring attention to its deleterious embodied effects. In 2012 in Rampur Camp, Truelove observed Muslim men from Bihar living on their own, having left wives and families behind in rural areas to tend land. Due to the absence of women from many households on this side of the neighborhood, the gendered labor of finding water (as well as other household tasks such as cooking) becomes suddenly reversed. As Muslim men took on the gendered labor of finding water due to their wives' absence, these men's water practices disrupt patriarchal norms and gain visibility as their male bodies stand out against the gender norm. For example, on any given evening Muslim men could be seen carrying heavy containers of water on their shoulders, accessed from the neighboring settlement's tube well. While Star (1999) indicates that infrastructures often become visible at the moment of breakdown, here the breakdown of infrastructure that brings visibility is the sudden rupturing of embodied and patriarchal reproductive labor, a breakdown in social structures that reverses the norm of the female body working as an infrastructure of household water provisioning. As Muslim men take on the typically feminized labor to procure and transport water after twelve-hour shifts working on constructions sites, they resort to a variety of strategies to gain even the most minimal amounts of water. It was common to hear expressions among this group that problem-solving water was the most stressful element of living in Delhi, and that it had become so dire they often did not have sufficient water to cook food, and instead had to use money to buy food from informal vendors, which further eroded their earnings and thus what they could send back home to their families in rural Bihar (Truelove 2016).

CONCLUSION

This chapter approaches intimate everyday infrastructures in urban Nepal and India through the lens of gendered bodies as infrastructure. As such, one of the primary goals of the chapter is to open up analytical space to consider the everyday politics and practices that shape, and become (re)produced, as bodies engage in infrastructural labor, care, knowledge networks, and social work. These are the often unseen yet critical infrastructures and embodied practices that help neighborhoods and cities to function, and they also reflect social relations and hierarchies, slow violences, and unequal patterns of urban inclusion and exclusion. In our comparative case studies of Bharatpur, Dhangadhi, and Delhi, we show how gendered bodies as infrastructure are connected to wider social, political, and economic processes at the neighborhood, city, and regional scale, demonstrating how the politics of the city are intimately connected to the gendered politics of the body, and vice versa. As such, we contribute to new work in feminist geography utilizing a gendered and intersectional approach to understand the bodily scale and sphere of urban infrastructures, and its associated gendered forms of slow violence in cities.

First, our respective case studies utilize a gendered intersectional approach to show how wider politics and governmental structures at the city and regional scale become unevenly experienced intimately at the bodily scale. Drawing on feminist political geography work on the body, we demonstrate the ways such wider politics profoundly shape how infrastructures are made in the everyday and whose gendered/casted/classed/racialized bodies disproportionately (and often invisibly) engage in circulating critical resources, materials, and knowledge in their communities. As such, we hope to contribute to De Leeuw's (2016, 16) call for "a deeper engagement with the political geographies formed in everyday intimacies." This analysis seeks to bring visibility to gendered infrastructural practices and networks that often go understudied and are rarely acknowledged in policy, planning, and research. It also allows us to think comparatively about how gender operates in tandem with other key identities (caste/class/race/ethno-religious identities) in relation to unequal embodied experiences of urban infrastructure. Notably, giving analytical attention to intersectionality at each field site reveals important differences in the ways diverse social groups in urban Nepal and India unevenly experience "infra-making" (Lancione and McFarlane 2016) in the everyday through wider gender, caste, and class politics. While gendered invisible infrastructural labor, patterns of care, and social relations all shape how infrastructures are built in each city of study, such networks are heavily inflected by caste, class, and ethno-religious politics in urbanizing South Asia.

For residents in Bharatpur, for example, middle-class Brahmin women (and homeowners) experienced particular caste- and class-based politics that provided complex openings and closures with regard to the social labor to build financial networks of support in mothers' groups. Many middle-class Brahmin women reported a lowering of perceived risks in the city and that a sense of economic security was achieved through the mothers' groups provision of informal financial infrastructure at the local and household scale. However, patriarchal governmental structures at the neighborhood and municipal government scale worked to curtail some women's power over this savings and credit infrastructure, with the tacit condoning of such practices by local male authorities, community leaders, and even husbands. Such findings speak to the necessity for urban scholars across locations to take seriously the ways differing patterns of intersectionality are tied to the everyday politics and uneven experiences of infrastructure.

In Delhi, social, political, and economic processes at the neighborhood, city, and regional scale shaped differing gendered infrastructures and embodied water practices at the intrahousehold scale. While governmental structures at the city and regional level have put in place laws that widely exclude the urban poor (specifically those living in unplanned areas of the city) from centralized water connections, our research demonstrates that the provision of public water even in planned areas of the city (which are assumed to receive adequate per capita water deliveries) nonetheless relies upon the gendered labor and time of women's bodies in order to circulate. The unacknowledged and unremunerated gendered labor of storing, managing, and distributing household water among middle-class women creates tensions between neighbors, interrupts and even hijacks women's routines, and curtails other life and income-earning opportunities. For residents of unplanned areas in the city such as Rampur Camp, the quest to piece together water infrastructures beyond the network disproportionately falls onto the bodies and daily practices of non-dominant-caste women and Muslim men of lower socioeconomic groups. For the few Brahmin women and many Hindu men living in the area, accessing water was not identified within research interviews as a major problem in their own daily routines, precisely because it was either handled by other household members or provisioned at relatively more secure levels through dominant-caste relations and connections in the settlement. Here, we see not only how intersectional gender/class/caste/ethno-religious politics come to matter in shaping the everyday life of infrastructure, but also how particular neighbor-hoods and household members benefit from the circulation of resources that are provisioned through the ongoing labor, care, and social networks of others.

Last, and related, our research shows that the invisibility of these every-day intimate practices of particular bodies to provision infrastructure is deeply connected to what we term "slow infrastructural violence." Here we contribute to feminist geographical work that gives attention to the gendered and urban dimensions of "confronting the often invisible, systematically maintained, and normalized 'slow violence' experienced by disposed and marginalized peoples" (Piedalue 2019, 2). Slow violence accretes over time as an unrecognized yet critical dimension of the embodied experience of infrastructural networks in the city. We show how it manifests through unequal gendered social hierarchies and relations coupled with forms of long-term and disproportionate forms of harm associated with practices such as waiting for and hauling water on a daily basis in Delhi, or providing unrecognized and unremunerated forms of care and maintenance that the municipality is failing to provide in Bharatpur's streets and lanes, or not paying health workers to do essential public sector work in Dhangadhi. These simultaneous infrastructural politics and material configurations reveal important dimensions of urban inclusion and exclusion that have to be understood at the intrahousehold and bodily scale, profoundly shaping the uneven experience of the city for urban residents. We thus call for not only more engagement theoretically and empirically with the multiplicity of urban infrastructures that enable resources to circulate and cities to be built in the everyday, but also extending our understanding of the socio-materiality of infrastructure to include bodies in order to understand the intimate and gendered infrastructural politics of the city.

NOTES

1. The municipality does not know how many mothers' groups exist in their city. This esti-mate of the value of financial schemes is based on Ruszczyk's knowledge from conducting research in this city for several years.

REFERENCES

Amin, A. 2014. "Lively Infrastructure." *Theory, Culture, and Society* 31 (7–8): 137–61. https://doi.org/10.1177/0263276414548490.

BBC 2012. "Our World's Water Crisis." https://www.youtube.com/watch?v=jscOuWpw_iU&t=725s.

Berlant, L. 2016. "The Commons: Infrastructures for Troubling Times." *Environment and Planning D: Society and Space* 34 (3): 393–419. https://doi.org/10.1177/02637 75816645989.

Bondi, L., and D. Rose. 2003. "Constructing Gender, Constructing the Urban: A Review of Anglo-American Feminist Urban Geography." *Gender, Place, and Culture: A Journal of Feminist Geography* 10 (3): 229–45.

Carse, A. 2017. "Keyword: Infrastructure: How a Humble French Engineering Term Shaped the Modern World." In *Infrastructures and Social Complexity: A Companion*, edited by P. Harvey, C. Jensen, and A. Morita, 27–40. Routledge.

Collective, the. 2019. "Interlude: Feminist Approaches to Infrastructure." In *Labouring Urban Infrastructures. A Workshop Magazine*, edited by A. De Coss-Corzo, H. Ruszczyk, and K. Stokes, 21. http://hummedia.manchester.ac.uk/institutes/mui/InfrastructuresZine191007.pdf.

Comptroller and Auditor General of India. 2013. Government of Delhi, Report of the Comptroller and Auditor General of India on Social Sector. Report No. 2 of 2013. Government of India.

Crenshaw K. 1989. "Demarginalizing the Intersection of Race and Sex: A Black Feminist Critique of Antidiscrimination Doctrine, Feminist Theory, and Antiracist Politics." *University of Chicago Legal Forum* 1989 (1): article 8.

Datta, A., and N. Ahmed. 2020. "Intimate Infrastructures: The Rubrics of Gendered Safety and Urban Violence in India." *Geoforum* 110 (March): 67–76.

Davies, T. 2019. "Slow Violence and Toxic Geographies: 'Out of sight' to Whom?" *Environment and Planning C: Politics and Space*, 239965441984106. https://doi.org/10.1177/2399654419841063.

de Leeuw, S. 2016. "Tender Grounds: Intimate Visceral Violence and British Columbia's Colonial Geographies. *Political Geography* 52: 14–23. https://doi.org/10.1016/j.polgeo.2015.11.010.

Edwards, P. 2003. "Infrastructure and Modernity: Force, Time, and Social Organisation in the History of Sociotechnical Systems." In *Modernity and Technology*, edited by T. J. Misa, P. Brey, and A. Feenberg, 185–225. MIT Press.

Elyachar, J. 2010. "Phatic Labor, Infrastructure, and the Question of Empowerment in Cairo." *American Ethnologist* 37 (3): 452–64. https://doi.org/10.1111/j.1548-1425.2010.01265.x.

Fluri, J. L. 2009. "Geopolitics of Gender and Violence 'from Below.'" *Political Geography* 28 (4): 259–65.

Fluri, J. L., and A. Piedalue. 2017. "Embodying Violence: Critical Geographies of Gender, Race, and Culture." *Gender, Place and Culture* 24 (4): 534–44. https://doi.org/10.108 0/0966369X.2017.1329185.

Fredericks, R. 2018. *Garbage Citizenship: Vital Infrastructures of Labor in Dakar, Senegal.* Duke University Press.

Graham, S., ed. 2008. *Cities, War, and Terrorism: Towards an Urban Geopolitics.* John Wiley and Sons.

Graham, S., and C. McFarlane. 2015. *Infrastructural Lives: Urban Infrastructure in Context.* Routledge.

Gregory, D. 2011. "The Everywhere War." *Geography Journal* 177 (3): 238–50.

Harvey, P., C. Bruun Jensen, and A. Morita. 2017. "Introduction: Infrastructural Complications." In *Infrastructures and Social Complexity: A Companion*, edited by Penelope Harvey, Casper Jensen, and Atsuro Morita, 1–22. Routledge.

Hyndman, J. 2019. "Unsettling Feminist Geopolitics: Forging Feminist Political Geographies of Violence and Displacement." *Gender, Place, and Culture* 26 (1): 3–29.

Lancione, M., and C. McFarlane. 2016. "Life at the Urban Margins: Sanitation Infra-Making and the Potential of Experimental Comparison." *Environment and Planning A: Economy and Space* 48 (12): 2402–21. https://doi.org/10.1177/0308518x16659 772.

Larkin, Brian. 2008. *Signal and Noise: Media, Infrastructure, and Urban Culture in Nigeria.* Duke University Press.

Larkin, Brian 2013. "The Politics and Poetics of Infrastructure." *Annual Review of Anthropology* 42 (1): 327–43. https://doi.org/10.1146/annurev-anthro-092412-155522.

Lawhon, M., D. Nilsson, J. Silver, H. Ernstson, and S. Lwasa. 2018. "Thinking through Heterogeneous Infrastructure Configurations." *Urban Studies* 55 (4): 720–32. https://doi.org/10.1177/0042098017720149.

McFarlane, C. "Fragment Urbanism: Politics at the Margins of the City." *Environment and Planning D: Society and Space* 36 (6): 1007–25.

McFarlane, C., and D. N. Robinson. 2012. "Introduction—Experiments in Comparative Urbanism." *Urban Geography* 33 (6): 765–73. https://doi.org/10.2747/0272-3638.33 .6.765.

McFarlane, C., J. Silver, and Y. Truelove. 2017. "Cities within Cities: Intra-Urban Comparison of Infrastructure in Mumbai, Delhi, and Cape Town." *Urban Geography* 38 (9): 1393–417.

Millington, N. 2018. "Producing Water Scarcity in São Paulo, Brazil: The 2014–2015 Water Crisis and the Binding Politics of Infrastructure." *Political Geography* 65: 26–34.

Mountz, A. 2018. "Political Geography III." *Progress in Human Geography* 42 (5): 759–69. https://doi.org/10.1177/0309132517718642.

Nelson, L., and J. Seager. 2005. *A Companion to Feminist Geography.* Blackwell.

Nixon, R. 2011. *Slow Violence and the Environmentalism of the Poor.* Harvard University Press.

Pain, R. 2019. "Chronic Urban Trauma: The Slow Violence of Housing Dispossession." *Urban Studies* 56 (2): 004209801879579. https://doi.org/10.1177/0042098018795796.

Pain, R., and L. Staeheli. 2014. "Introduction: Intimacy-Geopolitics and Violence." *Area* 46 (4): 344–47. https://doi.org/10.1111/area.12138.

Piedalue, A. D. 2019. "Slow Nonviolence: Muslim Women Resisting the Everyday Violence of Dispossession and Marginalization." *Environment and Planning C: Politics and Space,* 239965441988272. https://doi.org/10.1177/2399654419882721.

Public Services International. 2018. "Community-Based Health Workers' Struggle in Nepal Enters a New Phase," April 11. http://www.world-psi.org/en/community-based-health -workers-struggle-nepal-enters-new-phase.

Ranganathan, M., and C. Balazs. 2015. "Water Marginalization at the Urban Fringe: Environmental Justice and Urban Political Ecology across the North–South Divide." *Urban Geography* 36 (3): 403–23. https://doi.org/10.1080/02723638.2015.1005414.

Rodgers, D., and B. O'Neill. 2012. "Infrastructural Violence: Introduction to the Special Issue." *Ethnography* 13 (4): 401–12. https://doi.org/10.1177/1466138111435738.

Ruszczyk, H. A. 2017. *The Everyday and Events: Understanding Risk Perceptions and Resilience in Urban Nepal.* Doctoral thesis. Durham University, UK.

Silver, J. 2014. "Incremental Infrastructures: Material Improvisation and Social Collaboration across Post-colonial Accra." *Urban Geography* 35 (6): 788–804. https://doi.org/10.1080 /02723638.2014.933605.

Simone, A. 2004. "People as Infrastructure: Intersecting Fragments in Johannesburg." *Public Culture* 16 (3): 407–29. https://doi.org/10.1215/08992363-16-3-407.

Staeheli, L., E. Kofman, and L. Peake. 2004. *Mapping Women, Making Politics: Feminist Perspectives on Political Geography.* Psychology Press.

Star, S. L. 1999. "The Ethnography of Infrastructure." *American Behavioral Scientist* 43 (3): 377–91. https://doi.org/10.1177/00027649921955326.

Truelove, Y. 2016. "Incongruent Waterworlds: Situating the Everyday Practices and Power of

Water in Delhi." *South Asia Multidisciplinary Academic Journal* 14. https://doi.org/10.4000/samaj.4164.

Truelove, Y. 2019. "Gray Zones: The Everyday Practices and Governance of Water beyond the Network." *Annals of the American Association of Geographers* 109 (6): 1758–74. https://doi.org/10.1080/24694452.2019.1581598.

Truelove, Y., and K. O'Reilly. 2020. "Making India's Cleanest City: Sanitation, Intersectionality, and Infrastructural Violence." *Environment and Planning E: Nature and Space*, 251484862094152. https://doi.org/10.1177/2514848620941521.

Truelove, Y., and H. A. Ruszczyk. 2022. "Bodies as Urban Infrastructure: Gender, Intimate Infrastructures, and Slow Infrastructural Violence." *Political Geography* 92: 102492, https://doi.org/10.1016/j.polgeo.2021.102492.

United Cities and Local Governments. 2020. "Intermediary Cities." United Cities and Local Governments. https://www.uclg.org/en/agenda/intermediary-cities.

Wilson, A. 2016. "The Infrastructure of Intimacy." *Signs: Journal of Women in Culture and Society* 41 (2): 247–80.

World Health Organization. 2003. "The Right to Water." Office of the High Commissioner for Human Rights, Centre on Housing Rights and Evictions (COHRE), Water Aid, Centre on Economic, Social and Cultural Rights.

Zerah, M. 1998. "How to Assess the Quality Dimension of Urban Infrastructure: The Case of Water Supply in Delhi." *Cities* 15 (4): 285–90.

Zerah, M. 2000. *Water: Unreliable Supply in Delhi*. Manohar.

CHAPTER 11

LOOKING INTO WELLS: PICTURING THE GENDERED RELATIONS OF WATER INFRASTRUCTURE IN SOUTHWEST CAMEROON

Jennifer A. Thompson

INTRODUCTION

Figure 11.1, a photo looking into a well, was taken by a group of women in Southwest Cameroon. Critically, wells do not feature prominently in Cameroon's policy landscape or water scholarship, which both tend to focus on the politics of piped water delivery systems. Yet wells feature centrally in photographs and videos produced by women and men as part of participatory visual research about water in both urban and rural communities. Wells like the one depicted in fig. 11.1, currently a source of drinking water in Mudeka village, raise acute concerns about water quality and public health. Wells also provide alternative water sources for coping with unreliable piped networks. Women's portrayals of wells provoke many questions about why women's voices, roles, priorities, and concerns seem to be missing from much of the recent theorizing about water infrastructures. What does it mean that women photographed this well? What does this well signify in Mudeka, where the community-managed water delivery network has been defunct for decades? How might a gendered analysis and participatory visual study of wells inform the burgeoning infrastructural turn?

Recent anthropological and geographical theories of infrastructures expand understandings of infrastructures beyond static or inert entities that "reflect" or "mirror" particular politics or social relations to assert their

Fig. 11.1. Photograph captioned "Present drinking water" produced by Women with Action group, Mudeka village

productive role in transforming socio-material relations (Jensen and Morita 2016; Larkin 2013; McFarlane and Rutherford 2008). Within this scholarship, questions about in(visibility) highlight a politics of looking. Infrastructures can be invisible backgrounds that become visible upon breakdown (Star 1999). Infrastructures can also be spectacularly hyper-visible, symbols of modernity stimulating particular forms of desire and awe (Larkin 2013). Different ways of "seeing" infrastructures play an integral role in shaping broader urban political landscapes (McFarlane and Silver 2016). While much of this scholarship is motivated by questions about power and the everyday (Graham and McFarlane 2014), the general invisibility of gender within infrastructural theorizing is remarkable. Noting the limits of a visible versus invisible dichotomy, and even a linear spectrum of (in)visibility (Larkin 2013), in this chapter, I take up feminist methodological concerns about who is looking at what, and in what way. This framing emphasizes questions about positionality, voice, and the situatedness of knowledge (Haraway 1988) as intimately linked with the uneven complexities and hierarchies of knowledge and power.

In particular, participatory visual research traditions center a transformative "research as social change" paradigm (Mitchell 2011). Participatory visual methodologies such as photovoice and participatory video invite research participants to take photographs or make videos to identify and analyze the critical issues in their lives (see Milne, Mitchell, and de Lange 2012; Wang 1999). Often seeking marginalized perspectives, participatory visual methodologies simultaneously focus both on the content of participant-produced images as well as on the implications of opening up or "democratizing" research processes (Mitchell 2011). Expanding whose voices count also works to diversify the types of knowledges that are typically valued and produced in research. Participatory visual methodologies can provide opportunities for community and policy engagement through the visual (Mitchell, de Lange, and Moletsane 2017), as well as for participants to "speak back" to dominant narratives or misrepresentations of their lived realities (Mitchell and de Lange 2013). Amidst concerns about the appropriation or tokenistic use of participation (Cooke and Kothari 2001), participatory visual methodologies are certainly not a panacea or without challenges. Yet too often, research extracts, appropriates, and often misrepresents local knowledge all the while excluding participants—often those most affected by research topics—from making sense and use of the research findings. These colonizing histories of injustice in research compel transformative paradigms. Participatory visual methodologies offer opportunities for knowledge exchange, collective learning, and critical dialogue among participants and their communities. Visual methods can help to render everyday and sensory relations more tangible and visible (Pink 2004), and extend beyond knowledges produced through talk-based research methods such as interviews and focus groups.

In this chapter, I center women's and men's visual productions and interpretations to explore the gendered production of wells in the context of Cameroon. I first frame this inquiry at the intersection of feminist and hydrosocial theorizing around water, which both call attention to the socio-materialities of water and power. I then contextualize water access in Southwest Cameroon, how this study responds to the work of an interdisciplinary water collective, the Buea Water Resources Research Group, and the fieldwork design for working with photovoice and participatory video in four communities. The findings feature participant-produced photographs, videos, and analysis about groundwater wells that highlight the following: (1) As one of many water sources that women rely on, wells are "small technologies" that occupy ambiguous positions, both as a type of resilience for communities to cope with unreliable networks but that also produce forms of compromise; (2) Wells result from and produce multiple, complex embodied, and affective gender relations that have different outcomes for different people; and (3) Hydrogeological conditions play an important role in the gendered production of wells as well as how they connect with other underground infrastructures, such as graves and pit toilets. Within the politics of (in)visibility within infrastructural research, these findings demonstrate the importance of a gender lens and methodological questions about knowledge production within infrastructural research. Bringing women's perspectives and experiences into focus and conversation through participatory visual research can help make gendered everyday practices around infrastructures more visible and contribute to the critical need to widen the gaze of infrastructural research beyond the network.

GENDER, WATER, AND WELLS

Framing my inquiry looking into wells, hydrosocial theories of water emphasize the complex, hybrid relations between water and social power (Linton 2010; Swyngedouw 2004) and the constitutive role of infrastructures and technologies within water-society relations (Linton and Budds 2014). Much of this hydrosocial theorizing has focused analytical attention on political and economic processes related to urbanization, development, and capitalism with particular fascination about the complexities and reach of large-scale networked infrastructures. Fragmented and contradictory, these systems include assemblages of socio-materials forms, labor, and protest, for example related to pipes, valves, and hydraulic citizenship (Anand 2017), and the materiality of water meters as a site of struggle, technical knowledge, and reconfiguration (Von Schnitzler 2013). Despite the imperative to investigate diverse infrastructures across a variety of contexts, water infrastructures (perhaps infrastructures in general) seem implicitly theorized as networked, and often in relation to cities. This scholarly gaze risks overshadowing infrastructures like the well photographed by women in Mudeka village, depicted at the beginning of this chapter. Looking "beyond the network," Furlong and Kooy (2017) and Truelove (2019) draw increasing attention to the range of everyday water practices, actors, sources, and technologies around networked infrastructures that constitute urban waterscapes in the Global South.

Wells are also complex infrastructures, although in different ways than large-scale networks, and integral to everyday lived experiences in both urban and rural waterscapes. Wells also shape and are influenced by complex sociomaterial relations. In their anthropological study of the Zimbabwe Bush Pump, de Laet and Mol (2000) attributed the success of this particular type of well to its fluid boundaries that include the pump's adaptable and flexible mechanics, but that also extend to, for example, the changing gut flora of user communities and the character of its inventor. Yet not all wells attract the same levels of success and fame. In many African contexts, the reliance on borehole wells as primary strategies for rural development has resulted in catastrophic failure, with the majority of the tens of thousands of wells installed in African contexts every year falling into disrepair and failing just a few years after being installed (Skinner 2009). The status, success, and promise of wells have significant gender implications.

Feminist political ecologies of water emphasize the invisibility of, or silence about, how *gendered* social relations and structures of power differentiate water use, access, and control and shape gendered inequalities in the sociomaterial production of waterscapes. Gender-water relations operate at multiple scales that include bodies, households, communities, nations, as well as in the broader neoliberal context (Ahlers and Zwarteveen 2009; Harris 2009; Lahiri-Dutt 2011; Truelove 2011). An intersectional approach to gender resists homogenizing "women" (Crenshaw 1989). More complex views of the relationship between gender and water attend to social difference and account for the inseparability of gender, race, and class (Harris 2008; Joshi and Fawcett 2005), historic and ongoing colonial structures (Hawkins et al 2011; Mollet and Faria 2013), and how gendered social relations also entangle with hydrogeological systems (Coles 2005; Sultana 2009, 2011; Thompson 2016). An intersectional lens highlights the complexities of difference and how not all women or men experience or influence water in the same way. Bringing hydrosocial materialities together with feminist intersectional thinking allows for richer, more nuanced, and contextually sensitive understandings of gendered struggles and water infrastructures.

Within gender-water research, a small but important body of work articulates the gendered production of wells. Veronica Strang (2005) traces the gendered meanings encoded in water with the historic shift in the UK from surface wells associated with pagan fertility ritual practices and water goddesses to channels, spouts, and fountainheads that symbolize patriarchal forms of enclosure and control associated with early Christianity. Emily Van Houweling (2015) observes how the recent transition from customary hand dug wells to handpumps in rural Mozambique created new spaces for women and men to renegotiate their gender roles in relation to water collection work. Farhana Sultana's (2009; 2011) work in Bangladesh documents how the spatial differences in arsenic contamination of tubewells plays a critical role in producing gendered subjectivities. Building on this scholarship and the significance of women's systematic exclusion from water decision-making (Coles and Wallace 2005), I ask what it means to explore the gendered production of wells in a participatory way. In particular, involving women more actively in research processes and working with images as a method of inquiry offers opportunities to expand who is looking at what aspects of the waterscape and in what way (Thompson 2011). This methodological shift complicates the (in)visibility of water infrastructures by making the gendered production of infrastructures more visible, and by focusing on infrastructures often overshadowed by scholarly fascination with large-scale water networks.

CONTEXTUALIZING WATER GOVERNANCE IN SOUTHWEST CAMEROON

With the absence of a national water policy and a fragmented water policy environment, Cameroon's attempts to prioritize privatization and decentralization have been precarious. From 2008 to 2018, a Partially Privatized Partnership (PPP) involving a Moroccan-based consortium, *Camerounaise des Eaux* (CDE), governed water service delivery in urban and semi-urban areas. In 2018, Cameroon did not renew the PPP and returned to a public water delivery model. Decentralization also supposedly transfers power and resources to the lowest administrative level (municipal councils). However, decentralization has been characterized as ambiguous and conflicted (Mbuagbo 2012), particularly in Cameroon's minority Anglophone regions that have been marginalized by the largely Francophone central government, an ongoing legacy of British and French colonial rule. With recent protest and the resurgence of an Anglophone secession movement, and the government's militarized response spurring additional violence and suggesting the state's will for centralized control, the progress of devolution is even less clear.[1]

Drawing on traditions of community participation in the Southwest Region, community-managed water schemes also operate in both urban and rural areas. From independence to the 1980s, hundreds of community water systems were built and financed as "self-help" projects to service areas not covered by the water utility (Njoh 2003).[2] These schemes operate at a smaller scale than municipal networks using technologies appropriate for local technical capacity and offering viable ways for communities to manage water. However, many community schemes face ownership and maintenance challenges, with participatory practices often tenuously intertwined with hierarchies of state power. Community water schemes are sometimes coerced or appropriated by, for example, national authorities or agricultural corporations (Njoh 2011; Folifac and Gaskin 2011). Unfortunately, many rural schemes fail within a few years (Fonjong, Ngwa, and Fonchingong 2004). Urban community systems coexist with and supply areas not covered by the municipal network (Sally et al. 2014). The resurgence of urban and rural community water schemes reflects the high cost and limited reach of utility water, and systematic exclusion of rural areas (Njoh 2011).

Water research from Cameroon generally acknowledges women's central role in the daily provision and management of water (Fonjong and Ngekwi 2014). Through precolonial, colonial, and postcolonial phases of Cameroon's history, women have always been powerful water actors constructing water berms, digging water trenches, maintaining codes of behavior at water points, and cooking and participating in inaugural ceremonies for water systems (Page 2005). In particular, women's distinct forms of political organizing and naked protest (Ardener 1975) prevented the closure of public taps and shaped decisions about the management of water systems (Page 2005). However, scant research asks women in Cameroon about their experiences and concerns with water. Traditional research methods such as observation, surveys, interviews with (male) leaders, and document/archival review rely predominantly on men's knowledge and priorities (and are often conducted by male researchers). This methodological trend, while not unique to Cameroon or water and water infrastructure research more generally, leaves critical opportunities for qualitative, participatory research approaches that actively involve women in identifying, representing, and analyzing how water affects their lives. In this study, I work with participatory visual methodologies to explicitly ask women about their concerns and actively involve women in the research interpretation process.

FIELDWORK

This chapter builds on the work of the Buea Water Resource Research Group, an interdisciplinary research collective interested in how to support integrated, collaborative, and participatory forms of water governance in Cameroon. Bringing together engineers, chemists, geographers, and urban planners, this group drew on action research traditions that acknowledge the critical need to go beyond studying water to engaging with local water stakeholders in ways that might contribute to finding sustainable solutions. While this group did not initially set out to study gender, facilitating stakeholder dialogue requires a deeper consideration of social power and corresponding methodological challenges in bringing diverse groups together (Folifac 2009). For example, in a school competition involving youth as contestants and key water sector actors as jury members, gender issues emerged as central concerns, particularly in relation to girls' experiences of sexual violence while out searching for water in the context of unreliable water delivery (Thompson, Folifac, and Gaskin 2014). Yet this event also elicited patriarchal stigma around girls' sexualities, as girls were *also* sometimes accused of taking advantage of uncertain water schedules to meet up with their intimate partners to engage in sexual activities, ultimately reinscribing gender norms that control women's and girls' sexualities.

The school competition in Buea sparked concern and interest within local communities and organizations about the multiple and complex ways that gender influences social relationships with water.

In Cameroon, I worked in collaboration with a local women's organization, Changing Mentalities and Empowering Groups (CHAMEG), to build on the school competition and contribute to existing work within the women's movement. Alongside a team of predominantly female local fieldworkers and graduate students, I co-facilitated photovoice and participatory video workshops in two urban (Buea and Kumba)[3] and two rural (Mudeka and Bwitingi) communities each within a one- or two-hour drive of Mount Cameroon. In 2-day media production workshops in each of the communities, a total of 130 participants (96 women and 34 men) worked in small groups to take photos and make short, "no editing required" videos (Mak 2012) in response to a prompt, "What are some challenges you face with water? What are some solutions?" In total, the participants produced 233 photographs and 27 videos (2–8 minutes each). We also brought selected participants together to co-analyze the corpus of data across the sites and to select which photos and videos to represent the work (e.g., those pictured in this chapter). A dialogue event with local decision-makers, including traditional rulers, municipal councils, the media, NGOs, and representatives from various ministries culminated fieldwork. While a range of gender issues emerged related to water storage and transportation, gender-based and sexual violence, corruption and mistrust, the internalization of structures of power, and the politics of participation in decision-making (Thompson 2017; Thompson, Gaskin, and Agbor 2017), in this chapter, I focus on the gendered production of wells. I first contextualize wells among several water sources that women rely on to cope with unreliable water delivery networks. I then focus on women's photographs and videos of wells and the related discussions.[4]

RELATIONAL TECHNOLOGIES OF WATER ACCESS

Despite relatively abundant freshwater from high levels of rainfall and dense networks of springs and streams around Mount Cameroon, water access problems persist. All four of the research communities have infrastructures for piped water delivery but these systems are not consistently reliable. In Buea, Kumba, and Bwitingi, the presence of networked infrastructure and the partial reliability of water services have established expectations among residents that these water schemes can and should be functional. In Mudeka, the network has been dry for several decades. Certainly, the reasons for the unreliability of these networked systems differ from community to community.

Factors such as the utility's changing water service schedules, long queues at public taps, leaks and breaks that affect water pressure, technical problems with water networks,[5] and general governance challenges produce unpredictable water availability. While water access challenges affect all community members, women and youth are disproportionately affected because of gendered and age-related divisions of labor.

Many participants' photographs and videos portray shared narratives about the gendered stress for water that begin with a conflict: Women and girls arrive at a tap to find that it is dry. Exasperated, with their bucket in hand, they ask, "What am I supposed to do?!" Women and girls must inevitably go out into the neighborhood, an embodied and time-consuming task of finding and moving water. These journeys involve negotiating many uncertainties such as: What are my options? Where will I find water today? How far will I have to go? How many other people will be there? How long will this take me? How much money is in my pocket today? How will I get the water home? Is it enough water? Will the water quality be safe? Will I be safe? Will my daughter be safe? These relational questions shape the dynamic character of the waterscape. Women expressed a sense of urgency, describing the search for water using terms like *rushing*, *scrambling*, *struggling*, *stressing*, *hunting*, or *fighting*, particularly in relation to how women juggle the responsibility for water with the other responsibilities in their lives as teachers, students, businesswomen, and farmers.

To cope, women rely on several types of water sources to meet their household water needs including private taps, public taps, wells, springs, and streams. Each of these different technological interfaces means navigating compounding and intersecting factors related to water in the natural environment, infrastructural considerations, and social, political, and economic dynamics. Women distinguished between the cost and reliability of different water technologies as well as how they interact and change. For example, urban residents' monthly water bills do not ensure the regular distribution of safe water from municipal connections. Borrowing from a neighbor's tap or well might provide better quality water than a local stream, but this negotiation relies on either neighborly goodwill or some type of transaction. Many free public taps have been closed down or are considered by young women as unsafe spaces because crowds of men jostle to fill containers to sell and distribute on their motorcycles or pushcarts. The character of water access points changes at different times of the day, week, and season so that women must constantly renegotiate water access. Women's daily water decisions reflect particular spatial, temporal, social, and ecological moments that vary according to how sources are used and cared for, who is there that day, and what else is happening in the neighborhood, as well as dynamic ecological conditions.

PHOTOGRAPHS OF COMMUNITY WELLS

Within this dynamic waterscape, photograph after photograph depicts wells (fig. 11.2). Critically, most images depict *surface* wells. Relatively inexpensive and accessible, these wells can be dug by hand and access the water table directly with a bucket attached to a rope, without the need for expensive drilling equipment. Some wells provide good clean drinking water. Other wells generate problems. Often, wells present a conflicted compromise. Women's photographs peer down green algae-lined walls into dark cavernous wells. Others depict what participants call "traditional African wells" rimmed with old car tires at the surface opening. Well coverings range from fixed sliding covers to more temporary removable sheets of metal or wood. Some uncovered wells remain open and vulnerable to contamination from surface material. Other surface wells have been "modernized" with a wall of stone, concrete, or metal protecting the well and providing a higher ledge for access, which provides leverage for leaning over and lifting water. Women documented which wells are cleaned and treated, and others which are not. In Mudeka, located closer to the coast, many wells have been abandoned because of saltwater intrusion due to over-extraction. And women distinguished between the different waters coming from different wells, with some well water good for drinking, some for doing laundry and cooking, and other well water of such poor quality that it is simply unusable.

Women's concerns about wells articulate a range of socio-material complexities that make visible the integral role of gender in, for example, the often-invisible labor that constitutes many infrastructures (Fredericks 2014), the role of sense in what it means to know infrastructures (Schwenkel 2015), and the power and effect of infrastructural form in producing distinct experiences (Larkin 2015). Below, I elaborate women's concerns about negotiating (i) gendered labor, (ii) the variable quality of various well waters, and (iii) safety concerns with open surface wells.

Gendered Labor

Water's particular density requires heavy labor, which is gendered. Many images portray women walking with water containers in their hands or on their heads. Carrying water produces embodied physical strain, the sheer physicality of which requires appreciation. To supply a relatively small household of four, for example, a woman or girl might feasibly carry 160 lbs of water

Fig. 11.2. Photographs of wells taken in Kumba and Mudeka (Compilation by author. Photographs by research participants from the Faith Sisters, Friends of All, and Youths of Hope groups in Mudeka and from the Water is Life, Water Advocates, The Pathfinders, and The Hunters groups in Kumba, Cameroon)

daily.[6] As a liquid, water also shifts its weight when moved, creating additional sloshing forces for water carriers to contend with. Water's weight affects the embodied and emotional experiences of water carriers, strain that is unevenly distributed to lowest status household members. One group of women titled their video "*Wata Na Chest Pain* [Water Is Chest Pain]," naming both the physical pressure or discomfort on the sternum and spine from toting water on your head, and the emotional strain, including frustration, anguish, fatigue, and stress, of the struggle for water. Many participants laughed at the irony of this expression; it is not water that causes such pain, but the lack of water and broader failure of the systems supposedly in place to provide communities with reliable water. These physical and emotional layers of ache etch into the gendered waterscape.

Adding to this gendered labor of finding and carrying water, hauling water from wells requires physically lifting water up against gravity. This labor requires embodied strength and agility. Many images depict women and girls straining over open wells to haul water up to the surface. One group from Kumba drew attention to the situation of a young mother who has infant quadruplets. Looking at a photo of this woman leaning over the tires stacked around her well, Melina said:

> [She] gave birth to four children; White people call them "quadruplets."
> . . . She had four healthy girls. . . . Here she is, she is trying to haul the water—but her waist! She gave birth to four children, so she can't draw the water. She needs somebody to come and help her haul the water.

In the video "Matters Arising" (fig. 11.3), Melina portrays the woman with quadruplets, who struggles all day to simultaneously cook, haul water, and care for her children. When her husband, Gordon, returns from work, he is angry because Melina has not yet washed his shirt for his evening meeting. With one infant tied to her back and another in her arms, Melina argues that she is overwhelmed with her work and experiencing back pain. As the couple argue, a group of neighbors enter the compound and intervene. Each neighbor takes one quadruplet to relieve Melina, and the women negotiate with Gordon collectively on behalf of Melina to insist that he help with the household chores. Gordon agrees and as the video ends, he hauls one bucket of water from the family well.

This video emphasizes that women's labor has become normalized to the extent that it often does not warrant concern: the quadruplets (a relatively atypical scenario) literally amplify the gender issues at hand. However, participant interpretations of the video focused less on the specificity of quadruplets. Participants objected to inequalities in household water labor and men's unfair expectations of women's work negotiating childcare and water collection. Many women regarded these intrahousehold negotiations as exacerbating marital conflicts and sometimes domestic violence. And hauling water from deep wells compounds the nature of women's embodied labor. When we screen this video in Cameroon, audiences often count each of Gordon's arm-lengths of rope out loud (approximately 1 meter each) as he hauls a bucket of water. Melina's embodied strain is accentuated when it becomes apparent that her well is 13 meters deep—equivalent to a four-story building. The video reinforces how deep wells intensify women's heavy labor, particularly when other caregiving responsibilities magnify household water needs (in this case four-fold).

Melina's situation caught the attention and empathy of participants and

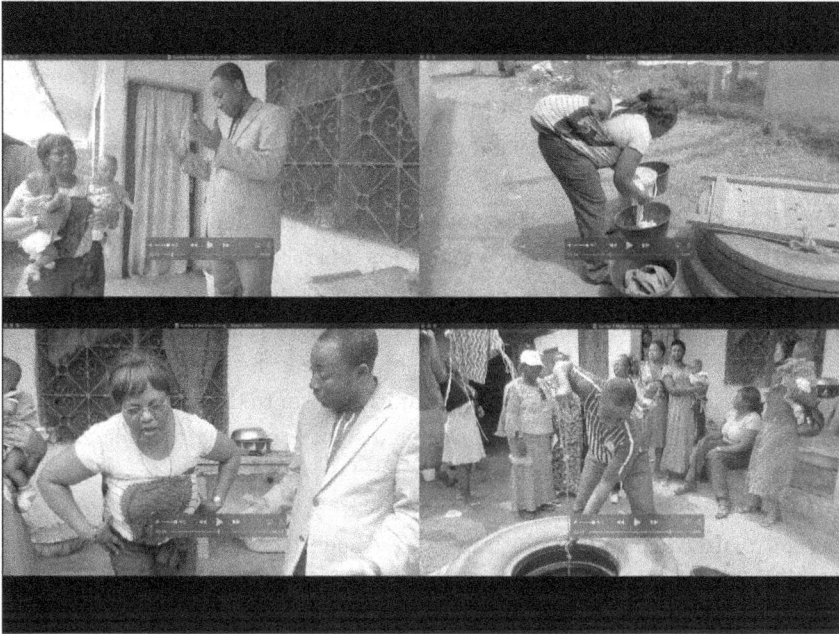

Fig. 11.3. Screenshots from the video "Matters Arising" produced by the Water is Life group, Kumba

audiences alike, motivating people to take action. One government officer who attended the Kumba workshop removed the photo of Melina straining over her well off the wall and brought it to her seat so that she could examine it more closely and inquire more about the woman's circumstances. In considering how to alleviate the embodied strain of gendered labor, this group also photographed a pulley as an accessible solution to the problem of deep surface wells. This technology did not require assistance from the government and had many women inquiring about the cost of pulleys and how they work. These conversations spurred questions about, for example, terms like *water table* and *water catchment*, language critical for engaging with water decision-makers. Photos like this offered participants inspiration that endogenous solutions to daily water problems could sometimes be found in a neighbor's backyard.

Doubtful Water Quality

Women often characterized wells as "doubtful" sources due to the variable and sometimes ambiguous quality of well waters. Wells sometimes offer good quality alternatives to springs, streams, and even piped networks. According to global health standards, wells can be considered improved drinking water sources if they meet certain design standards. A protected dug well that is "protected from runoff water by a well lining or casing that is raised above ground level and a platform that diverts spilled water away from the well" and "covered, so that bird droppings and animals cannot fall into the well" (WHO and UNICEF 2006, pp. 8–9). Yet many of the wells depicted in this study would not consistently meet this definition. Surface wells provide means for groundwater access but also serve as dynamic conduits that are vulnerable to seasonal changes in rainfall. Rainy season runoff risks contaminating unprotected wells with water-borne diseases. Dry season water tables lower and some wells dry up completely, or communities closer to the coast become more vulnerable to saltwater intrusion. Design distinctions are also complex; wells can produce changing qualities of waters. Many women's photos and videos surmised the *uncertain* quality of well water. Certainly, many wells are unambiguously unsafe. At our workshop in Mudeka village, several elders brought murky water samples from local wells as evidence of their health concerns. Yet, many photos depict a range of well arrangements. Several videos depict scenarios of people drinking well water that they thought was safe for drinking but who then collapse or end up in the hospital seeking treatment for water-borne illness.

A well's quality also varies depending on ownership and how wells are used and maintained. Seeking explanations for unsafe wells during our analysis workshop, Justine explained how public and private wells are cleaned and maintained differently:

> In Mudeka, the public wells are not treated. But private wells are being treated. People who own the well treat the well. Every year, they wash the well. Somebody enters [into the well and] drains the water. And then they go to the health center [to] get that chlorine tablet. Yes. [They] put in the well, cover [it] for some two–three days then we start carrying [water from] it again.

Well owners typically contract well cleaning to male laborers, further gendering the uneven benefits and burdens of this waterscape.

Several photographs also depict borehole wells, which require drill equipment for construction, are sealed at the surface with concrete headworks, and equipped with hand pumps to draw water from deeper aquifers. While more costly to build than surface wells, boreholes remain accessible for some

Fig. 11.4. Photograph captioned "Abandoned pumping well" produced by the Friends of All group, Mudeka

individuals and communities to build without financial support from the government or NGOs. Boreholes typically offer more protected and therefore better quality sources that require little ongoing maintenance compared with surface wells. In Kumba, participants photographed and celebrated borehole taps recently installed by local chiefs and businessmen. Women considered these wells as charitable donations that reflect volunteerism or personal initiative to alleviate community stress resulting from unreliable water networks.

However, borehole wells are not without challenges. In Mudeka, all three women's groups and one of the men's groups photographed the tubewell in figure 11.4, long abandoned because of unsafe water quality. This well produces water with a sharp, rusty metallic taste and smell so strong that the well has been unusable since it was installed. Figure 11.4 clearly shows rust staining on the cement apron around the pump, likely related to high iron content in the deeper aquifer (surface wells in Mudeka do not produce rusty water, but the now defunct piped network that also drew from a deeper aquifer did). Ma Fanny described this water as "carrying fire," and John exclaimed:

Do you see the quality of the water? Brown. This is water that you don't want to put near your mouth. If you put it near your mouth, it's like suicide [laughter].

The water from this well is unfit not only for drinking but also for cleaning and cooking. John went on to say he refused to use this well water even to wash his hands. Ma Fanny described how the poor quality water affects her cooking:

The water from that pump, do you see the color? Terrible! It will kill us [. . .] We don't know what's in there [. . .] When you put plantain in the water, it turns into something different. You go get the water, and it's just water. [But] when you put it in fufu,[7] it still doesn't soften after one month. You cook plantain and it turns black.

Abandoned borehole wells like this spurred community discussions about sustainability and the politics of infrastructures more generally, and how poorly planned projects waste valuable resources. Participants were unsure who installed this well—perhaps a politician wanting votes, perhaps a benevolent donation from abroad. Pa Eddy described his frustration:

Our policy-makers don't care for us! And then we go and vote! Tomorrow when I go and vote, they say "that man is this and that" [. . .] I don't really understand. So you see, we don't have water [. . .] Somebody came from nowhere to dig a borehole. We did not even know when he came to do that borehole. Oh! It is now just useless.

One day, "somebody" came and installed the well without consulting the community or conducting a feasibility study. Several participants also complained that once private wells are installed, communities cease volunteering their labor to maintain traditional drinking water springs. Often, water infrastructure development involves complicated arrangements that include community members, outside agencies, and government representatives, a combination that often leaves questions about ownership and maintenance unclear.

Within these discussions, women marked a gendered disjuncture between water infrastructure decisions made by men and women's water responsibilities. Reflecting on a video from Mudeka where women joined together to clean a spring, Justine called for women's increased power in community leadership:

If you look at the problems in Mudeka, you will find [. . .] abandoned wells, abandoned taps, abandoned boreholes . . . Abandoned, abandoned, abandoned! [. . .] But if a woman was made Chief of Mudeka, [. . . do] you think that that abandonment could have been carried out like that? [Women] would have been taking care of all of those things so that they would not have this problem of water.

Bodily Encounters and Safety

The gendered production of wells also involves other types of embodied encounters that intersect with form. Participants regarded surface wells with trepidation as unsafe technologies because of the physical risk of falling in. While deeper wells provide resilience during the dry season when water tables decrease, deep surface wells can also be quite dangerous. Reflecting on photographs that look into the wells, Veronique worried: "by the time you send your head to look into that well, your eyes are already turning [. . .] If I look into a deep pit, really, I'm scared. And you can easily fall into that pit." Indeed, a group of male elders photographed a well in Mudeka that had been abandoned and covered up because a community member had fallen into the well and died. Jackson described the men gathering around the abandoned well in the photo, grieving for the person who fell into the well as well as for the strain on their community because of the lost water source. He explained:

We say the solution is to have deep wells. [But . . .] the government provided [this well] for us and what did somebody do? They fell in and died. So they closed it up.

While surface wells provide important and affordable water access points, they also pose public safety risks. A number of high-profile cases of children falling into wells in Europe and North America have captured international attention. Yet many well-related accidents and deaths in the majority world do not make the headlines. In China, 35 children have reportedly died in wells since 2011.[8] In India, upwards of 100 children die every year from falling into well shafts, rates that reportedly increase with more and more private companies drilling unprotected borehole wells to extract water.[9] Ultimately, gendered and age-related divisions of labor around water collection and women's childcare responsibilities mean that women and children negotiate the safety and risks of open wells.

The men's photograph of the well in Mudeka that had effectively become

a grave also sparked discussion about the spatial relationships between infrastructures such as wells, graves, and pit toilets. While toilets feature frequently
in this study (see Thompson, Gaskin, and Agbor 2017) as well as in water and
sanitation infrastructures theorizing more generally, I focus in particular here
on the relationships between wells and graves. While perhaps a type of sanitation infrastructure, the functional and spiritual aspects of graves in supporting
death and bodily remains have particular implications. With few cemeteries in
Cameroon and cremation deemed illegal (Anyangwe 2011), families commonly
bury their dead within the family compound. Legally, graves must be six feet
deep and located at least 100 yards away from dwellings (Anyangwe 2011) but
participants expressed concerns about household decision-making. Justine
explained that in her village:

> Some wells are dug not very far . . . from toilets and graves [. . .] When
> you are digging a well in your compound, maybe the area of the compound
> is small. And maybe your father or mother have been buried there; their
> grave is in the same compound. And toilets [too . . .] Not, like, as if [you]
> *want* to go and dig the wells there. [You] just use the space that you have.

Indeed, many households install these types of infrastructure long after
homes have been constructed; changes in property layout and land management occur incrementally.

Locating wells and graves, participants emphasized the spatial relations
between infrastructures and local hydrogeologies. The unsettling idea that
graves might contaminate drinking water has implications given changing
burial practices in Cameroon. Grave sites signal particular forms of belonging
around claims to land and ethnicity (Geschiere 2005). Increasing numbers of
mortuaries enable corpses to be embalmed, transported, and buried at "home"
on family land (Page 2007). This practice suggests that rural areas might face
disproportionate responsibilities for managing graves and the impacts associated with the decomposition of bodies, such as the release of embalming fluids
like formaldehyde into the groundwater. Graves (and pit toilets) are designed
to manage and contain bodily processes and fluids but also act as point sources
of pollution that threaten the integrity of wells and the ecological systems they
depend on.

LOOKING AT INFRASTRUCTURAL DIFFERENCE

Eliciting women's water concerns and adopting a gender perspective through
a participatory visual approach makes the gendered production of wells more

visible and expands the politics of (in)visibility within infrastructural theorizing by: (1) drawing attention to smaller, decentralized infrastructures; (2) tracing the affective and embodied ways that gender social relations produce and are produced by infrastructures; and (3) connecting the relations between infrastructures as well as with their socio-material ecologies. These findings highlight to the need to disaggregate and attend to social and infrastructural difference within infrastructural research.

Smaller, Off-grid Infrastructures

First, women's focus on wells highlights the importance of smaller infrastructures beyond the network within infrastructural theorizing. In many ways a predominant focus on large-scale water networks risks replicating colonial, engineering interventions that privilege masculine norms of scale and control (Tennant-Wood 2011; Zwarteveen 2008). An infrastructural focus on massive, socio-technological innovation also positions particular infrastructures as inherently products of modernity (Larkin 2013), missing other infrastructural forms and technologies. Well technologies often reflect traditional practices yet maintain important and perhaps new and/or renewed functions within contemporary waterscapes. As women in Cameroon describe, wells often coexist with unreliable piped networks and provide critical alternatives to supplement household and community water needs and alleviate women's water labor and responsibilities. In this sense, wells offer relatively decentralized and accessible solutions to the challenges of centralized water networks. Wells seem to subvert the inevitable politics and fallacies of these systems and become intermittent, temporary, and sometimes permanent modes of access. In another sense, wells are produced relationally through the failure of larger political and socio-technical systems. While wells offer seemingly more independent sources, I also do not wish to imply an unbounded disconnectedness. Following de Laet and Mol (2000) and Redfield (2015), and as asserted by women in Cameroon, smaller water technologies also involve complex assemblages of matter, processes, and actors. Yet all of this suggests a need to perhaps distinguish between smaller technologies that attach to and constitute larger networked systems, such as Von Schnitzler's (2013) water meters and Anand's (2017) valve turners, and smaller, decentralized technologies such as wells that do not rely to the same extent on the coherence of larger networks. Wells may provide "small" alternatives for improving water access but might also be produced at significantly large scales globally with implications that are anything but small. Making smaller, decentralized infrastructures more visible brings networked conceptualizations into question and points to the need for increased visibility of "off-grid" infrastructures, such as wells.

Picturing Gendered Infrastructures

Second, women depict how wells produce and are produced by complex affective and embodied gendered patterns. Unlike infrastructures that mobilize and transport particular types of matter to or from the point of use, wells rely more integrally and intimately on human labor. Building on Frederick's (2014) attention to the devolution of trash infrastructures in Dakar into labor regimes, disaggregating laboring bodies as gendered bodies is essential for understanding the complex intersections between infrastructures and power. Gendered expectations shape the uneven distributions of embodied strain and responsibilities to negotiate the ambiguous quality of well water, often leaving women with difficult decisions and compromise in securing safe water for their households. Women are also tasked with the emotional labor of caring for sick children and family members who consume water from doubtful sources. Often, girls sent out to collect water are later chastised for fetching dirty water from the "wrong" source, ultimately shifting the responsibility and blame onto the shoulders and heads of the most vulnerable household members. Using visual methods in group settings urged participants to act out their lived experiences, making embodied knowledges more prominent on the screen. The effects of consuming poor-quality water, vomiting and diarrhea were portrayed poignantly in numerous photos and videos. Wells elicit multiple affective relations beyond Larkin's (2013) more enticing sense of fascination and awe, to less appealing forms of embodied strain, taste, smell and even vertigo or dizziness induced by deep wells that women have to deal with. And women also make clear the role of gender-based violence in disciplining water labor.

Infrastructural Ecologies

Third, women's concerns about wells focus centrally on ecological specificities. While water infrastructures often abstract water from its ecological context, wells interface intimately with local hydrogeologies at multiple scales. Drawing on Coles (2005), Sultana (2009, 2011), and Thompson (2016), the feasibility of and gendered labor associated with surface and borehole wells reflect spatial heterogeneities of groundwater resources. In women's photographs from Cameroon's Southwest Region, wells feature centrally in the drier and flatter city of Kumba and village of Mudeka. Wells feature less often in urban Buea and rural Bwitingi, both located on the side of Mount Cameroon where abundant mountain springs and streams and steep topography make gravity-fed water delivery systems more feasible. As in situ infrastructures, wells do not rely on moving water across landscapes, uphill or away from the source, but instead facilitate water access within particular ecological contexts. These findings complicate how water infrastructures scholarships tend to privilege urban geographies, implicitly distinguishing between urban and rural infrastructures and missing opportunities to explore infrastructural ecologies.

At the scale of individual wells, wells constitute multidirectional pathways, crossing the threshold between the surface and the underground and carving out opportunities for groundwater to be drawn up to the surface but also for the environment above to seep or fall in. Wells command attention to what are often invisible underground processes and infrastructural relations. Infrastructures such as wells, pit toilets, and graves are situated, fixed forms that connect through the underground, where groundwater moves matter between. Whereas graves and pit toilets are designed (albeit with limitations) to contain, wells require a certain amount of leakage and groundwater movement to recharge. The porous design of wells allows the surrounding groundwater to seep, infiltrate, or flow into and out of the well shaft. Yet the movement of hydrogeological and bodily fluids through porous materials produces inconsistent flows of things like sewage and human remains. Facilitating the movement of water, dirt, pathogens, and fear, wells constitute intimate socio-technical assemblages of life, death, water, and waste. Women's gendered and embodied experiences of wells are produced, in part, in relation to ecological materialities such as the weight of water and depth of the water table, as well as how infrastructures connect underground.

WIDENING THE GAZE AND CONTEXT OF INFRASTRUCTURAL RESEARCH

Women's attention to wells in both urban and rural areas of Southwest Cameroon requires critical pause. Women literally *looked into* wells and urged for more political attention to the construction and safety of wells to cope with unreliable piped water networks. Paradoxically, wells have the potential to both buffer and exacerbate the effects of unreliable piped water. Maintaining wells as one of several water access options provides resilience, absorbing some of women's stress for daily household water provision. Wells produce and are produced by gendered embodied and affective relations and agencies. This reliance on (or at the least, *looking towards*) wells suggests a subversion of the grid and in some ways *looking away* from networked infrastructures as communities search for more pragmatic and reliable water access. Wells are deeply gendered entities with multiple complex outcomes pointing to the need to (re)focus on the ongoing and possibly increasing relevance of wells in the gendered production of contemporary waterscapes across multiple contexts.

This chapter also highlights the methodological possibilities of participatory and visual approaches to research to widen and deepen the gaze of infrastructural research. This expansion positions the politics of (in)visibility as a question of who is looking at what, and how different research methods produce different types of knowledge. Participatory research that considers participants as co-researchers begins to address Harvey, Jensen, and Morita's (2016) concern about the epistemological distinction between infrastructure *users* and *analysts*. Visual methods (and other arts-based methods) create expressive modes for participants to represent their knowledge and lived experiences differently in ways that decenter the primacy of language. Overlooking a gender analysis, as much recent infrastructural theorizing seems to do, risks inadvertently producing infrastructural knowledge that reinscribes masculine norms. Gendered inequalities often become so normalized that they become invisible, or at least routine practice, and therefore difficult to study. Indeed, many of the women and men in this research had also just never thought about the gendered nature of water or water infrastructures before attending our workshops together. Many women learned new technical language about water, used digital technologies in new ways, and connected with other women interested in water advocacy. Finding accessible and engaged ways to study infrastructures *with* women and men is critical for both gendering and thus advancing infrastructural theorizing and for interrogating how infrastructural research might contribute to the lives of women and communities most affected by infrastructures in ways that are meaningful, relevant, and useful in their everyday lives.

ACKNOWLEDGMENTS

I would like to thank CHAMEG and the research participants for their important contributions to this work. I would also like to thank Fidelis Folifac, Sunday Shende Kometa, and Susan Gaskin from the Bueau Water Resources Research Group for making this fieldwork possible. This research was supported by a postdoctoral fellowship from the Social Sciences and Humanities Research Council of Canada (SSHRC), doctoral funding from the Fonds de recherche du Québec—Société et culture (FRQSC), and a doctoral research award from the International Development Research Centre (IDRC).

NOTES

1. This fieldwork was conducted prior to 2016, when the violence erupted.
2. The parastatal, Société National des Eaux du Cameroun (SNEC), operated from 1968 to 2008.

3. Politically and socially, the cities of Buea and Kumba are distinctly urban, yet in terms of infrastructure and housing development, they might also be characterized as semi-urban.
4. All participant names are pseudonyms.
5. At the time of fieldwork, one of the municipal networks in the city of Kumba produced brown and muddy water. While the intake filter in a nearby lake was eventually replaced, residents could not use municipal water for six months.
6. Based on an estimated an average daily water use of 20 L per capita in Buea (Folifac 2012). Given that 20 L of water weighs approximately 40 lbs, households of four people would need to carry about 160 lbs of water per day.
7. A staple starch dish prepared with cassava that has been boiled, soaked, fermented, and pounded into dough. Fufu is served with soup or stew.
8. https://gbtimes.com/35-children-killed-wells-china-2011.
9. Sudha G. Tilak, "India's Wells of Death," *Al Jazeera*, June 26, 2012, https://www.aljazeera.com/indepth/features/2012/06/201262518453409715.html.

REFERENCES

Ahlers, R., and Zwarteveen, M. 2009. The water question in feminism: Water control and gender inequities in a neo-liberal era. *Gender, Place, and Culture, 16*(4), 409–426. https://doi.org/10.1080/09663690903003926.

Anand, N. 2017. *Hydraulic city: Water and the infrastructures of citizenship in Mumbai.* Duke.

Anyangwe, C. 2011. *Criminal law in Cameroon: Specific offences.* Bamenda: Langaa Research and Publishing.

Ardener, S. 1975. Sexual insult and female militancy. In S. Ardener (Ed.), *Perceiving women* (pp. 29–53). New York, NY: John Wiley & Sons.

Coles, A. 2005. Geology and gender: Water supplies, ethnicity, and livelihoods in Central Sudan. In A. Coles and T. Wallace (Eds.), *Gender, water, and development* (pp. 75–93). New York, NY: Berg.

Coles, A., and Wallace, T. (Eds.). 2005. *Gender, water, and development.* New York, NY: Berg.

Cooke, B., and Kothari, U. (Eds.). 2001. *Participation: The new tyranny?* London, UK, and New York, NY: Zed Books.

Crenshaw, K. 1989. Demarginalizing the intersection of race and sex: A Black feminist critique of antidiscrimination doctrine, feminist theory, and antiracist politics. *University of Chicago Legal Forum, 1989*, 139–168.

de Laet, M., and Mol, A. 2000. The Zimbabwe Bush Pump: Mechanics of a fluid technology. *Social Studies of Science, 30*(2), 225–263. https://www-jstor-org.ezphost.dur.ac.uk/stable/285835.

Folifac, F. 2009. *Situation analysis of domestic water supply in rapidly growing municipalities in Cameroon, Case of Buea.* (PhD), McGill University, Montreal.

Folifac, F., and Gaskin, S. 2011. Joint water supply projects in rural Cameroon: Partnership of profiteering? Lessons from the Mautu-Cameroon Development Corporation (CDC) project. *Water Science and Technology: Water Supply, 11*(4), 409–417. https://doi.org/10.2166/ws.2011.061.

Fonjong, L., and Ngekwi, M. 2014. Challenges of water crisis on women's socio-economic activities in the Buea Municipality, Cameroon. *Journal of Geography and Geology, 6*(4), 122–131. https://doi.org/10.5539/jgg.v6n4p122.

Fonjong, L., Ngwa, N., and Fonchingong, C. 2004. Rethinking the contribution of indigenous management in small-scale water provision among selected rural communities in Cameroon. *Environment, Development and Sustainability, 6*(4), 429–451. https://doi.org/10.1007/s10668-005-0501-3.

Fredericks, R. 2014. Vital infrastructures of trash in Dakar. *Comparative Studies of South Asia,*

Africa and the Middle East, 34(3), 532–548. https://doi.org/10.1215/1089201x -2826085.

Furlong, K., and Kooy, M. 2017. Worlding water supply: Thinking beyond the network in Jakarta. *International Journal of Urban and Regional Research, 41*(6), 888–903. https://doi.org/10.1111/1468-2427.12582.

Geschiere, P. 2005. Funerals and belonging: Different patterns in South Cameroon. *African Studies Review, 48*(2), 45–64. https://doi.org/10.1353/arw.2005.0059.

Graham, S., and McFarlane, C. (Eds.). 2014. *Infrastructural lives: Urban infrastructure in context.* Abingdon: Routledge.

Haraway, D. 1988. Situated knowledges: The science question in feminism and the privilege of partial perspective. *Feminist Studies, 14*(3), 575–599. https://doi.org/10.2307 /3178066.

Harris, L. M. 2008. Water rich, resource poor: Intersections of gender, poverty, and vulnerability in newly irrigated areas of Southeastern Turkey. *World Development, 36*(12), 2643–2662. https://doi.org/10.1016/j.worlddev.2008.03.004.

Harris, L. M. 2009. Gender and emergent water governance: Comparative overview of neoliberalized natures and gender dimensions of privatization, devolution, and marketization. *Gender, Place and Culture, 16*(4), 387–408. https://doi.org/10.1080 /09663690903003918.

Harvey, P., Jensen, C. B., and Morita, A. 2016. Introduction: Infrastructural complications. In P. Harvey, C. B. Jensen, and A. Morita (Eds.), *Infrastructures and social complexity: A companion.* London: Routledge.

Hawkins, R., Ojeda, D., Asher, K., Baptiste, B., Harris, L., Mollett, S., . . . Sultana, F. 2011. Gender and environment: Critical tradition and new challenges. *Environment and Planning D: Society and Space, 29*(2), 237–253. https://doi.org/10.1068/d16810.

Jensen, C. B., and Morita, A. 2016. Introduction: Infrastructures as ontological experiments. *Journal of Anthropology, 82*(4), 615–626. https://doi.org/10.1080/00141844.2015.1107 607.

Joshi, D., and Fawcett, B. 2005. The role of water in an unequal social order in India. In A. Coles and T. Wallace (Eds.), *Gender, water, and development* (pp. 39–56). New York, NY: Berg.

Lahiri-Dutt, K. (Ed.) 2011. *Fluid bonds: Views on gender and water* (2nd ed.). Kolkata: STREE.

Larkin, B. 2013. The politics and poetics of infrastructure. *Annual Review of Anthropology, 42*, 327–343. https://doi.org/10.1146/annurev-anthro-092412-155522.

Larkin, B. 2015. Form. From the series: The Infrastructure Toolbox. Retrieved November 4, 2019, from https://culanth.org/fieldsights/form.

Linton, J. 2010. *What is water? The history of a modern abstraction.* Vancouver, BC, and Toronto, ON: UBC Press.

Linton, J., and Budds, J. 2014. The hydrosocial cycle: Defining and mobilizing a relational-dialectical approach to water. *Geoforum, 57*, 170–180. https://doi.org/10.1016 /j.geoforum.2013.10.008.

Mak, M. 2012. Visual postproduction in participatory video-making processes. In E. J. Milne, C. Mitchell, and N. de Lange (Eds.), *The handbook of participatory video* (pp. 171–182). Plymouth: AltaMira Press.

Mbuagbo, O. T. 2012. Cameroon: Flawed decentralization and the politics of identity in the urban space. *Global Journal of Human Social Science, 12*(11-C), 15–25.

McFarlane, C., and Rutherford, J. 2008. Political infrastructures: Governing and experiencing the fabric of the city. *International Journal of Urban and Regional Research, 32*(2), 363–374. https://doi.org/10.1111/j.1468-2427.2008.00792.x.

McFarlane, C., and Silver, J. 2016. The poolitical city: "Seeing sanitation" and making the urban political in Cape Town. *Antipode, 49*(1), 125–148. https://doi.org/10.1111/anti .12264.

Milne, E. J., Mitchell, C., and de Lange, N. (Eds.). 2012. *The handbook of participatory video*. Plymouth: AltaMira Press.

Mitchell, C. 2011. *Doing visual research*. New York, NY and London, UK: Sage.

Mitchell, C., and de Lange, N. 2013. What can a teacher do with a cellphone? Using participatory visual research to speak back in addressing HIV and AIDS. *South African Journal of Education, 33*(4), 1–13. http://www.scielo.org.za/pdf/saje/v33n4/10.pdf.

Mitchell, C., de Lange, N., and Moletsane, R. 2017. *Participatory visual methodologies: Social change, community and policy*. Los Angeles: Sage.

Mollett, S., and Faria, C. 2013. Messing with gender in feminist political ecology. *Geoforum, 45*, 116–125. https://doi.org/10.1016/j.geoforum.2012.10.009.

Njoh, A. J. 2003. *Self-help water supply in Cameroon: Lessons on community participation in public works projects* (Vol. 19). Lewiston, NY, Queenstown, ON, and Lampeter, Wales: The Edwin Mellen Press.

Njoh, A. J. 2011. Municipal councils, international NGOs and citizen participation in public infrastructure development in rural settlements in Cameroon. *Habitat International, 35*(1), 101–110. https://doi.org/10.1016/j.habitatint.2010.04.001.

Page, B. 2005. Naked power: Women and the social production of water in Anglophone Cameroon. In A. Coles and T. Wallace (Eds.), *Gender, water, and development* (pp. 57–74). New York, NY: Berg.

Page, B. 2007. Slow going: The mortuary, modernity, and the Hometown Association in Bali-Nyonga, Cameroon. *The Journal of the International African Institute, 77*(3), 419–441. https://doi.org/10.1353/afr.2007.0059.

Pink, S. 2004. *Home truths: Gender, domestic objects and everyday life*. New York, NY: Berg.

Redfield, P. 2015. Fluid technologies: The Bush Pump, the LifeStraw® and microworlds of humanitarian design. *Social Studies of Science, 46*(2), 159–183. https://doi.org/10.1177/0306312715620061.

Sally, Z., Gaskin, S. J., Folifac, F., and Kometa, S. S. 2014. The effect of urbanization on community-managed water supply: Case study of Buea, Cameroon. *Community Development Journal, 49*(4), 524–540. https://doi.org/10.1093/cdj/bst054.

Schwenkel, C. 2015. Sense. From the series: The Infrastructure Toolbox. Retrieved November 4, 2019, from https://culanth.org/fieldsights/sense.

Skinner, J. 2009. *Where every drop counts: Tackling rural Africa's water crisis*. Longon: International Institute of Environment and Development. Retrieved from www.iied.org/pubs/display.php?o=17055IIED.

Star, S. L. 1999. The ethnography of infrastructure. *American Behavioral Scientist, 43*(3), 377–391. https://doi.org/10.1177/00027649921955326.

Strang, V. 2005. Taking the waters: Cosmology, gender, and material culture in the appropriation of water resources. In A. Coles and T. Wallace (Eds.), *Gender, water, and development* (pp. 21–38). New York, NY: Berg.

Sultana, F. 2009. Fluid lives: Subjectivities, gender, and water in rural Bangladesh. *Gender, Place, and Culture, 16*(4), 427–444. https://doi.org/10.1080/09663690903003942.

Sultana, F. 2011. Suffering for water, suffering from water: Emotional geographies of resource access, control, and conflict. *Geoforum, 42*(2), 163–172. https://doi.org/10.1016/j.geoforum.2010.12.002.

Swyngedouw, E. 2004. *Social power and the urbanization of water: Flows of power*. Oxford and New York, NY: Oxford University Press.

Tennant-Wood, R. 2011. Silent partners: The fluid relationship between women and dammed rivers in the Snowy Region of Australia. In K. Lahiri-Dutt (Ed.), *Fluid bonds: Views on gender and water* (2nd ed., pp. 317–334). Kolkata: STREE.

Thompson, J. 2011. Picturing gendered water spaces: A textual approach to water in rural Sierra Leone. *Agenda, 25*(2), 43–53. https://doi.org/10.1080/10130950.2011.575996.

Thompson, J. 2016. Intersectionality and water: How social relations intersect with ecological difference. *Gender, Place and Culture, 23*(9), 1286–1301. https://doi.org/10.10 80/0966369X.2016.1160038.

Thompson, J. 2017. *Women and water wahala: Picturing gendered waterscapes in Southwest Cameroon.* (PhD), McGill University, Montreal.

Thompson, J., Folifac, F., and Gaskin, S. 2011. Fetching water in the unholy hours of the night: The impacts of a water crisis on girls' health and sexualities in semi-urban Cameroon. *Girlhood Studies, 4*(2), 111–129. https://doi.org/10.3167/ghs.2011.040208.

Thompson, J., Gaskin, S., and Agbor, M. 2017. Embodied intersections: Gender, water, and sanitation in Cameroon. *Agenda, 31*(1), 140–155. https://doi.org/10.1080/10130950.2 017.1341158.

Truelove, Y. 2011. (Re-)conceptualizing water inequality in Delhi, India through a feminist political ecology framework. *Geoforum, 42*(2), 143–152. https://doi.org/10.1016 /j.geoforum.2011.01.004.

Truelove, Y. 2019. Gray zones: The everyday practices and governance of water beyond the network. *Annals of the American Association of Geographers.* https://doi.org/10.1080 /24694452.2019.1581598.

Van Houweling, E. 2015. Gendered water spaces: A study of the transition from wells to handpumps in Mozambique. *Gender, Place, and Culture, 22*(10), 1391–1407. https://doi .org/10.1080/0966369X.2014.970140.

Von Schnitzler, A. 2013. Traveling technologies: Infrastructure, ethical regimes, and the materiality of politics in South Africa. *Cultural Anthropology, 28*(4), 670–693. https:// doi.org/10.1111/cuan.12032.

Wang, C. 1999. Photovoice: A participatory action research strategy applied to women's health. *Journal of Women's Health, 8*(2), 185–191. https://doi.org/10.1089/jwh.1999 .8.185.

World Health Organization and UNICEF. 2006. Core questions on drinking-water and sanitation for household surveys. https://iris.who.int/bitstream/handle/10665/43489 /9789241563260_eng.pdf?sequence=1&isAllowed=y.

Zwarteveen, M. 2008. Men, masculinities, and water powers in irrigation. *Water Alternatives, 1*(1), 111–130.

AFTERWORD

Anu Sabhlok and Yaffa Truelove

This book has its beginnings in conversations at a session on "Gendered Infrastructures" we organized at the annual meeting of the American Association of Geographers in early 2018. Five years have gone by since then, and a lot has changed. The pandemic transformed ways in which we think, move, meet, engage, and inhabit. At a personal level, many of our contributors dealt with sickness, loss, and fear as wave after wave of the virus swept the globe. In the context of this book, happenings around the world revealed to us even more clearly how infrastructures are gendered and intersect with other categories of difference and vulnerabilities. Globally, more women hold low-paying, insecure, and informal-sector jobs, often in the care, health, and sanitation sectors. The pandemic saw many women and men being laid off while the unavailability of childcare, increased illnesses at home, and closure of schools forced many women to quit the workforce. Others were overburdened with the increased demands on the cleanliness and care infrastructures in their cities and communities.

On March 24, 2020, the Indian prime minister Narendra Modi addressed the nation at 8:00 p.m. and announced a nationwide lockdown, starting within the next four hours, effectively stalling all movement in the country. For forty days, public spaces appeared abandoned while all those who had homes retreated into their private spaces. On our campuses, students in hostels scrambled for the limited flights to reach their homes—faculty and staff drove them to airports amid fear of police retribution for breaking the lockdown. Very soon, the reliance on *people as infrastructure* became evident when no one came to pick up garbage and gated communities (including at university campuses in India) started smelling bad. Migrant workers and daily wage workers in cities found themselves with no work, no money, no food, and no shelter. With the

Indian railways curtailing their service and a freeze on traffic, workers had no choice but to breach the curfew and begin a long walk back to their homes in the villages—an arduous, dangerous, and often violent journey. Roads as infrastructures became the conduits for thousands of *chappal*-wearing migrants lugging their children and luggage on the journey back home. This mass exodus caught the government by surprise, as it had failed to factor in the millions on whose back urban infrastructures rely for their construction, repair, maintenance, and operations. There was no documentation of the migrant workers that could be used to plan policy or bring relief to them after the draconian lockdown left them stranded. Migrant daily-wage workers on the long walk home experienced starvation, exhaustion, violence, illness, fears, and anxieties as they found themselves in an in-between space—forsaken and abandoned by the state, their urban workplaces, and often their rural communities, who worried that the migrants might bring the virus with them. The intersectional (gendered, casted, classed, regional, etc.) nature of this infrastructural violence was glaring when access to water, sanitation, shelter, and medical care were sporadic at best for those walking long distances on tarred surfaces or along railway lines.

Meanwhile, women bore the brunt of the pandemic, and many of them who worked as domestic workers lost their jobs. Housekeeping tasks in middle-class Indian homes that were earlier outsourced to working-class females, fell on the shoulders of the women of the household. Further, being trapped inside households and burdened with performing the embodied labor for homely infrastructures, women from all social classes saw an increase in domestic violence and psychological illnesses. Access to digital infrastructures that enable social and economic engagements too had gendered, class-based, and caste-based fractures and schisms. Families with only one cell phone at home had to choose between offering it to one of their children for online classes or using it for work-from-home tasks. Summer electricity cuts in many places interrupted children's access to education and people's work schedules. New infrastructural extensions became part of our everyday vocabulary: PPE, sanitizers, testing kits, N95 masks. With hospitals packed with COVID-19 patients, medical access including beds for those with chronic conditions or disabilities and for pregnant women were scarce. The pandemic made evident how infrastructural construction, maintenance, and operations rely on capitalism and patriarchy.

While the papers in this volume focus primarily on gender, we understand gender as intersectional and unequal relations as constitutive of infrastructural assemblages. The case studies discussed in this volume bring forth infrastructural intersectionality (Truelove and O'Reilly 2021) as they relate women's embodied, affective, and symbolic relations with infrastructure. In the chapter titled "Infrastructure of Recyclable Waste as Assemblages," Queirós et al. discuss how women waste pickers identify on the basis of gender as well as class to form associations and cooperatives. In the Indian context, waste picking and scavenging is strongly tied to caste and notions of untouchability. Even as it focuses on women waste workers, Fredricks's chapter also shows that "gender operates in intersection with other forms of difference, including class, religion, ethnicity, and age, to structure the value and power struggles surrounding different kinds of waste work in Dakar." In Truelove and Ruszczyk's chapter on bodies as urban infrastructure, intersections of gender, caste, ethno-religious difference, and class all shape the forms of "slow infrastructural violence" that different bodies in the cities of Nepal and India endure and resist. The women in Dávalos and Gamble's study are working-class women who use informal transport infrastructures, whereas Ahmed and Datta clearly situate their respondents as women living in low-income neighborhoods in the South Indian state of Kerala. Other papers in this book speak to colonialism, race, religion, and sexuality (Kirk's chapter) as also carefully delineating the temporal dimensions of gendered identity (as in the colonial and postcolonial gendered body in Vietnam in Schwenkel's chapter).

This book has brought into focus how gendered relations constitute and are constituted by infrastructures. Yet, there is a lot more to be done in terms of paying attention to infrastructural interactions with diverse social identities, embodiments, nonhuman lives, and ecology. For example, how do infrastructures shape, and become produced through, other intersectional social power relations that include heteronormativity, generational standing, and differing abilities? How do the multifaceted effects of climate change and unequal infrastructural access and burdens in the wake of disasters take on gendered dimensions? How do nonhuman lives and entities thwart infrastructural imaginaries and the differing embodied effects of networks as diverse as human health, transport, and digital systems? Looking at infrastructures as assemblages—as matter that enables circulations—has generated fertile ground for conversations across multiple materialities and diverse identities.

New methodologies need to be experimented with that allow for zooming into particularities while at the same time emphasizing vast networks and connections. As De Laet and Mol's (2000) work on the Zimbabwe Bush Pump B demonstrates, the boundaries and limits of infrastructure are inherently slippery analytically. Conceptualizing an infrastructure shifts according to one's gaze and how that particular infrastructure is situated in any given context. De Laet and Mol question whether bodies, the community, the nation, and the broader health system should all be included (or not) in how this water-pumping device functions. Such queries open up new methodological questions about how researchers can be attentive to the differing dimensions of infrastructure in the everyday, including the bodies, communities, and nations they shape and are entangled with. There is also a methodological imperative to distinguish how the symbolisms, discourses, and imaginaries concerning what counts as infrastructure are constructed to serve certain ends and means to the exclusion of others. Finally, feminist methods, including careful attention to self-reflexivity, building collaborative projects with communities, and attending to gendered dimensions of everyday life and practice, are all poised to make critical contributions to how we go about the complex study of infrastructure with its multifaceted gendered dimensions.

REFERENCES

de Laet, Marianne, and Annemarie Mol. 2000. "The Zimbabwe Bush Pump: Mechanics of a Fluid Technology." *Social Studies of Science* 30 (2): 225–63.
Truelove, Y., and K. O'Reilly. 2021. "Making India's Cleanest City: Sanitation, Intersectionality, and Infrastructural Violence." *Environment and Planning E: Nature and Space* 4 (3): 718–35.

CONTRIBUTORS

Nabeela Ahmed is a lecturer in human geography at Sheffield Hallam University. Nabeela's research focuses on questions of precarity (in terms of gender and race as well as class), citizenship, and state welfare in urban contexts and is currently looking at how these questions evolve in the digital age, primarily in South Asia.

Cecilia Alda-Vidal recently completed her PhD in human geography at the University of Manchester. Cecilia is a political ecologist interested in urban environmental challenges. Her research focuses on the everyday governance of urban infrastructures in the context of growing inequalities and climate crisis.

Alison L. Browne is a senior lecturer in human geography at the University of Manchester. Alison's research primarily focuses on practices, infrastructures, cultures, and politics of everyday life related to water, sanitation, and the nexus with energy, food, and waste. In a mixed methodological and transdisciplinary way, she plays with ideas of how such practices come to be disrupted, changed, and governed.

Linda Carroli is a research fellow at Queensland University of Technology (QUT) and visiting fellow at the QUT Centre for Decent Work and Industry. Her research examines sustainable and just transitions, regional planning, and the foundational economy.

Ayona Datta is a professor of human geography in University College London. Her broad research interests are in postcolonial urbanism, smart cities, gender citizenship, and regional futures. She received the Busk Medal from Royal Geographical Society (with IBG) in 2019.

Cristen Dávalos is a professor and feminist geographer at the Department of International Relations of the School for Social Sciences and Humanities in the Universidad San Francisco de Quito (USFQ) (Quito, Ecuador). She participates as a migration researcher in the Institute for Advanced Studies in Inequalities (IASI). Her recent publications and research projects are on migration, mobility, food security, and political ecology from a gender perspective in Ecuador and Latin America.

Rosalind Fredericks is an associate professor of geography and development at the Gallatin School, NYU. Her research and teaching interests are centered on development, urbanism, and political ecology in Africa. As an urban geographer, she conducts research that brings together discard studies, critical infrastructure studies, and feminist political ecology in examining the politics of waste work and discard infrastructures in Dakar, Senegal. Her book *Garbage Citizenship: Vital Infrastructures of Labor in Dakar, Senegal* (Duke University Press, 2018) was awarded the Toyin Falola Book Award for the best book in African studies by the Association of Global South Studies. She is currently producing her first documentary film about the transformation of Dakar's massive dump, Mbeubeuss.

Fernanda Regina Fuzzi holds a PhD in geography from the graduate program in geography at Universidade Estadual Paulista. Fuzzi participated from 2009 to 2012 as an intern and monitor at the Centro de Museologia, Antropologia, e Arqueologia, developing university extension projects. She also developed a scientific initiation project with funding from Fundação de Amparo à Pesquisa do Estado de São Paulo, under the guidance of António Cezar Leal, and a master's project with funding from Conselho Nacional de Desenvolvimento Científico e Tecnológico–CNPq. Fuzzi carried out, between 2017 and 2021, her doctoral project with funding from the Coordenação de Aperfeiçoamento de Pessoal de Nível Superior Brasil. She currently participates in the research group Gestão Ambiental e Dinâmica Socioespacial, linked to CNPq.

Julie Gamble is an assistant professor of gender and sexuality studies at Vanderbilt University. She is trained as a critical urbanist with research that focuses on questions related to urban inequality and social justice. She explores these issues through attention to the making of urban mobilities in Quito, Ecuador.

Deanna Grant-Smith is deputy director of the QUT Centre for Decent Work and Industry and Technologies of Justice Co-Program lead in the QUT Centre for Justice at the Queensland University of Technology. Her research focuses on exploitation ranging from unpaid internships to multilevel marketing and planning practices.

Gabi Kirk is a doctoral candidate in geography with a designated emphasis in feminist theory and research at University of California, Davis. Her research examines the political ecology of sustainable agriculture in Palestine-Israel.

Antonio Cezar Leal is a professor in the Department of Geography and advisor to the dean of University Extension and Culture at the São Paulo State University (UNESP), São Paulo, Brazil. He is a representative of UNESP on the State Water Resources Council and member of River Basin Committees with regional and interstate activities. He develops teaching, research, and extension activities in geography, planning, and management of water in watersheds and of solid urban waste, including actions with organizations of recyclable material collectors, municipal governments, intermunicipal consortia, and state and federal public agencies, among other institutional partnerships. He has participated in research projects and academic cooperation between graduate programs involving professors from universities in Brazil, the University of Havana (Cuba), and the University of Lisbon (Portugal).

Margarida Queirós holds a PhD in human geography from the University of Lisbon, Portugal. She is currently an associate professor at the Institute of Geography and Spatial Planning and a researcher at the Centre for Geographical Studies of the University of Lisbon. She was a visiting scholar at the University of Quebec at Montreal (Canadian Studies Grant—International Council for Canadian Studies), and at the Autonomous University of Barcelona (Calouste Gulbenkian Foundation Grant). She has been an invited professor at the São Paulo State University and at the Pedagogical and Technological University, Colombia in (cooperation with the Geographical Institute Agustín Codazzi). She was the editor in chief of the journal *Finisterra* from 2016 until 2021. Her research and teaching topics focus on gender, environment, and spatial planning. She has coordinated and collaborated in studies and projects (national and international) to support public policies focusing on gender, environment and territory indicators, gender mainstreaming in urban planning, inequalities in gender and mobility/work-life arrangements, and violence against women and domestic violence. She is the national representative of the Iberoamerican Network for Territorial Observation, a founding member of the Studies of Ibero-Latin American Geography, Gender, and Sexuality Network, and a recognized expert by the Portuguese Commission for Citizenship and Gender Equality as a reference on gender studies (List of Experts).

Maria Rusca is a lecturer at the Global Development Institute, University of Manchester. Her work focuses on political ecologies of water and hydroclimatic extremes, critical disaster studies, climate urbanism, and experimental political ecologies. Although her work is firmly rooted in human geography, she is committed to developing research at the nexus between social and natural sciences to further the fields of political ecology and nature/society.

Hanna A. Ruszczyk is a feminist urban geographer in the Department of Geography and the Institute of Hazard, Risk and Resilience, Durham University, UK. She explores governance techniques via accountability and digital cash assistance in the humanitarian system. She is also interested in urban risk governance and gendered resilience strategies in academically overlooked cities. Ruszczyk uses creative methods such as films and photography in her research. Before academia, she worked for two United Nations agencies, the International Labour Organisation and the United Nations Development Programme. For more info, see hannaruszczyk.weebly.com.

Anu Sabhlok is a professor in the Department of Humanities and Social Sciences at the Indian Institute of Science Education and Research Mohali. Her research lies in the domain of feminist theory, urban and labor geography, and the emerging area of critical infrastructure studies. Specifically, she focuses on the material and labor processes related to road construction in the upper Himalayas. She is trained as an architect, urban scholar, and feminist geographer. She was a Fulbright fellow at the University of Colorado in Boulder from 2017 to 2018, where the discussions on this volume first germinated.

Christina Schwenkel is a professor of anthropology and Southeast Asian studies at the University of California, Riverside, USA. Her work examines urban infrastructure breakdown and the legacies of Cold War circulations of people, objects, technologies, and design practices between Vietnam and socialist-allied countries. She is the author of *The American War in Contemporary Vietnam: Transnational Remembrance and Representation* (Indiana University Press, 2009) and the award-winning book *Building Socialism: The Afterlife of East German Architecture in Urban Vietnam* (Duke University Press, 2020).

Anshika Suri is an architect and urban development planner who works as the policy and funding advisor for the Unite! University Alliance (University

Network for Innovation, Technology and Engineering) at Technische Universität Darmstadt, Germany. She is also the co-lead researcher for Urban Morphosis Lab in the Department of Architecture, where her post-doctoral research focuses on intersectional perspectives in urban infrastructures and city development. She is currently co-editing a book on Rethinking Urban Transformations: A New Paradigm for Inclusive Cities (Springer International), focused on inclusion and diversity in planning.

Jennifer A. Thompson is currently a research associate with Myriagone, the McConnell-University of Montreal Chair in Youth Knowledge Mobilization at the University of Montreal. She wrote the chapter in this book during a post-doctoral fellowship in the Department of Anthropology at Durham University in the UK. Jen has worked with participatory visual methodologies to address gender issues related to water, agriculture, conservation, teacher education, and the COVID-19 pandemic in several global contexts that include Canada, Cameroon, England, Ethiopia, Kenya, Mozambique, and Sierra Leone.

Yaffa Truelove is an assistant professor in the Department of Geography at the University of Colorado, Boulder. Drawing on feminist and urban political ecology, her research primarily examines the connections between urban waterscapes and sociopolitical processes in cities of the Global South. Recent work includes research on the gendered and sociopolitical dimensions of water scarcity and infrastructure in Shimla, India, as well as the embodied dimensions of infrastructural violence in the cities of Indore and Delhi.

Mário Vale holds a PhD in human geography from the University of Lisbon. He is currently a full professor and president at the Institute of Geography and Spatial Planning (IGOT) at the University of Lisbon, and a researcher at the Centre for Geographical Studies. He is the coordinator of the PhD program in geography at IGOT. He was a visiting researcher at the Center for Urban and Regional Development Studies, University of Newcastle, in 2006 and a Fulbright visiting scholar at the Department of Geography of UCLA (University of California, Los Angeles) in 2013. He has worked on the topic of innovation and urban and regional economic dynamics, with special emphasis on European peripheral regions, combining institutional, evolutionary, and critical perspectives in economic geography. His research has been underpinned by several national and international research projects (fourth, fifth, sixth, and seventh Framework Programs, EEA grants, integrated actions, ESPON, and FCT). He has published works on these subjects in several international scientific journals. He was president of the Portuguese Association of Geographers (2004–2008) and vice president of the Regional Studies Association (RSA) (2008–2011) and is currently FeRSA (fellow of the RSA) and national representative of the association in Portugal. Since 2017, he has been a member of the Board of the Regional Studies Association Europe.

INDEX

Page numbers in italics indicate illustrations.

www.ingramcontent.com/pod-product-compliance
Lightning Source LLC
Chambersburg PA
CBHW050339270326
41926CB00016B/3524